Imagining the Kibbutz

Imagining the Kibbutz

Visions of Utopia in Literature and Film

Ranen Omer-Sherman

THE PENNSYLVANIA STATE UNIVERSITY PRESS

UNIVERSITY PARK, PENNSYLVANIA

Chapter 2 is adapted from Ranen Omer-Sherman,
Israel in Exile: Jewish Writing and the Desert
(Urbana: University of Illinois Press, 2006).
© 2006 by the Board of Trustees of the
University of Illinois. Used by permission.

Library of Congress Cataloging-in-Publication Data

Omer-Sherman, Ranen, author.
Imagining the kibbutz : visions of utopia in literature
and film / Ranen Omer-Sherman.
pages   cm — (Dimyonot: Jews and
cultural imagination)
Summary: "An exploration of the literary and cinematic
representations of the kibbutz movement in Israel.
Authors discussed include Amos Oz, Savyon Liebrecht,
Nathan Shaham, Avraham Balaban, Atallah Mansour,
Eli Amir, and Batya Gur. Directors discussed include
Yitzhak Yeshurun, Akiva Tevet, Dror Shaul, and
Jonathan Paz"—Provided by publisher.
Includes bibliographical references and index.
ISBN 978-0-271-06557-1 (cloth : alk. paper)
1. Israeli literature—History and criticism.
2. Kibbutzim in literature.
3. Kibbutzim in motion pictures.
4. Kibbutzim—History.
I. Title.

PJ5012.K53044 2015
892.4'09355—dc23
2014045413

The Pennsylvania State University Press is a member of
the Association of American University Presses.

It is the policy of The Pennsylvania State University Press
to use acid-free paper. Publications on uncoated stock
satisfy the minimum requirements of American National
Standard for Information Sciences—Permanence of Paper
for Printed Library Material, ANSI Z39.48–1992.

This book is printed on paper that contains
30% post-consumer waste.

VOLUME 2

DIMYONOT דמיונות
Jews and the Cultural Imagination

Volumes in the Dimyonot series explore the intersections, and interstices, of Jewish experience and culture. These projects emerge from many disciplines—including art, history, language, literature, music, religion, philosophy, and cultural studies—and diverse chronological and geographical locations. Each volume, however, interrogates the multiple and evolving representations of Judaism and Jewishness, by both Jews and non-Jews, over time and place.

For MICHALI

CONTENTS

ILLUSTRATIONS

Introduction

We did not attune our expectations to a distant morrow, but to their lifetime. As soon as today is over. Quickly, in our time. Not dreams of a far-off future or the Kingdom of Heaven at the end of a dark tunnel. It would all be right here, tomorrow. This little acre. This mule. This child. The redemption will come here and now and not in a generation that is all saints or all sinners or on the day that the tears of Jacob and Esau cease.

—*Nathan Shaham*

The impossibility of utopia is less a demonstration of the failure of conviviality than an ongoing proof of our determination to keep on trying.

—*Alberto Manguel*

Even more than two decades after leaving the kibbutz, I need only close my eyes for a moment or two for its rich textures and sensations to rush back in almost unbidden with startling intensity: the growling rumbles of tractors bearing wagons of sun-scorched and sweat-drenched laborers up the dusty road from our fields and orchards, the furnace heat under white desert summer skies, the gentle bubbling and hissing of the drip irrigation, the pungent aromas of rotting orange peels and manure in the cowshed. The dining hall's incessant scraping of moving chairs, small talk, excited debates, anarchic herds of roaming children, wicked jokes, and explosive laughter, all of it reverberating and filling the humming air, the bountiful refuse of eggshells, cucumber peels, olive pits, and globs of sour runny yogurt topped off with cigarette butts all stewing in the aluminum *kolboinik* atop each table. Then, at night, the drowsy and companionable silences of those sipping Wissotzky tea after being reluctantly roused for the early milking shift. The exhausting work—how ever did we summon the energy for those passionate arguments in the late nights of the members' assembly? Those seemingly endless days all came and went in a rapid stream, yet now they pause and linger because neither heart nor mind ever wishes to relinquish any of it.

In today's virtual community, however, idealists (academic or otherwise) increasingly inhabit their own hermetic worlds, and it has not been my good fortune to know very many (aside from a few aging red-diaper babies and veterans of the Civil Rights Movement) who have really lived their social vision consciously, day in, day out. To a great extent, this study is inspired by the many extraordinary years I was fortunate to share with some remarkable people, a few of them gone now, who actually acted on a fairly radical political vision. Although they could be as petty, scandalous, or annoying as just about anyone else, to a striking degree, they were also tireless and often even truly selfless. Sharing a preternatural utopian impulse, they were perfectly willing to spend their lives laboring on 110-degree days within the confines of an isolated settlement of homely prefabricated dwellings and sparse greenery, patiently rotating jobs and working unseemly hours whenever that was required of them, in plain view of the modest cemetery they figured to one day inhabit.[1] There is no other way to put it: we came to the kibbutz with a sense of joyful purpose. As if intuitively attracted to the kind of place where, to borrow from Frederick Buechner's spiritual imperative, "your deep gladness and the world's deep hunger meet" (95), we eagerly and, yes, so naively plunged into what is surely one of the more strangely optimistic but ultimately successful ventures in the history of human societies, for decades the most productive socialist system in the world (well outlasting the Communist regimes of the Eastern Bloc). It was world making at its purest, unhindered by nostalgia or our immediate pasts, every choice consciously, painstakingly made.

Like many others, during my kibbutz years, I often felt a sense of euphoria but sometimes also disaffection and withdrawal. As I gradually began to discover during that sojourn, there is a significant body of extraordinary literature brimming with a heady mix of ardent idealism and lonely alienation, richly illuminating the complex responses many of us have experienced. Over time, many of those works became intensely meaningful companions for me in periods of both faith and disaffection. First and foremost, there were the works of Amos Oz (a veteran of more than thirty years of collective living), his early kibbutz stories often written in the collective persona, an ironic voice leaving delicately veiled traces of malaise in its wake that, back in those days, struggling at times to hold onto my idealistic ardor, left me shaken.

That curiously supercilious tone immediately distinguishes the language of Oz's first novel, *Makom aher* (*Elsewhere, Perhaps*; 1966), guiding us on our first steps into the unfamiliar world and fraught psychological minefields of the fictional Kibbutz Metsudat Ram. Here we are made to understand the collective's symbolic place in the surrounding topography, the exacting but attractive surfaces of utopian engineering (a notable contrast to this frontier settlement's threatening existential situation in the ominous pre–1967 War period and to the inner torments of the souls within), and finally its unapologetic elitism:

> [Our] buildings are laid out in strict symmetry at one end of the green valley. The tangled foliage of the trees does not break up the settlement's severe lines, but merely softens them, and adds a dimension of weightiness.
>
> The buildings are whitewashed, and most of them are topped with bright red roofs. This color scheme contrasts sharply with that of the mountain range . . . at the foot of which the kibbutz lies spread. . . .
>
> Along the lower terraces on the slope stretches the border between our land and that of her enemies. . . .
>
> . . . There is a kind of enmity between the valley, with its neat, geometrical patchwork of fields[,] and the savage bleakness of the mountains. . . .
>
> The houses, as we have said, are brightly painted. They are laid out at regular intervals. Their windows all face northwest, since the architects tried to adapt the building to the climate. Here there is no agglomeration of buildings clustering or ramifying haphazardly down the ages, nor blocks of dwellings enclosing secret courtyards, for the kibbutz does not have family homes. There is no question of separate quarters for different crafts; the poor are not relegated to the outskirts nor is the center reserved for the wealthy. The straight lines, the clean shapes, the neatly ruled concrete paths and rectangular lawns are the product of a vigorous view of the world. That was what we meant when we stated that our village was built in a spirit of optimism.
>
> Anyone who draws the shallow inference that our village is stark and lacking in charm and beauty merely reveals his own prejudice. The object of the kibbutz is not to satisfy the sentimental expectations of town dwellers. Our village is not lacking in charm and beauty, but its beauty is vigorous and virile and its charm conveys a message. Yes, it does. (*Elsewhere, Perhaps* 3–5)

Notwithstanding the scattered hints of dread toward the internal human disorders and external hazards that invariably transgress the community's prudent geometrical designs (which do not altogether distract from the mischievous fun Oz perpetrates with this affectedly portentous voice), there is no mistaking his palpable reverence for its *essence*, the nobility of the historical mission underlying it all. Today, it deeply impresses that, as an "outsider" still in his twenties, Oz's mastery of literary art could achieve such equipoise. Forsaking the familiarity of his father's Jerusalem home to rush wholeheartedly into the alien life of the kibbutz, he yet remained enough of an individual to poke fun at that insular society's exasperating self-seriousness even as he so aptly captured its condition of anxious vulnerability: "The huts bestow a pioneering character on the whole picture, the air of a border settlement ready to turn a resolute face to impending disasters. So does the sloping fence that surrounds the kibbutz on all sides. Let us pause here for a moment to evoke your admiration" (*Elsewhere, Perhaps* 6). Yet, in spite of that light note of mockery, such "admiration" flowed forth from all over the world at the very moment Oz was writing—and for many years to come.[2] Attractive portrayals abound in the fiction and memoirs of even those writers most critical of the kibbutz, perhaps in acknowledgment of our intrinsic human yearning for utopia (sometimes even after we are disillusioned).

For who can resist warming to this classic snapshot of the kibbutz's indisputable pastoral allure, as seen through the eyes of Inspector Michael Ohayon of Batya Gur's famous mystery novels? Largely indifferent, if not altogether hostile, to the kibbutz as an institution that he finds markedly unwelcoming to Mizrahi Jews like himself, Ohayon is nevertheless charmed by its attractive spaces and alluring rhythm of life:

> Michael sensed the contradiction between the tempo of his movements and the surrounding serenity. Children rode bicycles on the paths, and three toddlers were being pushed in a mobile playpen. . . . The young man pushing it and the toddlers sitting inside were tanned and serene. . . . On the lawns . . . parents sat with their children. . . . Again Michael took in the cultivated landscape around him, the pruned, thick-trunked trees, the sign saying 'Six-hundred-year-old sycamore' on one of the massive trunks, the greenness of the lawns, the merrily dancing sprinklers. Once or twice old women in golf carts forced them to step off the path onto the lawn. [He] passed the culture center, the sports hall, and the spacious playing field, from which they could hear cheering and a thudding ball; [he] passed playgrounds with jungle gyms and slides. People in bathing suits were returning from the pool on their bicycles. (*Murder on a Kibbutz* 214–15)

Similarly, Avraham Balaban's memoir *Shiv'ah* (*Mourning a Father Lost*; 2000), though often a caustic and wounded account of childhood deprivation, affectionately conjures up the enthralling epic of labor and pioneering in the upper Galilee in language that washes over the reader in breathless ebullience:

> Imagine a group of people in a not very big house, who have committed themselves to sleeping together, eating together, bathing together, and toiling on the land together. . . . The ancestral land yields wheat and olives and milk. You can't know what it feels like to return home in the evening, sit on the shadowed concrete steps, and pull off your work boots, knowing that you've picked a quarter-tonne of apples, and the picking movements linger in the weary body . . . like a mild intoxication. The work does not give [the pioneers] a new heart, but it does sometimes produce a countryman's contentment, a countryman's joy and honest sleep. On feast days there is such rejoicing that the heart seems to melt, and even on working days, after supper . . . there is laughter and idle chat in the corners of the dining hall. An old comradeship envelops the inhabitants. (*Mourning* 34)

You would have to be completely obtuse not to be entranced by Balaban's language, so knowingly does his empathic portrayal of the zeal of the past rekindle the dream that once inflamed so many. Even the late Tony Judt, more famously known for his sharp criticism of Israel, was at first enraptured by the kibbutz experiment, toiling three long summers as a young volunteer during the 1960s. Judt's "Kibbutz" memoir recalls his early days, "proselytizing Labour Zionism as an unpaid official of one of its youth movements." Years later, like most anyone who sojourned on kibbutzim at some point during their youth, he simply cannot suppress his early romantic ardor, his giddy sense of adventure:

> For the neophyte fifteen-year-old Londoner encountering the kibbutz for the first time, the effect was exhilarating. Here was "Muscular Judaism" in its most seductive guise: health, exercise, productivity, collective purpose, self-sufficiency, and proud separatism—not to mention the charms of kibbutz children of one's own generation, apparently free of all the complexes and inhibitions of their European peers (free, too, of most of their cultural baggage—though this did not trouble me until later).
>   I adored it. Eight hours of strenuous, intellectually undemanding labor in steamy banana plantations by the shores of the Sea of Galilee,

interspersed with songs, hikes, lengthy doctrinal discussions (carefully stage-managed so as to reduce the risk of adolescent rejection while maximizing the appeal of shared objectives), and the ever-present suggestion of guilt-free sex.[3]

Fond kibbutz coming-of-age reminiscences by North American or British Jewish writers who, like Judt, became briefly acquainted with kibbutz life (whether or not they enjoyed amorous adventures in the volunteer quarters or orchards) are not all that uncommon. The American-born immigrant Yossi Klein Halevi launches his masterful historical study of the unraveling of national unity in the years after the 1967 War with this empathic scene, in which an Israeli paratrooper seems to find his greatest happiness toiling in his kibbutz's citrus harvest:

> In the orange orchards of Kibbutz Ein Shemer, Avital Geva, barefoot and shirtless in the early-morning sun, was frying eggs in a blackened pan. Turkish coffee was boiling in the aluminum pot, and his friends were laying out plates of tomatoes and cucumbers and olives, white cheese and jam. "Ya Allah, what a feast!" exclaimed Avital, as if encountering for the first time the food he had eaten for breakfast every day since childhood. It was mid-May 1967. Avital and his crew had been working since dawn, to outwit the heat of the day. Rather than return to the communal dining room for breakfast, the young men allowed themselves the privilege of eating together beneath the corrugated roof they'd erected for just that purpose. Could there be greater joy, thought Avital, than working the fields with one's closest friends and sharing food grown by their kibbutz? One could almost forget about the crisis on the Egyptian border. (3)

Here is the primal scene that allured so many other young people: the warm camaraderie in simple labor certainly, perhaps even the appealing hint of danger that was never entirely absent. Yet, more strikingly, we encounter the same kind of appealing utopian simplicity in the evocative imagery of a writer from a strikingly different background, Atallah Mansour (b. 1934), a young Arab journalist and native of Palestine who wrote one of the least known yet utterly remarkable works in the literary history of the kibbutz. Indeed, *B'or hadash* (*In a New Light*; 1966) was the very first Hebrew novel published by a Palestinian Arab and, though filled with its Arab protagonist's anguished struggle to belong, it is generously openhearted in setting the scene: "The sand is white and so are the houses. The red-tile roofs, abetted by the small vegetable gardens, turn the landscape into a naïve kindergarten drawing" (*In a New Light* 20). Whether or not they ever experienced the life of a kibbutz, those who read the novels of Gur and Mansour or the memoirs of Balaban and Judt will likely succumb to the warm tug of their alluring renderings of bucolic community life—that is, until things take a more dystopian turn, as they often do in the disenchanted nuances of many kibbutz narratives. For such writers (self-critical insiders and outsiders alike), writing honestly about kibbutz life demands keeping at least two central contraries in mind at once—the absolute necessity of euphoric dreaming and the mellowing inevitability of disillusionment.

These brief vignettes serve to illustrate that, for almost all who doubt whether they harbor a secret attraction to communal life, such uncertainty vanishes upon their first visit to a kibbutz, if only for a brief glimpse. What they perceive there will likely strike a deeply resonant chord even when they cannot imagine themselves actually living in such a place. Such encounters often elicit the sense of wonder and even wistful daydreams of alternative lives sometimes associated with visits to monasteries. After all, people since antiquity have sought ways to opt out of mainstream society to launch schemes of utopian communities (think of the Essenes, the late pagan Athenians, and other communities that formed in the ancient Mediterranean world), a trend that only intensified in the modern age (witness Samuel Taylor Coleridge's unrealized dream of a Pantisocracy on the banks of the Susquehanna and the actual proliferation of nineteenth-century communes in the United States).[4] Yet important distinctions between the self-understanding of these short-lived experimental antecedents—or even contemporary American exemplars such as the Twin Oaks Community, East Wind, and The Farm (whose members numbered 1,500 in the late 1970s)—and the kibbutz must be acknowledged.[5] As journalist Daniel Gavron points out: "Where other communes rejected society and retreated from it, the kibbutz embraced society and sought to lead it. The symbiosis between the kibbutz and the surrounding community is what gave it its strength and influence" (3–4).[6] Still, like any other human institution, the kibbutz in its fullest realization evolved in some ways and devolved in others, adapting to the internal and external forces severely buffeting it over a century of transformation. The study before you examines some of the most provocative narratives (created mostly by insiders but occasionally by outsiders), to imaginatively portray that ensuing struggle over generations.

And, to be candid, I wrote *Imagining the Kibbutz* in part out of a sense of dismay and even a degree of anger at how rapidly the kibbutz's extraordinary achievements are fading into mythic irrelevance. I share the sentiments of Yossi

Klein Halevi, who, in an interview that often stresses his roots in the Betar Movement and his onetime loyalties to Revisionist Zionism, paused to passionately affirm the extraordinary legacy of the kibbutz: "Did Zionism really produce this mass movement of egalitarian communes? What a story. How have we allowed this movement to fade away, without at the very least saying thank you. We are a society of ingrates. We owe our existence to the kibbutzim" (Green).[7]

Most kibbutz historians categorize the movement's development in relation to three social paradigms. In the early kibbutzim of the 1910s to 1920s, an intensely communal aspect prevailed; in the next two decades, with the rise of national and political aspirations, the kibbutz sought a role in the surrounding society; and in the 1950s, entrepreneurial ambitions competed with, and eventually overshadowed, the kibbutz's communal and political tendencies to culminate in the late twentieth-century *hafrata* or privatization model of our own time.[8] Whereas many have charted the atrophying effects of political events (in particular, the 1977 election of Menachem Begin as prime minister after three decades of supportive Labor rule) and economic stresses (the abrupt loss of subsidies, tax breaks, and other forms of government support), few have highlighted the acute psychological stresses these inflicted on kibbutzniks, who had once proudly considered themselves an aristocracy of pioneers (as already glimpsed in the passage from Oz's *Elsewhere, Perhaps*).[9] What followed was a debilitating blow to that pride. As historian Anita Shapira notes:

> The kibbutz was the crown jewel of the labor movement's social creativity. It combined a vision of equality, devotion to society, and recruitment for national missions. The values prized by the kibbutz were physical labor, a simple lifestyle, a culture of low-key restraint, and making do with little. There was no other sector in Israeli society whose values so opposed those of Begin and the culture he represented. Begin realized that if he wished to change the narrative of the state, he would have to undermine the status of the kibbutz as the most important creation of Zionism. (*Israel* 386–87)

It is not hard to imagine the sense of siege, the magnitude of estrangement that kibbutz veterans felt in the toxic atmosphere unleashed by what Shapira dubs Begin's "deadly criticism" (386) following so many decades of their service to the state's needs on so many vital fronts. They were bewildered to find themselves accused of living "off the fat of the land . . . their wealth originat[ing] in

. . . resources that had been kept from the development towns" (386). Shapira acknowledges "a grain of truth" in the stereotype: "but no more than a grain." With considerable justification, she argues that the kibbutzim "earned their relative financial robustness with hard work, and for many years had endured harsh conditions" (386). The new stereotypes that rapidly gained currency owed much to the fact that "their pastoral appearance highlighted the contrast between them and the development towns," which had indeed suffered years of neglect (a story we will encounter in chapter 3).

As Shapira shows, it was inevitable that Begin's discordant language "fell on willing ears" (387), the issue becoming only more complicated with the Left's initially unpopular protests against the 1982 Lebanon War since the kibbutzim remained "bastions of the leftist elite." Sadly, "the fact that the number of kibbutz members among the combat troops exceeded by far their relative proportion in the population did not prevent the incitement against them" (387).[10] But, as early as the 1960s, even before the Likud's crafty manipulation of the disenfranchised Mizrahim through its grotesque vilification of the kibbutz and Begin's distortion of historical memory, a severe internal shift in attitudes toward the individual and the collective had caused unprecedented turmoil within the kibbutz. And that interior metamorphosis bore unanticipated consequences, which later proved explosive in the drastically changed conditions of privatization that the surrounding society imposed.

Attentive readers of my study may conclude with some justification that, in the earliest kibbutz narratives, the individual is tested, whereas, in later decades, the collective itself seems to bear the burden of demonstrating its capacity to accommodate individual aspirations and even human weaknesses. By the 1960s, that shift seems to reflect the growing restlessness that swept through the movement. In his eminently worthy study of the post-1950s kibbutz, historian Alon Gan uncovers "the ideological roots that prepared the ground for the radical changes we are witnessing today" (43). Hence, amid the plethora of critical external transformations and pressures described by many kibbutz economists and sociologists, there also emerged the sharply divergent sensibility of the young kibbutzniks themselves. At a kibbutz youth conference held by the Ihud Movement in 1971, a member from Kibbutz Rosh Hanikra spoke of the need to satisfy the aspirations of members of a new generation no longer content to spend their entire lives working in a cowshed: "Until now it was customary to adapt the wishes of the people to the needs of the kibbutz, and they were dominant. This was usually accepted without opposition. But now the younger generation is promoting a new approach, calling for changes in the kibbutz structure that would provide more opportunities for the realization of a greater variety of aspirations in the occupational domain" (Gan 43). Writing in 1985 from the perspective of a much earlier generation, Zerubavel Gilead, who arrived at Kibbutz Ein Harod as an eleven-year-old in 1924, decries the

> worldwide skepticism of the younger generation about the validity of traditional idealistic values, and the worldwide permissiveness that springs from the skepticism. Although the kibbutzim, and indeed the country as a whole, have generally been free of the conflicts between the generations that have afflicted most of the world since the 1960s and beyond, the spirit of rebellion against accepted values has expressed itself among our young in a new tendency to insist on what they call self-realization—meaning the realization of what they deem to be good for them individually, without much reference to what may be good for the community as a whole. . . .
>
> This drive toward self-realization . . . has led to a significant increase in the number of *azivot* (departures). (Gilead and Krook 279)

Whether or not one bemoans the degradation of the traditional kibbutz, this critical shift clearly laid the foundation for the radical processes of privatization that followed the economic crisis of later years. In his elegantly succinct formulation of what ensued, Gan argues that "the idea of self-realization created an upheaval in kibbutz perceptions and discourse, diverting the focus from the individual as a means to the realization of the aims of society to society as a means to the realization of the individual's potential" (43). As we will see in chapter 1, intimations of this monumental swing—from the primacy of the collective to the primacy of the individual—surface as a source of anxiety in some of the earliest literary narratives by kibbutz writers.

Gan's exposition of the critical fundamentals underlying that notable shift is compelling:

> The kibbutz movement preserved the collectivist ethos as its formative and guiding principle. While opposition to this ethos was already in the air in Israel, the kibbutz movement fought against this "destructive tendency." The principles of the collectivist ethos were laid down by the pioneer generation. The 1948 generation made its own contribution by adopting the "culture of we," consolidated as the [Palmach] soldiers . . . gathered around the bonfire. The kibbutz made the collective tasks a top priority and demanded that the members comply—that they sacrifice their private desires and aspirations to the needs and demands of the

society. From the early sixties on, however, we can discern a growing tendency to divert the emphasis from "we" to "me." (38–39)[11]

Gan captures the individualistic departures from classic values, precedents leading to the subsequent dismantling of collectivization, in the starkest terms: "From the kibbutz as a meaningful way of life to the kibbutz as a home; from 'exclamation marks' to 'question marks'; from ideological discourse to psychological parlance; from 'we' to 'me'; from the collective to the self-realization ethos" (33–34). Whereas the founders conceived of their lives as a bold alternative to the debasing effects of capitalism, those born in the kibbutz regarded themselves as simply at "home," a natural way of being that did not demand "any ideological justifications" (34). And that difference gave rise to all the questioning by kibbutz writers, culminating in the critical narratives of doubt and recrimination addressed in the later pages of this study. Self-consciously, the earlier writers recognized that if the kibbutz was somehow intended to be a permanent departure from or a radical discontinuity with recent Jewish history, that grandiose revolution failed (and as we will discover in chapter 1, sobering misgivings emerged even in portrayals by writers who were among the most fervent ideologues). Yet such was the mythic power of that revolution that its allure persists for many.

Imagining the Kibbutz aspires to fulfill what I have long felt to be an urgent need—to provide an altogether different perspective from that afforded by the long tradition of kibbutz research amassed by social scientists and other investigators of various spheres of kibbutz life (industry, agriculture, education, economics). Inevitably, such investigations have neglected the *individual*, that precious and intimate realm to which the writer's imagination is invariably dedicated. Some of the most compelling works I address exhibit distinctly extranarrative lives that deeply resonate with their authors' very personal entanglements with the history of the kibbutz, lives that ensure the humanizing provenance of their art. The relationship between literature, the rise of the kibbutz, and the individual is a fascinating story, one whose beginning Iris Milner astutely recounts:

> The first decades of the kibbutz were marked by a consistent rise in its status as a leading, indispensable factor in the Israeli social and political milieu. Literature's commitment to the support and reinforcement of this status is apparent not only in its treatment of the kibbutz setting . . . but also in the dramatic narratives that it presents. This is particularly

evident in the historical novels that follow the development of specific kibbutzim through their initial stages. The chain of events these novels commonly recount starts from the very first steps of the communal group and leads to its successful establishment. The overt message thus relayed clearly relates to the advantages of kibbutz ideology and practices in "conquering" the land of Israel and in accomplishing the desired metamorphosis of the allegedly sick diasporic "Jewish" body into a vital, manly, cured Israeli one. (164)

Decades later, even though the kibbutz no longer held the lofty, commanding position Milner describes, I found myself as profoundly stirred by its values as countless other youths had been before me. So many of us were utterly enthralled by the kibbutz's revolutionary aura: "Egalitarianism and equality . . . presented not only as just and moral social causes, but as crucial conditions for the realization of national, Zionist aspirations" (Milner 165).[12] Accordingly, in the 1970s, I leaped at the opportunity to help establish a young kibbutz, Yahel, in the southern Arava Desert with other young people from Israel as well as the United States. And though every day seemed to present daunting challenges, both agricultural and social, in those halcyon and endless days, it seemed to many of us that everything was possible.

Some of us felt that we had found fulfillment beyond anything we had ever thought possible, and we could not imagine ever leaving, whereas others were soon discomfited by the lack of privacy for individuals or families or by the difficulty of adjusting to a life so far removed from urban pleasures. Years after moving away with his growing family, Ellis Shuman, a close friend with whom I once worked in the kibbutz cowshed and who had served for a time as kibbutz secretary, published a dozen stories in English examining the struggles of a variety of kibbutz members adapting to "new realities." Today, his collection *The Virtual Kibbutz: Stories from a Changing Society* (2003) strikes me as a profoundly perceptive portrayal of new developments, one that also grapples with the themes that have long preoccupied the literary witnesses to the rise and perpetual transformation (or deterioration) of the kibbutz. Since my friend is both a genuine autodidact and a natural optimist, it is hardly surprising that his stories are largely hopeful. Even as they range across the sharp vicissitudes faced by ordinary individuals (the turmoil of youth, the crisis of aging) as well as society (relations between Arabs and Jews, the wrenching shift from socialism to capitalism), more often than not, they conclude on notes of reconciliation or gentle open-endedness, tending to affirm the kibbutz's extraordinary ability to adapt. Yet, after experiencing thirteen years of communal life, I find myself more drawn to the few stories in his collection that are decidedly darker, more ambivalent in tone. These feature veteran kibbutzniks dreading changes that threaten the values they have spent lifetimes defending or former kibbutzniks looking in from the outside.

In a story representative of the sanguine majority, "The Kibbutz at the End of the Universe," Avi, a wealthy developer, tries to coax a kibbutz into converting its low-profit agricultural lands into a commercial center. This soured businessman bitterly dwells on how a kibbutz accident had drastically changed his life—he lost several fingers to the blades of a harvest machine. Now, years later, a reunion of his old Nahal comrades tempts him with the delicious prospect of flaunting the extraordinary success he has achieved since those distant days of dreams, sweat, and toil.[13] Yet the mere sight of verdant fields and hothouses in Israel's desert unexpectedly rekindles his long-extinguished idealism. Gradually, the desire to flaunt his success before old comrades wanes, and Avi comes to the happy realization that "business was not on the agenda . . . but friendship was" (*Virtual Kibbutz* 120). Along with the character's sentimental epiphany, this story highlights the remarkable vigor and bold experimentation of Israel's desert settlements.

In marked contrast to that story's sunny mood and its protagonist's redemption, Shuman's epistolary story "The Receding Shoreline" strikes a distinctly elegiac, even melancholy tone, as the narrator, one of the founding generation of pioneers (now reduced to a "few powerless idealists"), witnesses the death of his kibbutz. Based on the shores of the Kinneret (Sea of Galilee), it once withstood Syrian shelling, only to succumb to capitalism as it is woefully transformed into villas for rich outsiders (perhaps by the wealthy developer Avi?). At his brother's gravesite (a man who had sacrificed his life in a gruesome agricultural accident), the narrator contemplates the stark fact that "there is no younger generation to replace us" (137). In a similar mode, Genya, the ailing founder of "Requiem for a Dream," shudders at the construction project that will bring about the ruin of her world by selling off lots to outsiders eager to escape Israel's congested urban areas but not remotely inclined to join the social fabric of the kibbutz community: "The kibbutz was dead, of this Genya was certain. She had no need to look further than out of her kitchen window to see the most recent proof of the kibbutz's demise. There, barely a hundred meters from her home, was the construction site. The walls of the new houses were rising daily. Sweat-drenched foreign workers struggled with heavy bags of cement and pounded nails into wooden frames" (159). Of course (and perhaps even its author overlooked this irony), the fact that Genya's house even includes a kitchen from which to bemoan the demise of the kibbutz would itself have been cause for anguish in an earlier generation, a reminder to purists that, confronting one change or another, the kibbutz has *always* been in crisis.[14]

Beyond his spot-on portrayal of the social upheavals still corroding the kibbutz movement, what Ellis Shuman most successfully captures is the plight of disenfranchised individuals like Genya, who, lonely, frustrated, and aggrieved that, after a vigorous life of labor amid like-minded comrades, she must now rely on a walker to get around, dreads what is to come: "She held on to the metal bars of the walker, looking out at buildings that would serve their residents as nothing more than a physical place to sleep. These people, her future neighbors, would have no part of the kibbutz, its democratic institutions or its joint, collective future. They were purchasing the positive elements of life in her community—her home—while assuming none of the obligations" (159). In her anguished state, the dwellings under construction appear like "tombstones in a cement covered cemetery" (160). Shuman bookends the story with scenes of Genya hospitalized after a bitter ideological battle with her own daughter—whom she calls a traitor for "leading this anti-kibbutz revolution" (183)—leaves her broken in spirit. Slowly recovering, she recalls her late husband's advice fifty years earlier, to accept the fact that "a kibbutz is a living organism. Its members adapt and change. . . . You have to learn to embrace changes. . . . Changes are a part of going forward. Don't be afraid to allow changes to be part of your life" (190), an ethos that eventually guides Genya to reconcile with her daughter. And that would seem to be Shuman's own determined perspective on the way forward for the kibbutz were it not for the final story in the collection, judiciously titled "A Balanced Picture." Here a researcher for a television documentary finds himself inspired by the strategies with which many traditional kibbutzim staunchly *resist* the sweeping economic processes that might endanger their collectivist and egalitarian values, especially the well-being of their more vulnerable members.

It intrigues me that Shuman first conceived the idea for this collection long after he left the kibbutz. Writing my own book has led me to share his belated understanding (and apparently also that of many artists, filmmakers, researchers, and bloggers) that the kibbutz is never quite done with us, not even many years after we think we have moved on. We both consider ourselves fortunate to have participated in such an exuberant adventure. For so many of us, being former kibbutzniks remains an important part of how we identify ourselves later in life and of the values we try to uphold, no matter how much our paths eventually diverge.[15] Nevertheless, my friend Ellis wrote his stories in the wake of the transformative 1990s, by which time the kibbutz was the last surviving, nearly anachronistic institutional remnant of Israel's once-vital socialism, and, after the degradations wrought by privatization, many had come to view it as little more than a lifeless fossil.

The kibbutz writers inaugurated some of the first antiheroes in the Hebrew literature of the Yishuv and the early years of the Israeli state. Perhaps because of their often conflicted views on the kibbutz's social complexity, their narratives express a bold mixture of moods and modes of storytelling—exuberant and sour, confident and gloomily foreboding, blunt and sly, satirical and sincere. A great deal of their strength resides in choosing not to stack the deck—even in the most contentious ideological battles of the day, every camp makes its case, so that we must make our own choices as readers. And always we feel the ferment and urgency of acute social pressures, the sense that it all matters terribly. Even now, the raw power and urgency of their works sternly rouses us from our complacency and detachment. Not surprisingly, kibbutz fiction runs the gamut of styles distinguishing Modern Hebrew literature (social realism, psychological realism, mythic epic, magical realism, allegory, to name a few) and of its broadest thematic preoccupations (questions of identity and place, tensions between religious tradition and socialist secularization, the sacrifice of young lives, rifts between Diaspora and national homeland). Most memorably of all, its writers have contributed some of the most exciting perspectives on Israeli literature's enduring and troubled preoccupation with the fate of the individual protagonist, bearing the burden of collective obligations that sometimes put him or her in mortal peril. In that regard, their kibbutz narratives encode what Omri Herzog cannily identifies as the "deep structure" of Israeli literature, namely, the clash between individual desires and unyielding national imperatives, which forms the connective tissue of many of the works explored in the chapters to come.

At times, these writers shrewdly measure the surprising distances, secrets, and lies between individuals in their claustrophobic society, raising the question of the authentic self. Complications they present to us with great fidelity include protagonists who struggle with the stigma of some form of outsider status (ethnic or otherwise) deemed suspect by the insular elite or whose questioning of the collective mission or the national heroic ethos to which they are harnessed can prove self-alienating. Such urgent literary interventions are hardly surprising, given the extraordinary sacrifices the kibbutz has made in wartime, as well as its once potent role in the political sphere. And by placing some of the less familiar, antecedent works of writers such as Arthur Koestler, Meyer Levin, and David Maletz in conversation with more recent works by Eli Amir, Batya Gur, and Amos Oz, we can better gauge the extremely varied and sometimes surprising nature of the responses to the challenges and contingencies addressed in the kibbutz literary imagination over a span of more than eighty years.[16]

Though by no means pretending to be exhaustive, *Imagining the Kibbutz* is the first sustained study of imaginative portrayals of the kibbutz from its earliest decades to the present. Addressing both narratives by kibbutz "insiders" (including those born and raised there, as well as those who joined the kibbutz as immigrants or migrants from the city) and "outsiders" for whom the kibbutz is a crucial microcosm for understanding Israeli values and identity, this diachronic study addresses highly representative novels, short fiction, memoirs, and cinematic portrayals of the kibbutz in documentaries and in art as well as mainstream Israeli films. Wherever possible, I based my study on narratives that are the product of direct experience and observation and were written quite close to the time portrayed. Above all, I sought to underscore the strikingly recurrent themes that resound from the 1930s to the contemporary era, especially the many conflicts between individualism and the collective ideal, which often present us with a microcosm of the anxieties at the heart of Israeli society.

These are works for which those of us interested in the idea and reality of kibbutz (no matter what our disciplinary perspective) should be profoundly grateful, for they sift through the historical, emotional, and familial layers that have enriched it over time. In some narratives, ideological compromise gets a bad name, and in others, it proves redemptive. Yet there is also a kind of release in the fact that the messy jangle of kibbutz life and its processes is rarely idealized: kibbutz writers transcend the possibility of purity and remind us to acknowledge the inherent imperfection of the very best intentions even as we strive to achieve something greater. We see what is painful and shocking but also the undeniable blessings of collective living. And so often, in their most reverberating and morally imaginative moments, kibbutz narratives explore the urgent question of what individuals owe their society and what society owes them.

Chapter 1 launches this study of richly conflicted literature by tracing the earliest literary portrayals of the kibbutz and related developments from the late 1930s to the early 1950s, beginning with a discussion of Meyer Levin's 1931 novel *Yehuda* (the first American account of Zionist communal life) as well as S. Yizhar's very first story, the novella *Ephraim chozer le-asfeset* (*Ephraim Goes Back to Alfalfa*; 1938). Here Yizhar (still one of Israel's most revered writers) presents a romanticized view of a Negev kibbutz, leavened by a satirical edge that establishes the great theme that would grip later generations of writers: the conflict between exuberant, instinctual individuals and their virtuous, demanding egalitarian society. Or, in David Aberbach's memorable formulation, just "how does one become an individual while being ideologically bound, often painfully and nauseatingly, to strangers in a closed world from which there is little chance of escape?" From *Yehuda* and "Ephraim," we turn to the second-earliest (and arguably most provocative) novel in the history of literature written in English about the kibbutz, the prickly semiautobiographical novel *Thieves in the Night* (1946) by Hungarian-British author Arthur Koestler. Set in the final troubled years of the British Mandate, the novel juxtaposes the fervor of Jewish socialists with the increasing anger of the native Arab population of Palestine, creating a troubling connection between the dream of utopia and romanticized violence. This was the pioneering era of the "tower and stockade" settlements established in vulnerable territory, when the ever-mercurial Koestler was persuaded that Zionism should aspire to supplant rather than fulfill Judaism. In another novel of the 1940s, David Maletz's *Ma'agalot* (*Young Hearts*; 1945), an altogether more reflective, even meditative work, the author weighs in with a different perspective on the fate of Jewish continuity by raising the concern that the successful reestablishment of the Jew in the rhythms of agrarian life might bring about the demise of Jewish education and of self-development in other crucial realms. Maletz also sensitively explores the domination of the individual by the demanding pioneering society.[17] Though written in the same period of rapidly escalating tensions as Koestler's near-martial manifesto, *Young Hearts* focuses our attention instead on the complexities of daily life within a total ideological system. Thus, chapter 1 not only highlights the crucial role of the frontier kibbutzim and the individual farmer-soldier ideal in the Israeli imagination and public consciousness of the 1950s; it also draws critical attention to how some writers were more preoccupied by the struggle to create a life of meaning in the transition from traditional religious life to a thoroughly secular one during the rise of the political and cultural hegemony of the Labor Movement. Yet, above all, we come to appreciate the consolidation of the proud ethos, memorably captured by historian Zeev Drory: "The fundamental values of the kibbutz movement, on which its education methods were founded for many years, were socialism, the collective egalitarian way of life, work, volunteering, pioneering, and bearing the burden of national and societal missions. Security and defense have always been at the very heart of its ideology and endeavors. The dual symbols of the sickle and the sword have been intertwined since the founders' generation" (186).

Chapter 2 is devoted to the critical visions of Amos Oz, Nathan Shaham, and Avraham Balaban. Oz and Balaban are nearly of the same generation and are both former members of Kibbutz Hulda, whereas Shaham continues to live in Kibbutz Beit Alfa, his home since 1945. Until a son's severe asthma required relocating to the desert town of Arad in 1986, Oz thrived at Hulda, reportedly once telling his friend Balaban, who has a very different take on his early years, that "for you the kibbutz was a nightmare, for me it was redemption" (qtd. in Lori). Oz's short stories, essays, and novels from those years (*Where the Jackals Howl*; *Elsewhere, Perhaps*; *A Perfect Peace*) artfully probe the realization of egalitarian values amid the frail lives of maladjusted individuals and the idiosyncrasies of kibbutz society.[18] In his later, post-kibbutz career, Oz's critically acclaimed memoir, *Sipur al ahava ve-hosheh* (*A Tale of Love and Darkness*; 2002), partially illuminates his flight at the age of fifteen from his father's home in Jerusalem to Kibbutz Hulda, difficulty adjusting as an outsider with an artist's sensibility, and a recent collection of interconnected kibbutz stories, *Be'in haverim* (*Between Friends*; 2012), represents a significant return to his earlier wellspring of inspiration (though where the pervasive tone in the earlier works was pugnaciously acerbic, this late work is gently melancholic in spirit).

A recipient of the Israel Prize for Hebrew Literature and Poetry, Shaham served three terms as kibbutz secretary, and his *Kirot etz dakim* (*The Other Side of the Wall*; 1977) exhibits a deep and lively insider's knowledge of myriad aspects of kibbutz life from the Palmach era to the present. Shaham also offers us a rare glimpse of a kibbutznik struggling to cope when fate plunges him into an unexpectedly prolonged and unpleasant immersion in American capitalism (and the inner demons it arouses). The final work addressed in chapter 2, Balaban's *Shiv'ah* (*Mourning a Father Lost: A Kibbutz Childhood Remembered*; 2000), castigates the communal child-rearing system in which he was raised for having created adults who "evince the selfishness of people who never got enough protection and security."

Later chapters turn to "outsider" works by Atallah Mansour (*In A New Light*), Eli Amir (*Scapegoat*), Batya Gur (*Murder on a Kibbutz*), and Savyon Liebrecht ("Kibbutz"), none of whom lived for periods of significant duration in the kibbutz yet whose probing works nonetheless offer exceptionally penetrating and empathic considerations of both the trauma of childhood and the marginalization and mistreatment of outsiders. In chapter 3, we encounter contentious issues of ethnicity and national identity still festering in Israel today. One would think that Mansour's *B'or hadash* (*In a New Light*; 1966) would be of exceptional interest as the first novel written in Hebrew by an Arab citizen of Israel, but today it is largely forgotten. Born and raised in Palestine, Mansour lived on Kibbutz Sha'ar Ha'amakin, in northern Israel, from 1951 to 1952, and his vibrant novel, characterized by rich use of Hebrew slang (in those days still comparatively rare in Hebrew literature), vividly captures the fervent ideological debates that raged within the kibbutz as well as its role in national politics, all through the ironic gaze of an Arab "passing" as a native Jewish Israeli.

Israel is, of course, a nation built on waves of immigrants, but only rarely has that history been examined in relation to the kibbutz movement, which is one reason to be grateful for Eli Amir's *Tarnegol kaparot* (*Scapegoat*; 1983). A best seller in Israel, adapted for the stage as well as Israeli television, the novel is little known elsewhere in spite of its availability in a lively English translation. And that is regrettable because *Scapegoat* is one of the most heartfelt, thoroughly compelling, and often quite hilarious coming-of-age stories in the entire Israeli literary canon. With great psychological depth and insight, this picaresque novel provides a fascinating window into the cultural upheaval experienced by immigrant youngsters from Iraq and North Africa as they struggled to adapt to kibbutz socialism, leaving their parents behind in the *ma'abarot*, or immigrant transit camps. The chapter's analysis centers on how Amir's protagonist and his friends, hailing from traditional societies in Arab countries, are torn between traditional family frameworks and the demands that they conform to communal lifestyles that seem wholly aberrant to them. We also glimpse how their families were utterly dismayed by what they regarded as a condescending secular community's relentless hostility to faith and tradition, by the opposition to private ownership, and by the degrading life of manual laborers, which their sons and daughters were supposed to embrace. Poignantly, both Mansour's and Amir's novels conclude with their beleaguered protagonists still struggling to straddle two worlds, eyeing their futures warily.

Chapter 4 considers the breakdown of values in the traditional kibbutz as portrayed in two deeply empathic works by two of Israel's most popular women writers (intriguingly, both were born to Holocaust survivors around the time of Israel's own birth). Though perhaps never previously considered alongside one another, the two narratives of Savyon Liebrecht (b. 1948) and Batya Gur (1947–2005) are both highly attuned to Israel's political, social, and economic problems, especially to the marginalized and vulnerable in Israeli society, those struggling against ethnic discrimination, poverty, unemployment, and disability. Aside from these congruencies, both of these probing works (Gur's detective novel *Murder on a Kibbutz* and Liebrecht's psychological suspense story "Kibbutz") happen to feature strong female characters and to sensitively delineate the travails of new immigrants.

Chapter 5 considers classics of Israeli cinema such as Yitzhak Yeshurun's *Noa bat sheva-esrei* (*Noa at Seventeen*; 1982), Akiva Tevet's *Atalia* (1984), and Dror

Shaul's highly controversial and semiautobiographical *Adama meshuga'at* (*Sweet Mud*; 2006), a production that presents a starkly unsentimental view (as Gur and Liebrecht do) of kibbutz childhood and the collective's sometimes callous treatment of vulnerable individuals. The chapter goes on to explore exemplars drawn from personal documentary film and video art. Portraying important moments of crisis in individual lives and kibbutzim, they also mirror larger concerns and trends in Israeli society. For instance, set in 1951, *Noa at Seventeen* is both a gripping story of a young girl's adolescent disillusionment with the unquestioning collectivism of her friends and an incisive chronicle of the young state's ideological struggles, indelibly portraying the wrenching and sometimes violent conflict between the individual and the collective that was such a critical dynamic in the early years of the state, often forgotten today. The tense atmosphere Yeshurun creates is a faithful portrayal of the crisis of Israeli socialism in response to the Soviet Union's aggression and brutality on the eve of the Korean War, which ultimately shattered families and led to the breakup of a number of kibbutzim. Because Russia was both the ideological inspiration and country of origin of numerous kibbutzniks, they found it painful to relinquish their loyalty to the Soviet cause (many were still inspired by the heroic Red Army's struggle against Hitler and revered the Soviet Union as their "second homeland"), long after others became disillusioned by its social and economic failures. Noa, the film's heroine, wakes up to her own prickly individuality exactly when those around her demand unflinching loyalty to their cause.

In contrast to Yeshurun's reconsideration of the ideological wars of Israel's early years, Jonathan Paz's film *Eskimosim ba Galil* (*The Galilee Eskimos*; 2006; screenplay by Joshua Sobol) examines the decay of socialism in the contemporary kibbutz through a more nostalgic lens. A popular commercial movie that played at film festivals across the globe, it depicts a band of senior citizens who, wakening one day to find that the younger generation have sold the home they pioneered in the Galilee to a group of businessmen, struggle to rebuild their community and to defend their values against a greedy capitalist society that dismisses them as wholly anachronistic. Juxtaposing humorous and elegiac incidents, Paz makes a surprisingly resonant statement about the fate of ideology, while compassionately preserving the dignity and humanity of the nearly forgotten veterans who make a last, quixotic stand to preserve their dream. Paz's warm and evocative portrayal memorializes the culmination of a historical process pithily summarized by Anita Shapira: "The bond to the kibbutz was no longer preserved by ideology, which had collapsed, but by inertia and a sense of belonging [only] to place and family" ("Kibbutz and the State"). After considering the recent outpouring of critically acclaimed documentaries that reexamine the kibbutz movement in the light of new controversies over the much-vaunted institution of "children's houses" (or "children's homes") as well as the recent trauma of privatization, chapter 5 concludes with an appreciation of the melancholic vision permeating the poetic art videos of Oded Hirsch, a native son of Kibbutz Afikim.

Sadly, though their works continue to alert us to alternative ways of being, when it comes to the sense of literary vocation and purpose of kibbutz writers themselves, they felt their status within the community markedly deteriorate under the onslaught of unprecedented economic stresses and social transformations as early as 1987, when even prestigious kibbutz writers such as Nathan Shaham began to speak nostalgically of the past and uneasily about current trends: "There was a time when kibbutz society believed that literature was a sort of service to the society. It was thought that writers had an extraordinary capacity to benefit the society, and they had a hard time because of this exaggerated demand. Today, there is a certain indifference to the ability of literature to make a mark or to change anything in kibbutz society" (Rosenfeld 168). Shaham came from a generation of fierce dedication, for whom anything less meant living inauthentically in the world. Also responding to queries from *Shdemot*, writer Aliza Amir-Zohar spoke even more pessimistically about the ground shifting beneath her amid the fading values caused by economic duress and idealistic exhaustion:

> When matters of spirit and creativity, art and culture, held higher priority, every kibbutz was blessed with people who were creative in this area. It wasn't a question of whether or not they were given days [to practice their art] but rather that the society attached great significance to these things. Today—I don't know. There is no doubt that the order of priorities, the scale of values in the kibbutz, has been reversed. . . . Today you can find kibbutzim whose first step in dealing with the adversity is to abolish the poets' and the artists' and the writers' work days, because these things are perceived as superfluous when people are struggling for their existence. I say this in anger, with regret, and can no longer say that kibbutz society appreciates its writers and artists. I am very fearful of this process. (Rosenfeld 169)

In retrospect, Amir-Zohar's misgivings now seem prophetic. For, in spite of many who once viewed commitment to a life in the kibbutz as almost monastic-like in its demanding rigor (most notably, other literary writers addressed in this study), its ideological tenets have collapsed under deteriorating economic conditions. As researchers Richard Sosis and Bradley Ruffle pointed out in 2004: "Until a decade ago many kibbutz members would have considered the Marxist proposition 'From each according to his ability, to each according to his need' to be 'sacred,' in other words, beyond question. However, . . . as the economic situation on the kibbutzim has worsened, many kibbutzniks have challenged and ultimately rejected this fundamental proposition of kibbutz life, as evidenced by their decision to privatize their kibbutzim" (112).[19] In place of the old communal and egalitarian forms of economic and social governance, privatization (hafrata) led to the rapid (and some might say hasty) reclassification of the kibbutz, to kibbutzim that are today little more than suburbs where the members receive differential salaries and to a number that retain the old communal forms, with some variations. Perhaps the most regrettable aspect of privatization is that, even though a degree of economic support is provided to those struggling within the new kibbutz economy, this is now understood as a form of charity rather than the mutual social welfare that once encompassed everyone and won the admiration of the world. It is no exaggeration to say that for many of us, the once unthinkable has come to pass. And yet hope remains. Accordingly, my afterword turns to how many of the anxieties embodied in kibbutz narratives anticipate the present moment of a crisis that continues to fuel heated debates within the kibbutz movement in the aftermath of hafrata. In what amounts to a coda to the earlier chapters, the afterword considers these debates as examined both by novelists and poets and by kibbutz sociologists, taking heed of their arguments to present the fate of the kibbutz as an open, enduring, and urgent inquiry into the meaning of both collective and individual responsibility, of what has already transpired and what might yet be.[20]

Trepidation and Exultation in
Early Kibbutz Fiction

For Meir Avrahami the movement is all. Without it he ceases to exist. He is prepared to put up
with anything, be it work that is not to his liking or the company of people he does not respect,
as long as it helps to fill the ranks. His tastes are simple and his clothes look neglected and he
does not pay attention to mealtimes, and the resigned smile of a beatific monk spreads over his
face as they tell him that the boiler has exploded and there is no hot water in the shower.
—*Nathan Shaham*

Such is kibbutz: pretentious, obstinate, exposed and revealing, of variegated designs and
textures, of special and original human relationships, of expectations and disappointments,
pleasure and pain, rejoicing and sadness, togetherness and aloneness, liberty and
confinement. . . . Come, let's examine what truly lies behind all this.
—*Dan Shavit*

Given the imposing influence of the kibbutz in the fashioning of Israeli identity, it should come as little surprise that it has also been a pervasive and provocative presence in the formation of Israel's literary and, more recently,
cinematic culture. As Jo-Ann Mort and Gary Brenner observe: "Until the end
of the 1970s, most Israelis knew someone on a kibbutz. If you weren't a kibbutznik yourself, you had family on a kibbutz that you visited on holidays; or
maybe your parents sent you to spend the summer holiday with the kibbutz
cousins. And young people in the city were sent to the youth movements with
the possibility of going through the IDF [Israel Defense Forces] Nahal (agricultural settlement corps) and eventually becoming a kibbutz member" (14).[1]
Yet strikingly little attention has been paid to the fact that so many of Israel's

founding writers were raised or otherwise spent a significant number of their formative years on a kibbutz.[2] Though two decades transpired from the founding of the earliest communal settlements to the publication of the first kibbutz novels, the independent and often skeptical voices of writers have been an energetic presence in Israeli literature. Many of their works are notable for their moral seriousness, intellectual depth, and exciting candor about the gains and losses incurred by one of the most genuinely revolutionary achievements of the Zionist Movement. Still, why should the fact that the kibbutz inevitably entered the Israeli literary imagination really matter, no matter how robust its presence?

It matters precisely because reading the literature of the kibbutz can bring us profound insights into how ideology responded to historical contingency in different periods of Israel's history, to the tensions between the aspirations of the individual and the collective and between the Zionist socialist revolution and the Jewish Diaspora. To cite Bernard Horn, this phenomenon "would not matter much if Israeli literature were an 'art for art's sake' sort of literature in which society is either irrelevant or viewed exclusively as an impediment to the full realization of an individual's potential. But the contrary is the case for Israeli literature, which began and for the most part continues to be an engaged literature, a literature of allegory and advocacy in which the Jewish vicissitudes of Jewish identity in the Diaspora and Israel play an important role" (190). More than most other modern literatures, Hebrew fiction is tightly entwined with national and historical developments, and the pivotal role of the kibbutz within that realm merits far greater attention.[3] Indeed, Hebrew literature has much to reveal about the ideological construction of a new society, for, as historian Derek Penslar remarks, the kibbutz "has been one of the hallmarks of the Zionist project, and although it appears to have reached its end as a generative and innovative force within Israeli society, the kibbutz's historical grandeur and significance remain unquestionable" (7). Nor does the literature of the kibbutz show any sign of waning. This study addresses how some of its major themes (national identity, the clash between collectivism and individuality, otherness and discrimination, estrangement and alienation) have endured with surprising force as the steadfast concerns of the conscientious kibbutz writer. This is a literature of values, but one that has also reflected the troubled psyches of flawed strivers, the blemishes of the human condition as a whole.

For anyone who wonders just how a pastoral community like the kibbutz could contain the dramatic or even tragic ingredients that might instill the dark vision of life that many believe is essential to great literature, one need only look more closely at the extraordinary human costs and sacrifices involved in the kibbutz's birth, growth, and decay. Assaf Inbari (b. 1968; raised on Kibbutz Afikim) astutely describes the scale of that tumultuously epic history:

> Those who describe the pioneering period, or the early years of the state, under the leadership of Ben-Gurion, as a time of confidence and rejoicing simply ignore its terrible aspects. Internal and external conflicts, resounding failures, longing for parents or country of origin, waves of emigration, suicides, and the death of youth and children from all kinds of diseases always accompanied the activities of settlement and creation. The pogroms of the early twentieth century were among the childhood memories of many of the pioneers. Many veteran kibbutz members were, and still are, Holocaust survivors. About three thousand kibbutzniks fell in the wars and left, on every kibbutz, numerous bereaved parents and siblings, widows and orphans. The schism of the United Kibbutz Movement in the early 1950s was a terrible crisis in the lives of thousands of kibbutzniks and their children. The division of the labor movement in the 1960s, as a result of the furious abdication of Ben-Gurion, and the establishment of Rafi; the downfall of the Labor Party in the 1970s following the Yom Kippur War, until its defeat in 1977; the collapse of the stock exchange in the 1980s, which caused the economic breakdown of many kibbutzim and the consequent "kibbutzim settlement," which led to the privatization agonies of most kibbutzim during the last twenty years—all these painful events and processes have been no less central and critical in the lives of the kibbutzniks than the joyous ones of settlement, building, and growth. ("Kibbutz Novel" 143)

Inbari's own gripping novel, *Ha-baita* (*Home*; 2009), which draws with great skill from memoirs, letters, minutes of meetings, and other ephemera to relate the rise and fall of a kibbutz, was published to rapturous critical acclaim and spent ten months on the Israeli best-seller list.[4] For the most part, the narratives I address, though resolutely avoiding the distortions of nostalgic sentiment, evince a profound regard for the kibbutz's extraordinary achievements and daring in wartime sacrifice, communal innovation, cultural creativity and resilience, agricultural achievement, and what Yehudah Mirsky rightly hails as its "sheer stubborn life force." Indeed, although one might suppose that the kibbutz writer's frame of reference and themes would necessarily be quite provincial, Elisha Porat (poet, novelist, and founder of Kibbutz Ein Hahoresh) seems representative of many of his contemporaries in delineating how:

in the kibbutz there is a little of everything. It can be seen as a drop in the ocean, and it can be seen as a small universe, and I see it as a completely unlimited arena for all possible human events. I consider it above all as my birthplace: I was born here; I know every plot of land, every local story, every bit of its history. To me, the important thing is that it is a small village with which I am very familiar, which by way of artistic association can be turned into an arena for all the struggles in the world. (Rosenfeld 166)

An "arena for all the struggles in the world" seems altogether apt, for who didn't long to join a kibbutz in its glory days? Even the young centaur, the fantastical protagonist of Moacyr Scliar's 1980 Portuguese masterpiece *O centauro no jardim* (*The Centaur in the Garden*), longs to live that life, if he isn't first killed in heroic battle fighting for Israel's independence. We overhear him musing in 1947 (still the golden age of kibbutz socialism) that "I would be very useful there. I who knew farm life so well. I would be a dedicated worker, and the other members of the kibbutz would end up accepting me; in a new society there is room for everyone, even someone with horse's hooves" (*Centaur* 45). Alongside Scliar's improbable hero, whose condition brilliantly embodies the modern human vicissitudes of alienation and an impossible duality, it is worth noting that even *B'or hadash* (*In a New Light*; 1966) by Atallah Mansour (b. 1934), the very first Hebrew novel written by a Palestinian Israeli, memorably scrutinizes the kibbutz's willingness to live by its own values through the eyes of a lonely outsider.

In the mid-1980s, novelist Dan Shavit (b. 1944, Kibbutz Kfar Szold), contemplating the value of the growing literary canon of the kibbutz, seemed to find the greatest merit in that body's capacity to assess the distance between reality and the piety of ideology:

Such is kibbutz: pretentious, obstinate, exposed and revealing, of variegated designs and textures, of special and original human relationships, of expectations and disappointments, pleasure and pain, rejoicing and sadness, togetherness and alone-ness, liberty and confinement. . . . The average person tends to be attached to somewhat shallow formulas, superficiality, false beliefs, and the author responds stubbornly: Come, let's examine what truly lies behind all this. Has, indeed, reality caught up with the dream, or does it, perhaps, lag behind permitting a "critical distance" for the flourishing of the counterfeit, the hypocritical, the admissible falsehood. If this is the mission of the writer everywhere, then even more so in the kibbutz because of its pretentions to values and ethics. (4)

Although the canon of kibbutz literature and art has always been one of sharp contrasts stubbornly affirming the perseverance of ethics and communal solidarity, today most artistic accounts of the kibbutz vision and the fate of kibbutz values are far from sanguine. For instance, critically acclaimed Israeli video artist Oded Hirsch insists that "it's a little trite to keep talking about the shattering of the kibbutz dream. . . . I see it as a dream that was solidified in the early part of the last century. The update it is currently receiving won't last. The kibbutzim have become construction sites. Retirees take mortgages and expand their apartments, but their children live in New York or Tel Aviv and won't come back" (Karpel). How did we arrive at this juncture? In very recent years, there have been numerous obituaries and "postlapsarian" descriptions of the kibbutz's declining position in Israeli consciousness.

Karen Grumberg succinctly and lucidly highlights just what has transpired: "The morally upstanding image of the kibbutz has been tarnished . . . by revelations of systematic gender and ethnic discrimination, by disillusioned ex-kibbutzniks who remember with horror such experiences as the collective children's house, and by the economic disintegration of the kibbutz institution itself" (*Place and Ideology* 38). Alongside Grumberg's recent assessment (shared by many others), when we examine the entire trajectory of the kibbutz narrative closely, we uncover an early skepticism, directed toward even that most hallowed of collective institutions, the children's house. For instance, in David Maletz's novel *Ma'agalot* (*Young Hearts*; 1945), the omniscient narrator strikes a circumspect tone in describing the unintentionally competitive dynamics of collective child rearing, even in the infants' home:

> The infant brought to a collective home has an entirely different set of experiences from the child born into a family. For one thing, he does not come alone. Another infant has come just before him and still another is brought in the following day. His crib stands in a line of identical cribs. From his very first day he is in "society" and runs into social competition. To his parents he may seem the acme of perfection, but here in the home his personality is not outstanding. He is surrounded by other little personalities. . . . So far as the staff . . . is concerned, he is only one of many and he must win his place in life either by his unusual character or simply by force of arms and legs. (*Young Hearts* 226)

That hint of anxiety about the inherent aggression in the most innocent forms of collective life may surprise many who might imagine that, from the beginning, it was a sacred tenet of kibbutz society that was never challenged from within, at least not in the early years. Nevertheless, a sense of caution and uncertainty about utopia's hubris is palpable in Maletz's language.

Though the kibbutz commitment to strict equality through the socialization of its children in communal education may now seem to many a peculiar excess of twentieth-century socialism, that process might also with considerable justification be considered the fulfillment of a far more ancient dream of humanity that Joshua Muravchik notes can be traced back to Plato's imaginary republic. For Plato, the "Guardians" could overcome selfish inclinations by raising their children in common, in ignorance of who was biologically one's own (166); the children so raised, Muravchik tells us, "will not rend the community asunder by each applying that word 'mine' to different things and dragging off whatever he can get for himself into a private home, where he will have his separate family, forming a centre of exclusive joys and sorrows. Rather they will all, so far as may be, feel together and aim at the same ends, because they are convinced that all their interests are identical. . . . They will be free of those quarrels that arise from ownership of property and from having family ties" (331). As explained by Muravchik, Plato's hope is echoed in the rhetoric of the kibbutz movement's own guiding prophets. In bearing the burden of that ancient hope, however, "despite optimal conditions" that endured "seventy years," even those raised in socialism were somehow insufficiently "imbued with communal and egalitarian values" (D. Gavron 158). The kibbutz system began to collapse in the 1970s when a small number of kibbutzim began to make the transition to family sleeping. That ripple eventually became a tidal wave.

Significantly, there is an emergent critical discourse that, according to Rachel Elboim-Dror, expresses "a new and important dimension: the subjective and first-hand experiences of utopia's children, as viewed from their present, mature and adult perspective" (Review 158). Indeed, a number of narratives exemplify this transformative trend. Salient examples from the first decade of the new century include Avraham Balaban's wrenching memoir *Mourning a Father Lost: A Kibbutz Childhood Remembered*, the quasi-autobiographical film *Sweet Mud*, and Ran Tal's documentary film *Children of the Sun*; each embodies this late and frequently pessimistic inquiry. Yet these later works are not really radical departures from the creative engagements of the past at all. Indeed, a chief goal of this book is to demonstrate that the literature of the kibbutz, even in its relatively early years, sought not to reinforce collective kibbutz values but rather to raise complex and challenging questions, perhaps even to play an unexpectedly subversive role. But, most crucially, what emerges even in the more dystopian portrayals of the kibbutz is at least a grudging respect for what was attempted. Yehudah Mirsky argues that, "though the classical kibbutz foundered on the laws of economics, in both its successes and its failures it bequeathed a larger and richer sense of human possibility. And while its arrangements ran counter to certain basic human needs, they did answer to another need—the need, as Martin Buber put it, 'of man to feel his own house as a room in some greater, all-embracing structure in which he is at home, to feel that the other inhabitants of it with whom he lives and works are all acknowledging and confirming his individual existence.'"[5] The writers who themselves participated in enacting that visionary "all-embracing structure" have witnessed its achievement and eventual decline, often in gripping language and extraordinary storytelling endowed with undeniable verisimilitude.

It befits us to note, however, that literature, like the other arts, was not initially encouraged in the kibbutzim. Reflecting that earlier historical reality, in Nathan Shaham's novella "Kirot etz dakim" ("The Other Side of the Wall," the title story of the 1977 collection by that name, set in the early 1940s), the kibbutznik Theo is outraged by what he finds in a book of poetry, even though it is published by his movement's own publishing house: "This decadent poetry . . . has no connection with the lives of working people . . . bears no relationship to the values of Labor Israel. . . . These bourgeois diversions are published by a house that exists off the savings of people who are breaking their backs and living on bread and water. There is something wrong here" (*Other Side* 163).[6] He condemns the tropes of literary language—"metaphors, analogies, personifications" are "wasteful, confusing games"; they distract from the urgent reality of the collective mission: "To bring forth bread with honor; to rule over nature; to create clear, unambiguous, linear, perpendicular, cut-and-dried linguistic tools. To build anew that tower that was destroyed. To take the building stones and lay them out, each in its place. To grab people by the scruff of the neck and say here is electricity, here is manpower, horsepower, productivity, seeds, nails, ideas" (164). In her admirable study of the movement's formative years, Shula Keshet identifies the cause for literature's near-absence in the first two decades of the new utopia; the terms of her analysis are strikingly similar to the rhetoric of Shaham's fictional character. Keshet recalls how A. D. Gordon, the movement's most illustrious ideologue, heartily advocated against literary expression throughout the *entire* Yishuv:

In its first steps, the settlement enterprise swept up the kibbutz members
and imbued them, first and foremost, with endeavor, hard physical labor,
mainly on the land. Literary-artistic writing written by professional writers was rejected and halted. . . . The opinion became rooted in Hebrew
critique that the Eretz Yisrael reality did not yet possess permanence and
typification, and thus could not serve as a model for literary writing. . . .
A. D. Gordon's demand from writers was . . . stringent: he thought that
the transition to "right living," undetached from the land, from nature,
demanded man's all and that only when individuals redeem themselves
and become whole people, their work would in any case become living
work. Gordon accused the Hebrew writers who did not physically take
part in the new life of pioneering of having a sterile "aesthetic" approach
and demanded that they first of all invest all their efforts in creating life
itself. In his view, even Bialik's work did not pass the test. "If Bialik were
here," Gordon dared to say, "working and living a life of labor and nature
and seeing life purely as a life of work . . . and sing us the song of labor
and the life of labor, then I would now give all his poems for that."
("Freedom" 196)[7]

In the days when the devotees of the religion of labor sought to create the New
Hebrew, the writer was associated with the enervated Diaspora. This prevailing
ethos "drove kibbutz writers into silence, or at best to writing in secret, in
stolen hours, just before dawn before going out to work in the fields. . . . Only
after many years of paralysis of their creative power and their voluntary inhibi-
tion did some dare to critically address the early days" ("Freedom" 197).[8] Even
in Maletz's influential novel of 1945, *Ma'agalot* (*Young Hearts*), there are long
swaths of prose in which the author seems to aspire to prove himself a Gordonian acolyte. Thus the protagonist, Menahem, on a wagon ride with his companions home from the fields, drifts in his reveries between love of community,
Eros, and, most important, a feverish ardor for the countryside, all of which
blurs and coheres in a glorious whole, emanating from the miracle of collective
life and agrarian labor:

Silently they watched the peaceful rain descending over the entire
landscape. Someone began to sing, but the rest merely listened. Menahem sat wedged between the others. He felt that the warm rain was
softening the people as well as the soil, softening and fusing them
together. The rain touching them spread a pleasant sense of comfort
and contentment through their bodies. Menahem became aware of invis-

ible but nonetheless powerful bonds uniting the people who together toiled on this land; his heart overflowed with great tenderness for all of them. As during his first days with Hannah [his wife] he felt an urge to declare his love to everyone and to the entire landscape. "And I have betrothed thee forever." . . . He realized that he had struck deep roots into this soil and this society. The knowledge filled him with gladness. (*Young Hearts* 164)

For the *halutzim*, working the land symbolized the rebirth of both the individual and an entire people.[9] As Donna Rosenthal points out, the halutzim found special significance in the fact that "the Hebrew word for man, *adam*, is derived from *adama*, Hebrew for land. They took Hebrew names like Barak (lightning), Tamir (towering), and Oz (strength) or agricultural names like Karmi (of the vineyard) and Dagan (corn); the new names were symbols of a personal and collective rebirth" (103). Still, even in their most rhapsodic portrayals, what Maletz and other early writers seemed to recognize (whether driven into silence or not) was that, no matter how noble the kibbutz's mission, it would never be more than an imperfect veneer for the human frailties that composed its secret life.[10] Nonetheless, the writers struggled mightily to affirm the kibbutz's positive aspects, often siding with the collective against the disgruntled individual.

By and large, the literature of the early period steadfastly served to uphold the polemical goals of both Zionism and socialism, forging an indissoluble link between them. In her brief survey of kibbutz narratives from that time, Iris Milner describes how these strategically

establish the kibbutz as a place of a total realization of the Zionist agenda of fostering the collective over the private sphere, which is a crucial move in the formation of the collective, national identity and a crucial aspect of Socialist Zionism. Indeed, the constitution of a "collective family" in place of the private one—a change which this literature is deeply committed to portraying—represents the twofold ideological rebellion of Socialist Zionism against both Capitalism (represented by the traditional bourgeois family) and Diasporic Judaism (represented by the traditional religious Jewish family). (161)

Though, in our own time, we have witnessed the nearly complete transformation of Israeli society by the economic forces of neoliberal capitalism and privatization and by the overpowering demographic and political dominance of the Haredi (ultra-Orthodox),[11] kibbutz ideology once shaped Israel's national structures as well as its symbolic and mythic systems in myriad ways.

Beginning in the 1920s, Milner identifies "a wide corpus of prose fiction in which kibbutz life and ideology were a central issue. . . . These works accompanied the formation of the idea of communal life in the land of Israel, observed its initial practical applications, and testified to its growing role in the Israeli nation-building process." Yet, from the very beginning, this imaginative literature immediately "also gave voice to some problematic aspects of this revolutionary ideology and explored its limits. . . . Literary representations became an important virtual site where critical reflections on the benefits of the Zionist ethos, particularly in its [dominant] socialist version . . . were expressed" (159). Milner regards the earliest kibbutz narrators as already anticipating the "turbulent struggle for more pluralistic and democratic approaches to collective interests and goals" that beset the movement in its later years of development (161).[12] Moreover, whereas skepticism rarely surfaced in the portrayals of communal life found in the visual arts of the 1920s and 1930s, Milner finds strong evidence of critical doubt and questioning in literary narratives of the time.[13] At a 1986 symposium of kibbutz writers held by the Kibbutz Artzi Movement, the movement reported having found 222 creative writer members, 370 members occupied with "documentary, scientific, philosophical literature," and roughly a thousand other members active as musicians, dancers, choreographers, stage directors, as well as a range of visual and other artists in its ranks (Ring 150).[14] Yet, at the same gathering, poet Mira Meir (b. 1932) of Kibbutz Nachshon, alluding to an entire generation of "technologists, economists, computer operators," warned that very few of the children raised on the kibbutz had any viable connection to the humanities (Ring 161).

It is easy to see how such a utilitarian identity had taken hold. Indeed, as Grumberg argues, it would be hard to exaggerate the essential role that kibbutz society played in the Zionist drama of settlement, the self-realization of the Jewish laborer, and the birth of an enduring myth that remains popular in spite of the atrophy of later days:

> As the fertile breeding ground of Israel's mythical native sons, the Sabras, the kibbutz holds a special place in the national consciousness. Promoting idealism, brotherhood, collectivity, and social justice, the kibbutz founders and residents (called *haverim*, or comrades) oversaw the creation of settlements that were as self-reliant as possible. . . . The mythical value attached to the kibbutz remains forceful in Israel. . . . Part of the reason for this is that the idea of the kibbutz precedes the creation of the state by

almost half a century, and is thus associated strongly with the rough-hewn ethos of the *halutzim*, pioneers, who established the first kibbutzim in harsh conditions. This pioneering ethic constituted the initial expression of the desire to be close to the land, and to exorcise the studious and religious "Old Jew." . . . The kibbutz became a greenhouse for the cultivation of the New Jew and indeed of Israeli identity, the exemplar of the Jewish State that was being shaped, which would be characterized by a self-sufficient, principled collective existence. (*Place and Ideology* 37–38)

The inside testimony of generations of kibbutz artists lends even greater depth and complexity to that historical record. Given the circumstances Grumberg outlines, it is not surprising that, even when literature gained a modicum of respect within the kibbutz movement, it was invariably assigned a highly restricted pedagogical mission, one that excluded ambivalence, skepticism, interiority, or just about any of the psychological dynamics most of us would associate with modern literature. The imagination was to be placed in service to Jewish destiny. The famous Holocaust writer Jakov Lind spent four unhappy years in Palestine immediately after the war. In his autobiography, Lind wrote scornfully of the diminished role for literature and the visual arts that he found in the life of the pioneer, who "was a culture consumer (at its best). The aims of his culture and its achievements seemed very provincial to me. 'For the decorations of the dining hall, for this we need a painter?[,' he would say. ']Or to write a poem for the next anniversary of the founding of the kibbutz, for this one needs a poet, *chaver*?' The entire 'cultural air,' like in all small countries, in all provinces, was to entertain and to decorate only" (139). In compelling detail, Keshet explains how narrative art in the society that Lind despaired of was to have only one mission, "the mission of influencing and shaping the life of the entire generation, of becoming a lever for the greater needs of Eretz Yisrael reality, and contending with shaping the image of a new societal type . . . a unique synthesis of intellectual and farmer. . . . This ideological-didactical demand . . . called upon writers to keep any conflict quiet, ignore the psychological schism, and focus on 'externalized' descriptions of the wilderness" ("Freedom" 200). Even the unpleasant realities of their heroic struggle— "malaria . . . poverty . . . hard physical labor under the burning sun" (201)— were beyond the scope of this austere mission.[15] Rather than celebrate the individual voice of the writer's struggle with oppressive circumstances, "the total identification of the individual with the aims of the community" was to be stressed (201).[16] It helps to briefly consider the didactic nature of the earliest forays of the kibbutz narrative, a genre unique to its time, which Keshet argues sought to "heal the rift between the Jew and the world" ("Freedom" 201).

For example, Shlomo Reichenstein's novel *Raishit* (*Beginnings*; 1943), one of only three kibbutz novels written in Hebrew in the 1940s, is wholly devoted to the conquest of the land and the rhythms of agricultural life; its plot culminates in the "big ceremony" of the kibbutz's first harvest festival.[17] The main theme of *Beginnings*, the sanctification of labor, is craftily embodied in the title: "the re-creation of the world out of chaos, the creation of paradise on earth. . . . The secular pioneer has become a god on earth, and his deeds are praised in religious language" (Keshet, "Freedom" 202). In later years, the unbroken harmony of the New Hebrew taking root in the soil would be parodied to memorable effect by writers such as Amos Oz, whose young Sabra warrior-farmer in *Menuhah nehonah* (*A Perfect Peace*; 1982) spends much of the novel dreaming of being elsewhere, and whose earliest stories included a protagonist gruesomely sacrificed by his demanding kibbutz father.

Obviously critical to this mission of forming the New Jew was the first generation; in that context, Yael Darr offers a fascinating account of the literature on which these children were nurtured, in picture books usually written by educators who were members of the Kibbutz Education Committee (representing the major kibbutz movements):

> The children's story as told by the founding generation usually revolved around the glorification of the kibbutz way of life, depicting kibbutz childhood as the embodiment of heaven on earth. When a city-dwelling child appeared in these stories, his strong yearning for the kibbutz life or at least to the kibbutz was emphasized. The stories were based on collective adventures from the children's home and the children's society. Parents and their "room" were most often absent from the plots. Readers were often addressed by the plural "you," referring to the generational collective of the peer group. (131)

The ardent ideology expressed in the lives of the fathers and mothers of those raised on such narratives is vividly captured in an amusing scene in Moshe Shamir's novel *Hu halach ba-sadot* (*He Walked Through the Fields*; 1947) and the 1959 drama by the same name, set during the British Mandate, in which the young men and women in the kibbutz shower stalls squabble over the few unbroken sets of "shower sandals," which, like everything else, were communal property in the rarefied days when kibbutz socialism was at its height.[18] In later years, kibbutz writers grew increasingly attuned to the critical demands of reflecting the tensions rising between the individual (and nuclear family life) and the pervasive power of what Edna Barromi Perlman calls the "mythologies of collectivity" (102). It is these rifts which *Imagining the Kibbutz* investigates, in a range of popular as well as lesser-known literary narratives, each of which serves as a stirringly poignant portrait of a unique time and place whose norms and values may now seem utterly alien.[19]

Meyer Levin's novel *Yehuda* (1931), set in a fictional "farm commune" identified as "Carmel," provides the very first extended fictional treatment of kibbutz life in either Hebrew or English (it is such an early work that an explanatory note accompanies the greeting "Shalom"). Today Levin (1905–1981) is regarded as the most prominent Jewish American writer of his generation, renowned for novels such as *The Old Bunch* (1937), about the struggle of a group of Jewish characters to leave behind Chicago's West Side ghetto and assimilate into the American mainstream, and *Compulsion* (1956), inspired by the Leopold and Loeb case. In later years, Levin was deeply embroiled in legal conflicts over his dramatized version of Anne Frank's diary, but, as a young man, he labored on a kibbutz near Haifa, which directly inspired his subsequent literary representation.

Considering the number of Jewish American writers addressing the economic struggles of the Depression era, it is surprising that no other contemporary writer looked as closely at the early kibbutz experiment with its alternative egalitarian, democratic, and anticapitalist promise. It is not difficult to imagine that, in its day, *Yehuda*'s pastoral lyricism and unabashed Jewish nationalism would have appealed to readers already accustomed to the images of Zionist propaganda posters or popular documentary films such as A. J. Bloome's *Halome ami* (*Dream of My People*; 1934) and Helmar Lerski's *Avodah* (1935), yet who would otherwise have had few opportunities to encounter such a textured literary portrait of Jewish pioneering efforts in Palestine. Today *Yehuda*'s fervid prose provides a quaint but undeniably appealing portrait of the halutzim. Despite the relative youth of the settlements themselves, Levin's opening paragraphs convey an atmosphere of almost timeless rhythms of Jewish agrarian accomplishment. Through the eyes of narrator-protagonist Yehuda, we glimpse the commune of Carmel in twilight:

> The afterglow of the sun transforms the tin roofs of the cottages into shining sheets of mirror. . . .
> . . . The comrades coming home from work, getting their change of clothes, going across the yard to the shower. Across the yard, facing the

cabins, are the barn, the cow-stable, and the machinery sheds. And span-
ning the back of the horseshoe are the shacks where Rambam does his
carpentry, and Yossel the smith has his shop; there is the long cabin
used for mess-room, and as general gathering place. Who is in the
kitchen? Sarah Lieubovna tonight; she has surely made potato soup.
Above, perched over the whole meshek [settlement], is the bright new
children's house, built of white concrete, how it shines! . . . And then
scattered over the place like pebbles . . . are the sheds, the bakery, the
laundry, and further down in a corner the small house of Dvoraleh's
hennery. (*Yehuda* 2–3)

Levin's language deftly establishes the same halcyon imagery of utopian order
and routine that would later enliven the Hebrew literature of the kibbutz and
tantalize readers for whom such a community later beckoned like an oasis, in
contrast to the frenzied pace of the Israeli city, or even the violence of Israeli
history. Yet a careful reading reveals the origins of the painful conflict that
rages on into our own time. Yehuda's approving gaze sweeps cinematically over
the exotic surroundings, but then settles briefly on an "unplanted" field belonging to the neighboring Arab village.

The kibbutz comrades "are trying to annex" the land, an aspiration with
which readers are apparently intended to sympathize because it lies fallow, thus
serving up the classic Orientalist dichotomy of idle, unproductive Arabs and
redemptive Zionist labor. Still, that unfortunate note of condescending mythos
notwithstanding, readers familiar with the simplicity and ardent antimaterialism of early kibbutz days might still feel a surge of melancholic nostalgia in
Levin's attention to interior spaces of dwellings such as the room of "Aryay
[Arieh] and Aviva" a young couple, described as "white, neat. Their two narrow
beds that Aryay has painted white. A white enameled pitcher stands in a pan.
A stool. An upturned box neatly covered with a cloth. On the box, a small jar
in which Aviva has put blue flowers. A few books on a shelf . . . a small white
curtain" (22). As noted earlier, Levin himself experienced life on a kibbutz
during the 1920s and, in such passages, he is a keen witness to the unfamiliar
values as well as physical routines of communal life.

For instance, in his classic portrayal of a young immigrant male self-named
Maccabee, Levin captures the essential ingredients of Jewish self-transformation:

He had been a factory hand in Cracow. Some of the Jews in the factory
had formed a pioneer-unit, and asked him to join. Once he compre-
hended their idea, it became as integral a part of himself as his right arm.

A Jew, a labourer—of what use in the world was his labour unless it were devoted to the upbuilding of Eretz Yisrael? Their bold Jewish men and women would gather, there they would live, wed, produce a race of stalwart hero children. He dropped his name of Yankelovitch, and like many of the others took a Hebrew name for himself. (33)

A few pages later, "Daavid," another kibbutz youth infatuated with a female comrade, is described as having a "Cossack-striding figure" (49). His quaint vision of romance (which makes for unintentionally humorous reading today) conveys the essence of his generation's aspirations: "If [Sonya] would only come and live with him together, he would read poetry to her in the evenings; the soft words of all the newest Hebrew poets he would read to her. And in long, long talks he would explain his ideas to her of the life that lay before them, of the harvests they would reap from this their land, of the cattle that would increase under his care. . . . They would have children, they would become substantial, important comrades in the commune, whose opinions would weigh heavy on all problems" (57). No words could better sum up the idealistic will to create a new society of culture and labor, as well as its poignant commitment to duty (including procreation), the inescapably romantic yearning of young people in that astonishing moment, and ultimately their self-sacrifice.[20]

One of the more appealing aspects of this early rendering of kibbutz life (which may amount to a self-effacing act of wry mockery on Levin's part) centers on the figure of an American visitor, a character known only as "Mister Paley" (arguably the forerunner of all the lonely outsiders cast as protagonists in later narratives by Amir, Gur, Oz, Liebrecht, Mansour, and others discussed in later pages). Paley is as filled with curiosity about the experimental communes as he is with comforting platitudes about his own society. The first night of the American visitor's sojourn, Yehuda (together with his compatriots Feldman and Podolsky) eagerly questions the American: "What for instance was the condition of labour in America, how much did the average workman earn? Mr. Paley had only the vague knowledge that labourers were overpaid, but cheerfully assured Podolsky that in America all workmen owned automobiles. 'What was happening among the striking miners when you left the country?' 'I'll tell you, if the miners were striking it's their own fault. In America everyone has an equal chance to get ahead. An equal chance'" (93).

At Paley's last risible utterance, Podolsky turns away in evident disgust, calling on another comrade to toss him the latest edition of *Davar* (the newspaper of Eretz Yisrael Workers, which lasted through various incarnations from 1925 to 1996), whose contents are more sensible to him. But a few pages later, Paley, sensing a more sympathetic interlocutor in Yehuda, reveals to him the doubts about America that provoked his journey to Palestine: "America is supposed to be a great big melting pot where they throw in all the nations and they all form a big stew and after they stew a long time they come out all the same—Americans. But that proposition never worked with us Jews, because here after twenty-seven years of stewing I still got something in me that won't come out" (95). As if repudiating the assimilationist paradigm first coined by Israel Zangwill in his drama about Jewish immigrants, *The Melting-Pot* (1908), Levin voices the skepticism about national belonging that stirred a significant minority of second-generation Jewish Americans to reinvent themselves in Palestine. He comes across as a near relative to Ludwig Lewisohn (1882–1955), the popular novelist and essayist who was an impassioned foe of Jewish assimilation, an academic outsider, and who felt himself forever a foreigner in American society.

Yet, though often exultant, *Yehuda* never waxes naive or sentimental, a reminder that Levin himself faced the rigors of pioneering, nowhere more evocatively or effectively rendered than in this grueling description of midday torpor after labor: "The comrades lagged into the yard. Grimy, heavy, sleepy under the sun. No water for the showers. Perhaps to go bathe in the pool. Too far. They flung themselves tired sweaty on their cots. The rooms were stifling heat-clogged. Flies sat on their faces. They waited, waited for the flies to go away, then angrily beat their arms over their heads; the flies only came back. Some sought shade outdoors. No shade, no trees anywhere. . . . Exultant bully-horrible the sun beat down on them" (77). In such moments, A. D. Gordon's dream of the spiritualization of labor seems an impossibly naive doctrine at best. In fact, Levin's language evokes the disappointment of Nathaniel Hawthorne's mid-nineteenth-century novel *The Blithedale Romance* (1852), inspired by Hawthorne's brief dalliance with the failed commune Brook Farm, in which the disillusioned narrator admits that

> the clods of earth, which we so constantly belabored and turned over and over, were never etherealized into thought. Our thoughts, on the contrary, were fast becoming cloddish. Our labor symbolized nothing, and left us mentally sluggish in the dusk of the evening. Intellectual activity is incompatible with any large amount of bodily exercise. The yeoman and the scholar—the yeoman and the man of finest moral culture, though not the man of sturdiest sense and integrity—are two distinct individuals, and can never be melted or welded into one substance. (66)

Of course, unlike the grueling routine of labor that dampened the spirits of Hawthorne's character, the kibbutzniks' days did not end at sundown—indeed, their impassioned ideological debates into the early morning hours often substituted for sleep. One of the early classic arguments *Yehuda* touches on concerns whether some of the labor pool should be sent to work outside—"'That brings up the whole principle of outside work,' put in Shimshon. 'Question of economic theory. Is the group contained in itself, that is to say indigenous, or can it extend branches outside itself'?" (79). So very much would depend on the answer to this essential question by future generations of kibbutzniks.

Another important early writer whose work is redolent with the labor of the new Hebrew farmer of the Yishuv was the incomparable S. Yizhar (1916–2006), pseudonym of Yizhar Smilansky. Born in Palestine, Yizhar spent part of his childhood in Kibbutz Hulda. Aside from serving as a member of the Knesset during Israel's formative years, he is most renowned for his epic novel *Yemei Tziklag* (*Days of Ziklag*; 1958), which ostensibly follows the struggle of a unit of Israeli soldiers to protect a remote Negev outpost during the 1948 War but is primarily a deeply textured delineation of the landscape, flora, fauna, and even sunlight of the new/old country. In his shorter fiction, Yizhar's searing examinations of Israel's national conscience during wartime have been read by generations of students. His novella *Hirbet Hiz'ah* (*Khirbet Khizeh*; 1949), published just months after the war's end (and translated as *Khirbet Khizeh* in 2008), addressed the grim reality of Palestinian dispossession and the flawed behavior of the IDF toward civilians. In the decade prior to the war, Yizhar had already gained recognition for the almost feverish beauty of his language in portraying the intimate bond between human beings (frequently just surrogates for his own ardent subjectivity) and the landscape. Truly a writer's writer, Yizhar was called variously "the Beckett," "the Joyce," and "the Proust of Modern Hebrew"—and sometimes all three at once. Unfortunately, he has often been neglected even though critics have repeatedly identified him as the greatest Israeli writer of his era.[21]

Yizhar's 1938 novella *Ephraim chozer le-asfeset* (*Ephraim Goes Back to Alfalfa*; sometimes titled simply *The Choice* in translation) barely has a plot at all: the title character, a veteran member, simply requests to be granted his desire to switch from his assignment in the alfalfa fields to laboring in the orange grove. The kibbutz declines his request, Ephraim submits, and there the matter ends. And yet that spare plot proves a solid foundation for displaying Yizhar's keen grasp of the clash between the individual's aesthetic, libidinal, or moral impulses and the community's exacting demands for complete obedience and obligation (the heart of the dilemma that would invigorate the works of kibbutz writers

for decades to come).The language of *Ephraim* is quintessential Yizhar, especially his inimitable capacity for capturing what one character calls "feeling in
the flow of time a fragment of eternity" and another, "the fragrant beauty of
the distances" (43, 52). The story's "action" takes place during the deliberations
of the kibbutz assembly (many of its fifty-odd pages gleefully parody the numb-
ing pace of such deliberations, which is so even today), frequently interrupted
by long reveries in which Ephraim escapes in his mind to the Palestinian landscapes that the young Yizhar cherished. And it is for those precious vignettes
that contemporary readers will be grateful.

On the whole, *Ephraim Goes Back to Alfalfa* (collected in *Midnight Convoy
and Other Stories*; 2007) is a bold and sophisticated literary and philosophic
achievement for a twenty-two-year-old writer.[22] Yizhar deftly satirizes the self-
important socialists as they endeavor to quash Ephraim's modest expression of
individualism with their endless pontificating "in a variety of styles and a
multitude of original expressions, drawn from the vocabulary of the newspapers. . . . clad in weighty solemnity founded on reason and nothing else."
When it comes to agrarian routine itself, however, Yizhar strikes a more somber
note, accentuating its poetry. If the opposition between the instinctual protagonist and the prohibitively rationalist collective forms its intellectual back-
bone, the landscape of Palestine, especially the relationship between the first
Hebrew farmer in centuries and the soil, is its beating heart:

> Ephraim will leave the yard in the early dawn and go down to the alfalfa
> field in the valley, stepping in the same footsteps that the sand absorbed
> yesterday and the day before, continuing to tread in the rut engraved by
> the tractor wheels in this reddish soil, covered with the fine night dew, as
> the east, between the long-leaved eucalyptus branches, reddens and
> injects a blush into the greenish blue, while gray crumbly clouds evanesce
> on the cool horizon, their edges fluttering and falling away, and the whole
> land is filled with a quiet chill, and there is no wind. (12)

As is often the case in Yizhar's fiction (even to some extent in his wartime
narratives), the historical background is muted and the land emerges as irre-
sistibly beguiling and almost biblical, except for the quiet but persistent presence of Arab farmers and shepherds.

Ephraim Goes Back to Alfalfa is brimming with evocative passages celebrating the miracle of the first Hebrew-speaking Jewish farmer in modern times,
passages that are among the most memorable in all of Modern Hebrew litera-

ture. Thus "a practiced hand gets on with the job in a flowing rhythm: banking up and pulling down, releasing and collecting, breaking and raking, stamping down, scraping, weeding digging, filling up, and coating the water channel and the walls of the alfalfa bed. Muscles are tensed, your body pushes against your shirt, your vigor is skillfully directed and aimed, without a superfluous or inadequate movement" (37). Even when the assembly's tedious proceedings become most unbearable—"His place is with the alfalfa and nowhere else"; "This isn't the place for self-indulgence" (33)—Ephraim seems to exult in the very labor from which he seeks release. In fact, as the others carry on, Ephraim doesn't speak at all. When asked why he remains silent, he imagines himself far from them all, on horseback galloping through Yizhar's beloved Palestine: "over the open country, between budding cornflowers and a blaze of golden groundsel, and many-colored poppies and colorful sage and purple irises, and banks of wild radish and wild mustard, white and yellow—the entire space filled with shining patches, nothing blurred or pale, no mark or line to indicate limits or boundaries between the song of light and the color" (51). You cannot help but feel the rush of the escape from the assembly's mind-numbing chatter and claustrophobia in Yizhar's breathless, lyrically charged prose.

Ultimately, the trivial question of whether Ephraim should be allowed to work in the orange grove instead of the alfalfa fields veils a much deeper inquiry into just where the collective ends and the individual begins. Or, as David Aberbach expresses it, "how does one become an individual while being ideologically bound, often painfully and nauseatingly, to strangers in a closed world? . . . How can individual choice and freedom be reconciled with group consciousness and needs?" For the self-contained community, "Ephraim with a hoe is a byword" (37), but really, who is he otherwise? Noting that "'orange grove' in Hebrew is *pardes*, and from it, the word 'paradise' derives," Avishai Margalit explains that "Yizhar's great-uncle, Moshe Smilansky, a well-known writer, was also an agricultural entrepreneur who owned large orange groves in Palestine. Part of Yizhar's childhood, in the little colony of Rehovot, was spent in the shade of his uncle's trees. Orange groves were Yizhar's childhood Eden, from which he was expelled when he became an adult. For Ephraim, being assigned to cultivate alfalfa is to be told that there is no return to the lost paradise of childhood." Aside from Yizhar's gesture to his own lost origins, it bears emphasizing again that this many-layered story is especially noteworthy for its decidedly satirical approach to the socialism of its era. The kibbutz was supposed to emerge from the detritus of the Jewish past like a new butterfly unfurling its wings in the dawn. But, as Aberbach cogently asserts, "in its provincial self-absorption and high moral standards, the kibbutz as Yizhar describes it seems . . . almost an extension of the shtetl from which the *halutzim* longed to escape."²³

Indeed, despite their devotion to the New Hebrew, in rushing to quash the tentative expression of selfhood of one of their own, the members of Ephraim's hyperconformist collective seem to emulate the pious constraints, insularity, and exaggerated discipline of Jewish Orthodoxy.²⁴ With telling irony, Yizhar uses their own pronouncements to puncture the conformist presumptions of Ephraim's smug comrades:

> No one leaves, no one sets himself apart, no separate roads for individuals. We, at any rate, won't allow it. Here, with us, no one gets special privileges. There will be no change just for one—we've all got the same right to changes, concessions, a meaning in life and a way in life, work and rest. Do you want to read? So do all of us, and there's a "Literary Circle" and talks and "Mock Trials"; you want music—okay, Shmuel will bring the gramophone and we'll all stretch out on the grass, listen quietly, yawn surreptitiously and go into ecstasies together; didn't we sing beautifully this very evening in idle, sentimental improvisation! And that's not all—there's a Ramblers' Troop, and Circle for Nature Lore and the Study of the Homeland, and a Cultural Committee, and a Library Committee, and a Members' Committee, etc. etc. . . . —and as for general attitudes to the soul of man and inanimate nature, haven't we all read A. D. Gordon and know something about that too? But all of us together. No room for exceptions. (40–41)

Thieves in the Night: From Socialism to the Stern Gang

In the heated polemical drama that is Arthur Koestler's *Thieves in the Night* (1946), the young novelist appears to philosophically weigh the gains and losses of Jewish power and powerlessness for many pages. Ultimately, however, the novel comes down most decisively on the side of Jewish terrorism as the only force capable of shifting British policy in Palestine.²⁵ *Thieves* was a huge success, read and admired by Teddy Kollek and other Zionist officials in Palestine, received prominent reviews in the leading newspapers, and was praised by many cultural luminaries abroad (Billy Wilder and Ben Hecht, among others, were in a bidding war for the film rights, though a film was never made because the subject of Palestine was deemed too delicate by the Hollywood studio bosses). Born in Hungary and educated in Austria and Germany, Koestler first arrived at the port of Haifa in 1926; from there, he journeyed by horse cart to Kvutsah Hephizibah (Hebrew for "God will sow"), one of the earliest of the fertile Jezreel Valley settlements.

Though he would later claim to have spent at least four to five weeks in that notoriously rustic settlement, correspondence from that period indicates a stay of only ten days, and Koestler's esteemed biographer, Michael Scammell, asserts: "He was turned down by the members' assembly as unsuitable for settlement life, a blow to his pride but also a relief" (48).[26] On the other hand, according to Walter Laqueur, Koestler came to know a number of commanders of LEHI and the Irgun and "knew and admired Jabotinsky" (163).[27] After his apparent failure to adjust to the rigors of communal farm life, we know that Koestler spent his later months in Palestine as a foreign correspondent, deeply attracted to the Revisionist Zionism of Ze'ev Jabotinsky, to whose memory he dedicated the novel. Appearing just as the grim enormity of the Holocaust had begun to sink in, his impassioned kibbutz narrative highlights the indifference of the British to the Jewish refugees, and, accordingly, many American rabbis praised it from their pulpits.[28] A *New York Times* best seller, *Thieves* also proved immensely popular in France and other European countries. As for Israel, his biographer reports that during Koestler's arrival during the 1948 War "had . . . been news in the Israeli press. Every taxi driver in Tel Aviv had read *Thieves in the Night*—and was eager to argue with him about its conclusions" (Scammell 327).

Thieves consists of three interwoven parts. In the first, which echoes salient aspects of George Eliot's philosemitic *Daniel Deronda* (1876), we meet Joseph, the son of an English gentile woman whose family disapproved of her marriage to Joseph's father, a Russian Jew. Joseph's own encounter with anti-Semitism (a neo-fascist woman he is in love with is viscerally repulsed when she discovers he is circumcised) inspires him to emigrate to Palestine to join a new kibbutz. There he falls in love with Dina, a girl whose horrific experiences in Nazi concentration camps leave her unable to bear the touch of any man and who is later raped and murdered by an Arab.[29] Joseph's and Dina's destinies are closely aligned with the novel's second part, told through Joseph's diary entries, concerning the life of Ezra's Tower, a fictional colony of the new Jewish warrior-farmers. Koestler describes the stealthy nocturnal construction of Ezra's Tower quite accurately in the chapter titled "The First Day," which opens with its halutzim traveling under the stars on a convoy while singing:

El yivneh ha-galil,
An'u yivn'u ha-galil . . .

God will rebuild Galilee,
We shall rebuild Galilee,
We are off to Galilee
We will rebuild Galilee. (*Thieves* 4)

In Koestler's evocative description, these young people manifestly embody the early Zionist dream of the New Jew: "mostly under nineteen, born in the country, sons and grandsons of the first settlers from Petakh Tikwah, Rishon le Zion, Metullah, Nahalal. Hebrew for them was the native tongue, not a precariously acquired art. . . . Europe for them was a legend of glamour and frightfulness, the new Babylon, land of exile where their elders sat by the rivers and wept. They were mostly blond, freckled, broad-featured, heavy-boned and clumsy; farmer's sons, peasant lads, unjewish-looking and slightly dull. They were haunted by no memories and had nothing to forget" (9–10). They are joined by a few Europeans trained by youth groups such as Hashomer Hatzair, who struggle painfully with the process of rebirth, "unit[ing] the fervor of a religious order with the dogmatism of a socialist debating club. Their faces were darker, narrower, keener; already they bore the stigma of the things to forget. . . . They looked nervous and overstrung amidst the phlegmatic and sturdy Sabras, more enthusiastic and less reliable" (10). Much like Meyer Levin, Koestler creates highly oppositional portraits, between the Jews of exile and those who have successfully transplanted themselves as rooted beings in the soil of Palestine.

If the rooted ones excel in excitable intellectual verbiage, the Jews of exile are as laconic as the American cowboys of Hollywood. Koestler also introduces us to the major political actors of the days of the British Mandate: Arab leaders and village elders, British administrators, Jewish Agency officials, and the Haganah. In the third section of the novel, after Dina is raped and murdered, Joseph seeks revenge from an old comrade who has left the kibbutz to establish a militia closely resembling the Stern Gang. Eventually, Joseph also departs to join the Jewish terrorist movement as well, and we are meant to regard his repudiation of the moderate kibbutz as a laudable, even evolutionary act marking the authentic maturation of both a cause and the individual.

Nevertheless, Koestler pays substantial homage to the stockade and watchtower method of settlement to which his characters willingly sacrifice their youth, and he portrays them as both a cultural and territorial breakthrough.

Historically, the success of this model depended on the following elements, concisely enumerated by Henry Near in his magisterial history of the kibbutz movement: "official protection on the first day [an escort of armed police], completion of tower and stockade by nightfall, direct visual communication with a neighboring settlement, and reasonably swift access in time of emergency" (1:318). Near's historical account as a contemporary witness to the well-organized but labor-intensive process of settlement underscores the verisimilitude of Koestler's own version, notwithstanding the brevity of his sojourn:

> The day of settlement is fixed in advance, after the removal of all the many obstacles, and completion of the practical preparations: consolidation and evacuation of the appointed lands, confirmation that the necessary funds are available, the agreement of the (British) authorities, which is not easy to obtain, and preparation of the defensive equipment. For some time before settlement day, feverish preparations are under way. . . . In a near-by kibbutz . . . members of the settlement group, together with . . . mobilized members . . . from the neighboring kibbutzim, prepare all the components of the new settlement: the sides of the defense stockade, the watchtower, huts for accommodation, a searchlight, equipment for the barbed-wire fence, and all the basic tools required for work and defence. At the point of departure there is a powerful feeling of expectation. The members of the settlement group are to meet there. During the night, they and their hosts will finish off all the preparations, plan the final operative details, and allocate the different tasks. . . . During the night they load all the equipment on trucks. . . . Long before dawn, the whole convoy—in trucks and carts, some by vehicle and some on foot— moves off to the appointed spot. They are accompanied by many friends and comrades, dozens of police brought along from the kibbutzim in the neighbourhood, representatives of the settlement authorities and the Histadrut, and the commanders of the Hagana's forces.
> At first light . . . the camp's perimeters are marked out, stakes driven in the ground, and a double wall erected around the camp. The gravel is carried from the trucks in baskets and poured between the walls. Here, in the long line, passing the baskets from hand to hand, are old and young, veterans and newcomers, mean and women, all pouring with sweat and all radiating good spirits. In a short while the tower is erected, proclaiming afar that a new Jewish settlement has sprung up. . . . The song of these workers and builders bursts forth into the silent evening. (Near 1:317–18)

Koestler's *Thieves* vividly retraces these fevered activities of settlement while wittily portraying the self-seriousness and excesses of youthful idealism, and ultimately the pettiness and fractiousness lurking behind the heroic spectacle of Zionist fulfillment. In that regard, the narrative is often as psychologically astute as it is historically reliable. Set between 1937 and 1939, the third part of the novel invariably encompasses the grim historical events just unfolding on the world stage as increasingly desperate waves of Jewish refugees sought access to Palestine. Yet, even though the catastrophe of the Holocaust provides the moral rationale for the novel's unapologetic defense of Jewish terrorism, that unyielding militancy is softened to some degree by Koestler's strategic employment of certain characters who drive home the point that the budding Jewish settlements springing up overnight among traditional Arab villages will ultimately benefit the Arabs. Here, for example, is the non-Jewish American reporter Matthews lauding those substantive ameliorations to an Arab *mukhtar*: "You were the pariahs of the Levant and today you are the richest of the Arab countries. . . . [The Jews] haven't robbed you of an inch of your land, but they have robbed you of your malaria and trachoma and your septic child-beds and your poverty" (216).[30] (Similarly patronizing declarations inform Levin's *Yehuda* of the previous decade.) As for the motivations that bring the Jews to Palestine, at one point Joseph admits to himself that "I became a socialist because I hated the poor; and I became a Hebrew because I hated the Yid" (*Thieves* 279). Such moments bear out Ruth Wisse's tribalist argument that the novel as a whole seems to "grant Zionism the right to fight its enemies as a means of solving the Jewish question" (255), a phrasing which seems particularly apt considering Koestler's later notoriety in rejecting the Jewish religion.[31]

To Koestler's lasting credit, though frequently addressing similar themes (illegal immigration, post-Holocaust identity, the Jewish struggle against Arab and British interests), *Thieves in the Night* ultimately refrains from the stereotypes of heroism, à la Ari Ben Canaan, that James Bond of the Jewish Underground, and villainy that notoriously inform Leon Uris's more famous 1958 novel, *Exodus*. (Unfortunately, those very conventions may explain why *Exodus* has never gone out of print.) On the other hand, Koestler undeniably anticipates Uris's argument for the righteous necessity of Jewish violence in Joseph's bitter conclusion (en route to join the militant Underground) that "one can reach a point of humiliation where violence is the only outlet. If I can't bite, my wrath will bite into my own bowels. That's why our whole race is ulcerated in the bloodiest literal sense. Fifteen hundred years of impotent anger has gnawed our intestines, sharpened our features and twisted down the corners of our lips" (*Thieves* 229). In the novel's demonstrably unambiguous denouement,

Joseph becomes disillusioned with the universalist posturing of the kibbutz (tainted by the false values of the Diaspora) and embraces the purgatory force of terrorism, thus embodying the violently conflicting forces that divide Israeli society in our own time. And here is where Koestler's novel ruffled feathers with Israel's first government. Scammell suggests that "every member" of the ruling Labor government was dismayed by Joseph's "conditional endorsement of terrorism" and support of the Irgun. Adding to their consternation was the fact that Koestler continued to meet with his Revisionist friends, "who insisted that it was the Irgun's forces, not Ben-Gurion's, that had driven the British out of Palestine" (327–28).[32] Most intriguingly, Scammell also insists that Koestler personally and quite vigorously identified with the figure of Joseph (though he apparently intended for this character to continue to evolve): "Koestler transposed parts of his youthful self into the figure of Joseph, the half-English, half-Jewish protagonist, whose progress through the novel ends with him reluctantly embracing terrorism, but he didn't intend Joseph's development to end there. He . . . thought of the novel as the first in a series, probably a trilogy" (279). In any case, whatever Koestler did or didn't grasp about the idea of the kibbutz, it is clear that he well understood the situation in Palestine itself; as we now know, the novel's prophecy of violence and Jewish sabotage of the British colonial infrastructure was soon fulfilled, with the subsequent destruction of roads, railroad bridges, and the infamous bombing of the King David Hotel in Jerusalem by the Irgun, resulting in over ninety dead (almost unprecedented in its scale at the time). *Thieves in the Night* fully warrants our appreciation (and deserves far more attention from scholars of Israel studies, among others) as an unusually vivid, faithful, and evocative portrait of life in Palestine, of just what the establishment of a new kibbutz entailed, and of the escalating political tensions between Jewish factions.

Koestler's biographer (joining many critics) aptly hails *Thieves* as "Koestler's best novel after *Darkness at Noon*" (Scammell 282). Yet, today, it reads as a morally troubling document of its times, especially with its rather sympathetic portrayal of its hero's "progress" toward embracing terrorism; indeed, Scammell concludes that, by the third part of the novel, Koestler had clearly lost his "moral bearings . . . blinded by a sentimental loyalty to Jabotinsky and the Revisionist fervor of his youth. . . . What he was unwilling, or unable, to explain was how and when the defensive violence of the weak turned into the oppressive violence of the strong" (Scammell 283, 284). At one point, the leader of the novel's radical Jewish militia declares, "We have to use violence and deception to save others from violence and deception." As Orwellian as that phrase sounds to us now, Koestler was not being remotely ironic. After some inner struggle, Joseph is won over: "He was too weary to argue about ends and means. . . . This was no time for soul searching. Who was he to save his integrity while others had their bodies hacked to pieces? In the logic of the Ice Age, tolerance became a luxury and purity a vice. . . . To wash one's hands and let others do the dirty job was a hypocrisy, not a solution" (*Thieves* 283). Little wonder that the kibbutz vanishes entirely from view in the novel's third part. For, in the worldview that Koestler then embraced, the kibbutz's humane liberalism could secure little of lasting value. In the inevitable violence to come, the spoils of the world would be decisively fought over by revolutionary movements, whether those of the Communists, the Fascists, or the terrorist Zionists of the Irgun.[33]

It is instructive to consider that, in even the most doctrinaire children's stories written or endorsed by kibbutz educators during the most stringently ideological era of the kibbutz movement, we may glimpse occasional fissures of doubt, ambivalence, and self-questioning. In her exceptionally illuminating "Discontent from Within: Hidden Dissent Against Communal Upbringing in Kibbutz Children's Literature of the 1940s and 1950s," Yael Darr finds numerous exemplars of canonical picture books works that reveal surprising slippages. For example, kibbutz poet Fanya Bergstein's *Bo elay parpar nehmad* (*Come to Me, Sweet Butterfly*; 1945), illustrated by Elsa Kantor, breezily portrays "a free-spirited childhood" in which children "meander through the kibbutz outdoors as if it were their home" (Darr 134) without adult intrusion. (It is as if the children dwelled in some socialist version of *Peanuts*.) That absence is pointedly sustained even in the good-night scene, notably the only scene set indoors in this rhapsodic celebration of the Jewish child's rootedness in the natural world, which "shows the peer group of children going to sleep . . . in the children's home, with no adult in sight. Instead, the children are bid good night by 'our watchful dog' . . . Thus, the going-to-bed scene, which in western children's literature revolves around a loving parent attending to a child, here reflects just the opposite: it serves to emphasize the independence of the children's society" (134). Given the strictures laid down by the Kibbutz Meuchad Education Committee (which commissioned the book), it seems surprising that this paradigm was even mildly challenged in the final product. Whether this slippage is the result of unexpected disjunctures often produced in any collaboration between a writer and an illustrator or something more craftily subversive is hard to say with certainty.

Still, as Darr elaborates, Bergstein and Kantor

> wove into the book another model of parenthood diametrically opposed to the kibbutz childhood model. Under the guise of nature and namely ani-

mals, the book repeatedly shows a family model that reveals "home" scenes of mothers and their offspring. The kibbutz children (and through them, the readers as well) are shown viewing these scenes with pleasure. . . .

. . . The fact that every illustration simultaneously includes two enclosed spaces: the home space of the observed object, and the illustration itself as enclosed by an elliptical frame of color, emphasizes the sense of interior, of home, without the latter being mentioned. In this way, while formally the book glorifies the independent kibbutz childhood, it simultaneously also brings to light another childhood model, one based on family and home. (134)

I mention these traces of a surprising dualism because such moments are strikingly similar to the ambivalence revealed in even the most zealous narratives written about kibbutz life for adults. The narrative imagination, even when smitten by the project of utopia, cannot resist voicing skepticism and envisioning alternative ways of being. So it is with David Maletz (1899–1981; fig. 1), a best-selling novelist in the Yishuv and a recalcitrant figure throughout his lifetime. Though Maletz was a founding member of Kibbutz Ein Harod (1923) and an ardent follower of A. D. Gordon's spiritual exaltation of labor, his novel

FIGURE 1   David Maletz at Kibbutz Ein Harod, ca. 1925. Used by permission of Ein Harod Archives.

Ma'agalot (literally, "Circles" in English; *Young Hearts*; 1945) caused an unprecedented level of controversy within and even beyond the kibbutz movement.[34] Most readers encountering the novel today might find it hard to comprehend the furor that greeted publication of the original (Hebrew) edition, which sold out almost immediately and which in many respects seems an ardently ideological and even naive affirmation of the kibbutz project.

After all, *Young Hearts* features the characteristics basic to the genre of Zionist-settlement novels as described by Reuven Kritz: "At the center of the plot usually stands a couple of pure, innocent lovers, who have to overcome internal difficulties (too shy, temporary misunderstandings) as well as external ones: separation, temptation, and even . . . real intrigue. Their success in realizing their love is bound up with the success of the kibbutz in building itself" (32).[35] Even its infrequent moments of dissent, voiced by a youthful innocent, seem surprisingly mild when considering the anger it aroused. Yet that assessment overlooks the complete dominance of ideology in kibbutz society at that time. In her account of the remarkable heat generated by *Young Hearts*, Keshet notes that "even urban workers displayed great interest in it, and worker's councils throughout the country invited the author to literary gatherings to discuss the book and its conclusions about life in the kibbutz. . . . Many kibbutzim convened meetings and discussions attended by [Maletz], which took the form of a kind of 'literary trial' of the work and its author alike" ("Kibbutz Fiction" 148). Keshet cites a front-page article that appeared in the newspaper *Ha-Boker* under the banner headline "Stormy Debates in Kibbutzim over Maletz's Book":

> In the kibbutz settlements and the left-wing camp in general the book by Mr. D. Maletz . . . has generated a great storm. All the kibbutzim in the country have held, and are holding, literary trials of this book by one of the first members of the Third Aliyah [wave of immigration, 1919–1923], who in his book has condemned the kibbutz. At Ein Harod a week-long literary trial was held at which the members of Faction B [Mapam] condemned the book and the author, whereas the members of Mapai defended it. At the same time many voiced complaints against Am Oved for publishing a book such as this that vilifies the kibbutz. The book, *Circles*, extensively discusses kibbutz life and its negative aspects. Its conclusion is that the individual in the kibbutz is repressed and dominated by those able to push their way forward. The Hashomer Hatza'ir kibbutzim have even banned its entry to them, and it has been declared one of the heretical books proscribed for reading in kibbutzim. Despite all the proscrip-

tions, the book is in great demand and is being read extensively in the young kibbutzim. (qtd. in Keshet, "Kibbutz Fiction" 149)[36]

How did a fictional work have the power to raise such ire? Even in the era of Khomeini's fatwa against Salman Rushdie in the Islamic world and school library censorship in the United States, that passion can be hard for us to grasp today. Keshet explains that, in the aftermath of World War II and as "the terrible shock at the magnitude of the Holocaust" was painfully absorbed, the kibbutz movement had begun to feel deep anxiety about its enduring relevance and vigor, whether it could in fact still retain its central mission in the days of the Third Aliya, which had so heroically transformed the country's settlement landscape: "The questions were whether history would repeat itself and accord the kibbutz a central national role, as it had after World War I, and whether the developments that had taken place within the kibbutz since then would enable it to preserve the spiritual forces that had contributed to the realization of the Zionist project or whether the process of institutionalization would prevent it from returning to its pioneering heyday" ("Kibbutz Fiction" 149). Given that fraught climate, Maletz's readers could not help but be dismayed by such a singularly unworthy protagonist (even if the charges that Maletz had "vilified" or "condemned" the kibbutz were overwrought).

On one occasion, a kibbutznik serving as a soldier in the Jewish Brigade in Europe wrote Maletz from the site of the Terezin concentration camp (where tens of thousands perished) two months after its liberation to vehemently protest the novel's lack of ideological conviction. He pointedly chided him for overlooking the extraordinary scope that had already been achieved: "For us kibbutz members who are here, the kibbutz is such a beautiful dream that it is almost difficult for us to believe that such a thing exists in the world. We have seen the destruction of an entire continent, the annihilation of our people, with our own eyes, moral annihilation too. How, in a world such as this, I ask you, can there be a place where a person can live free of numerous cares, with communal education, with children like ours, with people who read literature other than detective stories, a place without prostitution, without drunkenness?" (qtd. in Keshet, "Kibbutz Fiction" 155). In such a wounded and fateful time, perhaps any deviation from absolute consensus could only be construed as heresy and betrayal.[37] Yet, by the time that Maletz's novel *Ma'agalot*, titled *Young Hearts: A Novel of Modern Israel* in the English translation, was published in the United States (1950), that furor had largely faded (and, in any case, its American readers lacked the ideological hypersensitivity and sense of emergency of readers in the Yishuv); without the weight of that baggage, its publisher touted it simply as "the first genuine modern Israeli novel to be printed in English."[38]

In later generations, many kibbutz writers would come to identify "outsiders" or nonconformists of one kind or another as their most compelling subject.[39] Self-consciously or not, they all likely owe a debt to *Young Hearts*. Although Maletz's novel (which not infrequently reads more like social commentary than imaginative literature) may ultimately sanctify the communal endeavor, it grapples most acutely with the plight of the lonely and alienated individual within collective life in ways that clearly anticipated Amos Oz's early writings as literary kibbutz insider/outsider. Indeed, Oz gratefully acknowledges Maletz's powerful influence in a note appended to his 1982 novel *Menuhah nehonah* (*A Perfect Peace*).[40] Menahem, the struggling but sympathetic protagonist of *Young Hearts*, is bewildered by instances of his comrades' thoughtless behavior to one another as well as a pervasive sense of cold institutionalization. Somewhat ironically, he comes to wonder whether "in striving after full equality and justice you lost all elementary human feeling?" (182). However in retrospect, *Young Hearts* also conforms to salient features of the formulaic phase of kibbutz novels that, Derek Penslar argues, tend to "follow the norms of social-realist fiction, that is, to generate melodramatic plots, rife with sexual and familial intrigue and discord, set against documentary backgrounds" (6). No doubt, *Young Hearts* contains each of these ingredients, yet, as a transitional work, it also offers strong hints of the rebellious questioning and dissent that would follow, beginning with the fact that, contra the New Hebrew, his main character (male), here and in later works, is consistently unheroic, weak of body and sometimes spirit.

In what seems a striking irony (which may not have been fully intended), Maletz's protagonist, who has long struggled to conform to the settlement's norms of masculinity, is assigned to work with the settlement's aged population. Menahem is viscerally repelled by their entrenched melancholy, bodily weakness, and shameful personification of the reviled Galut (Zionist epithet for the Diaspora); indeed, when he overhears the "shrill tremulous voices" of the old men at prayer, "he could not imagine anything more pathetic, more hopeless than this sound" and finds himself "saddened by the weak old voices, expressive of hollow hearts and desolation. . . . When prayers were over he would hear the heavy dragging walk, the sighs and coughs . . . as the old men returned to their rooms. They were laden with the dead weight of the past" (*Young Hearts* 205).[41] He further recoils from the old people's religiosity, which seems a fossilized relic of the vanished past: "The old Jews had lost all sense of what they were doing and kept up their rituals from mere habit. . . . They had lost their sense of personal worth and personal importance, deprived of that, their actions, even their worship, lost meaning" (204). For their part, the "old people" feel humiliated that, though all their material needs are provided for, "they counted for nothing to their sons, nor did they have any worth in their own eyes. They were nonentities, their doings were meaningless" (218–19). Moreover, they are appalled by their children's casual desecration of the Sabbath—"The clatter of a tractor on a Sabbath wounds the soul of Israel," one complains to the protagonist bitterly (209). Divorced from their former lives of dignity—"In the old days in Europe they were heads of families and sat at the head of their table"—the "old people" spend their days squabbling over food in their isolated dining area where "they made a last ditch stand . . . thus compensating for the general blurring of their social position and for their sense of futility" (211). Their caregiver, the protagonist, who raises the right questions but rarely finds answers, muses: "What had Eretz Yisrael done to these old people that food had come to matter so much to them? Why had these high-minded Jews . . . been suddenly turned to gluttons whose entire lives centered about their meals?" (211). Unbeknownst to him, in the face of their children's heresies and "grievous sins," the old men vow to study a page of the Talmud every day to "atone" for the community; the most pious among them even secretly fasts twice a week.

Maletz hardly exaggerates: such was the intergenerational war of secularism and religion waged on the socialist kibbutz in those early days. As Muki Tzur (a former secretary general of the United Kibbutz Movement) compassionately observes, "The kibbutz did not pay attention to the fact that ageing is an essential part of the human life cycle and [that] of the kibbutz. When members' parents appeared on the kibbutz, they were completely separated from [this] rebellious community. . . . This separation also existed because the parents demanded kosher food. [They had] lost their former traditional lives the moment they had immigrated to the kibbutz . . . [and] aged quickly. . . . [and] the parents lived as a community [that was] separated from the kibbutz" (qtd. in Bar-Gal 74–75). Yet, alongside its faithful adherence to the norms and codes of the secular Zionist enterprise of the day, Maletz's *Young Hearts* is also a novel that urgently and poignantly gestures toward the need for inner fulfillment even as it underwrites the goals of Jewish nationalism. Here a minor character pleads forcefully with his entire community to struggling to achieve a more spiritual life: "I know that if there is meaning to the life of Jews as Jews anywhere in the world, it is here. . . . I'm not denying the importance of bread and butter—aren't we giving our full time and effort to producing bread from the soil? Yet man does not live by bread alone and there's a pretty good likelihood that neither does he live by social and national ideals alone. He has to have a higher principle" (154). In regard to this speaker's call for "a higher principle," it is worth recalling that Maletz was enormously influential in his lifetime, credited with inspiring the kibbutz movement's Renewal of Judaism project.[42] In that regard, Maletz's critical interlocutors have weighed the considerable ideological and aesthetic tensions present in his work and the extent that one realm might undermine the other.

For example, Moti Zeira lauds the high moral seriousness of Maletz's literary mission, steadfastly pursuing "the question of whether there is a spiritual basis for this new life, which is devoid of the belief in God, that can be a solid foundation for a permanent, stable, and moral life experience" (Zeira 214; translation mine). In contrast, Iris Milner sees a rather banal adherence to the uniform plot of the kibbutz narrative of his day, in which "the necessary compromises in most of these texts are made by the individual, who agrees to pay the price of private inconvenience for the sake of participation in the collective project" (167).[43] On the other hand, philosopher Avi Sagi hails Maletz for capturing "the complex reality being created in the kibbutz, the gap between the life on the surface, which is dominated by solid rhetoric and practices, and the desires, horror and socio-cultural deterioration hidden below the surface. His heroes live on the margins and are symbolic of the ailments and lack of discipline Maletz identified under the healthy Sabra exterior." According to Sagi, Maletz was intensely dedicated to the kibbutz's bold reimagining of the ancient Jewish festivals for the new Hebrew agrarian society: "He rejects the viewpoint that the cultural effort invested in designing these ceremonies is a manifestation of 'purely folkloristic entertainment.' In his eyes, the design of these ceremonies expresses the 'strength of the group, of the community that works together and jointly weaves the tapestry of day-to-day life. Indeed, it is the spirit of partnership that confers human holiness on the six days of work and elevates the Sabbath and the Festivals."[44] If so, that concern seems manifestly apparent from the very outset of the novel, when Menahem, the first in a long tradition of troubled "outsider" yet primary characters in the kibbutz novel, returns exhausted from the fields in the evening to find his wife, Hannah, whom he considers the very center of his life, in "a black mood": "He knew that he ought to sit down beside her, stroke her head, find out what was the matter, console her. But at the moment he lacked the necessary strength. He felt unutterably tired" (*Young Hearts* 7). Maletz's anxiety that the dulling effects of labor and routine might pose a significant challenge to the spiritual and even sensual lives of the agrarian socialists, no matter how lofty their ideals, clearly informs his portrayal of the attractive simplicity of life in the early *kvutzah* (including the no-nonsense pairings off of young socialist male and female comrades in those days):[45] "Menahem's sturdy body seemed to be weighted down with lead. The work dragged painfully. This twilight hour . . . had been preceded by tedious hours of a hard day's work. Menahem was dead tired as he plodded home up the hill. Even seeing Hannah could not rouse him from the torpor of . . . fatigue. . . . The heavy toil in the terrible sun . . . made him so tired that he was indifferent even to Hannah" (8). In such moments, Maletz does not shy from the reality behind the romance of the "new Jewish peasant" in Palestine, the arduous struggle to transform the individual shtetl Jew within the Zionist ideal of reconstituted Jewish peoplehood and reclaimed masculinity.

If in many ways *Young Hearts* is a dutiful report on the progress of the Zionist project of reinvention, there is also a great deal of self-reflexivity in how Maletz portrays his characters' hidden anxieties and desires. Thus Avram Klein, an otherwise minor character (who seems to represent Maletz's own position), long troubled by a sense of spiritual incompleteness, experiences an epiphany that he shares with his comrades:

> The sun is setting. Twilight. A strange hour. From all sides people are slowly returning from the fields.
>
> I go up the hill a way . . . and the entire village is spread out before me, this place whither we have come from all the four corners of the earth. I see the barracks, the houses, the dining hall, the groves of trees we have planted. All is bathed in the dim light of this strange hour. The sight is a moving one and suddenly I am struck by the meaning of the entire scene. I have a great and moving experience. . . .
>
> Can such an experience serve as the spiritual basis for our lives? . . . We all have experiences like this . . . yet there is no spiritual basis to our lives. . . .
>
> What is a spiritual basis? When a man constructs his life on clear principles deriving from a more than human source, he has such a basis. (144)

This compelling attainment of a new and redemptive perspective in a "strange hour" on what the kibbutz lacks by a lone character's foray *outside* the kibbutz is not only repeated later in the novel but eventually becomes a prevalent trope in subsequent kibbutz literature, most recently, in Amos Oz's *Be'in haverim* (*Between Friends*; 2012).[46] Maletz portrays Klein's outsider perspective (ironically thrust to the margins of the novel's primary plot) in the tradition of the biblical prophets—who, having received their private epiphanies or mystical revelations, are called to plunge back into society, where they struggle to transform its vision or restore its dormant values.[47] Moreover, in a captivating admission, Klein relates his envy of the native Arab's instinctive piety: "Once I was on my way to Galilee when the train stopped near an Arab town. The station seethed with activity, for the hundreds of sacks of grain were being loaded on the train. Then I saw one of the Arab laborers turn aside, spread his upper garment on the ground, remove his shoes and bow in prayer. I envied that man. He had firm ground under his feet, while we, for all our highly developed consciousness, lacked it" (144). Here it is not the Palestinian's "nativeness" that is the subject of the kibbutznik's envy (as is often the case in Hebrew literature of the time) but rather his desire for what he perceives as the Arab's inherent spirituality.

It helps to consider the pre-state society that shaped the aspirations, restlessness, and inherent sense of loss of this and other beleaguered characters (who share the dedication of Maletz himself)—a radically "recruited society," in Edna Perlman's memorable phrase, whose members "were required to forsake their personal pleasures, their parental desires and personal development" to meet "the needs of the collective" (103). From the seminal decade of the 1930s until the establishment of the State of Israel, the kibbutz member was defined as an individual committed to extremes of self-sacrifice. *Young Hearts* does not sentimentalize the profoundly enervating conditions of that period: soon after Maletz's Menahem first comes to Eretz Yisrael from Poland, the young man's soft body is plagued by the miseries of heat, insects, and even boils, so that "he felt like Job on the dungheap, scratching his sores" (20). Worse, he is summarily rejected by the elite quarry crew and humiliated by one physical challenge after another. In Menahem's early struggles, it is sometimes difficult to find any hint of the Gordonian spirituality of labor in which the author so passionately believed.

In contrast to hapless Menahem, newcomer Hannah miraculously thrives and proves immensely popular: "Everybody wanted to work with Hannah. Her . . . generous character had blossomed out in the sun of her love . . . her face, her eyes, her manner of walking and talking seemed to scatter light about her. Everyone who saw her involuntarily smiled" (45). Most crucially, she embodies the archetype of the new Hebrew woman, a legendary worker whose earthy sensuality and joyful participation in labor seem to merge seamlessly with her surroundings in Maletz's naturalistic imagery: "She was a joy to work with . . . good to look at, with her shapely, full and pliant body. It was a pleasure to see her plunge her fork into the well-cured clover, carry it along and then deftly shake it into the mangers. It was a pleasure to watch her walking among the wholesome, pure-bred cows. She would lay her hand gently upon their rounded sides and they would quietly obey her orders" (11–12). That deft, nearly cinematic description poetically underscores not only the "nativeness" that Zionism eagerly sought but also the association between woman's body and earth's fecundity, calling to mind the ancient Near Eastern goddess figures and fertility symbols dug from the clay of kibbutz farms to this very day.

Elsewhere, Menahem is jolted by the jarring similarity between his mother's aroma (mingling with "fresh-baked white bread" and "golden fish sauce," remembered from childhood) and Hannah's. Indeed, throughout the novel, women are described, first and foremost, as nurturing figures and, not infrequently, with pantheistic ardor. Menahem recalls his mother's domestic rule as "like the pulse of the river and the warm peace of plowed fields steaming in the midday sun" (16). As this and numerous passages mingling erotic heat and maternity suggest, *Young Hearts* reveals the contradictory position of the Jewish woman in the Zionist imagination.[48] She was to participate in radical nation building without abandoning the traditional roles of wife and mother. Beginning in the 1930s, women like Maletz's Hannah found themselves deeply torn between fulfilling their "passive" biological role as child bearers and rearers (in the mounting demographic competition between Arabs and Jews) and their "active" role as Zionist pioneers. Yet, in most critical moments, the novel's gender dynamics vigorously confirm Yael Feldman's charge that "the liberatory impulse of Zionism has never 'overcome' the traditional Jewish valorization of motherhood" (*No Room* 107).

Though Maletz does not explicitly acknowledge this cultural schizophrenia, it nevertheless seems fully evident in his sympathetic portrayal of Hannah's subsequent breakdown as a young mother. In one of the novel's crucial expository sections, the author outlines the general situation: "The birth rate in the collective settlements had shot way up. In the early days, the atmosphere of the kvutzah, peopled largely by unmarried folk, had been perhaps too earnest. Now the young girl pioneers had, most of them, become young mothers" (*Young Hearts* 132). But Maletz reassures us that "the presence of children added a new dimension, a new lightness, to the communal life" (132). As this passage suggests, conflicting impulses abound in *Young Hearts*.

In salient instances, Maletz's language captures the egalitarian potentiality of the kibbutz's early days, such as this brief portrayal of the socialist comrades in one of the first primitive dining halls: "The big new tent was half dark, lit by two hanging kerosene lamps which made the shadows of the [servers] dance as they scurried between the dining tent and the shack which was used for a kitchen. Young men and young women, bundled in all kinds of old jackets and army coats, clustered at the tables and sang at the top of their voices, *vetaher libeynu*—purify our hearts" (23).

On the other hand, the male protagonist himself falls well short of the Zionist paragon of masculinity, as when he lies passively in the long winter nights, enfeebled by malaria. Yet more is going on here. For Menahem's state of weak dormancy is later configured by Maletz as the redemptive crucible that produces the toughened Hebrew colonizer. Indeed, Karen Grumberg reminds us that Zionism's project was dedicated to the "recuperation of a distinctly Jewish masculinity"; its "principal concern [was] the Jewish man and his body" ("Female Grotesque" 164), rather than a genuine new beginning for both men and women. Grumberg argues that Israel's "formation of a national body politic as an alternative to the 'disembodied' diaspora textuality" always prioritized the masculine over the feminine (164). Thus, egalitarian discourse notwithstanding, "the Zionist liberation of women from bourgeois life [remained] incomplete" (146).[49] And when a man is perceived as falling short of the Zionist ideal of the New Hebrew, he is inevitably viewed as effete. Because his proclivity for seeking a measure of happiness and personal fulfillment strays beyond the "effort" or "to build a new life," Maletz's protagonist, Menahem, remains "Menahemke" (*Young Hearts* 27).[50] The Yiddishized diminutive of his name effectively reifies his condition of unmanly dreaming and querulous hopes, "the fatal obstacle that barred him from the status which should have been his because of his seniority in the settlement" (27). Poignantly and paradoxically, Menahem is first drawn to Hannah not for her ostensible organic relation to her surroundings but because she shares his Diasporic memories of a childhood shaped by the life of a river—"She talked about the river traffic, about rafts and the songs of the raftsmen" (37)—a world of flux and movement unlike the stasis inherent in the permanency of the settlement and Zionist rootedness in the soil. In this and other representative moments, *Young Hearts* seems self-aware of the kinds of fascinating contradictions that Hannan Hever exposes in his study of Hebrew nativism:

> Zionists tried to live in peace with the tension between their faith in the new, Hebrew Jew, and the unbroken continuity of Jewish existence. But nativism, with its great emphasis on the new and revolutionary, is actually where these two poles were brought into a paradoxical coexistence that is embodied in the very figure of the native. Thus nativism, whose role it is to render organic and mainly to justify the link between people

and territory, is ultimately unable to do so in a smooth, unequivocal way. It oscillates uneasily between two opposites: on the one hand, the native is a new beginning—the beginning of the new Jew; at the same time, however, the native is perceived as indigenous to the particular place over which Zionism asserts a continuous, organic, and eternal ownership. . . . The "beginning" of nativism immediately also contains the denial of exile. The very appearance of this "beginning" constitutes an erasure of everything that did not exist "here," in the Eretz Yisraeli space, but belongs, rather, elsewhere: to exile, which is denied precisely because it is not the space of the "beginning." (4–5)

As *Young Hearts* makes abundantly clear, that "paradoxical coexistence" (which Hever eventually characterizes as an "erasure") had sharply wounding edges: the early *kvutzah* could be quite brutally judgmental toward outsiders, who still bore the stigma of exile, resulting in low self-esteem that might last for years, even for individuals who chose to remain.[51] That condition naturally sours Menahem on collective life, an attitude he reveals by "going off by himself, by standing aloof. And there is nothing like the sense of aloofness for making one look at things with a jaundiced eye. . . . People show up as petty, ludicrous, selfish, malicious, cruel. You fall into an attitude of general contempt; you hate and become still further alienated from your fellows. It is a closed circle, a squirrel cage from which there is no release" (*Young Hearts* 43). In the critical terms with which Maletz renders Menahem's defensiveness, we can find the vestiges of severe alienation reflected in the kibbutz protagonists of later years. Though in some respects naive, the protagonist's bewilderment as he clashes with his society's rules and cherished assumptions is eventually transformed by Maletz into a powerful social critique of the tyranny of ideology. As Keshet observes, Maletz's protagonist "is particularly sensitive to instances where social norms are formulated in harsh, even fanatical, ways that run counter to the founding principles of the society itself," and his grievances are voiced against "a kind of rule of the jungle" that threatens the spiritual and practical sustainability of the collective ideal ("Kibbutz Fiction" 151). Especially where Menahem lingers at the periphery of the mainstream, beleaguered by his outsider status, he seems almost a prophet of the disenchantment that grew in the later years of kibbutz life.

In contrast to those immediately deemed capable (who find no trouble gaining status and recognition), Menahem haplessly falls into the category of those immediately disparaged. Even his eyeglasses become a shameful marker of his enervated Diasporic nature:[52]

There are cases when a newcomer goes out to work for the first time and immediately creates an unfavorable impression. The whisper goes around: "That one is a real 'stopper'!" In a collective settlement a "stopper" is a person who does not succeed in getting a permanent place in any specialized labor; the work committee uses him to stop up all sorts of gaps that arise in the labor economy of the village. . . .

It took only a few days for Menahem to be marked down for a "stopper." Srulik, one of the senior members of the kvutzah . . . watched Menahem doing his first assigned tasks and sneered. Menahem's slow walk and measured movements made an unfortunate impression. And then his glasses. Menahem's glasses were a real curse. Srulik instantly decided that he wasn't much. . . .

And so it came to pass. Any work that the "permanent" workers disdained was given to Menahem. He was a Gibeonite—a hewer of wood and a bearer of water. (*Young Hearts* 29)[53]

Clearly appreciating the novel's unsparing gaze on the less appealing aspects of communal life (particularly its focus on the intolerance exhibited toward those struggling to adjust), Keshet hails Maletz for his "autonomous voice" and for presenting the settlement reality as "complex and highly problematic," even though he "was totally involved in the all-consuming endeavor of the pioneering enterprise" ("Kibbutz Fiction" 147). That stance must have required an unenviably demanding (perhaps in some ways, schizophrenic) balancing act. Undoubtedly, *Young Hearts* warrants our appreciation for its conscientious verisimilitude and balance, if not always its literary merit. Yet, ultimately, notwithstanding the critical ire of Maletz's contemporaries, *Young Hearts* unapologetically advocates for the "endeavor of the pioneering enterprise."

At the novel's conclusion, Menahem's uncomplicated redemption seems indistinguishable from the miraculous revitalization of the land itself: "All day Menahem had been irrigating the clover beds. The moment he let the water in the tall dusty plants lifted their heads to the sun and stood tall, bright and green. And as the plants revived, Menahem, too, seemed to straighten up and experience a strange exultation" (234). Throughout, the beleaguered hero endures the slights and animosity directed toward him and perseveres. His conviction that all labor is worthwhile sustains him, even though (notwithstanding kibbutz rhetoric) prevailing attitudes toward the worth of particular vocations were always strongly hierarchical. In his salt-of-the-earth naïveté, Menahem simply cannot comprehend "why these tasks were considered less dignified than others. Work was work. . . . All work has its own beauty and the very act of working brings peace. . . . Peace flooded his heart. So far as Menahem was concerned, he would be content to be a water carrier for a long time" (30). As Keshet suggests, in such moments, Menahem "acts from within the depth of spontaneous experience," out of an unseen spiritual or psychological realm not derived from the "ideological-rational" realm of official Zionist culture ("Kibbutz Fiction" 151, 152).[54] Despite his earlier diffidence toward both labor and the collective life, Menahem's rekindled dignity and pride stem from his organic relation to the land and his innate conviction that the least desirable tasks are eminently worthy.

And there is always Hannah, the vivacious young woman who works all day and dances till dawn, whose beauty and love redeem Menahem in the narrative's unworldly, unabashedly mythic symbiosis between human coupling and the fertile anima mundi. Her "nativeness" offers everything that his maladjusted condition lacks: Hannah "hadn't been sick for a day, no malaria, no ailments—she might have been born in the land" (*Young Hearts* 37). As noted above, Menahem's acculturation as a halutz was once halting, stymied by his inappropriate sensibility; he "felt only the dull indifference of the stranger," and was utterly "unable to feel any appropriate love for the homeland" (43). In those earlier days, the Palestinian landscape appears "barren and desolate and overgrown by white thornbushes. The sound of the dense thorns resulting in the breeze aroused a deep sadness in Menahem" (51). Yet, suddenly, the love of a good woman reorients his consciousness so that he can nurture the land with the proper ardor:

> In this time Menahem became wedded forever to Hannah. He envisioned life before him as a level, sunlit plain over which Hannah and himself, and everybody else, walked about and prospered. Now Menahem also made his peace with the landscape. Formerly he had been unable to respond to the sear, cracked, burning fields of Eretz Yisrael. His ideal was the green meadows and the prodigal river of his childhood. Against his will the baked, tawny land of Israel depressed him. . . . Now for the first time he saw the land's beauty. (43)

Inexorably initiated into "the great mystery of germination and growth" (54), Menahem not only emerges as a worthy partner for the novel's Zionist heroine but also emulates her vigorous fecundity.[55] In Maletz's rhapsodic prose, Menahem's own ripening incarnates the fruition of A. D. Gordon's vision:[56]

He felt almost feverish, trembling for the outcome. . . .

He waited for some signs of germination with the greatest anxiety and was terribly excited when the minute green shoots first pierced the surface of the earth. There were multitudes of them and they made rapid growth until they formed a solid green mass beautiful to behold. . . . He took up his hoe and . . . let the water in. Obligingly, the water surged through, circulating among the tender upright stems. They bowed their heads before the flow, as if unable to break the great joy of drinking. Then they again erected themselves toward the sun. (*Young Hearts* 54–56)

Although the narrative clearly extols Menahem's gradual redemption, a quiet yet distinct and lingering note of dissent over the petty prejudices of the collective accompanies that spiritual and bodily transformation. Indeed, the rancorous community Maletz describes anticipates the demythologizing by Meir Shalev in his epic novel *Roman russi* (*The Blue Mountain*; 1988), where, in Alan Mintz's memorable turn of phrase, the new society of agrarian socialists (in this case, a moshav) is immediately blighted by the "romantic self-dramatizing egos" of its founders.

In spite of the halutzim's "utter revolt against the benighted decadence of Diaspora Judaism, the village they create resembles nothing more than an Eastern European shtetl, a small, intensely provincial community held together by a shared set of beliefs (there religion, here socialism) but torn apart by hatred, passion, and intrigue" (Mintz 39). Moreover, in spite of their rhetoric about "brotherhood" and egalitarianism, some of Maletz's kibbutzniks take on the haughty role of elites based on their labor. Unhappily for Menahem, that includes Hannah, whose work in the dairy—"the pillar of their economy"— bestows her with "a certain superiority over the others" (*Young Hearts* 46). Moreover, she finds herself just a little embarrassed for Menahem, especially when she overhears the withering remarks directed by her comrades toward him and the other untrained vineyard workers. Though Maletz somewhat justifies the judgmental behavior of the community—"This development was only natural, since work and action were paramount here" (46)—his pointed critique of the collective and his sympathy for the cadre of weaker workers held in contempt by the strong is inescapable:

The idealism which brought these young Jews back to the homeland, to physical labor . . . did not do away with all their prejudices. Pettiness and selfishness crept in, even into the midst of their community based on equality and fraternity. The community gave rise to a rather mean competitiveness and arrogance toward the weak; the less assertive took a subsidiary place in the life of the kvutzah and the "successful" ones, the aggressive ones, were glorified. . . . The slower workers suffered keenly from the situation. (46–47)

Indeed, here, in Maletz's literary record of those earliest days, we might find a clear link between the haughty outlook toward less skilled labor and the embrace, decades later, of privatization by those whose potential earnings motivated them to desire differential salaries.

Meanwhile, Hannah's initial joy at finding herself pregnant begins to fade as nausea and weakness overcome her; she who long prided herself on her resistance to sickness now finds it impossible to work. The experience is shattering, and she even avoids the dining room. Here the story of Hannah and Menahem takes a decided turn for the sordid. After the birth of her child, Hannah remains deeply depressed and later struggles against her desire for another man, while Menahem suffers from a mysterious stomach ailment in his increasing isolation. Crises of one kind or another are woven throughout the narrative but, true to Maletz's convictions, there is no ordeal, however acute, that cannot be overcome by immersion in the land: after months of barely speaking, Hannah and Menahem briefly reconcile on a hike up a hill overlooking the settlement.

The tropes accompanying these developments, so evocative in all their painterly detail, would become a nearly constant feature of the generations of kibbutz fiction to follow. Yet even though many of those later works rapidly expose the lyrical setting as a very thin veneer for what festers beneath, Maletz's romanticized description is essentially a clarion call to participate in the project of utopia: "The cultivated fields and the cluster of red roofs gave a nucleus to the landscape. There was the yard of the settlement, outlined by the regular rows of the vineyards. The oblong barracks and the white tents looked like toys set down in geometric patterns. And the people circulating among the buildings were like tiny dolls. . . . With the whole life of the kvutzah spread out beneath her in such a wondrously beautiful setting, she suddenly felt the meaninglessness of all the compulsions that drove its people" (99).[57] The conviction that the socialist design, with all its attractive trappings, can ultimately harness the chaotic force of human frailty is upheld in Maletz's sanguine vision, even as he unhesitatingly portrays the serial adulterers and malcontents who were always present in kibbutz life. Hannah carries on a flirtation with a cynical comrade named Shmuel Grossman (a snake in the kibbutz's Eden), who casually advocates the "sharing" of the kibbutz's women, carries on frequent affairs, and has already left a number of ruined marriages in his wake.

The philandering Grossman (a stock type in kibbutz fiction) senses a beckoning opportunity in the rift between Hannah and Menahem. In each subsequent encounter, Shmuel's seductive rationales further unravel Hannah's devotion to Menahem and their family life as he attempts to persuade her that conventional morality is absurd and that the revolutionary collective has no place for traditional marriages:

> Just think how odd this is. We live in a kvutzah for years, perhaps for our entire lives. A man may live virtually under the same roof with a woman. They've breathed the same air, been surrounded by the same things. He knows her thoroughly, her frowns, her laughter, how she raises a spoonful of soup to her mouth, how her body flexes at work. Every day, all the time, she reveals herself before him. Yet, under the present set-up, she has to remain a stranger to him, unharvested fruit. He can never attain the final intimate knowledge of her. I call this both odd and unnatural. If we organized our collectives along really rational lines, we'd encourage physical union between all men and women. (113–14)

Though initially shocked, Hannah is ultimately entranced by Shmuel's blandishments and keeps returning for more, while Menahem is beset with nightmares in which the pastoral Galilee dissolves into a gothic black fog and he cannot reach his beloved. Suffering from postpartum depression and unable to nurse her first infant properly, Hannah is subject to bouts of weeping and hysterical laughter. Empathically, he imagines the plight of a pioneer woman trapped who feels degraded by the conspiring forces of the unfeeling institution of the children's house, her body's new role, her failure to nurse properly, and an unfamiliar inner turmoil: "It was a bitter solitude. She felt herself entirely superfluous—to herself, to the child, to Menahem. All of her, her body, her spirit, seemed paltry and unnecessary. Even her lovely breasts had no function" (73). In portraying the heroine's depressed state with notable candor, Maletz honestly confronts the kind of alienation that can arise in collective living—but he does so only up to a point.

Thus, just as soon as Menahem voices his unease, he immediately assures himself that the kibbutz itself is the remedy for estrangement, for whatever ails the individual: "Yet what could one do in a collective settlement where everything was interlocked and complex, where everything had its place in the general framework and even people's moods had their wide ramifications?

What could you do? Only talk it over, clarify the situation in the course of a conversation. There is much talking in a collective; conversation is almost the mainspring of order" (68). The author's admiring tone here, his manifest pride in affirming the kibbutz's self-sufficiency and healing capacities seems unmistakable. Yet Menahem experiences many peaks and troughs as he struggles to adjust. Indeed, for long sections of the novel, as we experience Menahem's travails and humiliations, especially over his lowly place in a hypercompetitive environment, it would be hard to imagine wanting to try out the kibbutz for ourselves. Pushing back against his stratified society, he asks: "Why should the settler be required to have special qualifications. . . . Why should his satisfaction depend upon his outshining everyone? . . . Wasn't sowing the field or planting the tree the main thing? For the ideal he held before him was of a son of Israel following his plow over the dry land of Israel and raising his bread from this land in the sweat of his brow" (157). Yet affirmation always follows, as if Maletz fretted over any lasting negative impressions he might be leaving with his readers.

For, no matter how beleaguered Menahem finds himself (whether in work, the daunting kibbutz hierarchy, or his marriage), Maletz takes pains to establish that his protagonist never comes even close to forsaking the glorious tenets of the kibbutz ideology: "Menahem sincerely believed in the superiority of collective living. He had a great and naive faith in this system which had wiped out the differences between rich and poor. In a kvutzah there was no such thing as an underprivileged child. Each individual, all the children, were wars of the community; and he held in especially high esteem the treatment of children in the kvutzah" (69). Further hardships arise for Menahem, from his ulcer and the humiliation of having to request a special diet from the communal kitchen to his physical separation from Hannah, who is sent in the vanguard of workers preparing to relocate the community to a permanent hill site. Moreover, a series of breathtakingly inconsiderate actions by members of the kvutzah toward one another lead many to doubt the entire collective enterprise: "Strange things happened, incidents that were talked about in shocked whispers. The settlers seemed horrified at themselves, at the ways into which they had fallen" (181). In the end, however, labor itself proves consolatory. Even a bloody skirmish with local marauding Arabs ends with the uplifting benediction "All in all, the incident did wonders in the way of strengthening the ties of the settlers with their land and their village" (191–92).[58]

As suggested by the novel's original Hebrew title (which translates literally as "Circles"), *Young Hearts* ends much as it begins, with a scene of wearied but content laborers streaming homeward from the orchards, fields, and vegetable gardens. Maletz describes their movement rhapsodically as "the slow sanctified motions of those who work with the soil" (236).[59] Accordingly, *Young Hearts* affords us a final, irresistible panorama of the kibbutz and its agrarian environs shaped by Hebrew labor: "Their fields lay, softened by twilight. The barley fields were already golden. The wheat fields were piebald with patches of green and patches . . . already beginning to yellow. The irrigated clover looked a brilliant green even in the dimming light" (236). The kibbutz is fecund in another crucial respect, for the infants' home is a virtual hive of procreation: "There was a constant coming and going of the nursing mothers, clad in white gowns which showed up their bursting breasts" (230). To Maletz's credit, his memorably unconventional kibbutz hero remains waywardly uncertain to the end, ever bemused by the spectacle of collective child rearing: "Its curious atmosphere both embarrassed and amused him. What was it, after all, he thought, but a glorified barn, devoted to milk production and the raising of sturdy young stock" (230).[60] Yet, for the most part, lingering doubts vanish. And, after all their travails, Hannah and Menahem are happily and permanently reconciled, feeling "the most intense sense of kinship" with the rest of the kvutzah, their three children growing up vigorously rooted in the verdant foothills and valleys of Mount Gilboa. The most genuine freedom, Menahem concludes, is expressed in the exhausted silences and "heavy steps" of the dedicated comrades at the end of a day engaged in "tilling a common farm." Maletz's focus on individual foibles and weaknesses now fades away entirely: "Menahem . . . Hannah and the children . . . became one with the crowd," solemnly affirming to one another that "in spite of everything it is good" (236, 237).[61]

2

"With a Zealot's Fervor"
Individuals Facing the Fissures of Ideology in Oz, Shaham, and Balaban

> They walk down the paths of the kibbutz on their way to work, to the children's houses and the communal showers, like monks intent upon their rituals and prayers in the hope that sanctity will enter their hearts, but sanctity never comes.
> —*Avraham Balaban*

As he tells it in his elegiac memoir *Sipur al ahava ve-hosheh* (*A Tale of Love and Darkness*; 2002), at the age of fourteen, a year after his mother's suicide, Amos Oz left his father's home in Jerusalem and moved to Kibbutz Hulda (fig. 2), changing his family name from "Klausner" to "Oz," the Hebrew word for "might"—an event he chillingly portrayed as a symbolic parricide. He raised a family there, quite content until 1986, when his son's asthma led a doctor to advise them to move to the small desert town of Arad, where the boy might benefit from the dry air.[1]

Though Oz is the grandson of a proponent of "muscular Judaism" and ardent follower of Ze'ev Jabotinsky (the revisionist founding father of contemporary right-wing Israeli zealotry), in many ways, much of Oz's subsequent literary career seems to have been devoted to a sustained critical engagement with the moral limits of that discomfiting paternal legacy and his nation's use of might and force. Because Oz is the most critically celebrated kibbutz writer in this study, and because he fled his father's home and joined the kibbutz at such a young age, his outsider status merits special attention.[2]

As Oz would recall many years later, the kibbutz was already an intimate and potent presence for most of his generation even before he arrived at Hulda. Indeed, the kibbutz was where the "real" Jewish story was taking place:

FIGURE 2   Kibbutz Hulda, 1945. Used by permission of Amotz Peleg, Kibbutz Hulda Archives.

> Sometimes my friends and I went to the Tnuva delivery yard to watch [the kibbutzniks] arriving from over the hills and far away on a truck laden with agricultural produce, "clad with dust, burdened with arms, and with such heavy boots," and I used to go up to them to inhale the smell of hay, the intoxicating odors of faraway places: it's where they come from, I thought, that great things are happening. That's where the land is being built and the world is being reformed, where a new society is being forged. They are stamping their mark on the landscape and on history, they are plowing fields and planting vineyards, they are writing a new song, they pick up their guns, mount their horses, and shoot back at the Arab marauders: they take our miserable human clay and mold it into a fighting nation. (*Tale of Love and Darkness* 6)[3]

Clearly, between this euphoric sensibility and his prickly, later fiction, the writer traversed an extraordinary distance. In reading Oz's earliest kibbutz stories, it is crucial to bear in mind that they are written by a *yeled hutz* (a lone youth who joined the kibbutz from the outside). Inspired by kibbutz values, Oz found himself in an unprecedentedly intimate, elitist, and sometimes xenophobic society, where it could be very difficult for an outsider to achieve acceptance. Indeed, his painful outsider perspective is often apparent.[4] Over the years, Oz emerged as one of the most self-conscious of the many writers who have documented kibbutz life from the inside. Interviewed in 1985, he remarked that his neighbors were his greatest literary resource: "I know three or four hundred very different people intimately. I know their secrets. The penalty is that they know a lot more about me than I'd like them to know—but that's only fair. After dinner, I sit down with these successful old revolutionar-ies who have outlived their revolutions and their success. They tell me their life stories, making me vow that I will not use them and secretly hoping, of course, that I will. I have a neighbor who combs his hair whenever he passes my studio. He tells me that in case I see him and use him as a character, he wants his hair combed" (Mitgang).[5]

Before coming to terms with the far-reaching and often startling qualities of Oz's literary intervention, however, it is worth briefly reviewing the portrayal of the kibbutz in the popular fiction of his formative years. One of the better known of the didactic novels Oz might have encountered in the kibbutz library is *Adama lelo tzel* (*A Land Without a Shadow*; 1951), coauthored by Alexander and Yonat Sened, a married couple born in Poland in the 1920s, who would collaborate on ten Hebrew novels.[6] Shula Keshet calls attention to the chief aspiration of the pioneers settling the Negev wilderness as the Seneds pietisti-cally portrayed them:

> Step by step, faithfully and accurately, the stages of the establishment of the place, the first plowing, the planting of the first tree, a carob, laying the foundation stone of the fort, establishing the experimental vegetable garden, storing water . . . and so on. . . .
>
> The struggle against the forces of the desert is described as a mythical struggle against the forces of chaos. The creation theme places the pio-neers inside an all-embracing framework of the tension between desert and culture, between Jewish detachment and the rooting of Hebrew, and turns the pioneering endeavor into a cultural pole advancing humanity. ("Freedom" 202)

Today Oz's 1963 short story "Navadim va-tsefa" ("Nomad and Viper"), also set in the Negev, reads like an acerbic recasting of the sanctimonious and naive vision of the Seneds' novel of the previous decade. Alongside A. B. Yehoshua (b. 1936) and a few others of the 1960s generation, Oz was instrumental in diminishing the heroic stature of the Sabra. As Adia Mendelson-Maoz and

Liat Steir-Livny observe, for these writers, "the macho-militaristic" dynamism of the Sabra became "a source of criticism and parody. Often the Sabra hero protagonist is replaced by a passive, weak anti-hero" as well as "non-authoritative narrators and characters who were primarily non-heroic protagonists, often unable to understand or control their environment" (121–23). Thus, in "Nomad and Viper," from the collection *Artzot hatan* (*Where the Jackals Howl*; 1965), Oz reveals the faulty comprehension of Sabras and their maladroit relationship to their Zionist homeland, and he parodies the hypocrisy of liberal humanism among kibbutzniks living on the borders of the Negev at a time when Bedouin still wandered the desert.

In much of Oz's early fiction, the kibbutz serves as a stage for his critique not merely of the utopian imagination but of the entire Zionist nationalist endeavor as well; even today, the stories gathered in *Where the Jackals Howl* resonate with disturbing moral force.[7] Some of them are ironic retellings of biblical episodes, casting a harsh light on Israeli idealizations of military force. On the occasion of the collection's republication in a fiftieth anniversary edition, critic Adam Kirsch memorably hailed it as "one of the most remorseless fictional X-rays of the Israeli soul." Whereas, in Maletz's *Young Hearts* and other kibbutz narratives of the day, the displaced Arab is taken for granted or nearly unseen as a relic of the past (with fleeting references to "ancient" village structures, routinely transformed into kibbutz outbuildings or dwellings), in "Nomad and Viper," the Arab is a *living* presence, a visible threat.

To further appreciate the subversive dimension of "Nomad," it is worth considering Robert Alter's argument in *Modern Hebrew Literature* (1975) that "the most crucial motif . . . in all of Oz's fiction of kibbutz life is that of enclosure. The kibbutz enterprise is seen as a dream of overweening rationality, an attempt to impose a neat geometric order on the seething chaos of the natural world . . . a reflex of turning away from the unsettling darkness of reality to an illusory light" (331). That dissident approach becomes even more apparent when we grasp the contours of the psychological geography of the typical kibbutz narrative, as outlined by Iris Milner: "The limited boundaries of the small settlement are often juxtaposed with the surrounding open landscapes, which are ambivalently experienced as both attracting and threatening, due to the dangerous maladies and potential enemies they hide. . . . The resulting oppositions that emerge declaratively reinforce and confirm the advantages of the kibbutz over any other way of life" (163). This is the rhetorical grain against which Oz wrote in his early career, demonstrating that a kibbutz artist could be both a fierce proponent of the kibbutz way of life and an equally fierce critic of the corrosive repercussions of its insidious complacency and cultural chauvinism.

For instance, in Oz's essay "Hakibbutz ha-yom" ("The Kibbutz at the Present Time") from the collection *Beor hathelet ha'aza* (*Under This Blazing Light*; 1979), he famously affirms that, for all its disadvantages, the kibbutz is the "least bad, the least unkind" social system that he has ever seen (*Under This Blazing Light* 128). Yet that lofty assessment never inhibited him from examining the deep social fissures and moral corruption that invariably arise within every kibbutz simply because of intrinsic human nature. In the essay "Machshavot al hakibbutz" ("Thoughts on the Kibbutz") from that same collection, Oz offers a sobering philosophic assessment of the disparity between the righteous ideals of kibbutz ideology and the predictable imperfectability of human nature: "This too is the revenge of the world on the redeemers of the world from days of yore, this is the ancient revenge of man's soul against all who try to redeem it. The necessary distance between words, slogans, doctrines and deeds [is] stripped away. 'Life' bursts through with its infinite complexity that shatters the most acute and rounded and all-encompassing of ideologies" (123–24).[8]

That "ancient revenge" is fully manifest in Oz's searing "Nomad and Viper." The story revisits the biblical tale of Dinah (Genesis 34), whose reported rape leads to the massacre of the male inhabitants of Shechem, an episode that undoubtedly counts as among the most outrageous of the myriad violent incidents in Genesis.[9] Oz's story is narrated by an unidentified member of the community, who, in lacking any apparent individuation, speaks in the collective "We" throughout, perhaps a subtle way of reinforcing the author's withering perspective on the failure of moral agency in an excessively conformist and self-righteous community.[10] After a nighttime encounter in an orchard with a young Arab in which her erotic attraction goes unfulfilled, Geula, a young woman living with other halutzim on a new Negev kibbutz, falsely accuses the Arab of sexual assault. A masterful cultural deconstruction, "Nomad" exposes the kibbutzniks' tenuous hold on their putative values (liberalism, egalitarianism, and rationalism) in the wake of that false accusation.

In an earlier scene, at a *sulha* (reconciliation ceremony) arranged to resolve tensions that have grown between Jews and Arabs, Oz portrays the pettiness of the commune's Orientalist condescension toward the indigenous Bedouin. Nehama Aschkenasy astutely observes that, in this scene, "Lévi-Strauss's binary opposition between 'savage' and 'cultured' collapses when the Bedouin elder phrases his elaborate, courteous remarks 'in careful, formal Hebrew' while the kibbutz secretary insists on replying in 'broken Arabic.'" Moreover, "the Arab's knowledge of Hebrew is [clearly shown to be] a tactic for survival, not an admission of defeat or inferiority. His insistence on using Hebrew rather than

Arabic may be understood as his exclusion of the Israeli from his own linguistic territory. . . . The Bedouin will neither be suppressed nor assimilated nor integrated into the inevitable march of history" (127).

In terms of the kibbutz's own defense of its values, it is important to note that, whereas their secretary, a man named Etkin, speaks benevolently of "the brotherhood of nations," promising to investigate an exchange of courtesy visits between the two communities, the young men of the kibbutz immediately begin to plot "an excursion one night to teach the savages a lesson in a language they would really understand" (*Jackals* 37). Thus, in this powerful early work, Oz thoroughly unsettles the readers' safe assumptions regarding the "civilizing" potential of the young Jewish nation's utopian efforts. Here it is worth noting that the Bedouin pose no real threat (certainly no violent one) beyond their occasional theft of crops and small tools. Whereas the story begins with the "distant drumbeat" (23) of the "savage" Bedouin out in the desert surrounding the kibbutz, it ends with a gang of kibbutzniks "crossing the lawn . . . to even the score with the nomads . . . carrying short, thick sticks." The unnamed narrator, an invisible member of the mob, tersely reports only that "excitement was dilating our pupils. And the blood was drumming in our temples" (38). Even before this ominous denouement, however, the narrator presents us with numerous instances of the witless groupthink that is escalating tensions. Though always masked by a rhetorical veneer of civilized restraint, the speaker's logic collapses, and we find ourselves in the unsettling realm of the "unreliable narrator," which Oz favored in those years:

> Decency constrains me not to dwell in detail on certain isolated and exceptional acts of reprisal conducted by some of the youngsters whose patience had expired, such as cattle rustling, stoning a nomad boy, or beating one of the shepherds senseless. In defense of the perpetrators of the last-mentioned act of retaliation, I must state clearly that the shepherd in question had an infuriatingly sly face. He was blind in one eye, broken-nosed, drooling; and his mouth—on this the men responsible were unanimous—was set with long, curved fangs like a fox's. A man with such an appearance was capable of anything. And the Bedouins would certainly not forget this lesson. (*Jackals* 24)

Oz is of a literary generation often identified with the Akedah motif (from Abraham's binding of Isaac in Genesis 2), decrying a situation wherein the Israeli founders bequeath a bleak future of inevitable violence to their reluctant sons. Yet, not infrequently, Oz's leftist humanism widens that responsibility, casting a skeptical gaze on his own generation.

Consider "Minzar hashatkanim" ("The Trappist Monastery"), in which Nahum, a "thin and bespectacled medical orderly," castigates a commando named Itcheh, a wild, Esau-like figure lately returned from a cross-border mission that has destroyed a Jordanian village. When Itcheh says he doesn't understand how the locals could endure such a life, Nahum lashes out: "Of course you can't understand. All you can do is destroy a village without knowing anything about its people or its history, without wanting to know. Just like that. Like a mad bull. Of course you don't understand. What do you understand? Fucking and killing, that's what you understand. . . . Because you're not a human being, that's why. Because you're a stupid wild animal" (*Jackals* 104). Similarly, in "Nomad and Viper," it is the younger members of the kibbutz (in other words, Oz's own generation) who have an appetite for conflict, whereas their elder, Kibbutz Secretary Etkin, embodies the conciliatory spirit of Labor Zionism, the "quality of neighborliness of which the peoples of the East [have] long been justly proud" (25). Etkin desperately warns the hotheaded Sabras against "lynch mob" violence, calling them back to their better natures. "It was fitting," he tells himself, "in view of the social gospel we had adopted, that we should put an end to this ancient feud. It was up to us, and everything depended on our moral strength" (37). Yet, despite the egregiously thoughtless, even thuggish nature of the younger members of the collective, the story is not a condemnation of the entire Zionist enterprise: as careful readers will note, the famine that caused the Bedouin to migrate from the south has moved the military authorities to open the roads to them: "A whole population . . . could not simply be abandoned to the horrors of starvation" (*Jackals* 21). Hence, even though "Nomad and Viper" has been rightly recognized as a relatively simple narrative of protest against the excesses of xenophobic nationalism, it also merits recognition as an intricately textured and complex statement about the tragic nature of cultural misunderstanding, the triumph of primal instinct, and humanity's apparently limitless capacity for dangerous rationalization.

"Artzot hatan" ("Where the Jackals Howl"), the title story in this collection (first written in 1963 and later revised), is enlivened by the collective voice that is predominant in Oz's early writing. Sashka, a founding member, sits in his room—a space the omniscient narrator calls "the heart of our illuminated world" (*Jackals* 11)—composing a chapter about "problems facing the kibbutz in times of change" (3). This old warrior (his pioneering era forty distant years in the past) counsels himself not to "mark time," not to "turn back upon ourselves," but to "be vigorous and alert" (4). Read today, the story is a potent reminder that even the hallowed institution of the kibbutz was already caught up in the crisis of transition. Indeed, when was it ever otherwise? But Sashka, like later protagonists in Oz's oeuvre, is further burdened by a sense of the precarious (perhaps ephemeral) nature of what those of his generation achieved, their inability to erase the Palestinian natives they supplanted, the incontrovertible enmity surrounding the Jewish state itself.

Writing in the evenings, Sashka succumbs to a sense of dread, oppressed by the "whispering voices" of realities easier to quash in broad daylight:

> At this twilight hour our world is made up of circles within circles. On the outside is the circle of the autumn darkness, far from here, in the mountains and the great deserts. Sealed and enclosed within it is the circle of our night landscape, vineyards and orchards and plantations. . . . Our lands betray us in the night. Now they are no longer familiar and submissive, crisscrossed with irrigation pipes and dirt tracks. Now our fields have gone over to the enemy's camp. They send out to us waves of alien scents. At night we see them bristling in a miasma of threat and hostility and returning to their former state, as they were before we came to this place. (*Jackals* 10–11)

In an ironic invocation of the familiar binary opposition we encounter in "Nomad and Viper," though Sashka's cherished writing desk and table lamp (emblems of enlightenment) might "banish" nearby shadows, as might the kibbutz's perimeter lights, ominous intimations of the collective's existential reality persistently intrude: "The inner circle, the circle of lights, keeps guard over our houses and over us, against the accumulated menace outside. But it is an ineffective wall, it cannot keep out the smells of the foe and his voices. At night the voices and the smells touch our skin like tooth and claw" (11). Dystopian harbingers of apocalyptic dread invade the dreams of many an Oz protagonist, and, in "Jackals," yet another character, Matityahu, a blacksmith struggling with a guilty secret, transfers his inner demons into a terrifying vision of an implacable force that threatens to sweep away the insubstantial Jewish settlements.

The ever-fraught demarcation between the "savage" and the "civilized," characteristic of Oz's fiction in this period, emerges in Matityahu's nightmare of

> a mass of ravines descending the mountain slopes, scores of teeming watercourses, crisscrossing and zigzagging. In a flash the throngs of tiny

people appear in the gullies. Like little black ants they swarm and trickle from their hiding places . . . sweeping down like a cataract. Hordes of thin dark people streaming down the slopes, rolling like an avalanche of stone and plunging in a headlong torrent to the levels of the plain. Here they split into a thousand columns, racing westward in furious spate. Now they are so close that their shapes can be seen: a dark, disgusting, emaciated mass, crawling with lice and fleas, stinking. Hunger and hatred distort their faces. Their eyes blaze with madness. In full flood they swoop upon the fertile valleys, racing over the ruins of deserted villages without a moment's check. In their rush toward the sea they drag with them all that lies in their path, uprooting posts, ravaging fields, mowing down fences, trampling the gardens and stripping the orchards, pillaging homesteads, crawling through huts and stables, clambering over walls like demented apes, onward, westward, to the sands of the sea. (*Jackals* 17–18)

Ironically, as the episodes surrounding this vision reveal, the true horror lies within, in the soul and actions of Matityahu, a predatory character who takes advantage of a young artist he lures to his lonely apartment. Once again (as in "Nomad and Viper"), the protagonist projects his own insalubrious nature onto the Arab Other: "And suddenly you too are surrounded, besieged, paralyzed with fear. You see their eyes ablaze with primeval hatred, mouths hanging open, teeth yellow and rotten, curved daggers gleaming in their hands. They curse you in clipped tones, voices choking with rage or with dark desire. Now their hands are groping at your flesh. A knife and a scream" (*Jackals* 17–18). Of such passages, Avraham Balaban contends that "the world's primal impulse opposes human consciousness and the culture it has built, manifesting hostility and malice to it" (*Between God and Beast* 97). Although that is indeed the essential conflict of Oz's oeuvre, especially his early fiction, it is also true that Oz often locates that conflict *within* the psyches of his Jewish characters. Moreover, Oz's evolving political consciousness plays a forceful role in many of his most memorable characterizations and plots. In Yaron Peleg's memorable reading of Oz's early stories, Oz employs "very clear distinctions between hot and cold, east and west, dry and wet." His kibbutz is ostensibly "an island. Green, cultivated, and civilized it defies the deadly east, a geographic hell of sorts, that spews hot winds and is crawling with vermin, which threaten to destroy the lush commune at any moment." Yet as the stories unfold, "we find that this ideal community is seriously flawed, and the rot that spreads through it dissolves the attractive patina that covers its defects. Could such characterizations . . . foreshadow the nationalistic excesses which would increase after 1967 and Israel's control of the Palestinian territories?" (301–2). To Oz's lasting credit, the critical energy Peleg celebrates is unwavering even from a kibbutz only two miles from the unstable Jordanian border, across which terrorists often launched their raids.

In one of the more evocative moments of his acclaimed memoir, one that touches on his early kibbutz years (fig. 3), it is easy to find vestiges of the stubborn resistance to the ubiquitous militarist ethos that would lead Oz to become a co-founder of Peace Now in 1978. "It was a fixed tradition in Hulda to support the bridal canopy on two rifles and two pitchforks, symbolizing the union of work, defense, and the kibbutz. Nily and I caused quite a scandal by refusing to marry in the shadow of rifles. In the kibbutz assembly Zalman P. called me a 'bleeding heart,' while Tzvi K. inquired mockingly whether the army unit I was serving allowed me to go on patrol armed with a pitchfork or a broom" (*Tale of Love and Darkness* 479). In deviating from the unquestioned tenet that one must harness even one's most intimate experiences to the national effort, Amos and Nily firmly assert that there is a private sphere of life that one must also defend, a stance that surely made ripples in an era of social-ist conformity.

The stark alternative, suffering the psychic costs of unquestioningly suc-cumbing to that pervasive militarization, informs the horrific logic of the senseless death portrayed in Oz's "Derech haruach" ("The Way of the Wind"; 1962), one of the most powerful stories in the modern Hebrew canon (also from the collection *Where the Jackals Howl*). Here "ruach," the Hebrew word for "wind," may also denote "spirit," "intellectual life," or even "ghost." Oz draws on all these meanings in exposing the corrosive effects of an unbend-ing ideology. The young soldier Gideon Shenhav wakens to a glorious sunrise, but one that rapidly gives way to a brutal khamsin; in what is surely Oz's most ominous beginning to a story, we are informed this will be the last day of the young man's life. His paratrooper platoon has been selected to par-ticipate in a celebratory jump on Independence Day, but Gideon can barely rouse himself, even though the jump is to take place on the outskirts of Nof Harish, his birthplace and home. In his diffidence, Gideon resembles other luftmenschen or nebbishy Israeli protagonists of the era—most notably, A. B. Yehoshua's irresponsible fire scout in "Facing the Forests," the title story of the collection *Mul haye'arot* (*Facing the Forests*; 1968)—who go strik-ingly against the grain of the heroic Sabra myth and whose malaise invariably dismays their fathers. As the narrative unfolds in "The Way of the Wind,"

FIGURE 3   Amos Oz as a teenager, center, at Kibbutz Hulda, ca. 1955. Used by permission of Amotz Peleg, Kibbutz Hulda Archives.

the focus shifts tensely back and forth between scenes of Gideon's preparations and his confident but impatient father, Shimshon Sheinbaum, who we are told is a founding father of the Hebrew Labor Movement, and who is every bit as ponderous and swaggering as his weighty name suggests. "For decades now Shimshon Sheinbaum's name has been invested with a halo of enduring fame. For decades, he has fought body and soul to realize the vision of his youth" (*Jackals* 41). Clearly, Oz wants us to be ever mindful of Shimshon's biblical namesake (Samson) and the highly charged resonance Samson carries in Israeli military culture.

In *Dvash araiot* (*Lion's Honey*; 2005), novelist David Grossman, preoccupied with denouncing the unending entanglement of Israeli society with the seductions of military might, offers a biblical exegesis of the story of Samson (Judges 13–16) to shed light on his country's troubling Samsonian psychology, whose implications reverberate throughout its tumultuous modern history:

In Hebrew, he is almost always referred to as "Samson the hero," and elite combat units of the Israeli army have been named after him, from "Samson's Foxes" of the 1948 War of Independence to the "Samson" unit created during the first Palestinian Intifada in the late 1980s. . . .

Yet there is a certain problematic quality to Israeli sovereignty that is also embodied in Samson's relationship to his own power. As in the case of Samson, it sometimes seems that Israel's considerable military might is an asset that becomes a liability. For it would seem, without taking lightly the dangers facing Israel, that the reality of being immensely powerful had not really been internalized in the Israeli consciousness, not assimilated in a natural way, over many generations; and this, perhaps, is why the attitude to this power, whose acquisition has often been regarded as truly miraculous, is prone to distortion. (*Lion's Honey* 88–89)

For Grossman, "Samsonian modes of behavior" are highly visible in the tendencies to "ascrib[e] an exaggerated value to the power that one has attained; to making power an end in itself . . . to using it excessively" and also in resorting "almost automatically to the use of force instead of weighing other means of action" (89). He traces this malady to the near-apocalyptic anxieties of his countrymen, transmitted from one generation to the next:

The well-known Israeli feeling, in the face of any threat that comes along, that the country's security is crumbling—a feeling that also exists in the case of Samson, who in certain situations seems to shatter into pieces, his strength vanishing in the blink of an eye. This kind of collapse, however, does not reflect one's actual strength, and often carries in its wake an overblown display of force, further complicating the situation. All of this attests, it would seem to a rather feeble sense of ownership of the power that has been attained, and of course, to a deep existential insecurity. This is connected . . . to the very real dangers lying in wait for Israel, but also to the tragic formative experience of being a stranger in the world, the Jewish sense of not being a nation 'like other nations,' and of the State of Israel as a country whose very existence is conditional, whose future . . . is steeped in jeopardy, feelings that all the nuclear bombs that Israel developed, in a program once known as the "Samson Option," cannot eradicate. (89–90)

Though written decades after "The Way of the Wind" (in the aftermath of two disastrous wars in Lebanon and two intifadas), Grossman's cultural critique has tremendous validity for those considering Oz's early portrayal of a militaristic and authoritarian personality.

Now seventy-five, Oz's austere authoritarian has spent a principled lifetime detesting the weaknesses of others and vanquishing them within himself. When we first encounter him, the old man is tormented by a dream of the previous night that he cannot quite recall but that prevents him from focusing on the day's work. In his austere ideological purity, Sheinbaum takes immense pride in never having been seduced into entering the political realm, unlike those who "cut themselves off completely from manual labor" (*Jackals* 43). Indeed, as related by the anonymously hive-like "we" that distinguishes the stories in this early collection, the very landscape is witness to this uncompromising halutz's indefatigable labor:

> Until a few years ago his days were divided equally between physical and intellectual work: three days gardening, three days theorizing. The beautiful gardens of Nof Harish are largely his handiwork. We can remember how he used to plant and prune and lop, water and hoe, manure, transplant, weed, and dig up. He did not permit his status as the leading thinker of the movement to exempt him from the duties to which every rank-and-file member is liable: he served as night watchman, took his turn in the kitchens, helped with the harvest. No shadow of a double standard has ever clouded the path of Shimshon Sheinbaum's life; he is a single complex of vision and execution, he has known no slackness or weakness of will—so the secretary of the movement wrote about him in a magazine a few years ago. (43)

Already a man's man in his youth, he attracted women as easily as he did political disciples. But, like so many of Oz's aging patriarchs—most notably, Yolek in *Menuhah nehonah* (*A Perfect Peace*; 1982)—Shimshon now has his moments of angst and despair, though he imperiously sets them aside every time.

His only son, Gideon, is the product of a sad affair with a lonely kibbutz girl thirty-three years his junior and has been a profound disappointment from earliest childhood—the poor boy is simply "not the stuff on which dynasties are founded" (45). Shimshon regretfully recalls the wretched discordancy between the boy and his environment:

> As a child he was always sniveling. He was a slow, bewildered child, mopping up blows and insults without retaliating, a strange child. . . . And from the age of twelve he was constantly having his heart broken by

girls of all ages. He was always lovesick, and he published sad poems and cruel parodies in the children's newsletter. A dark, gentle youth, with an almost feminine beauty, who walked the paths of the kibbutz in obstinate silence. He did not shine at work; he did not shine in communal life. He was slow at speech and no doubt also of thought. (45)

But, after eighteen years of disappointment, redemption seems close at hand. Gideon has enlisted in the paratroopers (with his father's permission and despite his mother's steadfast refusal)—"They'd make a man of him," Shimshon is quite certain—and now finds himself on this brilliant holiday morning about to take part in a triumphal display of parachuting. Yet, like other hapless protagonists, he retreats from the sunny Mediterranean present, struggling to extricate himself from the strange dream of the previous night: "All that night he had nestled in a half-dream of dark autumnal forests under northern skies, a rich smell of autumn, huge trees he could not name. All night long pale leaves had been dropping on the huts of the camp. Even after he had awakened in the morning, the northern forest with its nameless trees still continued to whisper in his ears" (47). This is Oz's quintessential rendering of Diaspora, Zionism's antithesis, the homeland of so many of his ill-adjusted dreamers, with its mournful evocation of autumn, a season that barely even registers in Israel. Having learned of his mother's discontent and her tragic suicide in *A Tale of Love and Darkness*, we can better understand the author's preoccupation with autumn and its usually sinister implications for his protagonists' fate or psychic health.[11] That northern clime of mist and cloud conspires to blur the Sabra's heroic identity, to leach away the certainties of the rooted native Hebrew.

Yet, despite his strange foreboding, Gideon relishes the almost spiritual ecstasy of transcendence that parachuting sometimes bestows, the tantalizing release from military routine, from the very limits of one's own self:

Gideon adored the delicious moment of free fall between the jump from the aircraft and the unfolding of the parachute. The void rushes up toward you at lightning speed, fierce drafts of air lick at your body, making you dizzy with pleasure. The speed is drunken, reckless, it whistles and roars and your whole body trembles to it, red-hot needles work at your nerve ends, and your heart pounds. Suddenly, when you are lightning in the wind, the chute opens. The straps check your fall, like a firm, masculine arm bringing you calmly under control. . . . The reckless thrill gives way to a more sedate pleasure. Slowly your body swings through the air, floats, hesitates, drifts a little way n the slight breeze, you can never guess precisely where your feet will touch ground, on the slope of that hill or next to the orange groves over there, and like an exhausted migrating bird you slowly descend, seeing roofs, roads, cows in the meadow, slowly as if you have a choice, as if the decision is entirely yours. (*Jackals* 47)

For a few precious minutes, the free fall through the void seems to afford this "migrating bird" the precious dissolution of self and place that beckon in his dreams. And he finds himself looking forward to the entire spectacle, the excited children, the kibbutz's welcome for his entire unit, to the consolation he will give his worried mother, and, most tantalizingly of all, to the rare gift of Shimshon's fatherly pride.

As the son ascends into the sky with his platoon, all the while daydreaming of the approval and paternal affection that will soon be his, the father stirs himself to join the onlookers, content that the months of military training must have performed its role in toughening up the diffident lad. But Shimshon has largely given up on Gideon's generation; his fondest hope is for future grandchildren: "The third generation will be a wonderful synthesis, a successful outcome: they will inherit the spontaneity of their parents and the spirit of their grandparents. It will be a glorious heritage distilled from a twisted pedigree" (49–50). He makes a mental note to jot down his profound musings about the new breed that will surpass Gideon and all his ilk, who "exude such an air of shallow despair, of nihilism, of cynical mockery," who "can't love wholeheartedly" nor "hate wholeheartedly" (50). But, as the father broods about their collective failure, the plummeting son yearns for individual affirmation. "A long wild scream of joy burst from his throat as he fell. He could see his childhood haunts rushing up toward him as he fell . . . the roofs and treetops and he smiled a frantic smile of greeting as he fell toward the vineyards and concrete paths and sheds and gleaming paths. . . . Never in his whole life had he known such overwhelming, spine-tingling love" (52). Yet that euphoria is soon overtaken by "a wild panic" that he will be lost among the other paratroopers. Suddenly, more than anything else, he wants to be fully visible—all by himself and on his own.

He releases both his main and his reserve chute (for use only when the primary chute fails to open), dramatically slowing his descent. As his fellow parachutists safely land, rapidly folding parachutes and forming ranks on the ground, Gideon hovers, "alone in the void, like a gull or a lonely cloud. . . . Happy, intoxicated, he drank in the hundreds of eyes fixed on . . . him alone. In his glorious isolation" (53). Drifting eastward, carried by a strong breeze and utterly oblivious to the danger that the crowd below already perceives, he sings in a sort of ecstasy—moments before his harness becomes entangled with the electric cables crossing the Jezreel Valley. For a time, as an officer below shouts out desperate commands and the other soldiers keep the gathering crowd away, the boy is protected by the rubber soles of his paratrooper boots. Sheinbaum quickly joins the officer and, together, they order Gideon to use his knife to cut himself loose and drop to the ground. Gideon obliges at first, but when he hesitates to cut the last strap, "his father's eyes filled with blood as he roared: 'You coward! You ought to be ashamed of yourself!' 'But I can't do it, I'll break my neck, it's too high.' 'You can do it and you must do it. You're a fool, that's what you are, a fool and a coward'" (55). Readers who doubt that the young author has more in mind than just the fate of his hapless protagonist need only attend to Oz's withering allusions to Israel's unremitting militarism. Indeed, fighter jets, a familiar trope in many of the stories from *Where the Jackals Howl*, are intrinsic to Oz's portrayal of Israel's militarized reality, the savage ordinary. And, as many critics have noted, precisely where his kibbutz imagery is most seductive is where Oz is most slyly subversive.

As Gideon fills the horrified silence of the crowd below with his heaving sobs, "a group of jet planes passed overhead on their way to the aerial display over the city. They were flying in precise formation, thundering westward like a pack of wild dogs" (55). Meanwhile, with similar ineptitude, the boy drops his knife, Shimshon hurls a stone at him, and the platoon commander fails to sever the electric cables with a burst of bullets from his machine gun. Struggling desperately to free himself, Gideon ends up suspended upside down, "like a dead lamb suspended from a butcher's hook" (57). And, after a series of grotesque incidents in which the collective proves disastrously incapable of acting together to rescue one of its own, he is indeed electrocuted. The corpse of the Sabra child dangles like an "upside-down Pinocchio," as a callous youngster calls him, or perhaps like one of Chagall's floating shtetl Jews, above his homeland.

Certain details in "The Way of the Wind" gain their most chilling impact only upon rereading. For instance, when viewed through the prism of Gideon's senseless death, even his father's seemingly benevolent qualities take on a sinister aspect. At one point, we are told that Sheinbaum had been the official kibbutz gardener in his day and that, even now, "he would not cease to scan the flower beds mercilessly in search of undesirable intruders" (50). Was Gideon one of those intruding weeds that Shimshon felt duty-bound to uproot? In any case, by now it should be clear that the intergenerational antagonism that figures more subtly in Oz's highly accomplished later novel *A Perfect Peace* is already fully present in this story—an antagonism that Adam Kirsch describes as proceeding "with the slow inevitability of a nightmare, or better, of a Greek tragedy, in which parentage is character and character is fate."[12] With similar force, in her superb account of sacrificial myth in modern Hebrew culture, Yael Feldman asks of this and related kibbutz narratives by young kibbutz authors: "Was the kibbutz environment too oppressive, rendering its young authors unable to imagine any way out for Oedipus/Isaac except through suicide/ self-immolation?" (*Glory and Agony* 181). For Feldman, who sees "The Way of the Wind" as one of the major exemplars of the stirring tradition of Akedah retellings in Israeli literature, the story's most critical element "is the chagrin of [the] aged father, a kibbutz founder, who is portrayed as a castrating, self-righteous tyrant." The vivid harshness of that portrait, Feldman argues, owes much to Oz's own position as "the young author-qua-son" (178)[13]—an altogether apt formulation, given that Gideon, the hapless son in this story, is a somewhat effete poetry writer who, like Oz, falls woefully short of the Sabra paragon despite his native status. Similarly, Nehama Aschkenasy illuminates the ironic force of the narrative's biblical retelling:

> Gideon, like Isaac, is his mother's only child, tame, gentle, and protected. Shimshon, a passionate Zionist and prolific writer of castigating, sanctimonious rhetoric, is self-centered and fiercely ambitious; like Abraham, he is the architect of the terrifying scene in which the bound son is about to be sacrificed. . . . Like Isaac, Gideon is only dimly aware of the imminent danger; both the biblical protagonist and his modern counterpart reveal a sense of foreboding—deeply buried under complete trust . . . in Isaac's case, and hidden behind naïve anticipation and excitement in Gideon's case. (129)

In Aschkenasy's exegesis, Oz's modern retelling of the Akedah is distinguished by a fatalistic sense of tragedy "because it starts with the sense of predestination; its opening lines already tell us that Gideon is doomed, and thus while Gideon is under the illusion that he is moving toward a glorious climax in his life, in reality he is only progressing toward his own destruction" (131). Hence, for Oz, the brutal and punitive dimensions of intergenerational conflict in his own time exceed those of its biblical antecedent. Though characters often contemplate suicide in Oz's kibbutz tales, they rarely commit it. I think that Gideon may conceivably be a salient exception, but even if that is true, it is impossible to isolate the way he died from the tremendous generational and nationalist pressures bearing down on him in his short life. Finally, so powerful is the disturbing resonance of "The Way of the Wind" within modern Israeli culture that video artist Oded Hirsch, known for his provocative films, created a haunting cinematic adaptation of the story in 2012, dramatically underscoring its primal and operatic dimensions to unforgettable effect (as we will see in chapter 5, on the curious reassessments of Israel's mythic past currently enlivening Israeli film).

Elsewhere, Perhaps

As might be expected from these predecessors, the first novel Oz wrote during his early Kibbutz Hulda years, *Makom aher* (*Elsewhere, Perhaps*; 1966), deepens his exploration of the kibbutz as a troubling realm of thwarted individual aspirations and raging sexual desire. Published shortly before the 1967 War, its varied tonal registers move abruptly between almost a travelogue appreciation of quotidian kibbutz life and an acute sense of the mounting dread and anxiety that Israelis felt in that era. The novel's spare plot is set in motion by the scandalous impregnation of a girl by a much older man and the complex responses of the community, ranging from harshly judgmental to tenderly compassionate (a theme Oz would later revisit in *Between Friends*). There are worrying developments from without, as tensions escalate on the Syrian border, and dangerous currents within. Yet, just as often, the novel looks beyond the travails of both war and scandal to linger lovingly over the simple pleasures of everyday life on the kibbutz. *Elsewhere* begins with the author's wily deconstruction of the demarcation between civilized settler and savage Other, contrasting Metsudat Ram's "neat, geometrical patchwork of fields" with "the surrounding bleakness of the mountains" and "the symmetrical architecture of Kibbutz Metsudat Ram" with "the grim natural chaos that looks down on it from above" (*Elsewhere, Perhaps* 4). In Keshet's astute reading, Oz has transformed the usual realism of the kibbutz novel to serve a largely allegorical purpose:

> The enlightened, sane world of the kibbutz is no more than a remote island in the land "where jackals howl," and the attempt to impose rational order on the forces of chaos—white, red-roofed houses, lawns, paths dividing the lawns into square, tilled, rectangular agricultural areas—is frequently divided by the hostile world all around, and the demonic and dark drives of the soul. Amos Oz elevates what was relegated to the subconscious by the kibbutz "superego." There are characters that uphold

the accepted norms and ideological dictates and impose the kibbutz super-ego on their soul, and there are plotting "others" that break the rules of the pioneering ethos . . . undermining the norms sanctified by the community. ("Freedom" 207)

As kibbutz memoirist Assaf Inbari has pointed out, Oz evokes contemporary kibbutz life "better than any kibbutz writer preceding him" ("Kibbutz Novel" 139). That is especially true for Oz's unerring portrayal of the positive as well as negative ways gossip shapes and regiments kibbutz reality: "With eyes like hawks' we observe our neighbors' actions. Our judgments take effect in a hundred and one devious ways" (*Elsewhere, Perhaps* 176). That concise declaration captures the essential truth of the social mechanisms of kibbutz life; in one way or another, each of Oz's kibbutz narratives reflects its force (fig. 4).

FIGURE 4   Amos Oz, first from right, harvesting peanuts at Kibbutz Hulda, 1956. Used by permission of Amotz Peleg, Kibbutz Hulda Archives.

Elsewhere's imagined kibbutz, situated two miles from the Jordanian border, is composed of two disparate and particularly tempestuous cultural groups, German and Russian Jews. Though they can barely get along at times, both are bound by a kind of exilic melancholy, especially when they gather to listen to music: "The older members . . . can see the far-off streets of their childhood, lashed by dark rain, perhaps, or shrouded in gloomy fog. Even the younger people, who were born here, feel a sad longing for far-off places, unknown, unnamed places that are far away and full of sadness. Silent sorrow settles on every face. They are human beings, tillers of the soil. They are weary. Their eyes are closed. Sorrow clasps their hearts" (82–83). Even as a young writer, Oz had little patience with the Sabra myth, hence his kibbutz characters (of all generations) cannot shake off their inherent connection to the long centuries of Jewish life in Diaspora. Moreover, Oz is always mindful of the sacrifices of previous generations, the precarious origins mythologized by the reverent processes of memorialization. Here he accurately evokes the stockade and watchtower days captured in Koestler's 1946 novel *Thieves in the Night*:

> The thirties—unforgettable years, years we shall boast of forever! Metsu-dat Ram: a tiny terrified encampment, lost in an empty expanse, braving the menacing mountains. A wooden tower, a double barbed-wire fence, dogs barking at the moon. Gray tents and dirt tracks, with billows of dust, four parched huts, scorched tin roofs, brackish, reddish water, smelling rusty in the common showers. A tumble-down shack with a few rickety tables. Frail saplings drooping in the heat. Tormented nights, filled with wild sounds, bathed in harsh moonlight, swarming with horrible movements. Strange noises from the Arab village nearby, the smell of smoke, damp vapors, our cheerful shouting in the middle of the night, wild dancing, party songs full of joy, full of sorrow, full of longing, a mixture of unbridled ecstasy and desperate orphaned sobbing. (*Elsewhere, Perhaps* 62–63)

Such impressionistic passages brilliantly conjure up the generation of the founders, the excesses of their passions and obsessions, the exuberant together-ness as well as hopeless isolation found in their near-impossible situation. Along with gripping accounts of terrorist infiltration and hostile actions by the Jordanian army, they go far to counter Oz's wry mischief elsewhere in deflating the heavily mythologized ideological past, almost as though a debate was still being waged within the young writer himself. As Alan Mintz argues, "much of Oz's best early fiction is an exercise in rapping vigorously on feet of clay. The job is done with great artistic sophistication, and with the best tech-niques in the modernist repertoire; but there is no disguising the fact that the encounter between father and son is not play-acting but a struggle for survival, in which the will of the father remains a potent force" (39). That Freudian dynamic, often with guilty repercussions, enlivens *Elsewhere*, which is not without its humorous moments of affectionate ridicule. Thus, on one occasion, the weary 1930s halutzim allow themselves the unprecedented treat of a night-time journey to Haifa for a production of the Habima Theatre Company. But, on the way home, the self-important vanguard of New Hebrews cannot refrain from grumbling: "Here we are building a new world, living a completely new life, and Habima still keeps harping on these ghetto themes" (*Elsewhere, Perhaps* 63). On another occasion, the kibbutz gathers to observe May Day, and, after the party anthem is sung, members rise one by one to speak portentously of the importance of observing the fellowship of international workers.[14] But, while all that is going on, a teenage boy, Ido, is suddenly overcome by the unbearable nearness of the female comrade beside him. In language that wit-tily captures the puritanical environment of the kibbutz in that distant time (so different from the culture most Western youths of the 1960s experienced), Oz draws an amusing contrast between the solemnity of the older members and the smoldering yearnings of a younger one: "Ido steals a glance at the woman sitting next to him. . . . Slowly, stealthily, the boy moves his thigh closer to Hasia's. His imagination runs riot. Stricken with alarm and remorse, he withdraws his leg, striving to avoid the slightest contact with his neighbor. But his fingers are shaking. He looks away, fixing his gaze on one of the flags flapping in the breeze. It won't calm down" (74). Still, Oz gives the final word to a veteran Labor Movement worker and his sense of the kibbutzim's prophetic mission: "The concept of social justice does not recognize national boundaries. On the contrary. Its aim is to eradicate false frontiers and to set up true fron-tiers" (75).

In other instances, Oz richly orchestrates the charged environment sur-rounding the halutzim, the disquietingly primal ways that human and natural worlds commingle: "The night stoops over you and blows its scents at you. An unpleasant, sour smell wafts from the hen house. A dense vapor from the cowshed, a damp smell from the stores. Various odors drift from all sides. A wild smell from the fields. The riotous air of the mountains provides a lively accompaniment. The cascades of mingled odors excite the furious barking of the dogs, which gives way to distracted and terrifying howls" (154). Passages like this abound, heightening a sense of barely contained ferocity and transgres-sions of all sorts. At night, the sunny illusions of utopian aspirations dissipate under the existential dread fueled by the mounting tensions of life on the border, which Oz portrays as an unending farce of mindlessly mechanistic enmity: "The beam of the searchlight on top of the water tower collided with another light. The yellow ray of the enemy searchlight. The two powerful lamps pointed their jets of light straight at each other's eye, as if trying to dazzle the other to death. . . . The two beams of light remained locked in a furious embrace, piercing each other's eyes, bitter and stubborn, like knives poised for murder or like drunken lovers" (189). By night, songs of enemy soldiers up on the Golan are carried to the kibbutz windows like the howling of jackals, filled with "simmering sadness" (291), and, by day, the kibbutz's fortifications are built up with ominous alacrity.[15] Greeting her son, home on leave from the IDF, a mother is saddened by his cold indifference to her hugs.

The sordid affair of a young woman and the corrosive gossip that ensues cast heavy shadows. Indeed, as we read of the often petty dramas that play out in Kibbutz Metsudat Ram, we often feel as though we are observing the Garden of Eden just before the humans spoiled everything forever. Or, as Christopher Lehmann-Haupt incisively describes the situation in his *New York Times* review, "the men and women of Kibbutz Metsudat Ram try to march in lockstep toward a new socialist utopia, but snapping at their ankles and tripping them into disarray are the traditions of their disparate pasts. Russian Jews are at odds with German Jews; the talkers are in conflict with the doers; the young don't see eye to eye with the old. . . . The women gossip and kvetch over trivia, the men stop speaking to each other over nothing." Ultimately, however, in the face of the looming existential emergency, their own dramas seem trivial, even to the kibbutzniks. When the sights and sounds of military jets and patrols intrude with greater frequency, they realize that "something was about to happen. The rhythm of our lives was about to change" (*Elsewhere, Perhaps* 292). Yet, throughout the novel, Oz counters his often surreal vignettes of nocturnal savagery, misconduct, and growing dread with homage to the gentle rhythms of days on the kibbutz, the small pleasures of daily interactions, the kind of serenity Oz himself might have savored at the very moment he wrote these lines: "At four o'clock in the afternoon, the time-honored rest; deck chairs on the lawn, the whisper of the wind in the trees, the scent of roses and of coffee, the clicking of knitting needles, evening papers, reading glasses, the twilight glow, answered by a blaze of light on the mountaintops to the east, Herzl Goldring's accordion, Herbert Segal's violin, the spray from the sprinklers" (185). Even so, the escalating threat of war and national unease sometimes overtake the quieter, more intricate human dimensions of the story (the young Oz himself would not escape the crucible of that war, serving as a member of a tank crew on the Golan Heights). Indeed, the novel often explores the psychological manifestations of that constant threat, particularly on the kibbutz children, whose play increasingly enacts fantasies of being at war: "All afternoon the kibbutz paths re-echo with their noisy games. Armed with stout sticks, they wreak havoc and carnage on the enemies of Israel under the orders of their young commander," reports the livid narrator, outraged that the kibbutz teachers do not encourage more constructive games (84). Later, when the children eagerly volunteer to help a local army unit dig in, that angry voice warns against "militaristic attitudes" and the steady atrophy of the soul under such circumstances (129). A young man, gazing up at an aerial skirmish between Israeli and Syrian planes, is described as "seized by demented joy" (164). Here and in related passages, we can see how Oz's dovish affinities, more publicly expressed in later years, were already firmly established in the pages of his first novel.

Yet, more often than not, for all its quarrels and pettiness, the warm humanity and genuinely benevolent spirit that have drawn so many to kibbutz life win out in the end. Thus a "straying" woman's affair and pregnancy may have scandalized the community, but, in the novel's later pages, "a flood of compassion broke over our kibbutz toward the end of summer. The women competed in good works and acts of kindness toward the straying lamb. She was surrounded by sympathy and warmth. Sincere invitations to come round and talk. You're so lonely. Why don't you come and have tea with us, come and have a rest, take a shower, look at pictures, pour out your troubles? The women in the sewing room acted beyond the call of duty" (241).[16]

Not only does the kibbutz rally around the individual in trouble, but we are made to see the value of such a tightly knit and giving community in the face of the growing threat of war. Following the death of a beloved member, Oz renders the kibbutzniks in all their shock, grief, and vulnerable imperfection, so organic a presence in their environs that the whole is summed up as a fully integrated and spiritual topocosm, the very land a participant in their loss. The touchingly spare language of the very young writer does not fail to move after all these years:

> No one . . . stopped working, because mourning does not interrupt work. But everywhere people worked silently, almost sullenly. Tsvi Ramigolski took Mundek Zohar with him to dig the grave. Tsvi had already telephoned a notice of the death to the newspaper of the kibbutz movement. Now he picked up a spade and went with Mundek to the cemetery. For a long time Tsvi had not done any physical work apart from gardening. His hands blistered, and he panted. He was fat, and his shoulders sagged

slightly. The soil was hard, dry, and stubborn. . . . The cemetery was on the edge of the pine wood. There was a continuous moaning from the pines. . . .

    . . . The spades gave out a metallic sound. And the stones gave out a stony sound. (261)

Toward its conclusion, *Elsewhere* immerses us in viscerally wrenching scenes of wartime violence and death. Yet, even here, one of the most inescapably stirring flourishes of this so often affecting novel is the prophetic utterance of its penultimate chapter, "My Brother's Keeper" (300). No three words have ever expressed the deepest core of kibbutz values quite so powerfully.

    In his 1973 review, after praising *Elsewhere, Perhaps* as "a charmingly unpious tapestry of Israeli life," Lehmann-Haupt summarizes its deficits in a way that also celebrates the emergence of a profoundly gifted voice, calling it "a young writer's book, not quite sure of its touch, too heavily freighted with literary symbolism . . . and quite evidently a departure toward better things." Thus today it seems altogether fortunate that this was not to be Oz's final attempt to capture the complexities and vagaries of kibbutz life in a full-sized novel.

A Perfect Peace

In Oz's *Menuhah nehonah* (*A Perfect Peace*; 1982), the long-festering seeds of today's Israeli-Arab crisis are fully present in the competing locales of organized kibbutz life and the ruins of a Palestinian village. From the perspective of the beleaguered young Yonatan, the desert wastes beckon as a desirable alternative space to escape the violence and purposelessness of the kibbutz life he feels he has unjustly inherited. From the outset, we plunge into a microcosm of Israel's fears, dreams, and anxieties as felt by this young citizen-soldier raised in the kibbutz's value system of unquestioning sacrifice.[17] In the course of the novel, Oz portrays the insular defensiveness of the modern Jewish state as smothering Yonatan, whose flight from kibbutz conformity toward desert space is seen by his comrades as a cultural and political relapse.[18]

    The tension between madness and sanity (whether that of the collective society or the individual) has long been singled out as perhaps the most distinct catalyst for Oz's imagination. Yosefa Loshitzky vividly identifies that critical dialectic, both in his fiction and in his "polemical essays," where Oz "celebrates madness (both personal and political) mainly through his use of poetically charged and excessive language that makes madness look more 'interesting' than sanity. One may gauge the evolving sense of Israeli personal and political identity in this tension between madness and normalcy" (111). The individual's moral resources are severely taxed by a society whose transcendental values of communalism, solidarity, justice, and ultimately democracy are themselves rapidly decaying.

More than anyone else writing in Israel today, Oz has an intimate understanding of the bold social revolution of the kibbutz, so often portrayed in the Hebrew novel as "Israel's quintessential social structure and the Zionist ideal in microcosm" (Brenner, "'Hidden Transcripts'" 105). After a hiatus of more than a decade, during which Oz dabbled with a variety of shorter forms including political essays, novellas, and even a children's book, *A Perfect Peace* marked a significant development in his novelistic oeuvre. Set between the winter of 1965 and the eve and aftermath of the 1967 War, *A Perfect Peace* is Oz's far-reaching exploration of the dangerous ideological and political divide between kibbutz generations as experienced by the unhappy young Yonatan, for whom, smothered by the communal responsibilities and ego-suppressing nature of kibbutz life, madness begins to appear more enticing than sanity. Centering on the internal crisis of this young citizen-soldier, raised in a kibbutz situated near the ruins of Sheikh Dahr, a (fictional) Arab village destroyed during the 1948 War, the novel raises important questions about the room for genuine political awareness (as well as self-consciousness) in collective life.

It is crucial to underscore that, as reflected in the ruins at the outset of the novel, the stark fact of the Nakba (the Palestinian exodus of 1948) is a quiet but increasingly urgent presence in the Sabra's journey (as we will see in discussing Ilan Yagoda's film *Rain 1949* in chapter 5). Indeed, writing of Palestinian hauntings in other contemporary Israeli novels, Gil Hochberg calls our attention to how such "emptied Arab villages . . . unfold a semantics of ambiguity located between presence and absence, the visible and the invisible," which in the disturbing effects of their afterlife are anything but "sealed fragments of the past" (66). As *A Perfect Peace* begins, Yonatan who feels empty and adrift, finds himself seduced by the exotic imagery of a religious broadcaster: "One evening, on the radio news, a certain Rabbi Nachtigall . . . used the phrase 'a desert wasteland and a wilderness.' For the rest of that night . . . through the next day, Yonatan absentmindedly recited these words as if they were a mantra: the magic of wilderness . . . the magic of wasteland" (*Perfect Peace* 15). Here and elsewhere, Yonatan imagines that he is being summoned by the voice of the desert, but to what purpose, he is unsure. In *A Perfect Peace*, as in "Nomad and Viper," the kibbutz and the wilderness embody the Apollonian and Dionysian polarities of Israeli culture that often course through many of Oz's characters and situations. We can feel the tensions between these polar opposites from the novel's first page, where we learn that Yonatan, kibbutz mechanic, army reserves captain and specialist in reconnaissance, wounded in war and decorated with a medal for his bravery under fire, is determined "to leave his wife and the kibbutz on which he had been born and raised" (3).[19]

Trapped in the smothering routine of kibbutz life and an unhappy marriage, Yonatan resents his father, Yolek, the aging but still vigorous kibbutz secretary, who, we are told, was a member of David Ben-Gurion's cabinet and of the legendary generation of political patriarchs. Little wonder that the son dreams of his father commanding him "on behalf of the secret service . . . to undertake a dangerous journey to some northern land and lay the serpent low in its lair with an ax stroke from behind" (21). For his part, Yolek is shaken by a nightmare in which "Ben-Gurion, red-faced and terrible, had sprung at him from a nearby Arab well and roared, 'I don't want to hear another word about it! You'll shut up and kill if you have to . . . just as King Saul killed his own son!'" (119).[20] Already we hear echoes of "The Way of the Wind," where another kibbutz father insisted on expunging his very seed of any hint of Diaspora's enfeebling traits, even at the risk of the boy's life.

The psychologically fraught dreams of both father and son in *A Perfect Peace* underscore the alienating militarist legacy of the legendary founding generation. We see the aggressive imprint of this martial ideology even on Yonatan's fantasy life. Tormented by rumors about his actual paternity—that his biological father may be a millionaire bearing the ironic moniker "Trotsky," who is living off the profits from his hotel in Florida—Yonatan feverishly dreams of escape to "a faraway place where anything is possible—love, danger, arcane encounters, sudden conquests" (6). He is torn between his rootedness in the kibbutz community and the allure of forbidden territories and identities. But before Yonatan flees into the alien desert, Oz makes sure that we learn a great deal about the moral cost of building a state, the existential toll exacted on both its founders and sons. How can the longing for self-determination be brought into harmony with the longing for shared community, particularly when community demands rigorous conformity? Through the rich delineation of the hero's crisis of entrapment, these questions are put to the test.

Yet another vital aspect of his hero's rebellion is signaled by Oz's rendering of Rimona, Yonatan's beautiful but disconcertingly vacuous wife. Yonatan sees her as a "barren desert," and their bedroom looks to him "like the bones of a cadaver in the light of the full dead moon in the window," as he lies "wide awake yet abducted by some white nightmare in a . . . wasteland, wide awake but alone with a corpse" (60). Through such charged imagery, Oz clearly implies that, when finally Yonatan exchanges the disappointing illusions of a marital wasteland for the bedrock truths of the real desert, it will be to exorcise the internal desert within his soul.[21] The young man's rebellion against his merely functional marriage is closely aligned with another source of dissatisfaction, for, very much like the kibbutz itself, Rimona is the perfect socialist subject, apparently content not to assign any special significance to any individual. And yet validation of his uniqueness is what Yonatan most sorely needs (echoing the tormented yearning of Gideon in "The Way of the Wind"). Rimona's matter-of-fact description of the harmony of routine, responsibility, and unceasing labor, of a life reduced to service, can only stir his unrest:

> When you're done working for the day, you can sit on the lawn with Udi and Anat and talk politics. You'll go to the all-kibbutz chess tournament and maybe win another medal. When you come home, it will be time for winter plowing. Your brother Amos will get out of the army and maybe he'll marry Rachel. You'll start picking lemons and grapefruit, and then oranges, and you and Udi will be busy all day getting the shipments out on time. . . .
>
> . . . And then winter will come back, and we'll light the heater and sit here together, and it can rain all it wants and we won't get wet. (67)

When Yonatan mutters an acerbic "And then?," Rimona replies with maddening logic: "Then it will be winter again." His resulting fury is exacerbated in part by guilt over his insistence that Rimona agree to an abortion, which later causes a second child to be stillborn.

It is surely revealing that, in spite of the kibbutz movement's manifestly egalitarian nature (still largely the case in the mid-1960s), Oz's Kibbutz Granot resembles more a decadent monarchy, presided over by Yonatan's father, the kibbutz secretary. Yolek Lifshitz is one of the Zionist founders of Ben-Gurion's generation, a scarred and embattled warrior of many ideological as well as martial battles. His generation lived and died by the logic of a Zionist motto, "For a people without a land, a land without a people," effectively rendering the indigenous Arab population invisible, a fateful denial that plays a role in his disaffected son's struggle with the harsh reality he has inherited.[22]

A paragon of his era, and long a man of unrelenting pragmatism and action, Yolek now languishes in his old age. Alienated from his son (about whose true paternity both he and the kibbutz are uncertain), he is beset with doubts as to whether any of his socialist accomplishments will endure over time. Although his body is ravaged by aches and pains, his discontent has a deeper source:

"Quite apart from his physical woes, some obscure worry was gnawing away inside him. He felt he had forgotten some terribly important, even urgent, matter, one that was imperative to remember lest some great harm be done. Yet what it was, and why it was so urgent, he could not for the life of him recall" (52–53). And the growth of his young country often brings him no pleasure. On one occasion, finding himself in an unfamiliar neighborhood, he recoils from the materialist values he feels are already undoing the hard-won gains of the Zionist dream of the New Jew:

> Its residents had taken all their savings, borrowed more money, obtained mortgages . . . to be able to live in these blindingly white high-rise buildings, in luxury apartments that would have made the local moneybags in the shtetl they had come from . . . turn green with envy in his unmarked grave.
>
> In vain, Yolek realized, had been the whole arduous attempt to rebuild Jewish life on a new foundation; in vain, the pioneers' tents and co-op restaurants; in vain, the creed of physical labor and life in the sun; in vain, the going barefoot, the peasant clothes, the shepherds' songs; in vain, the long nights of argument and debate. (112–13)

Back at home, Yolek's angst is mirrored by a weary malaise that has settled over his entire community. For, behind his back, the members mutter darkly to one another about his leadership, the growing scandal of his son's apparent ménage à trois, and the generally ruinous state of things: "Things are going to the dogs, my friend. . . . For all his big talk, Yolek never got off his butt to do a damn thing around here. Everything in sight is falling apart. The kibbutz. The country. The youth. I don't want to stoop to gossip . . . but just take a look at what's going on with a certain Very Important Person's son. *For the Lord hath created a new thing in the earth, one woman shall compass two men*" (177). Through such grumblings and expressions of resentment, the novel ruptures the illusory veneer of solidarity of kibbutz and nation, showing both to be riddled with social pretension, moral ambivalence, illness, and loathing.

Whereas Yolek bemoans the lack of idealistic fire in the young kibbutz members, for them, the large political organizations to which Yolek has selflessly surrendered a long and embattled life fail to provide the answers to the larger questions of life. The kibbutz's new generation has only contempt for the lofty realm of politicians and politics. Yolek's son, in particular, detests the kibbutz's formalism along with what he regards as its hypocritical and dishon-

est call for perpetual "selfless" commitment. Even worse, the Miami hotel mag-
nate Benya Trotsky, once intimately involved with Yolek's wife, Hava, hopes to
persuade Yonatan (who he imagines is his biological son) to join him in
America. Self-righteously, Yolek warns his nemesis, "Lay not thy hand upon
the lad!"—Oz's wry nod to the angel's call to Abraham as he prepares to sacrifice Isaac (Genesis 22:12).

The personal psychodrama of infidelity and paternity that divides Trotsky
and Yolek at times reads less like a clash between individuals and more like an
allegory, with seething layers of bitter ideological conflict between Diaspora
and Zion, kibbutz idealism and city materialism. Characteristically, Yolek
drafts a venomous letter, filled with sanctimonious rhetoric, to this long-absent
adversary:

> No power on earth can possibly forgive me for the moronic pity I showed
> in not digging your grave thirty years ago. . . . You are the lowest of the
> low. It's people like you who've been the poisonous cancer in the body of
> the Jewish people for generations. You're the age-old curse of the Exile.
> You're the reason the Gentiles hated and still hate us . . . You with your
> money grubbing, you with your Golden Calf, you with your foaming
> lechery . . . stopping at no betrayal, sleeping on your filthy ducats that
> spread like germs from country to country, from exile to exile . . . home-
> less, conscienceless, rootless, making us a laughingstock and a pariah
> among the nations. (191)

Raging against decades of unease over his Sabra son's paternity, Yolek is determined to exorcise the Diasporic demons that threaten the young man's stability
and native sense of belonging.

Above all, in Yolek's eyes, Yonatan embodies the first Sabra generation to be
born in freedom—"the first of a new line of Jews whose children would grow
up in this land to put an end to the malignancy of the Exile. And now the
Exile is back again, masquerading as a rich uncle. . . . Goddamn your soul,
Trotsky, may it rot in hell!" (192). From a different perspective, of course, it is
Yolek, not Trotsky, who would bind Yonatan to the altar of the first generation's hardened militarism. Yet, just as the angst felt by Yolek and apparently
everyone else in this ailing socialist kingdom is further aggravated by a preter-
naturally long rainy season, which reduces the kibbutz paths to rivers of mud,
and which brings both agricultural and social activity to a halt, a new hope
arrives in the strange form of Azariah, a young immigrant from the European

Diaspora (later revealed to be a Holocaust survivor), who suddenly appears at the ebbing of this winter of discontent. Yolek is soon won over by this Spinoza-quoting intellectual, who is brimming with precisely the kind of unfashionable socialist dreams now ridiculed by Yonatan and his comrades.[23] In spite of his slightly ludicrous appearance and mannerisms, the young feverish ideologue emerges as a champion of all that is sacred to Yolek.[24]

Eagerly, Azariah ingratiates himself with the father figure he wants to mentor him: "No job, if you asked him, could be too difficult in a place where one could go to work every day with a sense of joy and community. If he wasn't mistaken, that was the whole idea of the kibbutz" (42). Yolek is utterly entranced by this ideology-driven stranger, who stands in such marked contrast to the disappointing Sabras, those "hulking, tongue-tied, thick-skulled Huns, Scyths, and Tatars who had grown up in the kibbutz acting as though they were merely the most recent of immemorial generations of peasants" (43). Azariah is surely an incarnation of "those tormented soul-searchers from the small towns of Russia and Poland who had founded the first kibbutzim out of nothing, in the face of disease and desert heat" (44). For their part, although Yonatan and his friends at first find the stranger's hubristic rhetoric and quaint idealism highly entertaining, in the end, they, too, are won over when Azariah succeeds in fixing the broken tractor engine that has resisted Yonatan's best efforts and, later, when he manages to light a fire in damp weather where the Sabras have failed. Suddenly, it seems utterly logical to Yonatan, the alienated kibbutz son reared in a system reliant on the socialist logic of adaptive exchanges, that his new friend may also be the right man to light Rimona's erotic fire.[25] Oz deftly parodies the utilitarian mechanics of the collective system's beehive-like replacement of one individual by another.[26]

Yonatan is lately a poor vessel for his father's dreams. Raised on the highest ideals of human community and justice, he has loyally served his country as an army officer during various skirmishes. Yet now he struggles to regain a lost sense of at-homeness and selfhood apparently missing since childhood. Fully aware that he has been going through the motions of agrarian socialism like a man trying to walk underwater, he withdraws from the incestuous trivialities of kibbutz politics, the incessant debates on agendas and proposals, awakening one dazzling Sabbath morning of birdsong, breezes, and sunlight to a cynicism we find startling: "The kindergarten children sent up a solitary kite. It climbed tenaciously to heavenly heights, at which it seemed to be a flying genie or sea monster. Don't believe any of it, it's a trap, thought Yonatan Lifshitz as he dressed. . . . They're just decorating your death with the crepe-paper of love. If you don't make tracks now like an animal, they'll trick you into staying until you relax and forget that your life is your own" (115–16). Here Oz may be alluding to the heated debates over child-rearing practices that, as we will later see, increasingly troubled kibbutz members in the late twentieth century (certainly he does so in *Between Friends*). Little wonder that, with the movement's Spartan dedication to service in communal life and the rigor of elite military units, many individuals raised on kibbutzim later reported finding themselves in crisis, lacking the opportunity for personal development or the means of self-expression, and anxious about their ever-diminishing spiritual and cultural horizons.[27] As Balaban notes (almost certainly reflecting on his own youth in Kibbutz Hulda), the crux of Yonatan's unhappiness throughout the novel "is the feeling that he was never treated as a free human being, but as a 'human factor or manpower' . . . 'a means for implementing a fervent plan'" (*Between God and Beast* 120). Thus the individual's troubled childhood and the struggles and designs of the young state are deeply interwoven in one of Oz's most accomplished novels.

When at last Yonatan vanishes, his mysterious disappearance throws his father and the entire kibbutz into a state of deep unease and soul-searching, as if they had come across a previously unseen abyss at the heart of their society: "Maybe our whole way of thinking had a fatal flaw hidden in it right from the start" (*Perfect Peace* 282). Longing for his "perfect peace," Yonatan imagines himself "pierced" by a greater reality: he flees the everyday burdens of kibbutz life for the final consummation of self-transcendence. For a time, the young man seems to experience a humbling spiritual awakening, especially after his first night alone in the desert: "What have I done with my life all these years? From the citrus groves to the dining hall, to a dead double bed to this committee, to that meeting. Here, praise be, I've come home at last. Here, I'm no longer theirs. Thank you for all this beauty" (274). But Oz hastens to stress that this rarefied transcendence, perhaps because it is so effortlessly achieved, is an altogether untrustworthy realm, and, indeed, it soon evaporates.

In his emergence from the cultivated contours of kibbutz life into the vast landscapes of the desert, Yonatan becomes aware of his own perishable existence and insignificance, especially as a mere individual set apart from the enclosure of kibbutz society, the warm embrace of community. Ironically, where collective life previously threatened to smother him, now the sublime, untamed desert landscape threatens to do almost the same, by making him part of something "greater" than the self. Alone in the early desert evening, the young man recedes once again into a self-pitying reverie; the determination of an adult prepared to endure the gritty ordeal of genuine self-knowledge is replaced by the stubbornness of a delinquent adolescent: "I'm a nomad now. . . .

I'm as good as dead to them all, but I've never been more alive to myself. No one will ever tell me what to do any more" (338). Yet, in the stillness and solitude that gradually overtakes him during his flight into liminality, Yonatan achieves a certain grim self-knowledge. Perhaps no less a stranger to himself, he nevertheless begins to shoulder a measure of responsibility, especially for his callous treatment of Rimona. And his awareness of his individual failings is accompanied by a greater awareness of the kibbutz's significance in time and place.

In the haunting stillness, literal and figurative ghosts visit him. Subterranean images of an earlier Palestine urgently break into the present when the young man suddenly recollects visiting the site of Sheikh Dahr as a child to search for the lost treasure of gold coins the kibbutz children believed was hidden there (Oz provocatively reverses the popular anti-Jewish myth), only to encounter old agricultural tools and other signs of past human lives—and an uncanny sense of dread that lingers well into adulthood.[28] "Far-off jackals were howling," he recalls. "I was only a boy and those dead old villagers were thirsty for blood, for a bloodbath. . . . I was out of breath, and all I had to show from Sheikh Dahr in the end was a stitch in my chest and that terrible fear and sadness that keeps eating you, that keeps nibbling and gnawing at your soul to get up right away and go look for some sign of life in the wasteland" (24).[29] His restless angst can be traced to the shock of encountering the true meaning of the landscape that his kibbutz education had tried to erase.[30] Now he perceives what had always been there for him to apprehend, the expulsion of the previous occupants of the land, as witnessed by the silent ruins. For one educated in the proud certitude of socialist progress and achievement, awakening to the reality that his comfort hinges on the dispossessed Arab Others constitutes a violent existential shock.

Over the years, Yonatan has visited the ruins with friends who idly collect the "old Arab junk" they find scattered for garden decorations. What they read in the landscape confirms the triumphal Zionist narrative they have been raised with. For instance, Udi, a childhood friend who frequently expresses chauvinistic and worse sentiments, declares that "all the Arab terraces have been washed away, but that bottom course of stone still left down there must be from Second or First Temple times. Whatever Jews built, lasts" (125). Udi unquestioningly adheres to the kibbutz pedagogy he imbibed without questioning: nothing that transpired in the land between its eras of Jewish settlement has any enduring significance to him (just as the long centuries of Galut have no relevance to the reborn Sabra). In Yonatan's memory, however, the idyll of a picnic at Sheikh Dahr is disturbed by a foreboding which permeates the site, as if nature is intent on preserving the record of those who lived there before the Nakba: "On the hilltop, against the sky, backed by blue clouds, stood the ruins of Sheikh Dahr, light slashing through the gaping windows like an eviscerating sword, the out-of-doors just as bright on one side of the smashed, charred, homeless walls as on the other. Rubble from fallen roofs lay in heaps. Here and there an unsubmitting grape vine had run wild, cling with bared claws to a remnant of a standing stone wall. Above the ravaged village rose its shattered minaret" (127).[31] Only the tenacious straggly vine bears witness to the once vital, now vanquished Palestinian collective and its memories. Whereas, for Yolek, the ruins are a fitting end to what he calls "this murderer's den," their insistently disorienting silence stirs up feelings of guilt in his son: "From the ruins came not a sound of protest, not even the bark of a dog. Nothing but the silence of the earth and another, more subtle silence that seemed to blow down from the mountains, the silence of deeds that cannot be undone and of wrongs that no one can right" (127). As Yonatan awakens to the darker dimensions of the reversal of Jewish powerlessness and the triumph of the flourishing kibbutzim, the luster of the "glorious" achievements of Yonatan's father's generation grows ever dimmer for him.

In Yonatan's anguished consciousness, a conflict now wages over two conceptions of the same space; it conjures up a disquieting memory of the very last day the local sheikh, once a family friend, visited Yolek. The image of that old man dressed in a white robe, surrounded by notables, rises insistently in Yonatan's mind, even though he was only a child at the time:

> The sheikh touched my cheek with a hand that was furrowed like the earth. . . . Father told me to introduce myself, and Abu-Zuheir ran his weary old eyes from me to the bookshelf and back to father, who was the headman of the kibbutz. . . . It must have been Passover week, because someone brought matzos from the kitchen and a big jug of coffee. And now there's not a dog left in Sheikh Dahr and all of the fields, those we quarreled about and those we didn't, and all their sorghum and barley and alfalfa, are ours. Nothing is left now but those blackened walls on the hill and maybe their curse hanging over us. (129–30)

In contemplating this passage, it is worth bearing in mind that the films and novels of Yonatan's generation were replete with conventional images of corrupt Arab sheikhs and mukhtars who are overcome by idealistic and virile Hebrew farmers. In such narratives, the impoverished landscapes and Arab peasants overseen by inept or corrupt sheikhs are replaced by the abundant orchards and fields cultivated by competent, purposeful young halutzim. Clearly, in stressing the dignity and wisdom of the Arab Muslim village patriarch, as well as the fertile, well-tended fields of sorghum and barley and alfalfa handed over to the kibbutz, Oz is challenging that stereotype. His subtle, yet pointed layering of the Passover holiday of redemption from slavery and exile with Yonatan's memories of the old sheikh's poignant departure from his own land quietly underscores how the triumph of homecoming for one people ensures the tragedy of dispossession for another. Yonatan's sudden knowledge of this further destabilizes the kibbutz mythos that once nurtured him.

As it had at the kibbutz children's house, Yonatan's inner turmoil over this memory distorts his perception of the natural world: "A sickly-looking gibbous moon hung caught in the boughs of an olive tree, like Absalom in his oak. Ringed by craggy branches, it could have been a pale Jewish fiddler trapped by a band of peasants in some distant land of exile" (131). Meanwhile, his comrades idly speculate "about what the Arabs would have done to us had they won, and about what Udi proposed doing to them in the next war" (132). Udi is altogether enraptured by dreams of conquest and combat. Casually racist, he is a particularly woeful representative of the sad generation that so provokes Yolek's ire. In his brutal indifference to the history of the Arab village and its relation to his own story, he embodies the ominous disparity between the principled social justice of the Zionist present and the effacement, indeed the actual desecration, of the Palestinian past. For Udi, even a picnic excursion is an occasion to relish his fantasies of perpetual, unforgiving enmity: "Udi managed not to return empty-handed from his ramble on the hillside, bringing back a rusty wagon pole found among the rocks, some remnants of a leather harness, and the skull of a horse grimacing with hideous yellow teeth. All three finds were intended to give his front yard what he called 'character.' He was even considering digging up the skeleton of some greaseball from the village cemetery, wiring it together, and standing it in his garden to serve as a scarecrow and shock the entire kibbutz." The human remains have no more significance to Udi than the other ornamental relics of the destroyed village, but a mortified Azariah darkly warns, "If you don't watch it . . . one of the birds it scares may be the soul of a dead Arab and peck your eyes out" (134).[32] Udi's obtuse actions and Azariah's dark rejoinders stir Yonatan's long-dormant conscience, for, in his memory of that day, it is clear that the Palestinian village was just as vital a community as the Jewish kibbutz—surrounded by its own agricultural abundance, imbued with its own sense of belonging. In spite of the seductive powers of the pastoral landscape, the memory of the Palestinian peasantry unsettles him.

Unfortunately, where Yonatan expected to find solace and refuge in the wilderness, he finds terrifying black shadows and furtive movements, phantoms of the past breaking into the present. Even more unsettling are the "shadowy specters that split off" from his own consciousness: "the ghosts [of] the Syrians we've killed. The Arabs my brother bayoneted" (341)—the slain Syrian and Jordanian soldiers whose deaths contributed to making him a Zionist hero. The ephemeral peace of the moonlit night is morbidly transformed into "lifeless silver flow[ing] over the lifeless earth" (340). Overcome with mounting regret over his own past violence, his loss of innocence, and his abandonment of Rimona, Yonatan releases the safety catch on his rifle and fires rounds into the desert emptiness. Exhausting his ammunition, "pissing and puking," Yonatan nearly collapses. He suddenly panics; fully aware that he presents a perfect target for unseen eyes in the light of the full moon, he flees through the night (though there are no actual Arab pursuers). Apparently, he is not ready for death after all. Eventually, he makes his way home, seemingly reconciled to community and responsibility.

Whatever Yonatan's momentary coming into consciousness might have meant, the lasting significance of Sheikh Dahr itself is now pushed aside as the hero is summoned back to the imperious political "utopia" that birthed him. Yonatan's self-exile and wandering into the mysterious Eastern desert in search of a peace he cannot fully articulate now seems like a displaced version of the Zionist relation to territory.[33] In the end, Yonatan's struggle to leave the kibbutz—his father's house—to form an independent self collapses, and he returns to, as best he can, piece together the shards of his own identity and heal the social world he has hurt, a willed synthesis of the private individual and the coercive collective.

In the novel's gentle denouement, it is clear that life must be found with people, with one's nation, whatever the psychic costs that entails. (Does that also entail forgetfulness of the indigenous Arab? No more is said.) It is as if individualism itself, that great heresy of American Protestantism, has to be sternly pruned from the garden of the kibbutz. Here it is worth considering the intrinsic relation between Yonatan's brief isolation and the peculiar sociopolitical position of Amos Oz and, by extension, any artist in Israeli society. As Amos Kenan somberly observes, "Israel is, from a cultural standpoint, one of the most totalitarian states in the world," where, perpetually in thrall to the army (first as regular inductee, later as reservist), the artist perpetually vacillates between an identity as an autonomous, creative being and one as a soldier in complete service to the will of the state (11). The soldier, Kenan explains, soon learns "that it is possible to take him wherever they wish, to make of him whatever they wish—and he has nothing to say about it." Ultimately, the national imperative is always there to diminish the significance of the self: "This is a system of repression the like of which I am unacquainted with in any other country. It is very subtle, very democratic. There is no secret police of concentration camps. There is simply no need for them. In this state you can't become an other. Now how can a culture grow if a person doesn't become an other? What does it mean to be an other? It means first of all to be who you yourself are. Something that is not uniform. If there is no 'you,' then there can be no 'we'" (11). For Kenan, no one in this arduous position (especially no artist) can fail to resent the moral and psychic toll such repression entails. Little wonder that Oz felt compelled to create a kibbutz character as troubled and troubling as Yonatan; his flight from responsibility and national space toward the "otherness" of his own selfhood at once illuminates the psyche of the divided artist and that of all Israel's citizen-soldiers.

With his singular blending of irony with compassion, Oz rapidly resolves his restless characters' conflicts. Yonatan's homecoming is balanced by the impressive integration of Azariah, Diaspora's lonely orphan, into the kibbutz. In Yonatan's absence, Azariah has impregnated Rimona and taken over the tractor shed, a move he quietly signals by choosing to mount "a colorful picture of the sea" (*Perfect Peace* 358) in place of the snapshot of a public intellectual. Of Azariah's choice Yair Mazor writes: "The conjunction of summer and sea certainly typifies the Israeli experience, suggesting . . . an approach to life. It is the essence of the 'blazing light' that is the antithesis of the dark, wintry . . . world that Azariah came from . . . a transition from a 'wintry' . . . lugubrious nature that is associated with exilic, European, musty existence, into the height of Israeli summer with its white scorching light [and] golden Mediterranean beaches" (151–52). Homecomings of all sorts abound in the novel's mellow season of Zionist fecundity.

Yonatan returns just as the "agricultural season was at its height" (*Perfect Peace* 368), giving us a comforting sense that the crisis of the Fisher King has passed—the land restored to fertility. Nonchalantly resuming his old life, "as if he had never been away, [Yonatan] had as little to say as ever" (369). Thus, in the end, Oz's citizen-soldier and novel affirm the imperative that the individual's salvation depends on a return to community. In Oz's liberal perspective, the protagonist's flight from home is significant only insofar as the individual's homecoming asserts the primacy of the collective.[34] Despite Yonatan's pangs of conscience, the telos of the kibbutz remains undisrupted: images of the austere desert landscape are replaced by harmonious scenes of Azariah and Yonatan quietly laboring in the vineyard and of the birth of Rimona's daughter. The "self" that Yonatan claims is shown to be indistinguishable from the kibbutz "home" he originally fled. Indeed, when we see him restored to "sanity" and cleansed of his dangerous romantic infatuation with the desert, we may well wonder what has become of Yonatan's moral angst, his awakened knowledge of the Others' dispossession, in whose harsh reality his kibbutz flourishes.

Between Friends

In 2012, nearly fifty years after publishing *Artzot hatan* (*Where the Jackals Howl*; 1965), his first collection of short stories on kibbutz life, Oz returned to observe the kibbutz, not in its contemporary compromised form, but in its fresh vigor, as he first encountered it in the 1950s. Oz's transformative years in the kibbutz, following what he has always described as a painful betrayal of his father, have proved critical to his vocation and to his understanding of himself as both Zionist and writer, even years after moving away to his present dwelling in the desert town of Arad: "The truth is that I never completely left. . . . Many of my dreams take place there, and reflect an unresolved relationship with the kibbutz. . . . There were a few things I didn't like about kibbutz life. But I feel the absence of those things that I did like" (Lenir).[35] These enduring memories led to the delicately interwoven stories of the more slender collection *Be'in haverim* (*Between Friends*; 2012), where his gaze on the past is decidedly retrospective and melancholy, and where "Yekhat" serves as the name of his fictional kibbutz.

When asked what drew him to Yekhat, Oz (fig. 5) spoke enthusiastically of its singular duality:

> I chose it because of the distant association [in Hebrew] with something sharp and dulled. The first ideal of the kibbutz was sharp: to transform human nature instantaneously. Effectively, they [the founders] set out as a youthful camp, in the innocent belief that they would remain 18 and 20 forever. A camp of young people who were liberated from their parents, from all the prohibitions and inhibitions of the Jewish village and Jewish religion—a camp in which everything is permitted, suffused with perpetual ecstasy, and where life is always at a peak. You work, argue, love and dance until your strength runs out. It was childish, of course. In time, it became dulled. And then what came to the fore were the constants of human nature. The vulnerability, the selfishness, the ambition, the materialism and the greed. It was a forlorn dream, imagining that it

FIGURE 5   Amos Oz in his studio, 2014. Photo by Uzi Varon. Used by permission.

would be possible to triumph over all those forces, be reborn and create a new human being without the shortcomings of the old one. (Lenir)

Oz's answer seems altogether characteristic of his decades-long proclivity for paying heed to the ambivalences in politics, art, and life itself and for emphatically affirming the great promise of kibbutz life, even while honestly reckoning with its inability to fully overcome human weakness.

So many recent kibbutz narratives have been written by those who, raised on kibbutzim during their flowering, are now eager to grapple with the complexity of what they left behind. In Oz's case, there seems to have been a desire to honor the memory of the great "world reformers" without sentimentalizing their accomplishments:

At the funeral of Moshe Hess, one of the veterans of Hulda, with the grave surrounded by "old people" of 60–70, their faces flushed and all of them wearing caps, one of the young people burst out, "You have to know that you are the most wonderful Jews we have produced since the destruction of the Temple. No other Jews bore on their shoulders what you bore, and none ever will after you." In *Between Friends* I look at these people one more time. Not only at the burden they bore. Also at their zealotry, their dogmatism and their quasi-religious devotion. (Lenir)

In the emotionally resonant skein of the eight stories composing *Between Friends*, nearly all the characters struggle to uphold that formidable legacy (and be true to their better natures), yet with markedly mixed results. This time out, the interconnectedness between the stories of the collection brilliantly underscores the social and emotional intricacy of kibbutz life itself.

As was already evident in works such as "Nomad and Viper" and *A Perfect Peace*, Oz steadfastly refrains from portraying kibbutz society as somehow immune to mainstream Israel's racism, xenophobia, or its occasional militarist fervor. A few fraught exchanges in *Between Friends* allude to that darkness. Still others bear witness to the disappointing reality behind the myth of gender equality, as in "Ba-laila" ("At Night"), when a certain "man of principle who fought constantly to improve kibbutz life" and would never contemplate leaving nevertheless knows "in his heart that kibbutz life was fundamentally unjust to women, forcing them almost without exception into service jobs like cooking, cleaning, taking care of children, doing laundry. . . . The women here were supposed to enjoy total equality, but they were treated equally only if they acted and looked like men: they were forbidden to use make-up and had to avoid all signs of femininity" (*Between Friends* 115).

Throughout the 1940s and early 1950s, thousands of young North African and Iraqi immigrants were boarded on kibbutzim. The topic is nearly invisible in Israeli fiction, with the critical exception of Eli Amir's memoiristic novel *Tarnegol kaperot* (*Scapegoat*; 1983, as we will see in chapter 3). Long attuned to the plight of others, Oz paints an especially empathic portrait of a young Mizrahi boarder in "Abba" ("Father"). Sixteen-year-old Moshe Yashar copes with the kibbutzniks' condescension and discouragement whenever he wishes to travel to see his family. For a long time, his appearance and behavior are subjects of considerable controversy—"There was always something of the outsider about him. . . . When we lay on the grass at night and sang nostalgic songs under the stars, he was the only one who didn't put his head on the lap of one of the girls" (*Between Friends* 61)—although Moshe finds a measure of approving acceptance from the kibbutzniks for his good manners. His teacher David Dagan's patronizing attitude seems to speak for all: "On the whole, I have a very optimistic view of the Sephardim. We'll have to invest a great deal in them, but the investment will pay off. In another generation or two, they'll be just like us" (63).[36] All the while, Moshe quietly bears the condescension, shoring up his independent value system against the pedagogue's insistence on embracing the historical necessity of revolutions and the Marxist version of reality. Here, too, Oz seems to stealthily inscribe a part of his own story as Moshe disregards doctrinaire certainties, lured by the rich ambivalences of literature, and finds what he needs in the works of Fyodor Dostoyevsky, Albert Camus, and Franz Kafka: "Moshe was well aware that part of him still belonged to the old world because he didn't always accept progressive ideas, but rather than argue, he simply listened. . . . He was drawn more to unsolved questions than to glib solutions" (*Between Friends* 73). He is repelled by bloodshed and even dismayed by the cruelty of raising chickens for slaughter; indeed, a lesson on the French Revolution and his teacher's insistence on the necessity of historical violence only reinforces his "simple conclusion that most people need more affection then they can find" (65). A voracious reader, Moshe prefers the library to the kibbutz clubhouse or to joining his peers on their nocturnal raids on the food storeroom; his encounter with *Das Kapital* leaves him similarly skeptical: "He didn't like Karl Marx; he felt that there could have been an exclamation mark after almost every sentence, and that put him off. Marx claimed . . . that economic, social and historical laws were as clear and immutable as the laws of nature. And Moshe had his doubts even about the immutability of the laws of nature" (64).

Yet the precocious youth is already the kind of person who worries about the possible selfishness of his own misgivings, perhaps intuiting that such disaffection toward violence might ultimately lead to questioning the premises of the Zionist cause itself and to a more unbearable loneliness than he already suffers: "He was suddenly disgusted with himself . . . scornfully calling himself a bleeding heart, a label that [his teacher Dagan] sometimes applied to those who recoiled from the necessary cruelty of the revolution" (69). After a painfully unsatisfying visit to his ailing father in the hospital, a pious man who cannot begin to absorb the heresies and scandals of kibbutz life (it turns out Dagan is a philanderer who is sleeping his way through the kibbutz) that his son ineptly struggles to explain, Moshe begins the difficult journey back, distracted by thoughts of his peers' casual romantic dalliances on the kibbutz lawns as they sing the "nostalgic songs" of an intoxicatingly rich past he cannot claim. "He would give everything he had to be there now. Once and for all to be one of them. And yet he knew very well that it would never happen" (82). We leave him adrift between worlds. And sadly, there is a great deal of truth in

the youth's bleak conclusion; for, as we will see in Amir's more elaborate treatment in *Scapegoat*, the predominantly Ashkenazi kibbutzim failed to absorb
many Mizrahi newcomers.

So much for the fate of "outsiders" on the kibbutz. Yet, in "Yeled katan"
("Little Boy"), Oz makes it painfully clear that the kibbutz's native-born
members (especially the smaller, less secure, or "sensitive" ones) sometimes
endured traumatic forms of dislocation and even abuse.[37] As if written in
partial deference to his friend Avraham Balaban's grim account of his Hulda
childhood (Oz first became acquainted with Balaban when Avraham was eight
years old), "Little Boy" lays bare the heartbreaking fact that the children's
houses were for some raised there a nightmare of hounding and oppressive
rigor rather than an idealized community of support. The mother of five-year-
old Oded, Leah, immediately warms to the conventional counsel of the kibbutz pedagogues in response to the sensitive boy's bedwetting and inability to
cope with the bullying of tougher children: "The Committee for Preschoolers
instructed Leah . . . to be firm with him in order to wean him off this self-
indulgent behavior." Embracing the gospel of collectivist orthodoxy, she
"didn't like unnecessary touching and talking. . . . She adhered to all the kibbutz tenets with a zealot's fervor" (*Between Friends* 91). Thus, during the brief
time allotted for children to spend with their parents, "Leah saw to it that he
sat with his back straight, always finished everything on his plate and never
sucked his thumb. If he cried, she punished him for being a crybaby. She was
against hugging and kissing, believing that the children of our new society had
to be strong and resilient. She thought Oded's problems stemmed from the fact
that his teachers and childminders let him get away with things he shouldn't
and forgave . . . his oddities" (89–90). In contrast, Oded's tenderhearted father
rejects this thesis—"Roni believed that, here, cruelty is sometimes disguised as
self-righteousness or dedication to principles" (96). Indeed, Roni seems a
highly sympathetic character until a particularly egregious episode of bullying
suffered by his child causes him to lash out with shocking violence—another
of Oz's somber acknowledgments that the dangerous propensities lurking
within us all can be as easily provoked by love as by any innate sadism.

As was the case in his masterpiece *Sipur al ahava ve-hosheh* (*A Tale of Love
and Darkness*; 2002) and more recently in *Jews and Words* (2012; coauthored
with his daughter, the historian Fania Oz-Salzberger), Oz insistently aligns his
work with the totality of Jewish life (especially its European past) and the
imperative of memory. Fittingly, he delivers a cast of recurring characters with
disparate perspectives on the historical Jewish condition. Keenly capturing the
founding generation of ideologues warring with the youths who dared to seek

a measure of personal fulfillment, Oz mischievously intimates that the kibbutz, supposedly the wellspring of the New Hebrew, was little more than a reconstituted shtetl. Thus, in "Deir Ajloun," a temperate soul prophesies that, in the next generation,

> the kibbutz will be a much more relaxed place. Now all the springs are tightly coiled and the entire machine is still shaking from the strain. The old-timers are actually religious people who left their old religion for a new one that's just as full of sins and transgressions, prohibitions and strict rules. They haven't stopped being true believers; they've simply exchanged one belief system for another. Marx is their Talmud. The general meeting is their synagogue. . . . I can easily picture some of the men here with beards and sidelocks, and some of the women in head coverings. (*Between Friends* 158)[38]

It is as though the self-mythologizing halutzim are, in spite of themselves, caught up in the unbearable predicament of being incapable of shrugging off the identity and behavior patterns inherited from centuries of life in the Diaspora.[39] Indeed, philosophical questions concerning Jewish historical fate and solidarity intrude throughout this collection. Thus, again in "Deir Ajloun," Yotam, a young man anguished that the kibbutz's doctrinaire majority will likely refuse his request to study abroad, is told by an elder that, after the Holocaust, every member of his generation "must see himself as mobilized to a cause. These are the most critical years in the history of the Jewish people." Unwilling to live out his life in thrall to that trauma, Yotam confesses: "The thing is I can't take it anymore. I have no air" (146). In a similar vein, still other characters (though often unconscious of smothered desires) are beguiled in the quiet nights by dreams in which they inexplicably find themselves wandering through Diasporic landscapes of elsewhere: frothing rivers, valleys, mountains, and Polish towns. In their secret dreaming, the comrades seem bound to one another through an almost mandatory sadness.

No authentic portrayal of the kibbutz is ever complete without an honest account of the powerfully regulatory social role played by gossip. In the collection's title story, "Be'in haverim" ("Between Friends"), the members of Kibbutz Yekhat are both sanctimoniously outraged and titillated when high school girl Edna Asherov leaves her dorm to move in with David Dagan, a teacher her father's age (one infamous for his promiscuous affairs and six children sired with unmarried women). The story views that scandal from *Rashomon*-like perspectives, revealing the strained choreography between the individual and kibbutz society in the wake of scandal. We glimpse Edna's father, a grieving widower (further bereaved after his son was killed in war), wounded by his daughter's conduct with David, his only friend, in the kibbutz's quintessentially most public space, where the harsh judgments of gossip flow fast and furious: "Morning, noon and night he would appear in the dining hall to stand mutely in the queue at the serving counter, load his meal onto a tray and then sit down in a corner to eat, preferably in silence. He always sat in the same corner. People spoke to him gently, as if they were speaking to someone who was terminally ill, avoiding any mention or even hint of his problem, and he would answer briefly in his quiet, composed, slightly hoarse voice" (*Between Friends* 40). In Oz's portrayal, Yekhat's halutzim can seem as ruled by unwritten but unyielding norms of conduct as the gentry peopling Jane Austen's novels.

Throughout *Between Friends*, we become intimately acquainted with other characters torn between their private and public selves, and Oz masterfully takes us into the depths of their disquiet. The despairing nocturnal cries of jackals are an evocative refrain, a kind of ethereal soundtrack for the myriad sad, yearning, incomplete, and lonely feelings festering within, but unvoiced by, Oz's plaintive, sometimes grotesque, characters. Long an eerie trope in Oz's luminous prose, the cries of wild beasts, which seemed to symbolize violent passions in his earlier stories, here evoke his characters' restlessness, the inner tug of needs and existential quandaries for which their meticulously engineered, claustrophobic community offers no tangible recourse. Thus, in "At Night," as Yoav vigilantly watches over his community in the nocturnal silence; his apprehension of the stifling demands of settled routine and obligation, hitherto buried deep within him, suddenly surfaces with raw urgency:

> The night was cold and clear. The croaking of frogs punctuated the silence and a dog barked somewhere far off. When Yoav looked up, he saw a mass of low clouds gathering above his head and said to himself that all the things we think are important really aren't, and he had no time to think about the things that really are. His whole life was going by and he had never contemplated the big, simple truths: loneliness and longing, desire and death. The silence was deep and wide, broken occasionally by the cries of jackals, and Yoav was filled with gratitude both for that silence and for the cries of the jackals. He didn't believe in God, but in moments of solitude and silence such as this, Yoav felt that someone was waiting for him day and night, waiting patiently and silently, soundlessly and utterly still, and would wait for him always. (*Between Friends* 116)

Once such transcendent awareness arises, it is hard to return to complacency. The protagonists of kibbutz narratives are ever subject to the overwhelming political and social pressures of their demanding communities. Indeed, Oz's portrayal of Yoav's dawning awareness in the twenty-first-century story bears comparison with S. Yizhar's 1938 hero, Ephraim, who struggles with the knowledge that beyond the constraints of routine and obligation lie the dangers ever present in the siren-like call of the imagination, of the deeper recesses of an almost unfamiliar selfhood:

> Suddenly, one heart string would be loosened, and hum with the yearning of seemingly forgotten childhood dreams, filling the heart with one irresistible, almost lachrymose convulsion, lonely as an orphan, welling up and spreading through the veins, so that he had to take a deep breath and a broken sigh, immediately cut short, and then his hands went back to work. It felt good to work, and it was obvious that without work, without the assiduity that brings oblivion, without the act that is done, the world would gape like an abyss in which there was nothing to hold onto. ("Ephraim" 17)

Though most of the stories in *Between Friends* are imbued with interior drama as gripping as the inner life of Yizhar's Ephraim, the characters most likely to linger in our imagination are the richly realized ones of "Esperanto," a bittersweet threnody, which beautifully concludes this collection, and which explores the touching relationships between a dying idealist, an abandoned woman, and a young newcomer. The title itself seems especially apt because, for many socialists the kibbutz, the language invented in 1887 ("Esperanto" translates as "one who hopes") expressed a poignant dream of the universal more than it did a nationalist striving. Although characters in previous works express sentiments similar to those espoused by Oz the public intellectual, none does so more eloquently than the quixotic Martin Vandenberg, a deeply appealing figure devoted to the kibbutz's most visionary values, who dwells alone with a respiratory condition, dependent on an oxygen tank. Martin's post-Holocaust dream of spreading Esperanto (which he taught in Rotterdam before World War II) palpably echoes one of Oz's most powerful declarations on the often neglected nexus of ethics and language: "Martin said that imprecise words poison relations between people everywhere, and that's why clear, accurate words can heal those relationships, but only if they are the right words spoken in a language that all people can understand" (*Between Friends* 192). And here is Oz, in that most powerful declaration:

Each time and each place human beings are referred to as undesirable aliens, burdens or parasites, it's only a question of time before those humans will be actually persecuted. . . . It's always a certain distortion of language which heralds impending atrocities. Hence, the particular responsibility for the choice of words. . . .

Precision is a value. . . .

The moment we are precise with our nouns, adjectives, verbs and adverbs, we are closer to doing justice, in a small way. Not universal justice. Not international justice. But the way I describe a person, a mode of behavior or even an inanimate object, the closer I am to the essence, the more I evade either exaggeration or incitement. . . . Words are important because they are one of the main means by which humans do things to each other. Saying is doing. (Meyer)

Yet the stories of *Between Friends* are rich and complex precisely because the author seems to genuinely love all of his flawed and prickly characters even when they fall well short of their own ideals—and because Oz the polemicist never overrules Oz the imaginative artist. As in the Talmud, one voice is invariably supplanted by another in a potential infinitude of pluralistic discourse. Thus the ever thoughtful Mizrahi high school student Moshe of "Father" in "Esperanto" listens respectfully to the saintly founder's dying plea for a universal language but has come to his own conclusion: "Moshe Yashar said nothing, but thought that the sorrow in the world was born long before words" (*Between Friends* 192), which might well reflect Oz's own thinking, whether in his Hulda years or in this moment. Thus, too, as Oz portrays him and his comrades perceive him, Martin is the living essence of their ideology, but, in his universal yearnings, he resembles most of all the lonely immigrant iconoclasts and dreamers of the Jerusalem neighborhood Oz describes in a *Tale of Love and Darkness*. Perhaps for that very reason, of all the memorable characters Oz has created, Martin most embodies both the transcendence inherent in the farthest-reaching ideals of the kibbutz—and the impossibility of their genuine realization.[40]

For Martin, the dream of the kibbutz manifestly expresses a far more ambitious and perhaps more Jewish aspiration than the end point of nation building: "It was his belief that states should be abolished and replaced by an international, pacifist brotherhood that would reign after the borders between peoples were erased" (*Between Friends* 173). Faulting Ben-Gurion for his excessively hawkish policies, Martin passionately insists that "all governments, without exception, are completely unnecessary because the Jews had already shown the world how a people can exist and even thrive spiritually and socially for thousands of years without any government at all" (181). Though he considers the younger kibbutzniks to be basically decent, in his heart of hearts, he believes that, left to them, "the kibbutz was doomed to slide slowly into [the hands of] the petty bourgeoisie. . . . In another twenty or thirty years, kibbutzim would become nothing more than well-kept garden communities replete with material pleasures" (183). His comrades see Martin as a legendary paragon of morality; indeed, one good-humoredly dubs him "the Gandhi of Kibbutz Yekhat," while another observes that "Martin worked in the shoe-repair shop as if he had taken upon himself symbolic responsibility for every step we took" (196).

Stubbornly loyal to his unwavering conviction that "property was original sin," Martin left his former kibbutz when it allowed Holocaust survivors to keep their German reparation money in private accounts. Even now, he refuses to keep so much as a private kettle in his room. After a lifetime of labor as the kibbutz cobbler, he refuses to retire until ordered to do so by the kibbutz secretary. "Esperanto" serves beautifully as the coda to *Between Friends*: rendering up one of its most memorably iconoclastic protagonists, enabling its recurring characters to take their final bow, and offering a somber yet hopeful homage to the entire Jewish socialist dream. In the end, Martin is not alone: not only does he stir the moral imagination of young Moshe, but Osnat, a cynical woman whose husband abandoned her for a girl barely out of high school, is so touched by Martin's vulnerability and incapacitation that she emerges from her cocoon of self-pity to care for him. Juxtaposing them, Oz artfully contrasts their worldviews in ways that take us even deeper into the conflicts and contradictions of kibbutz life.

A kind of dialectic opens between them. In counterpoint to the dying Martin's idealistic fervor—"Man is by nature good and generous. It's only the injustices of society that push him into the arms of selfishness and cruelty" (177)—Osnat is convinced that there is more cruelty than compassion in the world and that the "kibbutz . . . makes small changes in the social order but man's difficult nature doesn't change. A committee vote will never be able to eradicate envy, pettiness or greed" (179). Yet we cannot fail to notice that, despite her hard-bitten view of humanity, Osnat is a deeply affecting model of compassionate selflessness. Thus she refuses to be compensated for taking care of Martin, saying that she did so "out of friendship, and there was no need for compensation. The evening hours she spent with the sick man, their brief conversations, his gratitude, the world of ideals and thought he opened to her—she treasured them all and trembled at the idea that their relationship might end soon" (188). When we consider the moral grandeur of characters like Osnat and Martin, it seems manifestly clear that *Between Friends* was born out of its author's desire to honor the memory of the great "world reformers" without sentimentalizing their accomplishments.

Ever as much a political pragmatist as he is a human rights champion, Oz has repeatedly called for a Chekhovian rather than Shakespearean ending to the tragedy of the Israeli-Palestinian conflict: rather than being left with a "stage heaped with dead bodies," both sides learn to adapt to a state of affairs in which "everyone is disappointed, disillusioned, embittered, heartbroken, but alive." Like Chekhov's, Oz's vocabulary in these stories is deliberately plain; only now and then does he indulge in the luxuriant metaphoric imagery that suffuses the fiction of his younger days.[41] As a whole, these are also *quieter* stories, their tender, lyrical fragility altogether less driven by the kinds of warring Apollonian and Dionysian polarities that distinguish Oz's earlier works. There are few decisive victories here, only a bittersweet, antitriumphal mood. Heartbreak endures, but so does life. We can savor these moody miniatures of the kibbutz past for their jazzlike variations, their haunting conclusions cumulatively underscoring the uncertain fates and destinies awaiting both the lonely individuals and the community to which their lives are ultimately dedicated. Yet, as Alberto Manguel declares, we emerge from *Between Friends* with the wistful recognition that "the impossibility of utopia is less a demonstration of the failure of conviviality than an ongoing proof of our determination to keep on trying." In many of the stories' denouements, we leave their pensive protagonists enshrouded in the stillness of night, each soul caught up in his or her own moment of silent anticipation, hoping, vacillating, querulous, indecisive. They seem terribly disconnected and isolated as they grope for answers in the dark. Yet, ultimately, Oz's brooding characters and the ever-metamorphosing institution of the kibbutz itself receive the justice of open-ended futures—the bare hint of hope that the best writers have always bestowed on their characters and readers, granting them a kind of melancholy grace.

Ideology and the Lonely Individual in Nathan Shaham's Novellas

The kibbutz should be of interest to almost any writer: It is a different society; this way of life is in itself innovative. And the society is changing, which makes it even more fascinating. From the inside you see things better—although there are those who observe from the outside and claim that they see things better, that love blinds, and that the positive decision to stay in the kibbutz would seem to dazzle

one's vision. To this claim I always reply that just as a person who writes out of
despair cannot be accused of inconsistency if he doesn't commit suicide, so a
person who lives inside the kibbutz is entitled to criticize it; the fact that he hasn't
left doesn't mean that he has denied himself the ability to see things as they are.
                                                    —*Nathan Shaham*

So many kibbutz narratives present scenarios in which the pastoral fabric of a
high-minded community is rent by the intrusion of eros that it is tempting to
compare this tendency to the Arthurian epic, wherein the noble order of the
Knights of the Round Table is sundered into factions by adultery, incest, and
other sexual misconduct. As they did to the chivalric warriors in the centuries-
old Matter of Britain, matters of the flesh perpetually undo the high-minded
socialist kibbutzniks. The literature of each, no matter how distant in time and
space from the other, examines human beings dedicated to upholding ideals of
the virtuous life, whether determined by the codes of chivalry or by twentieth-
century socialism, to reveal the tragic imperfections of their humanity.
Although Amos Oz is perhaps the most famous of insider writers deeply sympathetic and even loyal to the kibbutz way of life who have exposed how the
inevitability of human failings exacerbates the complex challenges of that life,
there are others whose work warrants greater attention than they have received
over the years, both in Israel and internationally. As the incisive reflection on
the singular optics of inside witnesses in the epigraph above hints, the conflicted fiction of Nathan Shaham (b. 1925) is also of considerable interest.

Like Oz, Shaham examines the most difficult quandary at the heart of collective life: "The kibbutz cannot admit to the existence of loneliness; the principle of togetherness makes it ideologically impossible to be alone, and so
forbidden loneliness becomes as sharp and as physical an experience as
asphyxiation in a closed room" (Herzog). Author of some of the first genuinely
sophisticated literary explorations of the kibbutz condition, Shaham has been
a member of Kibbutz Beit Alfa since 1945. Shaham's *Kirot etz dakim* (*The Other
Side of the Wall: Three Novellas*; 1977) frequently seems to pay ironic homage to
the notoriety of Oz's earlier stories of grotesquely marginalized lives and lonely
souls. Tellingly, in one salient instance, kibbutz member Meir Avrahami complains of the work of a certain kibbutz author whose portrayals focus on the
"miserable, lonely, morose ones," the "marginal people, who are absorbed in
themselves, in their sorrow and their isolation. . . . There is no point in having
literature 'latch on' to them and blow them out of all proportion." Meir would
prefer to see literary portraits of those he deems the majority, "stalwart, cheer-
ful, courageous, persevering, dedicated," who he insists are more representative

of his society (*Other Side* 149–50, 150). Although this might seem a reasonable complaint, the mischievous irony underlying it is fully apparent; indeed, Shaham's own work is a perspicacious window into the human frailty eating away at the lofty moral edifice of kibbutz society.

The three novellas of *The Other Side of the Wall* portray kibbutz life from the brink of World War II through the 1970s and are positively brimming with heartfelt yet levelheaded convictions about the prospects of the kibbutz revolution to transform Jewish life. Here, in a passage from Shaham's "Melah ha'aretz" ("The Salt of the Earth"), is an especially memorable declaration of how the Jewish socialists redeemed Judaism's ancient messianic impulse and translated it into secular terms that wielded an immediate impact: "We did not attune our expectations to a distant morrow, but to their lifetime. As soon as today is over. Quickly, in our time. Not dreams of a far-off future or the Kingdom of Heaven at the end of a dark tunnel. It would all be right here, tomorrow. This little acre. This mule. This child. The redemption will come here and now and not in a generation that is all saints or all sinners or on the day that the tears of Jacob and Esau cease" (*Other Side* 222).[42] "The Salt of the Earth" concerns the travails of this unnamed speaker, a seventy-year-old veteran of the kibbutz and a diehard socialist. He has lately taken on the burden of conserving the kibbutz archives, a task weighing most heavily on him, for the ideals and accomplishments of the past are already slipping into obscure irrelevance: "The job took him over as if the collective memory had been put in his hands" (227). Yet that quiet, unseen effort on behalf of the dusty obscurity of the archives is a poor substitute for the manifestly vigorous relevance of his earlier life:

> The young people didn't listen. And sometimes they interrupted without any shame. They had no time for an old man's trouble. A generation passes; they owed him no respect. The best of them listened quietly, but with impatience. As if he had been condemned by his age to espouse outmoded views. . . . Not even at the anniversary of the kibbutz, where he came to remind them of things gone by, were they ready to hear stories out of the past. These were tolerated only as jokes at the expense of some poor schlemiel. (229)

As if masochistically intent on acting out that uneasy sense of exile and estrangement, the protagonist travels to late twentieth-century America for the first time (he has not even been outside Israel in the previous fifty years), the symbolic antithesis of all he has labored for. Once there, he immediately finds himself utterly at odds with the dispiriting forces of capitalism, which, as it happens, his own children had rushed to embrace decades earlier. Everything he has despised from a distance for all those years is at once satisfyingly confirmed: "the loss of individuality . . . solitude in the crowd, alienation, simple fear for one's livelihood" (236). Yet, even before he departed from Israel, he had been tempted by the allure of that capitalism, as personified by an actor in a televised film who seems almost a perverse doppelganger: "an old man, like himself" but "glowing with health and decisiveness . . . confident, understated power," who sits behind the wheel of a "shiny, big car" (229). The fleeting memory of how easily he had been enticed by this seductive capitalist fantasy of virile American individualism embarrasses him now.

In any case, that illusion is soon replaced by a less congenial reality, for the protagonist finds himself stranded and helpless en route to Boston and meets only with rudeness or indifference from strangers. First, there is his encounter with the alienating anonymity of urban travel: a ticketing error results in his flight being cancelled—"As if he were an obstacle that time would remove. . . . Nobody offered help" (196). Not only does his expectation for help from the manager, a young Israeli expat, soon vanish, but the encounter grows surprisingly more unpleasant when his countryman discovers his kibbutz affiliation:[43]

> He wondered where this hatred was coming from. You have a swimming pool? A public auditorium? Tennis courts? The man even had something to say about income tax. And he could hardly get a word in edgewise. We built it all with our own hands. The manager laughed. And the subsidies? . . . He just managed to say that he had worked all his life, and worked hard. He wasn't happy with the apologetic tone that emerged. And could one imagine living in the Jordan Valley without a swimming pool? Today, that he has an air conditioner, he is amazed at how he survived for so long. Fifty years without one. A hundred and ten in the shade, in summer, in the banana groves. In that sweltering heat. And it would be shameful to mention the wars. And what for? And why must one hate so much, here in New York, in a plastic armchair, with gold buttons on a haughty blue blazer? (200–201)

The protagonist's umbrage reflects the deep dismay of kibbutzniks in the wake of Prime Minister Menachem Begin's dismissive slur that they were "millionaires with swimming pools" (a strategic appeal to Begin's Mizrahi constituents, who had long felt ostracized by the kibbutzim and the Labor Party's various coalitions).[44] Later, he spends his first night alone and frustrated by his experience in a New York hotel because, however irrationally, he finds himself unable to ask others for help: "Angry, depressed, hating his loneliness. He could have lifted the receiver and asked for room service. They could have fixed the drape, the faucet, the air conditioner. . . . From now until morning, he will just await the new day. He would not have been capable of disturbing room service in the middle of the night. Some habits become second nature. The ingrown taboos of an old halutz" (*Other Side* 194). This old "halutz" once dreamed of being the A. D. Gordon of his day, "a man whose attachment to labor and whose fidelity to the values of the kibbutz would be an example to others" (267). In the heyday of Zionist congresses, "he would harass the founding fathers of the movement. . . . He always judged them by the dirt under their fingernails—the more the better" (267). Now, in the waning days of this glorious dream and already feeling the fierce tug of the little pleasures of his autumn years—"morning exercises . . . salad with onion and garlic, an afternoon nap . . . an important performance of *Habimah*, with the old timers in the leading roles" (227)—he misses most of all the enduring daily rhythms of kibbutz life, the physical and social security for which his generation has toiled so hard: "There is nothing better for a person than a regular schedule, his own bed, a caring spouse, a strip of lawn, meals on time, fences to protect an old man's life" (227). Lately, he has become accustomed to letting issues slide that "used to be matters of life and death" (267). Nevertheless, the old socialist feels guilty over his absence from a crucial meeting of the *asefa* (the kibbutz's general assembly) in which an important issue of ideology would be raised: "He would miss the opportunity of making a resounding condemnation of hiring labor from the outside" (227). Then there are the very self-compromising terms of his visit to America.

For one thing, it was a present from his children—and, for his generation, such outside gifts were deemed highly controversial. Having allowed himself to be persuaded that "neither the image of the kibbutz nor its values would be hurt by a gesture of goodwill on the part of children who had left it" (211), he initially rationalized that it was better after all to accept their largesse than to drain the kibbutz's public funds. Yet, in the days prior to his departure, he is overcome with shame for having betrayed the lofty principles he so proudly defended in the past: "He went about like a man disgraced. Accusations made against others, of wanting to enjoy the best of both worlds, abnegation on the one hand and acquisitiveness on the other, came home to roost. When he was reminded of things he had written in the kibbutz newsletter a few years earlier he experienced genuine anguish" (212–13). Though we first meet the protagonist when he is already in America, the narrative is structured in such a way that we are soon immersed in all the vacillations, self-doubt, and hesitations that led up to his departure, in the curious inertia that links him so closely to many famous characters in Israeli literature.[45]

To escape his current unease, Shaham's protagonist revisits the amorous adventures of his youthful days, especially his tempestuous love affair with a free-spirited woman named Sylvia. He recalls the heat of their romance in unabashedly paganish terms: "When water was found as the result of an experimental drilling he took Sylvia with all the coarseness of a peasant, and she kissed the blisters on the palms of his hands as if she were continuing an age-old tradition. Sometimes they did it on the threshing floor. . . . When he returned at night . . . she washed the soles of his feet. At the full moon they would steal away to the swimming hole and bathe in the nude, as if enacting some pagan rite" (214). In their early days, they become a kind of magical couple, the "first family" or near-royalty of the kibbutz. They produce its first progeny and their famously hospitable tent is the heart of the community's social life (every kibbutz has such celebrities). Yet German-born Sylvia's fierce independence soon opens up a fissure between them. Besides addressing their children in her native German instead of Hebrew, she favors sensual wear such as a kimono, audaciously out of step with the ascetic kibbutz. Not unsympathetically, the protagonist grows to perceive her as one among the many naive celebrating ideas deemed intrinsic to a world revolution who were caught up in the easy spiritual fervor of the Youth Movement. With the passing years, he distantly observes Sylvia's disenchantment with how all that fiery rhetoric of radical transformation "had been elaborated into a row of humdrum tasks whose only reward lay in the doing. No longer did one speak of socialism in our time . . . or moral renewal or return to the soil. The people of the settlement spoke of workdays and nutritional units and the shoe budget and the clothing budget and petty cash" (216). Soon Sylvia becomes utterly detached from both the community and him and turns to artists, poets, and others for new distractions.

Increasingly, their ideological rift over tenets he regards as sacred leads to intense quarrels about the children's upbringing: "Especially hard on him was her sarcastic tone when she spoke to the children about kibbutz values. Concepts that were sacred to him were in her view conventional lies and empty chatter" (219). In his old age, he bleakly recollects how they bickered back and forth: "Sylvia used to say: You and your principles! Children come before principles. And he would say: That only means raising children without principles" (231). In the end, their children choose to leave the kibbutz shortly after the War of Independence—they "picked themselves up and left without acknowledging his sorrow" (222)—for which he blames Sylvia, though we are led to speculate that the probable cause is postwar disenchantment. Recognizing that she has no hope of repairing their relationship, Sylvia can only prophesy that a day when come when "he would give in and admit that what he called 'values' were nothing but a mask. A mask for tyranny and nothing else" (215). Thus, on his guilt-ridden trip to America, he ruefully conceives of his children's generosity as "belated revenge from Sylvia" (213). His condemnation of what he dubs her "victory" becomes a bitterly obsessive, literal refrain throughout the narrative. In Shaham's kibbutz, as in those of other writers we have seen, the Diaspora is forever the uncanny corruption, creeping back to unsettle halutz values.

Now the embattled protagonist makes his way to a relative whom he has not seen in a quarter of a century, a man who, like many others, has fled the American central city for the milk and honey of the whitening suburbs "in order to breathe clean air, play golf, grow flowers and fruit trees, and keep a wolfhound 'with a goyish soul'" (235). There he discovers that the houses are regally spacious, yet, inevitably, "the offspring were invariably in another part of the country" (240). As he moves from city to city, from one distant relative to the next, with not a little self-loathing, he begins to assume his token role as the "old pioneer" from whom "a bit of crudeness was expected." With the passing of time, he comes to regard Jewish American life as a sort of worthy adversary. Even though everything in him rebels against that society, he readily acknowledges that "two kinds of victory over Exile were facing one another, without Jew-fears or the equivocating of the underdog, proud in their strength, their wealth, their uprightness, with everything that America and Israel do to Jews, with everything that America does to Israel and Israel to America" (239). Here it is worth stressing that, at the time Shaham was writing (mid-1970s), rarely was that oppositional sense of two eminently worthy, warring Jewish destinies given such memorable voice by an Israeli writer. Indeed, to a degree that has not yet been sufficiently appreciated by critics, Shaham's provocative language even anticipates the bold terms of Philip Roth's famous explorations of Diaspora versus Zionism in later novels such as *The Counterlife* (1986) and *Operation Shylock* (1993). For example, in this exchange between the protagonist and a man named Webster, whose immigrant father "took the first name he came upon in the dictionary" to hide his Jewishness (*Other Side* 249), Shaham's narrative anticipates Roth's bickering Zuckerman brothers in *The Counterlife* (Henry, a dentist who has transformed himself into a zealot West Bank settler, and Nathan, a famous writer who is uneasy about Israel and Jewish absolutism) in their advocacies of competing Jewish homelands: "Webster smiled. . . . The only hope for the Jewish people lay here. Israel was raising soldiers and peasants. In America we had been liberated. In America there was no such thing as one kind of work being less worthy than another. Whatever led to freedom and prosperity was respectable. Only in America could Jews be unafraid of the same things as the goyim. . . . Israel is the only country in the world where Jews are killed because they are Jews, said Webster" (*Other Side* 249). Shaham is positively Rothian not only in this but also in other related moments. For instance, in his outraged response, the veteran kibbutznik resembles no one so much as Roth's Neil Klugman, who, lured against his better nature into the postwar affluence and shallow values of the Patimkins, reluctantly awakens to the darker shadows of the American Dream in the novella "Goodbye, Columbus":

> He could not bear the overweening pride and complacency of property owners who believed that the whole world operated according to their values. He hated those smug faces and the lady-bountiful expressions glittering forth out of covetous eyes. As if they were assaulting his own values—life without competitiveness, or class symbols, or the drive to dominate, life on a modest scale. He would let them brag about their wealth and shrewdness and resounding victories on invisible battlefields: banks and insurance companies and stocks and bonds and real estate, things he knew nothing about. And he would remain silent, as if in awe, and would have to agree that this big house, in which he got lost on his way to the bathroom, and the crystal chandeliers, and the swimming pool, and the horses and dogs and Japanese servants and Chinese cooks, and the private road and the private woods and the parties written up in the local paper, were all a valid way of getting back at the goyim. (*Other Side* 240)

Sickened by the vulgar hedonism of his near and distant American relatives—even when they treat him "with the reverence and awe reserved for an ancient relic from the Holy Land" (255)—the protagonist longs for the sparse and simple comforts of home. Even as he greatly admires the heroic spectacle of American construction workers poised many stories above the ground, he feels the absence of "a lofty purpose that would justify the risk" (243). He wearies of all the kitsch, incessant "Jewish 'command performance' dinners" (265), where he is compelled to deliver rhapsodic spiels extolling the glories of Zionist achievement. Whether in spite or because of those painful public charades, the longer he stays, the more uprooted he feels from his Zionist identity. Disconsolate and homesick, he returns hopefully to the El Al office "with a sense of belonging" (250) yet is put off once more, still with no promise of any definite return. As helpless as Kafka's subject thwarted by the mysterious gatekeeper in the enigmatic parable "Before the Law," he faints dead away.

Later, as he recovers in a hotel room, the unaccustomed idleness fills him with self-loathing. Nevertheless, he allows himself to be lured into a naughty adventure by Anna Steinhardt, an aging American siren who persuades him to stay a while longer because he has "only been shown 'Jewish America'" and missed the real America "of magical primeval landscapes and of marvelous tranquility." She cannily promises to show him the wonderful realities of the great American story, with its "simple, strong tie to work and the soil" (258). Initially reluctant, he soon falls under Anna's spell and that of the utterly unaccustomed, irresponsibly boundless nature of the adventure that beckons:

> The thing took hold of him in all its obvious idiocy: the hasty decision, the spontaneity of his reaction and the fast, insolent acquaintance with a woman rich in both charm and a sense of humor. He saw the thing as a kind of diverting return to the foolishness of youth, with its license to fall in love at first sight and to take all kinds of eccentric turns. . . . to live for once without keeping tabs on himself and without a sense of obligation bearing down from every side, like a man who had plenty of one thing at least: his own time, his own life. (259–60)

What, for Anna, amounts to just a carefree lark is, for him, the very essence of decadence and irresponsibility, utterly antithetical to all that his seven dedicated decades on earth signify: "A sense of adventure for its own sake was something that his strict way of life eschewed. The guiding principle required them to discover the light concealed in a humdrum life of purpose" (260). Only now is he willing to admit that in the days when he and his comrades eagerly competed for leading roles in the dangerous smuggling of illegal immigrants from Syria, it was not for the sake of "good works and lofty obligations" after all. "What they really wanted was a chance to run around at night and to quicken the pulse through exposure to danger" (260). As he travels with the American temptress in her land of vast spaces and forgetfulness, his "stories about the kibbutz sounded, even to him, like descriptions of some imaginary utopia" (271). Freed "from the mantle of serious objectives," the high drama of "Israel and Jewish rebirth and justice for all Mankind" (271) somehow dissolves away in Anna's company. As they restlessly rove across vast forests and rivers and prairies, the kibbutz shrinks into a strange new perspective: now it is simply "a village that had good people in it as well as peculiar and ridiculous people, and even a few damned chiselers, may the devil take them. He no longer needed anybody to praise, laud, adore, or uplift him and his kind for their role in building a home for the Jewish people" (272). After his road trip and American idyll come to their inevitably disappointing conclusion in New York and before his flight to Israel, he endures a debasing encounter with a prostitute and is beaten and robbed by muggers.

Adding insult to injury, the unsympathetic police take him to task for overstaying his visa and for foolishly wandering the streets at night. Humiliated and fearfully agitated, he collapses onto his hotel bed. America's spell and the allure of wandering have utterly unraveled (Shaham darkly hints that he may even die there). Yet though we are clearly invited to sympathize with the protagonist's ordeal, something about his self-pity and petulance rankles and, in the end, we cannot help wondering whether, despite its portrayal of the decidedly seedy and dangerous streets of New York, the story is not also a quiet indictment of kibbutz society, so sheltered and insular that it has left a grown man embarrassingly unprepared for the exigencies of the modern world. That is a question that has been raised by more than a few who once lived on kibbutzim and later struggled to adapt elsewhere.

Taken as a whole, Shaham's collection reveals a keen understanding of the lives of both veterans of the kibbutz and marginal newcomers. Both, it seems, are susceptible to deep turmoil, loneliness, and doubt. The most psychologically intricate of Shaham's three novellas, "Kirot etz dakim" ("The Other Side of the Wall"), takes place much earlier in a kibbutz caught up in the tumult of Mandatory Palestine, a time when the British were still losing ground to the Germans in the Western Desert Campaign of World War II. However, it chiefly concerns the travails of its unnamed protagonist, a maladjusted young woman who finds herself intimately absorbed in the sordid details of her married neighbor's sexual adventures. Through her experiences, Shaham traces the fate of a lonely individual caught between romantic fantasy and the austere demands of collective life and responsibility. Desperately searching for love and connection, the young woman finds herself instead the unlikely guardian of the sordid secrets of others as she drifts away from the values of her religious upbringing. In the light of day, her kibbutz is a society so resolutely dutiful and so principled that, even when the comrades harvest rows of carrots side by side, "it is customary not to choose one's partner, in order not to make people who are less popular feel left out" (Other Side 159). At night, however, things are altogether different.

The unnamed young woman spends all of her quiet and uneventful evenings in the kibbutz reading room, fitfully scanning kibbutz movement publications by the dim light of a kerosene lamp, waiting for drowsiness to overtake her. A few other bookish members gather there, but their camaraderie seems limited to greeting one another in the reading room. Living in the kibbutz for less than a year, she is proud that she has already been allotted a room for herself, whose sparse furnishings consist of an army cot, a rough-hewn "closet" composed entirely of agricultural crates, and an uneven table (104). Proudly embellishing the dreary little room with tablecloths and pillow covers of her own making, she secretly yearns for the kind of transformative creative expression that she knows will elude her: "She will never have the nerve to write a poem in the startling, flashy rhymes that are so much in vogue. . . . If it were still possible to write simple, melancholy poems like Rachel used to write, then she might write a poem" (105). Instead, she keeps a diary where she reveals her acute self-consciousness (she describes herself as "emotional, dreamy, hypersensitive"). She painfully acknowledges that she is the antithesis of idealized kibbutz womanhood, one who "can work on a tractor or in the machine shop, who can listen to a dirty joke and respond with boisterous laughter" (106). Assigned to an isolated bungalow with few neighbors, the young woman masochistically memorizes painful verses about stilted lives and unrequited desire. Even from her own perspective, her life often seems to take place in the subjunctive: "If she had let life take its course . . . she could have learned a respectable profession or even have been a lady of leisure" (109). Though she had grown up in an upper-middle-class religious home, she always felt drawn to the secular mystique of kibbutz life. Once proud of her independence in choosing the austerity of kibbutz life on her own without benefit of the ideological persuasions of a Zionist Labor Youth Movement, the young woman now doubts her earlier sense of superiority. Neither "fanatic nor ascetic," she longs only for genuine intimacy and passion that have so far proved elusive. Lacking any romantic life of her own, she is increasingly preoccupied by the sexual activity of her neighbors Raheli and Big Yitzhak, a young couple whose room is separated from hers by only the thinnest plywood, through which she overhears everything. Especially now that Yitzhak is away on active service in the British army, the protagonist is eager to befriend his attractive, though "not talkative," lover (113), Raheli, who she ruefully recalls had once teased her for explicating a poem that appeared in the literary supplement of *Davar* (newspaper of the Histadrut Labor Movement). That teasing stings even more since Raheli embodies the ideal kibbutz woman. In her diary, the protagonist enviously captures Raheli's unwavering equanimity and legendary beauty: "Three days of sunshine and she is tanned the color of a ripe date, encased as it were in a clinging garment that caresses the round breasts, the narrow hips, the long, slender legs. The repertoire of local folklore places her in a tale about a poet who was much taken with her appearance. 'I know that girl from somewhere,' said the man, who had a reputation for his bon mots. . . . 'Oh yes,' he said, as if suddenly reminded, 'from the Song of Songs'" (114). Though the mousy protagonist finds herself altogether wanting in contrast to her sensually earthy comrade, who laughs easily at her male comrades' scatological humor, alarming events in the region force her out of her petty self-absorption. Tobruk has just been lost to Rommel and there are contingency plans in preparation to evacuate the settlement and hide in the forested areas of Mount Carmel should the Nazis overtake Palestine. For just a few moments, somewhere along the "hundred and fifty paces" between the dining hall and her room, she dutifully contemplates enlisting in the British women's corps. Yet, consistent with her nebbishy nature, by the time she reaches her bungalow, she has persuaded herself that the kibbutz probably won't allow her to represent them in their quota as she hasn't lived there long enough. More to the point, she shamefully acknowledges, "she would never have the nerve to drive a car or to go about in a foreign city where she doesn't speak the language" (117). Fortunately, she is prevented from probing further into her own shortcomings by the startling appearance of a figure lurking in the shadows. She rushes over to Raheli, who, irritated by the late-night intrusion, impatiently dismisses her. Soon after returning to bed, she overhears the tantalizing sounds of Raheli's door opening and ardent whispers exchanged with someone who is definitely not Big Yitzhak. Instantly, she is ashamed.

Rather than harshly judging Raheli, she is embarrassed to have caused the lovers anxiety about exposure: "She pictures them to herself naked, panic-stricken, clinging to one another without moving, like terrified animals caught in a beam of light." She overhears the man: "'These rooms are like echo chambers.' And Raheli's voice, 'Sometimes she sighs in her sleep'" (120). Now she lies awake in the dark as the man departs, regretting only that she will probably not earn Raheli's respect for her noble silence. After a number of such episodes, we cannot help but cringe at the humiliations heaped on this lonely woman both by her kibbutz and by her own masochistic nature. For some readers, the portrayal of the protagonist's abjection will likely raise questions about Shaham's gender politics. After all, where his male characters are immersed in the big public issues and national struggle of the day, the female protagonist of "Other Side" is absorbed by gossip and erotic fantasies, incapable of acting on her fleeting dream of wartime service.[46]

In her astute critique of the novella's gender dynamics, Smadar Shiffman expresses disappointment with Shaham's portrayal of his unnamed female protagonist, who, though a pioneer as much as the men, is not afforded the respect offered to her male comrades:

> Precisely because Shaham's heroine is given such an impressive starting point, and is so clearly placed at the center of the novel, it is ultimately even more disappointing to find out that Shaham's idealistic *halutza* has remained a woman who thinks only about her love life, who is easily filled with what she herself calls "self pity, worry about the morrow, miserable fear for her own existence, and yearning for a male. Neither ideology nor creative self-realization fill the emptiness of the heroine's life, but rather spying on her pretty neighbor's love life. . . .
>
> . . . One might say, a bit bluntly, that whereas the male pioneers in Shaham's novella act out of ideology and abate their loneliness through taking social and ideological stances, Shaham's *halutza* acts out of "yearning for a male," is impressed by the discussions of social and ideological issues in a hazy, emotional way, "whose meaning she does not entirely fathom," and abates her loneliness by peeping into her . . . neighbor's life. (134–35)

Though initially professing dismay that, by the late 1970s, the "international feminist movement," which had taken root in Israel, apparently had no influence on the development of Shaham's literary heroine, Shiffman eventually concedes the painful truth that (at least from this kibbutz novelist's genuinely experiential perspective) even a pioneering woman cannot play a truly public role in the "main plot of Zionism."[47] Thus Shaham's protagonist is abandoned "on the margins of the national revolution" ("Forging the Image" 139, 140). Although this seems an apt assessment of the gender politics of Shaham's novella, Shiffman's critique overlooks the fact that "The Other Side of the Wall" is mostly concerned with the plight of the lonely outsider who does not fit in, whether male or female; that condition is only exacerbated by the lack of romantic attachments.

When Shaham's protagonist cries in solitude at night, beset by erotic imaginings, the amorous laughter from "a big party" in her neighbor's room leaves her even more bitterly aware of her own isolation. That consciousness carries into her careful observations of the following morning as the partiers exchange their familiar greetings "with bloodshot eyes . . . walking stiffly to work. Business as usual. The ability to say good-morning without overtones of the night before is required as a kind of denial of the self." She wonders whether the criterion of successful belonging requires the thoughtless suppression of what really happens between men and women, which she perceptively calls "this dulling of sensibilities" (*Other Side* 132). Ultimately, the dimming prospect of true belonging seems to be what really ails this forlorn young woman. Thus, when it comes to her complex feelings about Raheli, it is not so much awareness of Raheli's famous beauty that rankles (though she resents this, too), as the profoundly enviable at-homeness Raheli radiates in her very essence: "She seems packed into her skin, ready to be sent somewhere else, there to be transplanted painlessly, without homesickness, without the torments of adjustment" (132). The question of true belonging is the uneasy and haunting question perpetually raised by Israeli writers in each literary generation, without ever quite being answered. Indeed, that abiding unease is a far-reaching, disturbing dynamic in Israeli literature.

Shaham's alienated protagonist frequently retreats to her room, where she composes "long diatribes against the foolish pride of young people, who see no need to respect the feelings of a woman who is not beautiful" (157). Once the hapless protagonist discovers that Theo, the object of her secret desire, is sleeping with Raheli, she struggles against her growing sense of desolation by creating a Walter Mitty–esque fantasy for herself, the nature of which strains to blend the austere terms of socialist self-sacrifice with the tropes of romance fiction, yet which ends on a dismal note of disunity:

> And then she sees herself as the heroine of a romantic novel of great souls and courage and refined sentiment without limit and self-sacrifice and dedication and altruistic self-denial, and deep dark secrets that formerly could have existed only in gorgeously frescoed marble halls, in immaculately starched muslin gowns and small, diamond-encrusted tiaras, with dark, mysterious perfumes and tiny feet encased in sparkling silver slippers and dainty hands, heartrending in their limpness, held out to be kissed. And here are all these things in her poor shack, permeated always by an odor of dust, with mice gnawing away beneath the wooden floor and a coarse mat covering it, and sweaty work clothes and big clumsy shoes waiting at the door. (141)

The lonely young woman's growing disaffection is exacerbated by the kinds of incremental changes, or "progress," that fill the kibbutz's most ardent ideologues with the kind of deep foreboding most outsiders never seem to comprehend. Passively observing the elaborate festivities commemorating the historic occasion of the kibbutz's connection to the national electrical grid (in those days, kibbutzim were adroit at fashioning various anniversaries and holidays to strengthen their sense of identity and community), she is struck by the "gibberish" of the kibbutz secretary's rhetoric, the "childish" nature of the fireworks display. And, later, she is disenchanted by how the nocturnal kibbutz meetings lose their warmth in the absence of the "sputtering Lux lantern." Even the artificial lighting in the kibbutz reading room causes "certain poems [to] lose their magic" (143). Yet, most of all, she dreads the new outdoor illumination, which she fears may prevent neighbor Theo from resuming the scandalous affair that has become the sole source of passion and meaning in her life.

That Theo seems to be a misfit (a figure strikingly reminiscent of Maletz's maladjusted Menahem) much like herself, not at all cut out for the rigors of kibbutz life, excites her. Constantly "shifted from place to place like the teenage visitors who have no fixed place of work," Theo lacks a trade and his Galut essence seems woefully evident when, at the end of a day of fieldwork, he has "strength for only the most essential things, like those books that are needed in his struggle for existence." Yet the protagonist secretly adores him, even though he teases her for admiring "good manners" more than the "relations of production" as the true determinants of civilization (161). Theo has no inkling that she is besotted with him and obsessed with the affair he carries on with her neighbor in the small hours of the night. This romantic vacuum in her life (and her essential alienation from the community she yearns to be accepted by) is made more poignant by the forbearance of her pious father, whose tolerance of her apparent embrace of secular socialism is only due to the fact that the Russians are fighting the Nazis.

Father and daughter remain very close, however, even enjoying their affectionate feuding over the wisdom of "the rabbis of old" versus the modern poetry she quotes, which to his mind lacks "true Jewish feeling" (146). At one point, she briefly contemplates confessing her shameful spying on her neighbor's scandalous lovemaking, just "to test his love for her" (146). Hoping her kibbutz sojourn is just a passing phase, he is saddened by the spiritual vacuity at the heart of kibbutz life: "Your festivals are profane, and your Sabbaths are desecrated. Inspiration is on the decline and in the end materialism will prevail, and then there will be no room for even the tiniest bit of the Sabbath Soul" (144). In ironic juxtaposition to her father's concern over "materialism," his loving practice of bestowing her with lavish care packages containing almonds, olives, chocolate, halvah, and dried meats leads to one of the novel's moments of ideological crisis. On the one hand, she anguishes over letting the comrades devour the almonds her father has "cracked so patiently, so lovingly" for her. On the other hand, her father "is a class enemy . . . religious . . . employs Arab laborers . . . and in the articles he publishes . . . he attacks the policies of the governing [socialist] bodies of the Jewish community" (147). She cringes in guilt upon recalling that she once tried to appease those same disdainful comrades (who happily consume her father's gifts) by cynically declaring that the "love of a man of property for his daughter" is merely "egotism extended biologically" (147).

Thwarted romantic longings aside, there are all sorts of reasons for estrangement in the kibbutz portrayed in "The Other Side of the Wall." The protagonist seems happiest on the rare occasions when the comrades take cultural trips to the city because those afford her precious proximity to the exotic allure of private life. During a ballet performance, she cherishes the "folding seat that, for two hours, will be her preserve, a piece of private property within the public domain," fully aware that the comrade sitting next to her is utterly indifferent to "luxuries and nonutilitarian pleasures" (173). In contrast to this brief sense of possibility and expansiveness, her pleasure dims considerably on the ride home in the crowded kibbutz truck, where she finds herself nearly smothered between the very individuals whose adulterous entanglement obsesses her. This fleeting exposure to the joys of the arts and the urban scene seems to symbolize the wrenching contrast between private experience and collective life; indeed, the entire scene reads as a parody of the normative social claustrophobia that distinguishes kibbutz life:

> Theo's lips are forced into a pained smile, and Raheli's eyelids are lowered, although she can feel the fury mounting in Raheli's eyes as she opens them. . . . She tries with all her might to extricate herself but Big Yitzhak is blocking her way like a stone wall. Her body is squashed between Raheli and Theo. She can feel Raheli's supple breasts pressing against her back and Theo's thin, stiff body against her whole body, taut and raging and ready to burst. She wishes with all her might that she could get away . . . but the whole group is rocking like one mass, and there is no way out. (174)

And then there is the protagonist's intellectual friend who yearns to be sent out from the kibbutz to study at the university, yet knows he will likely be passed over by the secretariat because he is politically out of step with the majority (165). Although Shaham's compassionate portrait of individuals left unsatisfied by a callous community is much like other portrayals of the disaffected in kibbutz fiction, it would be hard to find a more damning rendering of the art of gossip whose corrosive presence seems almost ubiquitous in kibbutzim.[48]

Here is Shaham's impressionistic portrait of the explosive atmosphere following a night guard's public revelation of the adulterous affair that the protagonist has fetishistically savored through her thin wall and "guarded like a sacred trust" (189):

> Everybody goes at it in his or her own way: like discoverers of buried treasure, eyes sparkling, nostrils quivering in anticipation of the scent of a scandal, rejoicing at another's downfall, with a nod, in sorrow, in disappointment—with a look of reproach, angrily, with jealousy. . . . The men speak with contagious enjoyment, facetiously, with much rolling of the eyes, with moral indignation, and with coarse humor. . . . What an appetite she has. If she wants volunteers, count on me. They all give themselves the right to discuss these delicate, painful matters in the grossest, most arrogant language. But there are high-minded words too. Holier-than-thou repugnance, self-righteous offense. Nerve, disgraceful, shame, disgusting. . . . Some speak with an air of triumphant moral superiority, pure and innocent as the cheek of a newborn babe. Some make their remarks in Yiddish, that salty, peppery language that holds, in its attic, an expression for every occasion. . . . Discretion and tact do not seem to enter the picture. For adultery belongs in the public domain, and everybody is allowed to grope and feel and spit. Anyone who shies away is an accessory to the crime and denies the public its due. (183–84)

Though it makes for painful reading, no one who has ever lived for a significant period on a kibbutz will find this portrayal of malicious seduction and cruelty greatly exaggerated. Notwithstanding this bleak rendering, Shaham's narrative warrants recognition as one of the more multifaceted and nuanced portraits of kibbutz life, conscientiously striving to balance the sordid with the more benevolent side of kibbutz life. Thus, alongside the pettiness of the kibbutz's ruling elites and the private pain of its individuals, Shaham gives equal space to its reliable system of caring that rallies to any member in time of need. When the protagonist suffers an attack of malaria, she actually relishes her weakened condition because it brings the collective rushing to her side: "She is enraptured by her helplessness and enjoys the pampering she receives. She falls in love with the kibbutz and with each of its members all over again every time she sees the trays of food they bring her. Even though she is incapable of eating more than a mouthful she can appreciate the intent behind this lavishness, which the kibbutz certainly cannot afford" (176–77). Thus, in spite of Shaham's unwavering attentiveness to the social misery, moral failings, and loneliness that lurk within the community, the words of Meir Avrahami, an unapologetic ideologue, who earlier found fault with the shamelessness of an Amos Oz–like writer, seem to speak for Shaham himself: "We are engaged here in an under-taking that has neither precedent nor parallel anywhere in the world" (150).[49]

"The Affection He Reserved for His Trees": The Contortions of Childhood in Avraham Balaban's *Mourning a Father Lost: A Kibbutz Childhood Remembered*

There are a great many people in the world who to this day are settling accounts with the kibbutz and with their caregivers. I am not one of them. The anger is over the fact that we were promised something. We were part of a marvelous dream—the beautiful and the just and the spearhead, part of the utopia. But we were promised something that could not be fulfilled. The anger is at our hard childhood, which was sometimes also beautiful and ecstatic, but at the same time had a chicken coop morality. In the chicken coop there is a very clear hierarchy: the weak hen gets her tail pecked and will always reach the food last, and in the end you will find her sprawled on the ground, scratched all over.
—*Avraham Balaban*

Many years before the explosive outpouring of memoirs, novels, and films that have lately placed the experience and outcomes of collective child rearing in a critical light, there were early grumblings. For example, in a 1986 symposium of kibbutz writers, Amira Hagani (b. 1934) compared the outcome of collective child rearing to the fate of the title character of Victor Hugo's relatively obscure novel *The Laughing Man*, who is mutilated in childhood so that his face bears the permanent grimace of a laugh:

> Pardon me for the comparison: I've often thought that the problem is not that we were brought up in the framework of collective education. The problem is that the educators wanted to cast us in a mold—I admit it was an ideal mold, a dream of another type of person, a new person, strong, liberated, free, laughing, happy. . . . They wanted to mold us into clear-cut shapes, defined and undeviating and by means of rigid methods. It is extremely hard to liberate oneself from that. It is also difficult to hold anyone to account. Can one hold one's parents to account? After all, what they wanted was for us to grow up into people who'd be more successful than they were themselves. . . .
> A highly Spartan line was taken in educating us. . . . The main problem is our education towards self-restraint, our education towards camouflage,

towards covering up what hurt most, what was most sensitive and vulnerable. The real problem . . . is that this wall, this hard shell we had to produce, was the aim of our education. In order to break through this armor and liberate oneself, to summon up the courage . . . I don't know how much acid one needs to produce to melt such armor. (Ring 157)

Though she insisted that the kibbutz system in which she raised was "built on a vision of love, belief, and ideology," Hagani was clearly outspoken about its punitive consequences, the ironic and unexpected outcome of what her parents dreamed for her, declaring that "yes, we were harmed by collective education" (Ring 157). Speaking even more bluntly, another symposium participant, Miriam Dror, called hers "a castrated generation" (Ring 159), especially in terms of the stunted nature of its imaginative expression: "Those few attempting to liberate themselves from this state of castration not only pay a heavy price for it . . . the marks are deeply engraved and negatively influence their ability to function as creative individuals. And the reason for this is that kibbutz education and experience create a much more 'functional person' than a 'creative person.' . . . This framework prevents—or at least fails to encourage—individualism so vital for creativity" (159). Based on the critical ruminations of Dror, Hagani, and others in this and other kibbutz forums, it seems clear that artists approaching their middle years and beyond had begun to reflect on the path that shaped them. Yet it also seems clear that the distance of many more years was required for such reflection to fully ripen into a work like Avraham Balaban's *Shiv'ah* (*Mourning a Father Lost: A Kibbutz Childhood Remembered*; 2000).[50]

Ostensibly dedicated to the author's difficult relationship with his late father, whose death bookends the work, Balaban's exceptionally painful literary memoir is actually one of the most sustained and far-reaching examinations of the afflictions of kibbutz childhood (most often alluded to only obliquely by writers of Hagani and Dror's generation).[51] Although its aesthetic achievement might serve to challenge Dror's pessimism about the fate of the kibbutz artist, it is also true that this memoir was written many years after the author left his kibbutz home.[52] And readers be warned, it is a significant departure from the rhapsodic accounts by outsiders such as Yossi Klein Halevi: "As soon as the last rains ended around Passover, the children went barefoot and didn't put on shoes again until the first rains of autumn. In winter they ate oranges and grapefruits off the trees; in summer they roasted fresh-picked corn on campfires. Work and play were interchangeable: the children would be placed atop a pen filled with just-picked cotton and jump up and down until it flattened, while a comrade played the accordion. They learned to cherish the hard beauty of the land of Israel, wildflowers growing in porous stone, meager forests of thin pines clinging to rocky slopes" (*Like Dreamers* 5). In marked contrast to that reverent adulation of childhood in the kibbutz, *Mourning a Father Lost*, teeming with anger, compassion, and irony, is an unsparing examination of the alienating childhoods the kibbutz's utopian dreamers inadvertently bestowed on their progeny. Balaban's parents were immigrant halutzim from Bessarabia who arrived in Hulda with a Romanian settlement group. Because Balaban himself was raised in the classic days of the children's houses (fig. 6), it seems altogether fitting that his story begins with scenes that immediately establish the socially engineered distances between children and their parents.

Balaban's was the generation that Alon Gan describes as growing up with "the burden of constant tension between their desire to fulfill their parents' expectations and their awareness that they were forgoing their distinct individuality" (35). That angst is very much present in Balaban's sense of the past; as he once told a reporter, "We were young and the country was young and everything was very intensive and totalistic. I am still moved when I talk about my kibbutz childhood—a kind of inner trembling" (qtd. in Lori).[53] Given that context, it is not surprising that, on learning of his father's death, Balaban returns from the United States, only to feel a familiar sense of dread "as the old mechanism of suppression, camouflage, and detachment, a mechanism cultivated by the kibbutz children's homes, went into operation" (*Mourning* x). From this discomfiting adult awareness, Balaban sends his readers back through time to a primal experience of childhood terror.

It is nighttime in Kibbutz Hulda and the darkness is filled with the wailing of jackals, a surprisingly prevalent motif in the memoirs of Zionist childhoods of that period:

> The jackals know when the nurse leaves the children's house, as if her departure were an agreed signal. The first wail comes over the kibbutz's rusty fence, which passes near our children's house, rises at once to its pitch, drops for a moment, gathers strength, and tries to reach its peak again. It is joined, before it falls silent, by fresh wails from the dark field. Now they rise and fall continually, rasping the darkness. The shadows in the room move around, the scraping of their nails on the floor makes the air tremble. I breathe softly, I don't turn to the wall, to avoid exposing my back to the room beasts. They stir restlessly. . . . They stop beside the beds, stand and crouch. . . . I don't move my arms and legs. (7)

FIGURE 6   Avraham Balaban, standing second from right, in the *gan yeladim* (kindergarten) of Kibbutz Hulda, 1949. Used by permission of Amotz Peleg, Kibbutz Hulda Archives.

In characteristically poetic prose, Balaban makes childhood dread a visceral thing: we can readily understand why the "New Jews" of the kibbutz, given no choice but to rapidly learn how to suppress outward signs of fear and other forms of neediness, grew up with an acute sense of deprivation. Kibbutz Hulda was one of the communities influenced by famous revolutionary theorists of utopian Zionism such as Siegfried Bernfeld (1892–1953) and Boris Schatz (1867–1932), who vociferously insisted that the kibbutzim would succeed as revolutionary utopias only if they overcame the bourgeois institution of the family and raised the children apart from the corrupting influences of their parents.

Balaban takes stock of the insidious power with which this ideology took hold and the glib self-assurance of its advocates: "'A child cannot long for what it has never had, it cannot miss what it has never known,' the lecturers at the ideological seminars . . . persuaded one another" (*Mourning* 13). Achingly, he evokes the chasm separating parents from children and the missed opportunities for love between them under the rule of ideology. With remarkable candor, the memoirist recounts his own experience with this objectifying dogma, its chilly logic of duty, sacrifice, and substitution serving as an ironic echo of the emotional detachment with which he and his peers were indoctrinated:[54]

> Mom and Father are busy building up this place, and if they can't finish their work in time to fetch their children from the nursery or kindergarten, they ask a friend or neighbor to do this—for are we not all brothers? The few visits by people from their hometown . . . offer the nearest thing to a hug from an uncle or aunt. Mom and Father are very busy, laboring to put flesh and sinews on the skeleton of this settlement, and normally they only see their children for a little while before they put them to bed. These few moments are all it takes to remind the children of the existence of a warm body to snuggle against and all it takes to revive the fear of abandonment. The children are sheltered by the finest theories, surrounded by nurses and educators but. . . . The children develop survival strategies, like street kids, toughening their skin to the best of their abilities. When they grow up they will evince the selfishness of people who never got enough protection and security. (8–9)

Many who were kibbutz children in that era would later recall parents who withheld emotion and even physical affection. Balaban is no exception.[55] He recalls painfully brief visits with his parents, when affection had to be expressed in hasty, largely symbolic gestures at best: "During those years I saw Mom only at the end of the day, mostly at bedtime. Before leaving . . . Mom would squeeze my hand, compressing all her caresses into one. This is the immemorial parting gesture of those who must leave too soon. How did I call out to her in those years? From under the blanket, soundlessly, with my whole curled up body" (65). When encountering such painful childhood memories, we cannot help but wonder what the parents themselves felt about the rigid parenting model they were required to uphold.

After all, as Yehudah Mirsky suggests, it was not the parents but the stewards of kibbutz ideals who created the oppressive circumstances of separation: "The ideological bureaucrats" who "squeeze[d] every living moment into the service of the revolution left the kibbutz youngsters searching and frightened, and, in the parentless precinct of the children's house, cast back on their own devices." Still, diary entries written in this period often reveal anguish and conflict, as in Fanya Bergstein's posthumously published reflections:

> While with the group, at work, you weren't worried about your child. You knew his day was good, organized and plentiful, and he spent his time productively, without you. He longed for the evening hour he would spend with you—but still, he went on without you. You were completely immersed in your work—yet a distant sound of crying, the crying of a child among the group taking a walk with the caretaker, made you tremble; and you searched, from within the mix of cries and shouts that reached you, for the sound so familiar to your heart: "maybe it's mine?" And then you were struck with shame at your own relief; for it was "someone else's child" crying. (qtd. in Darr 134–35)

It is hard to know with any certainty just how Balaban himself might assess such a confession. Still, today he readily acknowledges that the days of such parents in his childhood's generation were so arduous that they simply were too exhausted to conjure up what was missing. His own mother, though a young woman,

> never played ball or hopscotch with me, never laughed with me. Eventually I understood that when she came to me at the end of the day her gravity was purely exhaustion—her love had been drained during the day by a dozen greedy mouths. The movement's gurus also did the damage. The old family is obsolete, the educationalists proclaimed. We shall create a new family, the education committee told her. Away from mother's apron strings we shall bring up natural, healthy children, echoed the general meeting. And she believed everything she was told, as a Hassid believes his rabbi. (*Mourning* 12)

The same tone of near incredulity is expressed by one of Balaban's childhood friends: "What amazes me, when I think about our childhood, is the members' conviction that we were a clean slate on which they could write whatever they saw fit. So they wrote on us: be brave and not afraid of the dark and the jackals . . . be loyal to the kibbutz. And they were naïve . . . or stupid enough, to believe that this is what would happen" (97).[56] As for his father, Balaban describes a distant figure fiercely devoted to the collective good and protecting the kibbutz apple orchard, yet ill at ease and impatient during the short periods his children were home with their parents:

The time assigned to his children was the gap between his shower and supper. He would lie down, cover his face with a sheet or a newspaper, and we would walk around on tiptoe, as in a sickroom. We clearly felt we were a nuisance to him. . . . The apple varieties, Delicious, Nonpareil, even the delicate Galia Beauty [sic], reached the Tel Aviv market safely, despite all the hardships of . . . picking, sorting, and packaging. But how to touch us, his children, that he didn't know. On stormy nights he would rush out, like a true farmer, to ensure that his tender saplings were unhurt by the blast. (21)[57]

The wounding effects of that memory linger on, for Balaban claims that, even today, whenever he cares for a plant or a tree, he simply cannot repress the unfailing eruption of the memory of his father's "sunburnt hands showing me how to plant a cypress tree, or stroking a cluster of apples with the affection he reserved for his trees" (23). Nor does Balaban find himself the sole guardian of such painful filial memories.

On the whole, fathers come off worse than do mothers in *Mourning*, and, in that regard, at one point an old classmate still living in Hulda mentions that his wife pressured him into attending "one of those workshops women go to" (80). He was entirely aloof from the proceedings until the moderator encouraged him to sit across from his wife and speak to her as if she was his late father, telling her everything he had never had the opportunity to reveal. After initially resisting: "I . . . thought I'd say a few words and get it over [with]. I thought about my Father and I couldn't say one word. After a minute I simply fell apart. I sat opposite my Father and cried. I blubbered, you know what I mean? And my Father was never such a big thing in my life" (81). Both men spent most of the subsequent decades of their life out of touch with their fathers who seemed to have remained remote figures to them. Moreover, unlike traditional notions of extended Jewish families, he and his classmates all had "abbreviated families: parents and one or two siblings" (103). Balaban recalls only one classmate with grandparents. Factors contributing to these small units include the fact that the founding generation of halutzim left families in Europe as well as "boys who took part in the fight for the state of Israel detached themselves quite early" from family life (103). Perhaps self-consciously, the kibbutz educational system Balaban describes (fig. 7) sought to create a compensating illusion of substitution for these absences. So just what took the place of the radically diminished family and the minimum daily time they were allotted to spend together? The answer seems to have been, at least in part, the weighty emphasis on a collective

FIGURE 7   Classroom at Kibbutz Hulda, 1955. Used by permission of Amotz Peleg, Kibbutz Hulda Archives.

sense of belonging to a maternal homeland, whose soil would receive "every battle casualty" as "another root in the ground" (103).

Balaban explains that this sense of belonging was instilled through songs that created a fierce identification between "mother" and "homeland." Or, in the operative pedagogy of Balaban's generation, "the children of [the kibbutz] family are . . . the sons returning to the bosom of their mother, to plow her fields and protect her home. The identification of homeland and mother suited the purpose of the kibbutz educators and the leaders of the Youth Movements: it was the shortest way to forge a bond between the generations, to create an illusion of family where there was none, an illusion of roots in a place of sand and rocks" (103). Yet the system that seems to have so cruelly impinged on family life is often viewed by the author through a distinctly nostalgic prism, especially when Balaban returns as an adult to find the older kibbutz generation (his mother's contemporaries) in rapid physical decline: "Like the last leaves falling from the branches, the remaining founder members were passing away" (43).

The remnant that remains mourns the ways that the forces of privatization have wreaked havoc on the cultural and social life of the community: "The kibbutz, they tell me, red-eyed, is no longer what it was: all the services have been privatized, the dining hall is only open for lunch, the last Passover Seder was celebrated by each family separately" (41).[58] No matter where Balaban turns, the communal fabric seems poignantly threadbare, and nowhere is that more apparent than in the fading institution of the dining hall.

As Ofer Vardi, author of a Hebrew-language collection of recipes and stories from the halcyon days of the kibbutz, asserts, "The importance of the communal dining hall runs much deeper than the food. . . . The dining hall played an important unifying role in the culture that developed in each kibbutz" (qtd. in Kessler). Balaban grimly notes an announcement in the newsletter of his former kibbutz: the institution of Friday night dinners has been eliminated; he senses the writer's "defeated tone, his awareness that there is no remedy" (*Mourning* 42). Acknowledging his powerlessness to prevent the social breakup of the kibbutz, the writer states simply, "I am deeply sorry about the cancellation of the Sabbath supper in the dining hall. I remember it as always a festive occasion, the gathering of all the members around the laid tables and sometimes a short ceremony of Kiddush" (42).[59] Plaintively, he concludes by confessing "a longing for the atmosphere of the past which will not return" (42).[60] Other instances of deterioration that Balaban encounters may seem less dramatic, but their cumulative impact conveys a decline of almost immeasurable consequence. One telling example recalls a touching custom according to which each newly wedded couple inherits, and subsequently passes on, a marriage scroll inscribed with the names of all kibbutz marriages. But when Balaban asks to see it, no one remembers who might have it—and, anyway, it has been years since the last kibbutz wedding.

Only toward the end of this psychologically wrenching story does a tantalizing hint of how Balaban and his father might have reconciled emerge. By then, it is too late, both for Balaban and for his readers, but that is the point—the narrative circles around a yearned-for figure who was never there.[61] Yet, in spite of its aching notes of loss, this intelligent work is written by a gracious and nuanced writer who never descends to self-pity.[62] Instead, *Mourning* triumphs as a moving chronicle of complex, sympathetic individuals caught up in a well-intentioned social experiment whose promise was never quite fulfilled. Moreover, for all its apparent bitterness, there are moments of unabashed love for the proponents of socialism's most daring experiment, for what they attempted. At one point, delivering a lecture to the old people on his former kibbutz, Balaban is struck by what they represent: "They were humanity's finest dream in this century, the most consistent attempt to forget humanity's inglorious origins" (37).[63] After so much pain and disappointment, this belated affirmation seems all the more authentic.

3

The Kibbutz and Its Others at Midcentury
Palestinian and Mizrahi Interlopers in Utopia

B'or hadash (*In a New Light*; 1966) by Atallah Mansour (b. 1934; fig. 8) would be of significant interest if only for its status as the first novel written in Hebrew by an Arab citizen of Israel. For reasons elaborated on below, this lively novel can also be usefully considered alongside other milestones in the "literature of passing" written by African Americans and others of divided identity. Born and raised in Palestine, Mansour lived in Sha'ar Ha'amakin, a kibbutz in northern Israel, from 1951 to 1952.[1] Like his contemporary, well-known contemporary Arab Israeli journalist and novelist Sayed Kashua, Mansour was a correspondent for *Haaretz*, indeed, the very first Arab Israeli journalist to work for what is perhaps Israel's most respected and influential newspaper. For both writers, their education in Israeli schools and their vocation as Israeli journalists made Hebrew a natural choice for their literary aspirations. Immediately after the Six-Day War, Mansour moved to the conquered Old City of Jerusalem, reporting on Palestinian affairs there as well as in the West Bank.

In his wide-ranging analysis of the historical and sociopolitical factors that contribute to the minority literature of Israel, Mahmoud Kayyal describes the situation of Mansour and other Arab writers in Hebrew as "exceedingly complex"; such writers are

> part of the Palestinian people, which is engaged in a violent conflict with Israel, and, at the same time, they constitute an ethnic minority which aspires to become integrated into Israeli society—a society which itself is a minority in the hostile Arab region surrounding it. Thus, there exist within it conflicting tendencies, both to alienation and to integration. On the one hand, the tendency to alienation stems from Israeli Arabs' links to the common Palestinian narrative, beginning with the Nakba, which is a part of their own experience, and continuing with the point of

FIGURE 8 Atallah Mansour
at home in Nazareth, 2014.
Photo by Bader Mansour.
Used by permission.

view of the State that they constitute a military and demographic threat, which was expressed in the Military Government imposed on them from 1948 to 1966, the expropriation of Arab-owned lands, and the limitation of the area of jurisdiction of Arab towns. On the other hand, the tendency to integrate stems their aspiration to attain economic, educational and cultural standards on a level with those of Jewish society. (32)

This dynamic of marginality, which seems to have become more oppressive in recent years, plays out with memorable psychological force in the uneasy relation of Mansour's protagonist to the Hebrew socialist dream.

As early as 1956, Eliyahu Agassi, an Arab Israeli establishment figure, pondered the fraught question of whether his community would ever succeed as a voice within the Hebrew language or how, for that matter, it might absorb Hebrew influences. Perhaps because Kayyal was writing less than a decade since the founding of the state, he observed that Agassi "does not give a clear answer to this question; but he does point out that the influence of modernistic verse in general, and of Hebrew verse in particular, can be discerned in local Arabic verse" (32). Yet considering what transpired within the space of just ten years, Agassi's tentative affirmation might be deemed a prophecy. After the publication of Mansour's *B'or hadash* in 1966, the first Hebrew novel by an Arab writer was rapidly "followed by dozens of Hebrew works written by Arabs: short stories, novels and verse. Moreover, several Arab intellectuals wrote on current affairs or were involved in theatrical performances and films, in translation, and in other cultural activities in the Hebrew language" (Kayyal 33). The importance of this critical shift in culture cannot be exaggerated. Yet, in retracing the basic adversarial divide between kibbutz insiders and outsiders, Mansour also joined in a growing mainstream trend that reconsidered whether the kibbutz could actually live up to its lofty ideals.

Like many of the works discussed in this study, Mansour's novel highlights the poignant failures of the kibbutz to realize the Zionist dream of utopia, even as it empathizes with those who struggle on its behalf.[2] At one starkly revealing moment, a kibbutz character ruefully acknowledges the disillusioning reality: "We wanted to redeem the land, to protect Jewish labour and to secure peace, and it looks as if it isn't easy to fulfill all three wishes" (*In a New Light* 63). But, for many pages, the predominant focus of the novel is on the limited horizons set for Israel's internal Others by the Jewish state. Mansour quietly crafts his narrator-protagonist's outlook as a prospective candidate for kibbutz membership while keeping us in ignorance of the protagonist's Arab identity. Years later, Mansour would publish an essay in Arabic, emphasizing that "Arabs in Israel have become bilingual without impairing their Arabic national identity" and "that Arab writers aspire to present an alternative narrative, and to tell the Israeli public about the special problems of Arab citizens in its own tongue, since most Jews do not know Arabic; in this way the Jews will identify with these problems, or at least, understand them" (Kayyal 35). Clearly, in imagining the plight of a young Palestinian struggling to integrate into the institution long regarded as the crowning glory of the Zionist state, Mansour sought to create a sympathetic portrait of the divided identity of the Others within Israel, whose presence the majority culture still struggles to accommodate nearly a half century later.

Characteristic of a number of other examples we will encounter, Mansour begins uncritically with the attractive surfaces of utopia: "The sand is white and so are the houses. The red-tile roofs, abetted by the small vegetable gardens, turn the landscape into a naive kindergarten drawing" (*In a New Light* 20).[3] Only on revisiting such serene observations, with the subsequent knowledge of the protagonist's distance from his actual origins and indigenous belonging (revealed much later in the narrative), can readers appreciate how thoroughly and ironically hegemonic ideology permeates his consciousness. For many pages, known to the kibbutz comrades only as "Yossi Mizrahi," the protagonist appears to fully embrace the political and mythic codes of their Zionist society. For example, while enduring one of the doctrinaire lectures so ubiquitous in the kibbutzim of the 1950s, the narrator sounds like one of

Edward Said's notorious Orientalists, reporting that he "loved to gaze upon the lands of our neighbors beyond those of the kibbutz. I enjoyed the sight of those shapeless fields, the clusters of trees strewn here and there with pitiful haphazardness. Poor ignorant louts who know nothing about the Laws of the Universe, who always mistake the casual for the causal! But they, too, must not be left out of the scheme of things, and it is incumbent on us to bring our gospel to them whether they like it or not" (*In a New Light* 14). Even his memory of his native village is distorted by the lens of colonialist ideology: the domiciles of the settlers seem to follow a rational, enlightened design, a clear improvement over the fearful ignorance that ruled over the Arab peasants for centuries. Whereas the kibbutz "houses are built far apart, meticulously planned, my father's village did not even have a master plan: people just built their houses to suit their needs. They wanted to live close to one another because they were afraid of drifting apart" (40). Echoing the essential terms of Theodor Herzl's prophetic pronouncement that "for Europe we will constitute a bulwark against Asia, serving as guardians of culture against barbarism" (23), the narrator's ideological purity and collectivist ardor is blemished only by his inconvenient lust for Rivkah, a comrade's wife who teaches him English.

Guiltily, he rationalizes away this transgressive desire because, after all, he has not yet shouldered the burdens and privileges of a full member of the kibbutz—"I did not as yet 'belong.'" (*In a New Light* 22).[4] For her part, Rivkah casually assumes that he was born in Yemen but that identification triggers his "guilty" awareness of his indigenous origins. That realization sends him into a downward spiral of self-doubt and longing:

> "No," I said with some confusion. I had wanted to say "Yes." "But I was born in this country."
>
> All the happiness was oozing out of me. I could never get accustomed to my life story. Why did everybody insist on questioning me about where I came from? (27)

Yet, of course, the American-born Rivkah sees only a dark-skinned "Jew." Thus, when she confesses her envy of his native roots in the Arab world, the narrator tells us, "Her words cut into my flesh like a rusty hacksaw" (27), a trope repeated twice more as his feelings for her intensify, especially upon discovering that she, too, has dallied with the transgressive frisson of passing. Rivkah explains that in the United States "her appearance wasn't Jewish and she could easily masquerade as a Christian. . . . She had actually taken advantage of this fact more than once" (27–28). Innocently, she tells the besotted narrator that "it wasn't pleasant to be different from anybody else, and it was only human that the one who was different should try to imitate the others" (28), which causes the narrator even greater turmoil: "Great God, this was too much!" (28). Worse still, she reveals that when her father learned of her deception, he was so hurt that he persuaded her to travel to Israel to find herself a Jewish husband. Much later, after we have at last learned the secret of the narrator's origins, the nexus of patrimony, obedience, and betrayal is intensified as Rivkah presses the protagonist to bring his aging father to settle on the kibbutz. When the young Arab continues to deceive her about both his father and his identity, Rivkah misinterprets his refusal to bring his father to the kibbutz as shocking evidence of filial neglect, and tensions between them rise. Yet, in the end, both Rivkah and the narrator will "betray" their fathers in pursuing the taboo Others.

In obsessively hungering for Rivkah or perhaps for her privileged world, the narrator seems to be trying to purge the wounding memory of an earlier dalliance. Like the Arab protagonists of much later fiction—such as Sayed Kashua's young surrogate in the novel *Aravim rokdim* (*Dancing Arabs*; 2002), whose condition as the sole Arab in a Jewish boarding school places him on the margin of Jewish Israeli society—Mansour's narrator spent part of his adolescence in an Israeli youth movement, when he briefly became the boyfriend of an Israeli girl named Yael. Painfully, he recalls that, even though she made a point of appearing with him in public, whenever they were alone together, Yael "took great care to set up a barbed-wire fence between us. . . . She labored hard to bring it home to me that we were strangers" (*In a New Light* 67). Later, it turns out that she had been using him all along to make a Jewish boy jealous.[5]

One of the many ironies surrounding the narrator's yearning to create a life for himself on his own terms is that it mirrors the dream of the New Jew, whether refugee from Europe or city dweller from Israel, to embrace the agrarian life of egalitarianism and self-sacrifice. He anguishes over why Rivkah seems so reluctant to recognize his own struggle to belong: "Why should she care about my father? Why should she care whether I was an orphan, a bastard, a foundling or just a bad boy who had run away from home and joined a kibbutz? Hadn't we been taught that we are there to set up the vanguard to the world of tomorrow?" (68). Of course, the Arab protagonist's central tragedy can be traced to his presumption that he, too, might be absorbed within the utopian socialist dream of the "We."

But his ardent efforts to suppress or deny the past, to overcome the constraints of his Arab identity, often come to naught when vestiges of an earlier existence break into his present. Thus he learns to avoid the organized kibbutz poetry readings because they remind him of his distant childhood, when "I used to sing when I was a *ghaffir* [watchman] in the vineyards, but these verses were different. . . . I would have liked to forget even those early songs" (34). Only when he is nestled together with Rivkah in the kibbutz vineyard can he bear to open up to the dangerous intensity of poetry. Yet, even then, the lyrical language of sorrow and loss conjures up unwanted, repressed memories: "I recalled my father's blood spurting from his stained shirt. I could see my mother tearing out the hair of her head. The British police-sergeant pushed her away with his bayoneted rifle and addressed the doctor, but the latter did not answer. . . . I had not seen my father and mother since that terrible day. They told me my mother was dead but I did not believe them" (35). Those unwanted vestiges of the past subvert Israeli readers' own complacency even today, but they did so especially at a time when the Nakba had not yet been absorbed into Israeli culture. Indeed, this much-neglected novel warrants the kind of recognition Lital Levy ascribes to later novels—such as Emile Habiby's *The Secret Life of Saeed the Pessoptimist* (1974), originally written in Arabic, and Anton Shammas's *Arabeskot* (*Arabesques*; 1986), originally written in Hebrew—that "enjoy a dual status as Israeli novels and . . . as Palestinian novels; both are in dialogue with Palestinian oral culture and collective memory. . . . As such they present literary critics with a particularly compelling opportunity to reconsider the utility of national language as the primary hallmark of novelistic identity" (Levy, "Nation, Village, Cave" 13).

Indeed, *In a New Light* gives voice to the interpenetration of Jew and Arab Palestinian through its protagonist's frequent attempts to insinuate himself within the majority culture, as when Mansour's bereft youth is taken into the home of "Old Mizrahi," a Jewish widower and father of three, whose daughter Ruth becomes his close friend. Ruth calls the boy her "brother" because he devotes more time to her than her siblings do: "She used to quarrel with the other children whenever they called me a 'goy'" (35–36). Ruth proudly tells them that her "brother" is the son of a man who had been in business with her father selling eggs to the Jewish farmers. She even encourages him to attend the Youth Movement's Hakhsharah (agricultural training program for youths interested in joining a kibbutz), but that is a step too far for Ruth's father. Whether out of discomfort at the prospect of causing the youth undue confusion about his identity or Old Mizrahi's own latent prejudice, they drift apart. Even so, the village space is the past; the door "Yossi" keeps firmly shut because it poses a great psychic threat, offering up only fragmentary impressions of oppression and atrocity: "He said that I should go back to my village but I didn't like the idea. I was afraid of seeing our house, afraid of remembering my father's blood spurting out of his stained shirt. Every British soldier reminded me of the police sergeant who had beaten my mother. . . . I didn't want to remember, I didn't want to go back to the village. I hated the village just as I hated the British" (36). Later, the narrator will forcefully suppress the visceral memory of his Arab father's death by declaring to the kibbutz members that his Jewish family is the only family he has ever known and that the reason for his estrangement from them is his Jewish father's disapproval of the radical ways of the kibbutz. The kibbutzniks seem ready to relate to this familiar story of rebellion; indeed, each one of them "used it as a pretext to sit down and tell me for hours . . . how he, too, had revolted against his parents in the Diaspora and came to Eretz Yisrael to participate in the building of a bright future" (37).

Here I should note that my approach to Mansour's complex mapping of Arab and Jewish identities in relation to kibbutz socialism is aligned with Rachel Feldhay Brenner's deeply illuminating reading of *In a New Light*, especially her observation that Mansour's Arab and Jewish characters are ironically twinned by attempting

> to construct their subjectivity on the basis of a deliberate, joint decision to suppress memory. Thus, Mansour's story line signals a movement neither toward a rediscovery of the forgotten nor toward a remembrance of the erased past. . . . Mansour's novel ironically suggests that social coexistence is conditioned upon a mutual consent to "forget." . . . Whereas the membership of Yossi is predicated upon suppression of his Arab identity, the membership of the "new" Jew in the Zionist movement is conditioned by the repudiation of the Diaspora Jews. (*Inextricably Bonded* 193)

Mansour's narrator persuades himself that his Arab identity is safely confined to the past; Jewishness, or at least the sanctification of kibbutz membership, is the future he dreams.

Meanwhile, persuaded that he is a Jewish immigrant from the Arab world, Rivkah, the married woman he is in love with, condescendingly misses no opportunity to remind him that he came to Israel from a "backward feudal society" based on "social values no longer compatible with the customs of the industrial pre-socialist society in which we live" (*In a New Light* 38). In such moments, Mansour slyly and astutely equates the marginality of Israel's Mizrahim with that of the indigenous Palestinian population. As the narrative proceeds, the cultural schizophrenia of "Yossi Mizrahi" requires him to accept the rigid binary logic of Zionist historiography and ideology (which inevitably proves impossible to sustain), beginning with Old Mizrahi, who "was undeniably a fine man; why, then, did he refuse to accept me as his son?. . . . Why couldn't he finish the good deed he had begun? But he said he could not lie" (100). When the old Jew sees the extent of the youth's anguish, he promises to consult a rabbi over the possibility of a conversion. But because the kibbutz is profoundly opposed to interference by rabbis and what they perceive to be the tyranny of religious authority, the matter remains unresolved.

The bifurcating crisis, of being torn between two fathers, on the one hand, and between two homelands, on the other, surfaces incessantly in Mansour's portrayal of his protagonist's psyche. At one point, the narrator recalls the destruction of the now abandoned Arab village of his birth by an Israeli bulldozer (an image and reality that have sadly become even more dominant in the history of Israeli-Palestinian relations since Mansour's novel first appeared). Yet he is so alienated from his origins that he tells himself that the village was his father's, not his own childhood home. One can only wonder what Jewish Israeli readers of the 1960s would have made of Mansour's irony-laden passages, such as when his narrator strains to persuade himself that the bulldozer is the benign agent of civilization, opposed to the Arab past of primitive violence. Again he recalls his father's violent end: "My father's blood stood for war and destruction, whereas the bulldozer was a vehicle of peace and construction" (40).[6] But the fact that the bulldozer is painted red seems to wield a charged mythic significance, an overwhelmingly visceral reminder of the past; indeed, the memory threatens to unravel the neat categories to which he has devoted his life. In spite of all his willful efforts to escape the past, he knows that his father "bled to death and his blood was red like the bulldozer which cleared the debris in the abandoned village. Why did I have to remember all this? I had no right to remember. . . . It looked as though I had not yet succeeded in becoming a 'well-organized person.' I was beset with longings for my mother, just as the bulldozer's operation reminded me, for no apparent reason, of my father's blood squirting out of his shirt. . . . I was being ridiculous. Why on earth did everything red make me think of my father and mother?" (40–41).

The protagonist's intense aversion to blood has consequences for his status in kibbutz society. During a mission in the 1948 War, he collapses at the mere sight of a friend wounded in combat, and he is subsequently removed from combat patrols. When a young female kibbutznik also questions his manhood, he acknowledges the essential truth of the charge, admitting to himself that even the red flag his socialist comrades carry in their demonstrations agitates him. He tells himself that here, too, the color embodies progressive values, a symbol that he must embrace in spite of himself:

I hated the red flag! No, I must not think that way. Without the Movement which aspired to brighten the future of the world people like me had absolutely no hope. Why was I thinking along such childish lines? Who was I and what was I without the Almighty Movement? The fate of man is preordained. Human society is marching forward in anticipation of a rosy morrow. It follows in the wake of the Progressive Forces and its flag is red. . . . The bulldozer, too, was painted red and so was my father's blood and Shmulik's blood. But what was the connection, anyway? The bulldozer clears away the debris for the purpose of planning and execution. One must not besmirch it. . . . I was glad there were brave bulldozer-drivers who were not afraid of the red colour. They were pulling down the world of yesterday to build the carefully planned future of mankind. It was foolish to nurse a grievance against the red colour. It was pure coincidence that the bulldozer and my father's blood were tinged with the same dye. (44–45)

The hapless young protagonist's struggle to maintain his convictions against the upwelling power of memory is made more poignant when we realize that, because his Palestinian home has been destroyed, no other future is available to him. But all he ever tells anyone of his past is that he is irreparably alienated from his "*petit-bourgeois* parents." Even when his Arab father's relatives try to coax him back to their village, he refuses the opportunity to return to his origins, clinging to his troubled identity without a clear stake in the Zionist national future. Once again, it is as if he is incongruously mimicking the Zionist paradigm of the "New Jew," fashioning himself anew. Instead, he seeks out Old Mizrahi, the Jew who sheltered him, only to discover that the old man's memory has long faded—"A mysterious hand began to wring my heart" (59). Only when he conjures up memories of Mizrahi's enduring friendship with "Muhamed from Ein-al-Hirba," only at this point—sixty pages in—do we learn the names of his Muslim father and his native village. Indeed, it is only at this juncture that the narrator calls himself "Yusuf" (born "Yusuf Mahmud"). Both men well up with emotion, overcome by the reunion, until Yusuf quietly declares to Old Mizrahi, "You are my father," to which Mizrahi vigorously protests, "Your father is dead" (60). The narrator pleads that he has no other living relations. Softening, the pious old man expresses his unhappiness that the young man has joined the company of the "godless" kibbutzniks. All the while, Mansour never suggests that Yusuf is overly enamored of kibbutz ideology, only that he is in thrall to Rivkah herself. In Old Mizrahi's home, Yusuf asks for tea with lemon because he recalls that this is how Rivkah drinks it.

Rivkah continues to give the narrator English lessons in spite of the growing signs of his ardor for her. She and her husband, Yehudah, seem to be part of a continuum of unhappy married couples whose lives have been blighted by childlessness due to the scarring psychic trauma of war. One evening after a domestic fracas interrupts the narrator's English lesson, she tells him that her husband "has been through war and destruction. In fact he has taken part in two wars and that's why he doesn't want any children. . . . He says we mustn't be cruel to others . . . that his parents had no moral right to bring him into such a ruthless world if they couldn't protect him against wars" (62–63).[7] In this and subsequent encounters, Mansour's Jewish characters reveal the same spectrum of beliefs and attitudes that readers would come to expect many years later from Jewish writers like A. B. Yehoshua (b. 1936) or David Grossman (b. 1954). For, as this intense exchange proceeds, the narrator begins to realize that his lover actually harbors deep sympathies for the position of the Arabs, especially when she asserts that, had she been born an Arab, she would surely have fought against the Zionists.

Although overjoyed by the prospect that Rikvah might not outright reject his Arab identity, Yusuf is almost shocked by her skepticism: "This seemed unacceptable, almost incredible. Rivkah's speech implied that she didn't believe in all those fine words that the Comrade Lecturers had preached . . . about the rosy future which would be shared by every human being!" (*In a New Light* 70). It was that egalitarian vision that had drawn him to the kibbutz community in the first place. Thus Mansour's portrayal of Rivkah's own Palestinian memory includes a nuanced consciousness of socioeconomic grievances in which kibbutz ideology itself has played an ironic role: "From whom did we buy the land to establish on it the justest form of life on earth? From the big landowners. The poor tenants remained landless as before. They also ran short of work because we stuck out for Jewish workers" (62). This remarkably sympathetic speech underscores the novelist's respect for the depth of his characters' self-interrogation and their capacity for comprehending the stories of others. Indeed, we can only wonder what it was like to read these words in a Hebrew novel during the 1960s, for there is a palpable generosity in Mansour's portrayal of Rivkah's self-interrogation and empathy.

Still imagining that she has to persuade "Yossi" of the just claims of Palestinians, Rivkah exclaims, "Look, these people have been living here for the last fifty years, for the last hundred, two hundred, one thousand years, maybe more. Do you think they wanted to keep this country [only] until we, their cousins, came back from exile? I mean these simple people who were born here and suddenly all these foreigners come and claim the country for their own and drive them out—" (62). Here Mansour ably renders Rivkah's historical consciousness, empathy, and perhaps even guilt in ways that bear historical witness to the ideological questioning that has always been present in Israeli culture. The presence of such passages throughout *In A New Light* shows Mansour to be as capable of portraying the warm humanity of kibbutzniks as he is attentive to their hypocrisy and biases. Perhaps it is for this reason that most Arab Israeli critics have excluded his novel from critical recognition, and that some have even chosen to ostracize Mansour himself.[8] On the other hand, Yusuf/Yossi's dualism and irresolution might pose an equally uncomfortable challenge to Jewish Israeli readers. After Rivkah inadvertently stirs up the unsettled past, peace-loving Yusuf wonders whether he might have more personal dignity had he participated in a war—"Perhaps I would still be somebody, would have some rights of my own" (69). Even after twenty years of living in the shadow of his father's death, uncertainties still torment him, sending him into frustrating Hamlet-like vacillations over the hopeless task of untangling the actual perpetrator amid the fatal entanglements of Arabs, Jews, and the English that marked the violent chaos of the final days of the British Mandate:

> Who killed my father? I didn't know. Was it the English? The Jews? The Arabs? The Jews killed Arabs, the Arabs killed Jews, the Arabs killed Arabs and the Jews killed Jews. The Arabs killed Arabs who were suspected of collaboration with the Jews. Was the selling of eggs by my father to Mr. Mizrahi regarded . . . as treason? Treason against whom? . . . Perhaps it was the English who killed my father. I didn't know. Or was it the Jews? Why not? Didn't my father go from the village to the settlement in the dark. They might have thought he was contemplating an act of sabotage. (69)

Yusuf faces the prospect of killing his father a second time, at least symbolically, when he realizes that the only way to prevent intrusive investigations by the kibbutz secretariat is to announce his father's sudden death. The haunting burden of his father's unsolved killing, coupled with his painful knowledge of his own antiheroic qualities, intensifies his desperate conviction that only Rivkah's love can heal him. Anguished over whether her expression of understanding for the Arabs' position might have further implications, he wonders if he dare test that love by revealing his real identity—whether the same woman who recognizes "their right to hate" might also recognize "my right to love and be loved" (70). And, as if that predicament were not complicated enough, it is further complicated by Yusuf's growing sense of self-alienation. After the kibbutz secretary warns him that, for the kibbutz to bestow the prize of membership, "we have to know everything about you. . . . Everything" (76), he is left doubting whether even he knows "everything about myself" (77). At this point, the crisis of Yusuf/ Yossi's indeterminacy and deep ambivalence nearly echoes Franz Kafka, who famously expressed his own minority quandary in his diary: "What have I in common with Jews? I have hardly anything in common with myself and should stand very quietly in a corner, content that I can breathe" (*Diaries* 11). In that regard, it never becomes clear, either to us or to the protagonist, whether Yusuf's fervent struggle to belong is driven by love for Rivkah or by a genuine ideological affinity for the kibbutz, especially when he admits to himself that "I was not inclined to believe the comrades when they prated about their burning desire and readiness to plan the future of humanity" (*In a New Light* 77). As we will see, this acerbic admission lies at the very heart of the novel.

Yusuf/Yossi's disillusionment grows during a confrontation between the kibbutz and a neighboring Arab village over a wandering ox that has trespassed upon kibbutz pastures. When the village headman approaches the kibbutzniks to retrieve the ox, they immediately dismiss him, rationalizing that he is a "parasite [who] sucks the life-blood of the peasants" and that, as the "avant-garde of the proletariat," it was their duty to refuse negotiations and hold onto the beast (78–79). Matters only escalate when the villagers call on the police, culminating when a hot-tempered comrade named Shlomo shoots the ox and later brags to his comrades, "We have won the war to put an end to the damned insolence of these Arabs" (79). Mansour's portrayal of this incident—especially the narrator's terse report that "there was a lot of talk . . . about 'us' and 'them'" (80)—recalls Amos Oz's similar inversion of the "civilized" versus "savage" binary in imagining the tensions between the Negev Bedouin and the violent, headstrong, sanctimonious young kibbutzniks of his early short story "Nomad and Viper."

The narrator, though long accustomed to the tendency of kibbutz ideologues to identify " 'we' as anything that was good, the aspirants-to-general-welfare-and-justice, whilst 'they' were the Sons of Darkness" (*In a New Light* 81), is upset that Shlomo, the cynical slayer of the ox, has introduced racism into this polarized situation, sadly noting that nobody else seems to object. Ironically, Shlomo is chosen by the kibbutz cultural committee to serve as political liaison to the Arab villagers, with Yossi designated to serve as his driver and body-guard. This leads to the novel's most richly farcical, though perhaps also truthful, scenes in the Arab-Jewish contact zone when the kibbutz (as instrument of the "Party of Equitable Unity") conducts a series of propaganda visits to the (fictional) village of Nur-Allah.[9]

These two have barely spoken to each other in the past. Shlomo's distrust of Yossi intensifies when he witnesses Yossi's horror at accidentally hitting a rabbit in the road. Observing that his "bodyguard" fears the sight of blood, Shlomo wonders how Yossi can possibly be relied on in the event of an attack: "It's a strange world. *I* am sent to make propaganda among Arabs while *you* are sent to defend me. . . . Listen, Yossi, I am no more qualified for propaganda than you are to defend yourself. I am not a hypocrite and I cannot lie to the Arabs. I simply don't like them" (83). That candid admission is uttered just as the pair drive into the Arab village. Arriving late, they receive a perfunctory welcome. The expected audience has already dispersed, and an old man ushers them into a nearly unfurnished room where a "strange stillness" prevails—except for an acetylene lamp that "sounded like the protracted sigh of a languishing patient" (86), as though a synecdoche for the fate of the entire Arab population. A variation of that impression of encroaching desolation appears on a later visit in the narrator's almost Keatsian observation of autumnal melancholy and abandonment: "The grass has wilted long ago. Fruit has ripened on the fig and pomegranate trees. The bird's nests have fallen into ruin since the fledglings flew away" (104). It is hard not to read Mansour's language as anything less than a stirring elegy to the passing of Palestinian culture from the land.

Eventually, a few young Arabs from the village return; when politely asked about their livelihoods, they complain bitterly that, in the Israeli economy, there are no employment prospects for Arabs apart from temporary construction work. Shlomo, presumably there to exploit precisely such a grievance, not only calls on the young men to support the "Party of Equitable Unity" (a thinly disguised stand-in for Mapam), which he cynically assures them will campaign "for equal opportunities for employment for all," but also declares that, should they wish to establish a kibbutz, they would be granted that opportunity. Here it bears emphasizing that Mansour's quiet critique of such duplicity would have been fully apparent to his Israeli readers, whether or not they knew that such support was never actually made available to the Arab minority.

Unsurprisingly, the kibbutz holds no allure whatsoever for the assembled audience. Moreover, contra the lofty status of the kibbutz within Israeli ideology—which cast the enterprise as the country's beacon of heroism, self-reliance, and pioneering spirit—a young Arab teacher offers this helpful clarification: "Once upon a time, when the Jewish immigrants could not make a go of it in this country, they set up collective settlements so that they could lean on one another—" (89). Upon hearing that irreverent portrayal of the movement's origins, Shlomo becomes apoplectic, for, as the narrator wryly observes, "all his attempts to enlighten the people of Nur-Allah" have been "in vain," even inducing some of the youths to doze off. Although the delegation's failure already seems palpable, matters become even worse when a furious stranger bursts into the room. He turns out to be the owner of the straying ox that Shlomo killed, and though he does not realize that Shlomo is the culprit, he angrily insists that the investigating policeman has determined that the kibbutzniks were guilty.

Blustering, Shlomo denounces the "dirty lie! . . . It's a frameup by the police. . . . They help to make propaganda against us." Shlomo then "proceeded to quote Marx and Engels: 'Policemen are the watchdogs of the ruling classes'" (*In a New Light* 91). His desperate tirade earns him only the disgust of two teachers, who leave without saying a word. As the delegation's official Arab minder explains: "They left the room because your friend began to speak against the government and the police. It's forbidden to speak against the government. Those teachers are civil servants" (91). Urgently, the minder declares that such rhetoric threatens the village's precarious relationship with the state. Yet Shlomo, who increasingly resembles the trespassing ox with each belligerent utterance, carries on oblivious to the effects of his denunciation. Eventually, he is stopped in his tracks by the ox owner himself, who reveals that the policeman Shlomo has railed against is both an Arab and a village resident.

With Shlomo silenced at last, the narrator speaks up for the first time, restoring harmony by tactfully assuring the Arabs that the kibbutz will conduct an inquiry and indemnify the ox owner in the event that one of their own is found responsible. During the traditional coffee drinking that follows the formal meeting, the conversation shifts from the momentary distraction of the ox controversy to the village's more pressing crisis of unemployment. Here the narrator receives an instructive economic and historical lesson in the contrast between earlier Arab prosperity and the straitened present from his official village host:

> When the British were here . . . people used to work in the fields or be employed as policemen or teachers, or else they had their own vehicles as a means of livelihood. They worked in peace and security, whereas today they don't. One day they work at Har-Or, the next day they run out of work, then they find a few days' employment with Herschel, the building contractor, which may last for a month or two. In short, they are looking for work nearly all the time. And how long can one be a builder? It's a murderous occupation—. (93)

Mansour knows that he doesn't need to account for the narrator's own internalization of these inequities; by this point, most readers will have imagined for themselves how such knowledge inevitably adds more layers to his guilt and mounting identity crisis. And for such readers, the narrator's growing disillusionment is compounded by the late revelation that he was drawn to this particular kibbutz because of its relative "innocence" in the Zionist project: "Its members had come to Israel after the War of Independence . . . they belonged to the left-wing party which was seeking a *rapprochement* with the Arabs" (129). Yet Yusuf's love for Rivkah keeps him from reaching what might seem to be an inevitable conclusion about his "place" in the world. After a strained period of remoteness, Rivkah tearfully reveals that she is pregnant. Mansour thus boldly ventures into the taboo issue of miscegenation between "Arabs" and "Jews," which has subsequently emerged as a pervasive theme in Jewish Israeli literature and cinema—famously in A. B. Yehoshua's novel *Hameahev* (*The Lover*; 1977).

When the clearly agonized Rikvah abruptly departs, her romantic and naive lover exultantly leaps onto a horse "and galloped toward the fields. . . . The cool air imbued me with a strange feeling of pride. I had given life to a new creature" (*In a New Light* 103), without a thought to spare for her marital complications. For a time, it seems to Yusuf that he does have a prospect of participating in the Zionist dream of fecundity and virile belonging. Yet that hope vanishes at their next meeting when Rivkah declares that she has told her husband "the whole truth" and that she intends to remain with him. For the besotted narrator, the rejection "was like a stream of fresh water gone with the desert mirage. . . . The earth would flourish again in the spring, whereas I had no hope" (108). In the final third of the novel, that incessant phrase—"the truth"—echoes like a guilty refrain. Soon after this incident, when confronted by Zelig, the kibbutz secretary, who demands "the truth" about his identity, "Yossi" slyly evades him by describing his previous sojourn in another Jewish community. At first, we are uncertain just what Zelig really knows or even suspects until the moment he declares simply, "You're not Jewish" (111), which "Yossi" nonchalantly concedes. Still, Yusuf's true identity goes unvoiced even as Zelig tells him: "We found an old man by the name of Mizrahi who claimed to have taken you in after your father was murdered and said that you had actually run away . . . with his daughter" (112). Like the ghost of Hamlet's father, like Sigmund Freud's "uncanny," the Palestinian father can simply not be put to rest.

When the kibbutz official alludes to receiving "a clearance from the Ministry of Defense" on the youth's behalf and assures him that the kibbutz movement itself "is extremely liberal in its views" (113), it isn't clear just what he knows or seeks. The delicate choreography of query and evasion between

Zelig and Yusuf continues until the moment the novel's enigmatic title is at last illuminated: "'Listen, we cannot propose a motion, accepting you, without knowing the whole truth. Give the kibbutz a chance to think it over, to see you in a new light, and then we shall be able to bring the matter before the general assembly—.' Of all this new speech only four words caught my ear: *In a new light*" (114). As "Yossi" lets the implications of this charged phrase settle between them, Zelig blusters on, offering placatory liberal rhetoric about the kibbutzniks wanting "peace with the Arabs" and about practicing "no discrimination," even as he builds toward a stark ultimatum: "We cannot ignore reality," which "Yossi" immediately understands as exposing his identity as an unalterable essence: "So that's it. I am *A-r-a-b*" (114), his inner voice proclaims. A moment later, Zelig utters the same: "You are an Arab, aren't you?" In the ears of "Yossi," Zelig sounds "as if he were cajoling a baby to mimic" his truth (115).

No sooner have the discriminatory implications of Zelig's concern settled in than "Yossi" responds with a stinging rebuke, which lays bare the hypocrisy behind the kibbutz's noble socialist rhetoric: "I was grateful to Zelig for having mentioned the future. Hadn't we all listened to his lofty speeches about the rosy future awaiting us all? . . . I started quoting from memory the highlights of his last lecture. I presented him with a verbal memorandum about the world revolution, the red flags that would soon be hoisted on the strongholds of the reactionary forces, the new cultural prosperity, the new type of humanity—" (115). In the wake of his rebuke, we realize that "Yossi" has probably never fully bought into the kibbutz's inflated self-image. His narrative voice grows increasingly distanced and ironic. For instance, when asked whether he wishes to stay, he says plainly, "I like it here," even as he admits to himself that this is "an unpremeditated lie," for he has come to believe that he remains only because he loves Rivkah (116). However, his desire to belong proves even more potent than his cynicism: not long after this exchange, the prospect that he might be regarded as "an unreliable alien" solely because of his Arab origins anguishes him deeply. Indeed, that "they were no different from me, yet they regarded me as a stranger" leaves him "racked by despair, alarm and a dead emptiness" (116).

At this low ebb, distraught upon discovering his ominous exclusion from the guard duty roster, the sight of Shlomo (slayer of the Arab village's ox), fills him with rage. Yossi Mizrahi/Yusuf Mahmud relishes what he anticipates will be a brutal but honest encounter with this racist, who alone seems capable of penetrating utopia's pretensions, who "wouldn't play the polite liar. He wouldn't stuff me with bedtime stories. . . . He would tell me in plain Hebrew:

'We are a frontier settlement and there is no place here for Arabs.' . . . Why should I go on giving them the pleasure of regarding themselves as good-hearted, progressive, benevolent? Shlomo could help me tear [away] their false mask. I was fed up with polite falsehoods, with sugar-coated sycophancies. By all means let Shlomo tell me point blank, 'WE HATE THE ARABS'" (119). And yet, strangely, the reckoning the narrator anticipates never arrives. The enemy he expected to confront is somehow replaced by a quiet and altogether amiable comrade who coaxes him to his room for coffee and conversation. "Yossi" is at first relieved to find himself treated sympathetically by such an unlikely host, only to learn that, against his comrades' wishes, Shlomo had taken it on himself to blow up the mosque of the deserted Arab village: "I told them this sanctimonious attitude didn't become a people who wanted to build their country" (123). Despite this abysmal act of erasure of another people's sacred life, history, and memory, it is a mark of the Arab novelist's essential empathy for his characters and respect for their complexity that he resists the temptation to portray Shlomo as a one-dimensional thug.

Like that of many of this kibbutz's American-born members, including Rivkah, Shlomo's immigration to Israel was motivated by the Holocaust: "We had to build our State on lands that had already been settled by another nation. We had no alternative whatsoever, except to go on living our rotten lives in Brooklyn, to wallow in a lagoon of Coca-Cola until the Americans decided to drown us in a sea of blood, the way it happened in Germany, Poland, Russia, etcetera" (123). Yusuf is grateful for his adversary's honesty and perhaps senses that, albeit for very different reasons, each of them is an outsider in kibbutz society. Eventually, they find a way to work together, stealthily conspiring to wean away the Arab village Nur-Allah from its political allegiance to their movement's nemesis, the Free Labor Party.

Back in his room, the young man's turmoil continues. Feeling himself under the gaze of an image of Stalin (this is in the days before the kibbutz movement broke away from its alliances with the Communist Eastern Bloc), he feels utterly unmanned not only by the icon's magnificent moustache but by Rivkah's husband and all the others who thwart his dream to assert what he perceives are his parental rights (though he still remains uncertain whether the child is even his). In his abject humiliation, he comforts himself that, though he now hates Rivkah, her pregnancy provides the vital "proof" he needs that he "was a man like anyone else" (126).[10] Like many exilic figures in literature, this protagonist is perpetually restless. And the depth of his turmoil is most clearly revealed when he wonders: "Perhaps I only loved myself, Yossi Mizrahi—sorry, Yusuf Mahmud" (126). However, it seems that Yusuf Mahmoud

THE KIBBUTZ AND ITS OTHERS　—✢　157

will prevail, for the more he thinks about it, the more he dreads the prospect
of having a son who "might grow up like Shlomo and lift his voice against his
own father. He wouldn't know that he was an Arab. I wouldn't be allowed to
live near him" (127). He vows that publicly he would call his son "Shalom,"
peace, but privately call him by the Arabic "Salaam."

At one point, the narrator's anguished reveries dredge up a troubling
memory of racism from his previous kibbutz sojourn. Here, anticipating the
postcolonial critique of Ella Shohat and others, who would point out that the
hegemony of Zionism (and indeed of the kibbutz) included internal Others,
Mansour has his narrator recall: "Our instructor, Yohannan, used to say, 'The
Arabs are a backward people.' Once a boy ventured to comment, 'They are like
the Sephardi Jews,' and Yohannan became very angry and retorted, 'No, no, a
thousand times more backward.' What if someone whispered to me that
Yohannan had taken offence because he was a Sephardi Jew himself? The
important thing was that *I* became ashamed and alarmed at the very idea that
somebody might say I looked like an Arab" (128). What is manifestly apparent
by now is that in Yusuf/Yossi's second attempt to make a home for himself
among the Jews, his identity in still in a state of chaos.

Obsessing over his Jewish lover's growing belly, the narrator bemoans his
alienated condition: "Everything appears in a new light. Even the vegetation
alongside the country lanes looks alien. My son will grow up among these
strange plants, yet he will feel that he belongs. I alone shall be a stranger to him"
(131). That estrangement grows when Rivkah, after coldly shunning him altogether, at last confronts him over his deception: "I am sorry for having trusted
you. . . . Haven't you lied to us for a whole year? How could you go on lying
throughout your life? . . . You have been standing on the stage playing a magnificent part and making fools of all of us" (135). In his defense, Yusuf bitterly
asserts that events caused him to be placed "on the stage from the day I was
born" and that he "must go on acting" to avoid falling off, which Rivkah rejects
as melodramatic self-indulgence. She, too, demands "the truth, the whole
truth," accuses him of being a traitor to his real people, and, in a crushing blow,
denies her pregnancy (135, 136). Some time passes before the two meet again, yet
on that occasion Rivkah's attitude softens considerably. Coaxed to join her on a
walk to the olive grove, Yusuf feels the "artificial stage of life" that has been
plaguing him in his sense of hypocritical performer both in the kibbutz and
Nur-Allah, overwhelmed by the beauty of the landscape and the love of his life:

> After a few steps she halted, seized my hand without uttering a word and
> pressed my fingers. Down in the valley a foggy cloud was emerging from

the woods and spreading into a hillside plantation. The sun-rays that caressed the fields broke up the cloud and dispersed it evenly upon the plateau like a wedding-dress. . . . She was standing still like some ancient goddess. I wanted to prostrate myself before her but found myself holding her in my arms. . . .

"I am tired of playing a part," I shouted. "I'll never go on the stage again. I am happy to be with you!"

We reached the . . . olive grove and lay down on the ground. Rivkah whispered in my ear, "*I love you.*" (146–47)

This sacred topocosm, the divine energy unifying all organic beings in time and space, the sense of the cosmic sanctification of their union—the mist resembles a "wedding-dress," the girl evokes an "ancient goddess"—encompasses even the fruit of their taboo union, as Rivkah exclaims to him that she wants "*your* child . . . swarthy like you" (147). Inevitably, the two must emerge from their pastoral idyll to face the extremely unlikely prospect that the kibbutz will ever accept an Arab. Rivkah suggests that they immediately take advantage of the advantageous political atmosphere leading up to the elections, when there is still "a certain value attached to slogans and promises" (148). In the end, he agrees and decides to confront Zelig to force the issue, to place the question of his membership before the secretariat and the general assembly. Yet, even when he does so, he uneasily recalls a fellow Arab who, when asked if he would ever join a kibbutz, replied simply, "It is an Arab's duty to stay with his people and help them" (166). Nevertheless, Yusuf soon finds himself directly making his own public plea for recognition (the secretariat votes not to take a position on his membership), while delicately acknowledging the matter of his "difference" to the members' assembly. His speech filled with brave rhetoric about loving "kibbutz life" and his desire "to cast my lot with the *avant-garde* of the Revolution" is made all the more poignant by his painful allusion to his father's unknowable end: "I would like to be a member of this kibbutz, the same as all of you. It is true that my parents did not fast on Yom Kippur or light candles on Chanukah, and I don't know what rituals they did observe. When I was five years old my father was killed. I don't know who killed him— it might have been the English, the Arabs or the Jews. . . . I heard good things about Har-Or and that's why I came here. I have been with you for a whole year" (171). His declaration concludes with the hopeful affirmation that if they only allow him the opportunity, he will prove to be "like any other member" (171), a hope immediately dashed by a bitter emotional outburst from Yehudah, Rivkah's recently estranged husband—"You are NOT like any other member!"

(171)—and the shrill demands by another member to know whether Yossi is a Jew or an Arab and what he really thinks about his identity. Yossi claims never to have known his parents, affirming that his documents indicate that he is a Jew. But this member, utterly dissatisfied, turns his back on the candidate and candidly insists that the lofty promise of kibbutz socialism is in fact separatist: "Comrades . . . we are facing a fundamental issue. It is true that we were brought up on the ideals of full equality between nations, but our primary duty is to serve as an *avant-garde* to our own people in their struggle for socialism. Yossi's place is not amongst us. He should live and fight with his own countrymen" (172). Fortunately, this naked expression of a separatist ethos is vehemently followed by the voices of other members, some of whom argue that, though Yossi may indeed not be a Jew, neither are the rest of them, at least not in any substantive sense. And Shlomo, of all people, quips, "Does any of you, Comrades, know that tonight is the eve of the Ninth of Av?" (172),[11] eliciting spontaneous laughter. Amid the ensuing commotion, Yossi leaps to his feet, shouting, "I shall try to bring up my children as human beings, not as Jews or Arabs" (173).

When a female comrade compares Yossi to an ostrich burying his head, Rivkah cannot keep silent any longer and rushes to his defense. Her protest penetrates to the heart of the deep crisis of Zionism and democracy that grows worse year by year: "National and racial divisions will continue indefinitely unless the people put an end to them" (174); she reminds the former Americans that many of them left the United States precisely because of racial animus and iniquities. As the tension in the room threatens to explode, Zelig proposes a compromise, one that eventually wins the day, yet he does so in terms that embitter Yusuf/Yossi. Even though Yossi has done nothing to cause offense, the secretary explains, the members are nevertheless "hemmed in by . . . unscrupulous attacks from right and left," and the kibbutz must not provide their political adversaries with any ammunition during the coming elections: "I [therefore] move that Yossi be accepted as a fully-fledged member, provided that nothing that has been said here will be put on record. The kibbutz will simply admit one more member, neither Jew nor Arab, and that's that" (175). Thus, in the end, Yusuf is allowed to stay, but at a price; the official kibbutz record of the deliberations will disregard the entire issue of his Arab identity. That dismays the increasingly restive Palestinian within the youth, forcing him, as it does, to live in the shadows, "stealthily, like a thief in the night" (176). Still, the narrative ultimately rests in an ambivalence that contains some hope, for he also gets the girl and even a cryptic hint from Rivkah that their biracial child, born of adultery and miscegenation, will prove redemptive, an agent of healing for the bifurcated land of Arabs and Jews: "I want your child.

. . . He will make the Revolution" (176).[12] Thus, at the novel's conclusion, Yusuf retains a faint, though somewhat ridiculous hope.

Even while noting that *In a New Light* ends on "an inconclusive and perhaps even pessimistic note," Rachel Feldhay Brenner affirms its resounding achievement: "For a brief moment the boundaries between the two peoples are removed, the definitions of victor and victim shift and lose their commonly accepted significations" (*Inextricably Bonded* 174).[13] For Israelis at least, the novel's prophetic allusiveness rests with how individual readers see their own identities and with how Israel's internal Others figure in their sense of national belonging. In his study of minority literature in Israel, Kayyal proposes that Mansour and the other Arab writers have inaugurated a "'third space.' . . . Within this space there has arisen a dynamic of attraction and repulsion, which leads to the blurring of boundaries and of the hierarchical relationships between ruler and ruled, and the creation of hybrid categories [that] bring together Orient and Occident, Arabism and Judaism, and Palestineness and Israeliness by means of processes of fusion and division that accompany the polar tension between the two sides" (34). Yet, considered today, the perpetual unease captured in Mansour's novel is certainly just as keenly felt by the Palestinian citizens of Israel, and it seems unlikely that the creative arts of hybridity will prevail over the politics of polarization.[14]

"My Father Sitting on an Empty Vegetable Crate Among Rubbish and Rotting Oranges": Youth Aliya and Mizrahi Dissonance in Eli Amir's *Scapegoat*

Though Israel is a nation built on waves of immigrants, including a tremendous influx from Iraq and North Africa, only rarely has its history of immigration been examined in relation to the kibbutz movement. A novel that does just that is Eli Amir's *Tarnegol kaparot* (*Scapegoat*; 1983), an Israeli best seller adapted for the stage as well as television but little known abroad, despite its availability in an exceptionally lively English translation. And that is regrettable because *Scapegoat* is one of the most highly entertaining and exuberant coming-of-age stories in the entire Israeli literary canon. With great psychological depth and insight, this picaresque novel by a writer who arrived in Israel as a young man and immersed himself in Hebrew, also offers readers a fascinating window into the cultural upheaval experienced by immigrant youngsters and their families as they struggled to adapt.[15] Most unusually, this semiautobiographical work examines a history little known to many Israelis: that of the newly arrived Arab youths who were sent off to live on kibbutzim under the auspices of Youth Aliya.[16]

That encounter proved difficult for kibbutzniks and newcomers alike, and in his introduction to the book's English translation, President Shimon Peres quietly observes that "reverberations of this confrontation are still heard in Israel even today" (*Scapegoat* 6). Much earlier, in one of her famous "Levantine" essays of the 1950s, Jacqueline Kahanoff decried the condescending, paternalistic, and hypocritical attitude of the dominant culture toward these newcomers:

> The Ashkenazi community in Israel, in identifying itself completely with the struggles leading to the establishment of the state, considered the state as its child. It is now imprisoned by a kind of parent complex, aggrieved when the child is growing up asserts its independence. Were it more firmly assured of its accomplishments, its attitude would be more rational and less emotional, and more understanding of the growing pains of another, newer section of the population. The perpetual bragging about the sacrifices of the pioneering generation, whom the newcomer sees living quite comfortably as an upper class in spite of the Socialist trappings, makes the latecomers feel not so much deficient and guilty, but resentful. (204)

A recent immigrant from Egypt herself, Kahanoff directly observed the clashing contact zones of Zionist socialism in those distant days. Jews arriving in Israel from the Arab world were often unprepared for the paternalistic hierarchy that awaited them. As Esther Benbassa and Jean-Christophe Attias explain:

> Israel, the country whose mission was to gather all the exiled together in a unified nation, created still more exiles within its borders. Each diaspora settled into its own particularism on this promised land of reunification. . . . The milk and honey of the dreamt-of promised land did not flow with the same abundance for everyone. . . . Exclusion grew out of [the] conflation of the Easterner with the Arab: exclusion from the camp of the privileged, the educated, the Westerners, of those who had inherited the benefits of "civilization." A kind of colonial view of the situation relegated the Easterners to the world of the "barbarians." (104)

Throughout the 1940s and early 1950s, when this ethos proved most consequential, several thousand young Iraqi immigrants were channeled to the communities of Hakibbutz Hameuchad (United Kibbutz Movement).[17]

By way of contrast, it is worth reviewing Eldad Kedem and Gilad Padva's discussion of the kibbutz cinema of the 1950s and early 1960s, wherein "the construction of a common denominator on the frontier is manifested by the socialization of the newcomer into the combat unit and the kibbutz, a metonym of their assimilation and subordination to the symbolic order of the State" (179). Kedem and Padva identify this dynamic in three representative films, Amram Amar's *Hafuga* (*Ceasefire*; 1950), Ze'ev Havatzelet's *Havurah she'kazot* (*What a Gang!*; 1962), and Menahem Golan's *Shmonah be'l'kvot ehad* (*Eight Against One*; 1964): "The Oriental (i.e., Sephardi or Mizrahi or Yemenite) protagonist in *Ceasefire* is a kibbutz member and a Palmach combatant who eventually returns to the kibbutz. The recruited bunch in *What a Gang!* and the children's group in *Eight Against One* absorb and educate an immigrant of Oriental Jewish origins who becomes an integral part of the group/kibbutz" (179). As we will see, the reality beneath the one depicted by these hopeful and sentimental films was quite different.

Once in the kibbutzim, as Esther Meir-Glitzenstein explains, the Mizrahi youths were doctrinally immersed in the Labor Movement's "emphasis on self-labor and a communal living framework"; they were encouraged to regard themselves as "the vanguard whose duty was to be the bridgehead for absorbing the mass immigration from Iraq . . . by establishing kibbutzim—in which, so they believed, the members of their families and other immigrants would find their place" (85).[18] In the end, however, this attempt at socialist resettlement, so radically different from anything the young Arabs or their families had ever known, did not succeed; by the middle of the 1950s, few remained:

> Despite their education toward life in the kibbutz and their basic willingness to change and adapt . . . the immigrants found it difficult to understand the complexity of kibbutz society and to decode the set of internal symbols that molded it. The shift from a closed, hierarchical family structure, in which each member had a set, clear role and standing, to the more open and egalitarian kibbutz framework, whose internal hierarchy was not unequivocal nor obvious, stimulated great admiration along with astonishment and confusion. (92)

> The gap between the cultural, social, and ideological world of the kibbutz and the world of the Zionist immigrants from Iraq could not be bridged. (97)[19]

Bearing eloquent witness to that confusion and destabilization, *Scapegoat* fittingly begins with an immediate sense of temporal and spatial displacement when Nuri, its teenage narrator, first glimpses the Carmel mountainside from the window of the bus that has only just removed him from his family, who are living in a ma'abara, or immigrant transit camp. Vaguely resembling familiar pictures of the Holy Land, what he sees momentarily calms him.[20] But, bewildered by the low status to which his once proud father has fallen in the Jewish "homeland" and frightened by the unknown life that awaits him, the forlorn youth quickly disengages from his surroundings, as his imagination brings forth a surge of memories from his childhood in Baghdad:

> Scene after scene flashed past my eyes but only one kept coming back: my father on the big bridge across the Tigris wearing his blue suit with the eternal white rose in the buttonhole of his lapel, and how different now, my God, sitting on an empty vegetable crate in the khaki tent among the piles of rubbish and rotting oranges, trying in vain to understand what was happening, his shirt unbuttoned, wearing the same blue trousers which suddenly seemed too big for his body, staring into space with only the clicking of the amber beads slipping through his fingers providing some sort of sign that he was still alive. I fumbled with my rucksack with a sacrilegious thought running through my mind: Why hadn't we stayed in Baghdad? And what was going to happen to me now? Out of the blue—a kibbutz. . . . And now I was being sent there, alone and already I was full of longings for my family and a wild desire to run back to them. . . . The only time I had ever left home in Baghdad was to go on a school excursion to Nineveh to see the antiquities. (10)

This passage, culminating as it does in the allusion to ancient ruins, quietly but unmistakably underscores the centuries-old rootedness of Mizrahim in the Middle East. But in much of what follows, Amir places the emphasis on the marginalization of Mizrahi Jews in the rigorously Eurocentric, socialist society with its aggressive absorption schemes, beginning with its humiliating DDT-doused reception of the newcomers at Lydda (Lod) Airport. The first occasion that Nuri joins in a sing-along, he wonders plaintively whether the "Israeli songs, foreign to heart and ear," will "ever be mine"? (13). Soon after arriving in the "Ahuza Immigrant Youth Transit Camp" (from where they are sent off to various kibbutzim), he endures a hazing in the form of the theft of his belongings and a subsequent beating when he protests.

As the other youths depart for the evening's cultural activity, Nuri remains behind to nurse his wounds, attended by fourteen-year-old Buzaglo, a recent immigrant from Morocco. Buzaglo's oldest brother arrived before the rest of the family and fought heroically in the War of Independence, but now his nine other siblings still languish in the ma'abara, as does his father, who had been a goldsmith at home in Morocco. Only his mother is a source of pride in the new land. Amir's translator, Dalia Bilu, takes great pains to portray Buzaglo's North African–accented Hebrew, which comes across as a lisp: "The'th [she's] going to get the Ben-Gurion prize—one hundred poundth! One hundred poundth!" (15).[21] Despite the comic overtones of Buzaglo's prideful lisping, its ironic force is profound: if the Mizrahim of the ma'abara are valued by their new society, it is for their reproductive capability and not for their cultural heritage or other intrinsic values.[22] Though Amir's novel doesn't dwell on the miseries of life in the ma'abara (perhaps reflecting his painful memories of those days), it is clearly a traumatic presence in the recent memories of his young characters. As Amy Horowitz explains, the "North African and Middle Eastern immigrants in the ma'abarot experienced profound culture shock. Lacking their former communal structures, Middle Eastern and North African immigrants came to form a pan-ethnic or Mizrahi subclass" (42). After his initial sense of injustice, Nuri's desire to flee and make his way back to his family is exacerbated by a fleeting encounter with a sexual predator. But Buzaglo catches up with him on the road outside the camp. Both are religious youths who have already prayed together, and the Moroccan's logic, drawing on his reading of the Book of Exodus, strikes a chord with the narrator: "I'll tell you thomething about the ma'abara. It'th like Motheth in the dethert. They'll all die there. You want to die?" (Scapegoat 18). This palpable sense of an impossible return and a sacred destiny always resides just beneath the surface of Amir's subsequent portrayals of the myriad painful readjustments made by the protagonist and his peers.

The pair rejoin the other youths, who have been gathered together to participate in an Israeli folk dance. Nuri is alarmed that even the girls have had their heads shaved, on suspicion that they harbor vermin—though one boy asserts that his mother "worked in the community clinic in Baghdad and she can't see any reason for shaving our heads" (20). Nuri is suddenly aware of how polyglot and multicultural the camp has become. He feels intimidated by the cultural sophistication of the newcomers from France and by the general babel of Polish, Romanian, and Yiddish he cannot understand. But within this microcosm (which closely resembles the growing cultural complexity of the larger society), he is relieved to discover "a whole hut full" of fellow Iraqis who welcome his dim view of the North Africans in the camp: "They're good for nothing but wagging their backsides and beating people up" (20). Of course, each population of young people carries with it the baggage of ethnic stereotypes; the Iraqis learn that they are viewed by all the others as "black-faced simpletons who can't dance, can't sing, and never hit back" (21). But the Iraqis have a distinct advantage in the guise of "Mister World Chest," a heavily muscled Iraqi Kurd who serves as their amiable Samson, "bending iron bars with flashing eyes" each evening for the entire camp's entertainment (22).

Days pass as the camp's young ethnic Oriental "inmates" come and go. Bored by the once alluring spectacle of the evening folk dance, repelled by the bland diet, and beset with homesickness, the narrator worries whether his turn to be sent to a kibbutz will ever come. Whereas some of the youths fill their time with amorous escapades in the nearby woods, Nuri's close friend Buzaglo seems to vanish into himself and memories of his distant homeland, "fingering his beads for hours at a time, utterly serene, singing dreamily . . . in a strange Moroccan dialect" (26). The monotony is relieved only by occasional tensions flaring up between the young people and the camp's authorities. The flagrant use of ethnic slurs and stereotypes among the inmates themselves seems largely benign—an "equal-opportunity" affair that levels the playing field and tends to calm rather than exacerbate serious tensions. But things take a turn for the worse the day Mister World Chest's mother arrives unannounced, wearing the dress and golden bracelets of her native Kurdish culture. When the officious Ashkenazi gatekeeper calls her a "dirty Asiatic!" (28)[23] and refuses to admit her, Mister World Chest throws him to the ground. Further violence is averted, however, by the arrival of "Aunt Olga," who shrieks at the gatekeeper in Yiddish and opens the gate to let the Kurdish woman and the others waiting into the camp. Although we immediately understand that Olga (who works in the camp kitchen) is a Holocaust survivor, the narrator is confused by the number tattooed on her arm. He pesters the barber until he finally learns what it means and what happened to all of Olga's children in Auschwitz. When the gatekeeper later conspires to have the Holocaust refugee dismissed, the young people organize a protest on her behalf and eventually prevail.

This triumphant display of collective will later proves a valuable precedent for the protagonist and his peers in their struggles against what they perceive as Ashkenazi injustice. In the meantime, ennui settles over the camp once more; the narrator grows increasingly frustrated as trucks filled with other young people drive past the camp on their tantalizing way to the kibbutzim. Although he wants more than anything else to be chosen by the kibbutz representatives who arrive every day, the narrator nevertheless doesn't quite grasp just what a kibbutz really is: "All I knew was that HaKibbutz HaMeuhad—'The United Kibbutz Movement'—was one big kibbutz where everyone was united; that on the kibbutzim of HaShomer Hatzair—'The Young Guard'—everyone was young, and on guard all the time; and that Ihud HaKibbutzim v'HaKvutzoth—'The Union of Kibbutzim and Kvutzoth'—was both things together" (33). He does learn that some kibbutzim are more desirable than others, as "mysterious lists of obscure origin" with those alluring names are furtively passed from hand to hand. The youths all hope to be sent to the prosperous and established settlements (since those mean better living conditions), and, indeed, whenever representatives arrived from "a remote or border kibbutz," they "would take off . . . like a flock of frightened birds" (34). Yet when Nuri realizes that only he and four others remain from those he arrived with and that, aside from Moroccan-born Buzaglo, they all happen to be Iraqis, he marches into the office to demand justice: "Have the Iraqis got a special place in the queue—last?" (34). The Youth Aliyah counselor tries to placate him with lofty rhetoric about patience as well as "group consolidation and cohesion and suitability and frameworks" (35), to no avail. Finally, the day arrives when the boys learn they are selected for the "big, rich, established" (fictional) Kibbutz Kiryat-Oranim (35).

Though all of the youths are eager to be chosen, they only have a fragmentary sense of what a kibbutz is all about: "'Everybody equal, they're all the same, they eat the same, do the same things.' . . . 'A kibbutz is a big house where everybody lives together.' 'Everybody in one house? Boys and girls?'" (40). "Never," vows one scandalized girl, who seems to speak for all the other female comrades. Deeply embarrassed, the girls break into the reassuring lyrics of a youth movement song: "I'm from Morocco and you're from Iraq and we're all in Israel. I'm from Romania and you're from Poland and we're all protected by the God of Israel" (40). But that carefree melting-pot balm cannot quite soothe their anxiety over sordid rumors of what lies ahead for them (reports of cultural taboos such as mixed living quarters are especially troubling), and they all lapse into a foreboding silence, save for a young man named Masul, whose sad voice fills that silence with a distinctly mournful threnody of longing and displacement:

> *Ya hali al-thullam hinu alayya . . .*
> Oh my cruel family,
> Why have you sent me into distant exile? (41)

Like Nuri's, Masul's father enjoyed greater prestige in his native Baghdad (as a lawyer), but he, too, remains in the ma'abara, relegated to menial labor. Masul's song clearly expresses the narrator's own anxieties: he doesn't understand why he is being told that the kibbutz is his "new family," and whether this means it is supposed to replace his mother and father (41). As the truck carrying the five youths winds its way through Haifa, he desperately looks for anything that will remind him of his beloved Baghdad.[24]

In the novel's early sections, Amir vividly captures the mixed trepidation and joy experienced by many young immigrants in Israel. When their transport truck arrives at Kibbutz Kiryat-Oranim, the youths are giddy with excitement. The protagonist, who in the early days of the narrative, spends much of his time plaintively searching for any signs in the human or natural landscape that evoke his homeland, is pleased to glimpse date palm trees just like those in his native land. All too soon, however, that sense of the familiar is pushed aside by the sight of an austere fortress encircled by barbed wire: "Not a street, not a shop, no café smells, no hawker's shouts" (42). As the youths clamber excitedly down from the truck and begin to explore their new surroundings, Amir stresses their outsider status though their Hebrew, richly laden with Arabic expressions. But it is their first encounter with a kibbutznik that really drives the point home. Thrilled to discover a *gauja* (plum) tree, the youths fall upon it and ravenously devour its fruit, ignoring the angry shouts of "Animals! Animals!," which are the first words anyone says to them on the kibbutz (42). Immediately, they are assigned two minders, doctrinaire counselors named Sonia and Yishai, whose role it is to mediate between the unruly youths and the orderly kibbutz society.[25]

Their excited questions of the welcoming staff give rise to a stunning discovery: their new home has no synagogue—"'God of the Universe, what kind of people have we landed among?' lament[s] the rabbi's son" (44). Even as the children struggle to understand what it might mean to live in a community of Jews without a synagogue, they are further dismayed to learn that the names their parents gave them are somehow deemed unsuitable for life in the Jewish homeland. Ofer, their official kibbutz liaison, calls off their names from his list and, as they answer, he instantly fires back their new Hebrew names, the classic Zionist remedy of erasing the unwelcome lingering vestiges of Diaspora in constructing the New Jew. Abed el-Aziz, the rabbi's son, is rapidly transformed into "Avner," Fawzia is designated "Ilana," Jamil becomes "Yoram," and so on. Only Nuri stubbornly refuses to accept the new name chosen for him— "Nimrod" (44).[26]

The notion of Hebraizing or otherwise rejecting one's original name is familiar to many who choose to immigrate to Israel, but, in the case of these youths, that decision has already been made for them—one youth intervenes before his name is called, haughtily informing one and all that, henceforth, he will answer only to the name "Herzl, the father of the state" (44). Perhaps because their renaming is accomplished so rapidly, the children barely process what has happened and are otherwise distracted by being introduced to their living quarters, where the narrator rejoices to discover that, for the first time since leaving Baghdad, he will live in a real room with electric lights rather than a tent lit by a smoky kerosene lamp. Yet, unexpectedly, amid and perhaps because of these comforts, Nuri feels himself weighed down by sadness and guilt, haunted by his father's face: "Mute and accusing. . . . I saw him standing like a beggar" (45). In the coming hours and days, there are so many wrenching adjustments to make—collective showers, living quarters that cannot be locked—that Nuri and his friends have little time to think of the families they have been forced to leave behind. And when they confuse the underwear they have been issued with outdoor sportswear, it causes a minor scandal.

Nuri and his friends are both hurt and enraged to find themselves repeatedly dismissed as "savages," "Asiatics," or "primitives"—as if Baghdad was not then perhaps the most cosmopolitan and sophisticated city in the Middle East. Even in his dreams, Nuri is uneasily stirred by memories of his father's humiliation back in the ma'abara at the hands of a haughty Pole who cursed him and refused to let him listen to the *Voice of Israel* Arabic news program on the camp's sole radio. The next morning, Nuri wakes up shaken by a nightmare in which he wreaks vengeance on his father's tormentor. By the end of their first day of working on the kibbutz, the young people are in a rebellious mood, having been put to tasks, such as shoveling manure in the cowshed, which they regard as demeaning, but which are merely routine labors in kibbutz life: "From the thit of the *ma'abara* to the thit of the kibbuth," Buzaglo lisps in scorn (63).

Through the coming days, the youths continue to pine for their parents, but the kibbutz strongly discourages family visits. When at last the visits do take place, the youths feel a sense of shame over their parents' appearance: "The visitors were conspicuous in their strange clothes, and we knew that the kibbutz members felt awkward with them and with us too, and we were torn between two worlds" (60). Some of the young people are abruptly removed by parents discomfited by the "outlandish" nature of kibbutz life or shocked and dismayed to find their daughters' thighs casually bared to all. Here, too, *Scapegoat*'s representations reflect the historical reality described by Meir-Glitzenstein: "The secular, permissive kibbutz lifestyle drew criticism and opposition from the parents of some of the HakhshHarah [agricultural preparation] girls. These parents . . . suggested or demanded that the young women join them in the city—anything so they should not continue to live in a framework that shook the foundations of traditional life" (95). As for the young women themselves, their revealing kibbutz shorts "troubled and confused" those "who, on the one hand, wanted with all their might to look like kibbutz members, and yet, on the other, were aghast at the extreme abrogation of the rules of modesty in which they had been raised" (93).[27] Nevertheless, many of the youths choose to remain, including the protagonist, who is enticed into shoveling the reviled manure by the promise of being taught to ride a thoroughbred Arabian horse. Dolek, who abandoned his studies in chemistry back in Warsaw and who now spends his days collecting and treating manure, lectures Nuri on the strange tenets of classic labor Zionism—"Too many merchants, too many members of the liberal professions. . . . In Eretz Yisrael we need farmers, workers" (66). Under Dolek's warm and approving gaze, Nuri takes some degree of pleasure in pouring all his energy into work. On the other hand, even though he sees the necessity of the work, he is confused by Dolek's insistence that he also take pride in being the "assistant manure-man"; when Nuri writes his father, he claims to be working as a garage mechanic instead. Even though never fully enamored of this starry-eyed idealist's rhetoric ("the righting of the inverted pyramid and the creation of a broad base of workers and peasants instead of the top-heavy structure of middlemen which existed in the diaspora"), he is impressed by Dolek's passion: "The look in his eyes was clear and direct, the look of a man whose awareness was profound . . . whose faith was perfect" (144).

Though the newcomers are encouraged to forge friendships with the kibbutz youths at the regional school, they hold back, "shy, embarrassed, mute, like country bumpkins on a visit to the metropolis" (69), excruciatingly self-conscious of their otherness. Gazing at the strong, proud, and tanned natives, whose Hebrew "ran easily and surely off their tongues, with a different rhythm," they are immediately cowed (70). One of Nuri's friends whispers in awe, "Walad Allah—the children of God," and Nuri himself is struck by the disheartening contrast between his friends, "a lost herd, straying in alien pastures without a shepherd," and the Sabras, so confidently rooted in their environment. "The children of God indeed," he muses. "And why not? It was their home, after all. Here they had taken their first breath, imbibed their Hebrew with their mother's milk, here, in this earth, they had put down their roots, they had leapt upon its rocks and galloped over its fields. It was all theirs" (70).[28] This reverie seems as poignant an expression of displacement and envy of those who never have to question their entitlement as any immigrant has ever expressed.

Though it is the task of the "regionals" to successfully acculturate and indoctrinate the youths from the ma'abarot, like so many immigrants in other times and places struggling between worlds, between disparate ways of being, Nuri and his friends naturally rebel against the Sabras' condescension: "Their efforts to teach us how to behave, what to sing, how to dance, what to read and how to be different from what we were imposed a strain on us. . . . They tried to provide us with ready-made identities, which we were supposed to put on like a new suit of clothes in order to be like them. We had, indeed, shed our old clothes, but the new ones were too new, as uncomfortable as brand new shoes" (72). The immigrant youths are overwhelmed by the lofty slogans inscribed on huge cloth banners—"Work and Pioneering," "Patriotism and Equality," and "The Integration of the Exiles"—that accompany them everywhere they go and by the portraits of Stalin (who the youths assume must be the heretical movement's prophet, or even God) that adorn all the public buildings. The ponderous slogans remind Nuri of "the texts of the Koran which decorated public buildings, government offices, cafes and clubs in Baghdad" (123). Throughout the novel, Amir artfully captures the Mizrahi youths' first exposure to a bewildering plethora of exotic phenomena such as May Day, clearly the "holiest" day on the socialists' secular calendar. Though nobody has offered them a clear explanation of the doctrine that underlies the workers' holiday, they are nonetheless compelled to participate in an urban May Day demonstration. Yet even those external pressures do not always result in group solidarity among the youths, taken aback by how quickly they have become divided into "those of us who had decided to adjust ourselves to our new surroundings, and those who had been thrown off balance by the difficulties of the transition. The first group had already begun speaking Hebrew among themselves. The second argued that even the kibbutz members sometimes spoke Polish to each other, that Arabic was just as good as Polish, besides being closer to Hebrew, and that they would 'show them.' The truth, alas, was different. It was hard for them to learn the language" (77), and their linguistic affinities were fragmenting the group's internal cohesion. As time passes, the protagonist and his friends grow intensely homesick and demand "home leave" to visit their families. Nuri boldly drafts a manifesto to the general membership—"We, the Iraqi youth group on Kiryat-Oranim, request to be given home leave once a month. We're not used to being away from home. We miss our families very much" (92)—which infuriates their counselors, Sonia and Yishai. Amir's portrayal of Nuri's terse confrontation with those figures vividly reveals the intransigence on both sides: "'We want to go home,' I said. 'Your home is here,' said Sonia. 'Our home is in the ma'abara,' I insisted. . . . 'You're instigating a revolt,' said Sonia sternly, 'and you're acting against your own best interests. . . . It's not enough to be a citizen of this country in order to be integrated into it'" (93). The Zionist youth leaders wish to curtail family visits altogether. Sonia tells Nuri and his friends that such visits amount to cultural regression: "After every trip to the *ma'abara* all our work here is undermined." An ardent proponent of the melting pot theory of citizenship, she declares, "I too discarded the old world I came from and put it behind me and you'll discard it too, and in the end it will be for your own good" (93). Here it is worth pausing to note here the irony that Kahanoff directly observed in the 1950s: "The kibbutz is definitely not proletarian compared with the *ma'abara*. Its members know where the next meal comes from and represent, paradoxically, a conservative force which defends the status quo" (205). Thinking that he is acting with the full support of the group, Nuri continues to demand the right to home leave. When at last he learns that his friends have been thoroughly cowed by Sonia, he feels utterly abandoned and retreats to his room in despair. In the coming days, bitter and lonely, he waits for the kibbutz to exile him permanently to the ma'abara as an unfit citizen.

Yet, back at work filling the manure carts, he is welcomed by Dolek, who regales him with ardent tales of early Zionist glory: "the second and third waves of immigration . . . dancing the hora until dawn, bitter ideological arguments, malaria and fights with the Arabs about living in tents, hunger and back-breaking work and pride, selflessness and the exhilarating feeling that they were building a homeland, a nation, with their own hands" (95). Nuri finds Dolek's stories as "extraordinary as the Arabian Nights," though whenever he is again alone in his room, they "fade and wither like flowers in the burning sun" (95). Nuri grows greatly conflicted over the power of an epic story that seems to both claim and exclude him, which causes him to feel a strange resentment toward his father, languishing in the ma'abara. On his solitary night walks in the silence of a pine forest, Israel's founding drama "came back to haunt me, poignant and frustrating. . . . In spite of myself I compared Dolek to my father. Although I loved my father very much I had a certain buried resentment towards him. I would never be able to take pride in him and say, like the 'regionals': 'My father began all this, he was one of the founders'" (95). Fearing he will be expelled, Nuri sometimes imagines himself taking his friends from the ma'abara to establish a kibbutz in the empty Negev. As soon as it becomes a flourishing oasis, he will take "revenge" by inviting the kibbutzniks who disdained him to visit.

At other times, his imagination resurrects his beloved hammock in his Baghdad home: "I would sink into the pile of bright cushions, doze off to the monotonous creaking of the hammock, and breathe the cool air into my lungs" (96). Thus he drifts between dreams of rebirth and rootedness, on the one hand,

and origins and Diasporic longing, on the other, while the kibbutz youth leaders remain coldly aloof from him, "as silent as Trappist monks" (96), his sense of exclusion and dispossession from the two worlds rapidly intensifies. He envies the "princes of the valley," the native kibbutz youths: "They were the new and I was the old, they the redemption and I the diaspora. I wanted to be like them, a new man, and I was neither one nor the other. . . . I was neither here nor there, a drifting plant in a no-man's land" (125). Though once he swore that he would take root in the kibbutz, Nuri fears that he will only feel at home in the ma'abara. At best, though still a young man, he can only hope that his future children will be counted as true "regionals" and fully belong. Yet even when he is nearly heartbroken, he cannot resist the seductions of utopia. While climbing the kibbutz water tower one day, he is assailed by the unadorned beauty of his surroundings. Like each of the other writers in this study, Amir conveys the artfully blended surfaces of engineered community and pastoralism that allured so many, as his lonely protagonist examines the source of his tormented journey to belonging, from high above:

> Mesmerized I watched the sun rising in the east like a floating ball in the milky morning mists, and when the mist cleared I saw the fields like a chequerboard of squares in different shapes and shades, from dark brown to brilliant green. In the distance the orchard looked like one vast tree spreading its branches for mile after mile, and close to the tower the palm fronds rustled in the breeze. . . . Among the trees, lining the kibbutz paths, were beds of bright flowers whose names I did not know, but whose scents filled me with an intoxication which was at once soporific and stimulating. (97)

Gazing at this panorama from the water tower becomes a comforting morning ritual; the "magical dawn world" (97) gradually softens his sense of grievance and resistance. Here the novel's thrust is perhaps at its most assimilationist.[29] The day arrives when Nuri awakens to the realization that he is, in spite of everything, at home: "A new love, whose like I had never known, gushed out of me for every plant, flower, and tree. . . . A love for this valley which had become my land, my country" (96). The ideologue A. D. Gordon could not have hoped for better human material for his pantheistic vision of organic Zionism than this rhapsodically smitten Iraqi youth. Even Nuri's outrage over Ashkenazi bias and the kibbutzniks' failure to uphold true egalitarianism pales alongside these fierce attachments: "From the heights of the water-tower all our complaints paled into insignificance—the food, the work and even the struggle for full equality. . . . The valley was freedom, and it was ours no less than theirs" (98). Soon his "holiday revolt" begins to fade from memory, and, as Sonia warmly reaches out to him, he feels that "the sword of expulsion had been removed" (98). Yet the sense of the kibbutz's pervasive prejudice endures; he and his friends are constantly viewed by the kibbutz members as a racialized group of primitives, never as individuals: "In their eyes we were all the same, as if we had no private names or individual identities and every slip by one of us was a bad mark against us all" (103). Moreover, even when the Mizrahi youths make a sincere effort to show their enthusiasm for learning about European Jewish heritage by portraying a Galician Hassidic court, they are ridiculed during their performance. Stung by the roars of laughter over their Kurdish accents, the youth named Masul persuades the group to turn the tables by creating a musical play entirely in Arabic (to be performed with Middle Eastern instruments) that will not only immerse the kibbutzniks in their Mizrahi culture but will clearly demonstrate their people's own sacrifices for Zionism.

Masul's play concerns the exploits of a young Iraqi Jew from Basra who pays a Bedouin to lead him through the desert to Eretz Yisrael, which he successfully reaches, only to be killed shortly thereafter in the War of Independence. Although the play seems utterly inoffensive, Nuri frets over the kibbutz's response to its exotic materials until a compromise is reached that incorporates familiar Israeli folk dances. In the end, however, nobody from the kibbutz attends their performance. Yet, rather than allow themselves to be demoralized, they hold a *hafla* (Middle Eastern dance party) featuring love songs accompanied by Arab drums and lutes. Rather than drawing the kibbutz into their world, the celebration affirms their own culture enclave within, their proud connection to their origins: "The party was a great success and redeemed us from our disgrace, if not in the eyes of others, then at least in our own eyes. And that meant a lot. On the following nights too we celebrated, catching fire as if we had withdrawn from the kibbutz into another world, the world from which we had come. With flushed faces and dreamy eyes, yearning for a distant and forgotten way of life, we were swept away on the currents of sound" (115). Although their musical celebrations rapidly become an evening ritual of consolation, the kibbutzniks, even the younger ones, coolly maintain their distance. Once, after an outburst of ululations and cheering, they overhear the Sabras' scornful judgment, just outside their window: "We wanted to turn them into human beings and just listen to them: howling like a pack of jackals" (118).[30] Confronted by their kibbutz "comrades," who sneer at their "Arab café" and "caterwauling," their high spirits collapse. Yet Nuri and his friends persist, perhaps because the kibbutz has never truly welcomed them and there is no alternative: "I felt the need, like all my friends, to huddle close together, and the deeper [they] stuck their daggers into our flesh the more we stuck together in our *haflas*. It was a time of consolidation. We closed ranks and doors, we became a tight, defiant group" (119). When all the community seems aligned against them, their kibbutz youth leaders rush to their defense and, turning "white with anger," Sonia confronts their worst persecutor: "You won't insult them or the Arabs either. What do you mean 'bloody Arabs'? Is that what you learnt in the movement?" (120–21). Undefeated, Nuri and his friends stubbornly sing the plaintive lyrics of their Arab homelands—"Wahshit baladi nar / A burning fire is my longing for my motherland / Oh, my sad and lonely soul" (120)—drumming their "wild rhythm" into the night.[31] Yet the next day, Sonia delivers a stern lecture to the young Mizrahim about the imperative to assimilate and to leave their origins behind. She insists that there is no hatred for Baghdad, that her movement demands equality and cooperation between Arabs and Jews. Yet, in the end, she leaves no doubt just where things stand for the youths. Their new life is a revolution in progress, and they must participate by assimilating and embracing new identities:

> There's simply no room in our lives here for Baghdad or for the way of life in the Jewish *shtetl* of Eastern Europe either. We came to this country because we rebelled against that way of life. Zionism is a revolt, a revolution, and every revolution has a price. . . . Do you think we didn't suffer the infantile diseases of cultural adjustment ourselves? Didn't we try to imitate the lifestyle of the East when we first came here? I told you about the mounted guards of HaShomer who wore *abbayehs* and Circassian hats. Didn't they put up Bedouin tents and try to imitate the Bedouin way of life? And it was precisely the HaShomer people who fascinated us in Poland. We didn't bring Poland here with us, and you're not going to bring Iraq with you either. We cast the yoke off our necks for the sake of the future, and that is your mission too. We rebelled against our parents. (121)

Sonia softens the impression of outright rejection by reassuring them that Jewish European musicians have sought to incorporate "the colors of the Orient" (122); she even professes admiration for Masul's craft with the lute. But her condescension is palpable when she warns Masul that he must ultimately embrace Western aesthetics and its tradition of "musical geniuses"; indeed, he must relinquish his heritage and embrace the new (122).

Quite late in the novel, we learn that another ma'abara (not the one where Nuri's family lives), a "remote and lonely island," is actually only an hour away from the kibbutz by foot. Sometimes the youths approach it during their premilitary training runs (Gadna), but they prefer to turn their backs on it. As with other characters we have encountered, being reborn as new creatures is not easy:

> The dark side of our lives. The nightmares from which we tried to escape. The dirt, the hunger and all the rest. . . . Quickly, quickly back to the kibbutz. All we wanted was not to smell its smells, not to know that it existed. But it was in our souls. It looked down on us from its hill as we ran along the road, taking its revenge on us simply by being there, breathing down our necks, refusing to let go, so far away and yet so powerful, drawing us towards it again and again. But something even stronger held us back and prevented us from crossing the area of ambivalence separating it from the kibbutz. (157)

In a development strikingly similar to the plot of Mansour's *In a New Light*, the kibbutz prepares to send liaison delegations to penetrate the "primitive" world of the Others. On previous occasions, the kibbutz met with failure when it sent its own party leaders as ambassadors into the ma'abara, but now they are set on sending its own "insiders" to penetrate and overcome its obstinacy: "The movement decided to conquer it. One of the party leaders announced: 'We must take the movement into the ma'abara.' . . . The ma'abara stood threatening and obscure, wretched and rejected, a blot on the pure souls of the kibbutz members" (*Scapegoat* 157). Naturally, Nuri is selected for the mission, but, utterly dismayed by the prospect of patronizing his "relatives . . . neighbors, teachers who had come down in the world, human beings who had lost everything" (160), he stubbornly resists serving as their political lackey. Instead, he proposes that, if they truly want him to serve as a movement leader, he will happily do so in the regional school. But, in the end, he humbly resigns himself to the fate decreed by the "Ineffable" (160). Nuri's reluctant journey back to his origins produces the kind of acute psychic conflict endured by Mansour's young hero in similar circumstances—the necessity and impossibility of synthesis. In this scene, Nuri ironically contemplates the encampment's hopeless condition in the wake of the Labor Party's cynical manipulation of the impoverished inhabitants' faint hopes:

> A few solitary cypresses rose into the air, as if rebelling against its barrenness. As I approached I was greeted by a crowd of hawkers sitting next to

piles of pots, boxes, shabby suitcases, and all kinds of odds and ends, advertising their pathetic wares at the tops of their voices to anyone who passed by. Huge tattered posters waved from their noticeboards with pictures of Ben-Gurion: "Labour, We're all Labour!" cried the posters. Here and there trampled bits of Ben-Gurion's face rolled about in the dust. The tin shanties huddling one on top of the other, like a frightened, beaten herd of animals, were boiling hot. . . . Ragged, barefoot children ran about in the narrow passages between the shanties. (161)

In Nuri's absence, the ma'abara hasn't changed; it remains a stagnant collection of hovels, where wild dogs roam and rudimentary canals flow with stinking sewage. Venturing into a typical shanty belonging to an old neighbor from his Baghdad days, Nuri finds "a pile of mattresses, two heavy Baghdad trunks, a muddle of clothing and blankets . . . jute sacks and a kerosene lamp" (162–63). It is Friday afternoon and, saddened by the sight of demoralized fathers returning from a day of menial labor, whose woeful appearance evokes that of "a chain gang, quiet as wilted leaves," he is ashamed to think of the kibbutzniks who at the very same hour must be "taking their clean Sabbath clothes out . . . humming Polish and Russian tunes on their way to the showers" (161). Asked by an Iraqi worker whether he is from the kibbutz, his first instinct is to lie. His second is a splenetic outburst, a guilty torrent of all his confused desires and suppressions, the utterly irreconcilable past and future:

> Did my father look like them when he came back from working on the roads?. . . . I felt a wild urge to run to the kibbutz and smash up their tractor-shed, break down the barbed-wire fences, smash the sheep-pen, the cowshed, chase the horses out of the stable and sent the tractors charging into the houses to smash everything up and avenge my frantic pain. I began to run like a madman . . . savagely eating up kilometer after kilometer until there was not a drop of breath or strength or anything else left in me. Suddenly I stopped. What did I want of them? What harm had the kibbutzniks done me? How was the kibbutz to blame? Why was I mad at them and the "regionals"? My father could have come here thirty years ago and established himself, like them, and I could have been a "regional." But he didn't . . . and they were the bosses. (161)

Pressure continues to build on Nuri to gain a foothold for the movement in the ma'abara. When he stubbornly attempts to cobble together a compromise between the kibbutz's mission and the traditional values of the Iraqi immigrants (whom he promises that they will have separate activities for boys and girls and that the girls won't be required to bare their thighs in the scandalous kibbutz short pants), he is denounced for "acting in opposition to the principles of the movement" (172). Yet, in spite of the inevitable fiery exchanges that ensue among kibbutz ideologues over the need to defend their vision of "revolution and evolution and the mechanism of human change and human adaptability" (172), Nuri perseveres with his struggle to achieve a middle ground. Unfortunately, when he returns to the ma'abara, he finds its youngsters dumbfounded by the notion that, like the other kibbutzniks, Nuri works for nothing. After knocking on the doors of countless tin shanties, he makes torturously slow progress with their parents as well: "Promises were one thing and sending their sons to join the movement another. They arrived in dribs and drabs, like the first rain on parched earth. And for every one who came another left and was swallowed back into the shanties" (175). Even as Nuri struggles to answer all the immigrants' anxieties, the rabbi of the ma'abara counsels him to leave the kibbutz, where the "people desecrate the Sabbath, they eat non-kosher food, and the girls are wanton" (176). Eventually, after endless negotiations, Nuri manages to bring the ma'abara youngsters to the kibbutz. But the stiffly staged welcome collapses into a welter of misunderstandings before the political speeches can even be heard. Nuri is left to ruefully contemplate his own lack of true belonging to either of the "two alien camps" (182).

Two weeks before the jubilee of Kiryat-Oranim, in a private meeting with Nuri, Sonia reveals her own ambition for the Mizrahi youths, who are now at a crossroads. Bluntly acknowledging that the "regionals" and the immigrants will never be able to work together—"an unavoidable tragedy" (198)—she proposes that, rather than remaining where they are, or even joining an existing kibbutz, the Youth Aliya immigrants should stand up at the jubilee celebrations to declare their intent to establish a new kibbutz of their own in the remote Negev. As Sonia attempts to sway Nuri with a carefully rehearsed speech about the available paths to acculturation (each clearly positioned in kibbutz socialism's ascending hierarchy of values), from which he and his friends must choose, he only hears a message of implied failure that drives home his sense of being a Mizrahi outsider. "If you don't become kibbutz members," Sonia tells him, "it will prove that the doubters were right."

If you join an existing kibbutz it will be like coming to a half-cooked meal. [But i]f you set up a kibbutz of your own, it will prove not only that the kibbutz is capable of changing people, but also that you are capable of changing. Nurik, I believe in you, in all of you. Think about one thing:

commitment to the kibbutz is the peak of our movement education, the greatest of our aspirations. It will be a personal failure for me if after all the work we put into you . . . the group scatters and disappears in the ma'abarot. The kibbutz and settling the land are the only answers to the problem of the ma'abarot, the true answer. (198)

This lofty mission is clearly a heavy burden for a sixteen-year-old to bear. When he leaves Sonia's room, Nuri feels weighed down by his sense of being judged as inherently unworthy: "God in heaven, what does she want of me? . . . I wasn't born a princess like her, nor a prince like them. I didn't have their sense of belonging, their history, their self-confidence" (199). He angrily rejects Sonia's plea to prove the "regionals" wrong: "They would win the argument? So what? So we weren't the same as those sweet little sabras who had given us a taste of their poisoned thorns"—as he knows all too well, "no one could teach me how to escape the world from which I had come" (199). The melancholy teenager spends hours tormented by the question of just what separates people like himself from the kibbutzniks. The next day, he shares his painful realization with Sonia. Whereas she and the other kibbutzniks had the luxury to act as independent individuals in joining the collective, he and his Iraqi friends came from a more unified, interdependent world, however fragmented it was now: "I came with my family . . . and friends, all of Jewish Baghdad moved out here, and now it's in the ma'abarot. Which makes it much harder to burn our bridges. You've built a society founded on individuals, because you came here alone. I belong to a clan. But to tell you the truth: I don't belong to the clan anymore either. I don't know who I am any more. I'm always running between the hilltop where the 'regionals' are and the ma'abara" (199–200). Sonia, who prefers to call Nuri "Nimrod" because it means "we will rebel" (naturally, she thinks of that in terms of Nuri's relation to his Iraqi origins, not the kibbutz), sympathetically but firmly declares to him, "It's only the torn who make revolutions . . . because they realize that they have to mend the tears" (200). She demands that he understand the great enterprise of world making that is his to command: "The great question is what kind of world your children will live in—in Kiryat-Oranim or in the ma'abarot and the slums of corrupt cities. In unending envy and a capitalistic rat-race, or in an egalitarian and revolutionary society" (200). In the weeks to come, Sonia beleaguers both Nuri and his friends with "her demands in words of fire" (201), yet the day of the jubilee arrives with no group decision. They are invited to a party where the first generation of kibbutzniks commemorates their long-departed comrades who were killed in armed conflicts with the Arabs and extols the fruition of their vision with elaborate pageantry. Nuri is stunned when his beloved mentor, Dolek, after ranging from the Holocaust to the triumphs of the present day, warmly concludes with praise for Nuri and his friends: "These boys and girls have proved that they are a true proletariat, people of work and labour. May they realize the ideals of our movement in their personal lives and join us in building the kibbutz and the land" (202). Yet, when his turn comes to speak for the group, Nuri feels forced to express everything that has wounded him and the others: "Haverim! In Bagdad I dreamt of a world where everyone worked without competition, without exploitation, caring about each other. In Kiryat-Oranim I found my dream. You, the founders, built the land for us. We love you and admire what you've done here. . . . But I have to say, even on this day of celebration, that in one thing you failed slightly: your children don't know how to welcome new immigrants. They're supercilious, contemptuous, sneering" (202).

In the days to come, undiscouraged, Sonia spends hours wheedling Nuri and his friends to dedicate themselves to the cause, tirelessly expounding on the "inverted pyramid" of workers and the Zionist revolution until Masul finally cuts her short with a prophecy of his own: "Leave us alone already with your pyramids. It doesn't mean a thing. Your kids are on the top of the hill looking down on us in the valley. They'll be the bosses and we'll be the workers" (205). Sonia looks to Nuri for support but he remains silent, knowing that his friend has spoken the truth. He has long been awed by Sonia's personal example. Somehow her life seems to have encompassed the entire Zionist revolution, from clearing stones and plowing with mules, to fighting for gender equality and working with delinquent youths and Holocaust survivors, to journeying back to Poland, where she discovered that her entire family was annihilated, to dedicating herself to redeeming the Iraqi youths. Yet, in the end, her rhetoric of "self-realization"—which, she tells him, means "accepting the burden of physical labour like a religion, like prayer, like a daily creed. Self-realization means tying your lives and futures to the land, and committing yourselves utterly to our way of life, our principles and beliefs" (206)— leaves him cold. In the end, this is what he knows:

> I, Nuri, the son of Fahima from Iraq, knew that my parents, who were waiting for me to come home to help support the family, would never in a million years understand the ideal of "self-realization" and that they would never forgive me if I abandoned them to their fate. . . . My mother

refused to set foot in the kibbutz and blamed everyone on it as if they had robbed her of her child. My parents would never understand why parents lived apart from their children on the kibbutz, why the family was split up, why children called their parents by their first names, and why the "regionals" were always referred to by the names of their groups, as if they had no family names. (206)

Yet, despite his profound regard for Sonia, he expresses none of that directly to her, and she remains unaware of the guilt he feels for betraying his family. Nuri knows full well that, even if he were to pledge himself to founding an Iraqi kibbutz in the distant Negev, none of his friends would ever follow him—"Masul wanted to be a lawyer, Herzl wanted to eat shashlik and kebab, and Buzaglo was looking for his lost God" (206). In the final chapter, after an absence of three months, and two days before Yom Kippur, Nuri journeys back to the ma'abara where his family lives. Again he feels the familiar "choking sensation" (209) that overcomes him whenever he returns. He encounters Abu-Jamila, a legendary figure in Baghdad, beloved for his rhymed verses and elegance, but now "a deposed king" (212), reduced to begging for charity, like all the other Iraqi immigrants. Taking in their pathetic efforts to grow a few herbs and tomatoes, he realizes yet again what was lost: "They would never approach the abundance of fruit and vegetables in Baghdad, not even on the kibbutz. Pile upon pile, rich and juicy, rising as high as hills, behind which Nabil and I would play hide-and-seek, running to and fro among them until darkness fell, when the amount of food abandoned in the market-place would be enough to feed an entire ma'abara" (210). When he learns about the abysmal state of schooling in the ma'abara, like a true kibbutznik, he vigorously advocates for communal activism and the establishment of committees. Facing his defeated father, he tries to inspire him with the industrious self-sufficiency of his comrades: "On the kibbutz we have committees for everything—social problems, education, work" (217). To which his father cries out in despair, "There's no one to talk to, my son! The only thing that counts here is parties. The religious party, the labour party, the general Zionists, the communists. Only the ma'abara is an orphan" (217). In the end, Nuri, too, seems on the verge of succumbing to his parents' alienation, tormented by "oppressive feelings of guilt," haunted by the image of his mother "standing silent at the entrance to the tent, wringing the flap in her hands . . . it was like talking to a wall, a fortress without windows or cracks" (215). Thus, caught between the equally unsatisfactory polarities of ma'abara and kibbutz, only the past has legitimacy. At the novel's conclusion, nothing has been resolved, no clear path forward has emerged, and Nuri falls into an indeterminate sleep that aptly underscores the liminal state of his divided consciousness.[32]

Despite the dystopian aspects of the youths' encounter with kibbutz socialism in *Scapegoat*, it is worth noting that personal reflections by Iraqi immigrants in the newsletters of this era often express a rosier perception. Meir-Glitzenstein quotes one young woman's recollection of her first year in Kibbutz Givat Hasheloshah:

> If we look a bit at kibbutz life, it seems that the aspirations we dreamed of for so long are now being fulfilled in this new lifestyle. There is no difference between poor and rich, pauper and patrician, all live together a life of freedom and cooperation, with everyone sharing one grand goal—redemption of the land. . . . I never thought I would live this way: among many fathers and mothers, brothers and sisters who live jointly a cooperative, egalitarian life, on a large piece of land on which are found Jews from all kinds of countries, who work by the sweat of their brow in agriculture. . . . By our lives, the lives of a laborer in the kibbutz, we feel the beauty of nature, the taste of communal life, the realization of Zionism. . . . One forgets the difficulties in this type of life through love of nature, labor, and homeland. (87–88)

This seems as ardent and assimilationist a declaration as Mary Antin's *The Promised Land* (1912) was for Americans in the early twentieth century. As Meir-Glitzenstein argues, the rhetorical intensity and familiar tropes of the young woman's ideological fervor reflect "the educational indoctrination process the immigrant trainees had undergone. The kibbutz was presented as the ultimate and only way for achieving both the national and personal solution. . . . City life, in contrast, was depicted as the continuation of Diaspora life and was vehemently disparaged" (88). At the same time, it is worth bearing in mind that kibbutz newsletters of that time rarely published expressions of dissatisfaction from their own youngsters, let alone from immigrant youths. Nor is it hard to find other literary voices from Amir's generation that affirm the loneliness of their ordeal as younger immigrants. Thus Ella Shohat, the renowned scholar of postcolonial and cultural studies, reflects on the contradictions and ambivalences in her acculturation:

The planes that were arranged to transport Iraqi Jews to Israel uprooted millennia of life in Babylon, leading to a new diasporic existence. Overnight, we were no longer Iraqis, but Israelis; a new citizenship coupled with a strict poetic national-culture meter. The Israeli-Arab conflict formulated a new grammar of belonging where Arabness and Jewishness composed a mutually exclusive syntax, in excess of each other. Upon their arrival in Israel, my grandparents did not speak Hebrew and never learned it until their last day. My parents, while becoming more fluent in Hebrew, persisted to speak it with a heavy Iraqi accent, unable to erase the traces of their "Bilad al-Rafidein" (Mesopotamia) birthplace. My father and his friends, during their first days as construction workers, communicated among themselves in Arabic but were disdainfully ordered by their Euro-Israeli boss to "Stop speaking Arabic! We are not in an Arab country." Arabic, needless to say, was the language of the enemy. A Jew could not speak it, and a Jew could certainly not claim it as an identity marker. "In Iraq," my parents often lamented, "we were Jews. In Israel, we are Arabs." ("Remembering")

Shohat's memory of her early years in Israel is that of traumatic rupture, erasure, and silencing:

In our own fragile and disoriented apprehension, we the children were recruited for the making of a new identity that was to clash with our parents' Iraqiness, Arabness, and Middle Easternness. At home we turned into a domesticated linguistic police force, the secret agents of Euro-Israeli hegemony. Back from school, we voiced what was expected of us: "Stop speaking Arabic!" When my grandparents took the bus with us, we wanted them to remain silent, anxious that they would forget that we were not at home, and could be heard. We virtually ordered our parents to forget that alien linguistic baggage of Iraqiness. Unknowing targets of mental colonization, we were the children who were expected to delete not merely the past across the border but also the transplanted Baghdads, Cairos, or Rabats of our homes and neighborhoods. Our bodies, language, and thought were regulated to the rhythms of a disciplining, corrective, normalizing machine designed to erect us into proud Israelis. ("Remembering")

Like Amir, Shohat delineates the impossibility of a truly hybrid identity in her new society, the imperative to repudiate the alien within. In the end, in ways congruent with the pressures exhibited by mainstream Israeli society that Shohat describes, despite their much-vaunted project of "universalism" and assimilation, the predominantly Ashkenazi kibbutzim failed to overcome their own ethnic condescension toward the Mizrahi immigrants: "Casting a pall over the network of relations were the Ashkenazi veterans' feelings of superiority and the Eastern immigrants' feelings of inferiority. . . . The kibbutz was found to be a closed ethnic unit whose members reacted intolerantly to cultural difference" (Meir-Glitzenstein 97, 98).[33] Having examined the larger picture of the immigrant Mizrahi experience of the 1950s, Jacqueline Kahanoff notes the sad irony that some of the country's most economically vital "pioneering" was not carried out by the Ashkenazi socialists after all:

> Today, paradoxically, the hard labor of building up new settlements and developing the arid Negev devolve[s], in fact, upon newcomers, most of whom are of oriental origin. The old-timers of Ashkenazi origin, because of their experience, constitute the managerial class. Although the harsh conditions of the new settlements are softened by the welfare state, the young Oriental who aspires to social recognition is too often denied appreciation by his fellow citizens for the tremendous role he plays. In spite of all appeals, it is not the settled population on the whole which goes to live in and build up the land, but the newcomer, who surmounts his first fears and disappointments to grapple with its starkness, and who, in doing so, has a claim to his country's gratitude. (205)

Among the categories of workers Kahanoff finds forgotten or underappreciated are the Moroccan laborers, the layers of the nation's water pipeline, those who toiled in the Sdom–Dead Sea Works or the Negev phosphate mines. These are Israel's genuine "austere workers" (205), whose extraordinary role the condescending Zionist narrative was reluctant to affirm. But it is also worth recognizing that there were kibbutzniks who were keen on supporting the later Mizrahi arrivals. Alfy Nathan, a founding member of Kibbutz Kfar Hanassi, recalls: "I was one of those who strongly favored hiring outside workers. Why? It was not just a matter of need. The people who constituted our labor pool were predominantly . . . from North Africa and the Middle East. I felt we were helping these people by providing good, steady employment. The state had brought these people over and had made certain assurances. . . . [They] were promised decent housing and gainful employment. I saw our hiring them as helping to fulfill those promises. More importantly, I saw this as a mitzvah that we needed to perform. I am pleased to say that . . . my side won out" (Nathan and Sklare 165). Yet Nathan also acknowledges the condescension, bias, and mistreatment that the Mizrahim experienced elsewhere. In an even more confessional mode, Meron Benvenisti, who later became deputy mayor of Jerusalem, recalls that "we wanted to assimilate new immigrants from Iraq and North Africa. We brought them to our kibbutz and believed that in teaching them how to behave like us we were doing the right thing. It was a sincere, if misguided, attempt . . . that injured their self-respect and bred pure hatred" (qtd. in Joffe).[34] It is undoubtedly one of Zionist history's saddest and more ironic chapters that the most pioneering communities of the Galilee and Negev peripheral communities—the kibbutzim and the immigrants from North Africa and the Arab Middle East—were political and cultural antagonists rather than regional partners.

The immigrants were settled in remote development towns during the 1950s, where they languished economically, in large part due to the shortsighted neglect of the Labor Party. Later, they formed an important voting bloc that was loyal for many years to the Likud, the kibbutz movement's greatest political enemy.[35] Why? Perhaps because, when they first arrived as refugees and became Israel's instant underclass, they were never regarded as equals by the Ashkenazi establishment of the Mapai (Land of Israel Worker's Party) and the Labor Party (of which the kibbutz movement was an important wing); indeed, they saw the kibbutzim as a sort of landed gentry upholding class stratification,[36] never witnessing the prodigious pioneering labor of this once vibrant and admirable socialist expression. Moreover, the Likud came to attract the working masses far more than the Labor Party did, which led to its triumphant ascendancy to power in 1977.[37]

Finally, it is worth noting that, in another significant Hebrew novel of the 1980s, *Hitganvut yechidim* (*Infiltration*; 1986) by Yehoshua Kenaz (b. 1937), similar Mizrahi grievances are raised by a young conscript.[38] Also a coming-of-age story set in 1950s Israel, *Infiltration* traces the evolving relationships, disparate cultures, and gradual maturation of a platoon of soldiers deemed unfit for combat during the challenging physical and emotional rigors of basic training. Kenaz's wide cast of brilliantly realized characters includes Sabras—notably, the proud kibbutznik Alon (who tragically commits suicide)—and others from big cities, as well as new immigrants from Europe and Arab countries. At one point, an Arab youth named Rahamim Ben-Hamo, who has unhappy memories of his sojourn in a kibbutz boarding school, confronts Alon: "I suppose you think if you're from a kibbutz you're too good to talk to Ben-Hamo. I was on a kibbutz too. Six months" (241). When the kibbutznik presses him for the reasons that he did not remain, Rahamim gives him a lesson in the sharp contrast between the Mizrahi reality in the Arab colonial world and their status under the bigotry of Israel's Ashkenazi establishment:

It was hard for me. . . . I didn't even know Hebrew yet. In the middle of the year they sent me home. For not fitting in. They didn't give me a chance, that's the truth. But I wasn't so sorry. A kibbutz is no place for me. You people are too conceited. You look down on the whole world, as if you're sitting up in the sky and everybody else is lying in the mud, in the shit. You know what, in the old country everybody knew our family. Wherever you went everyone knew the Ben-Hamo family. We had a shop and a big house with Arab servants. We only spoke French. Not Arabic. People came from all over to ask my father's advice, they came to ask him to settle arguments between people, Jews and Arabs both. Everybody knew my father. He died before we came here. His grave stayed there. (242)

After Rahamim's elegiac portrait of his father's illustrious days and his lament for what has befallen that father's son—"In all my life I never felt like I was such shit as I felt on the kibbutz" (243)—proud Alon can only blandly counter that, had Rahamim only stayed a little longer, he would have recognized that the kibbutz adhered strictly to its ideals of equality and that, at the very least, Rahamim's family should have embraced the "healthy, new life" that Israel offered the immigrants in the Negev. Of course, written in the 1980s, that remark of the oblivious young Sabra carried only intended biting irony; by then, most of the peripheral development towns had long become infamous for their social neglect and economic marginalization by the establishment.

Though at first disconsolate in the aftermath of his ouster from the kibbutz—his own sister berates him: "Go home, the kibbutz isn't for you. It's too good for you. Here there's people with education, refined, Ashkenazis. The place for you is the transit camp, with the gangsters" (247)—Rahamim is stirred by a late epiphany:

I had about half an hour for the bus to come. So I sat in the room by myself and thought and suddenly I felt happy. Because I was going away from there already. Like a person let out of jail. Before then I didn't even know how shitty it was for me there. And now that it was over I was as happy as if I'd had too much to drink. I was like some drunk, I couldn't sit still. All our songs from the old country that I like so much came back into my head, and the taste of food from home came into my mouth, and how I wouldn't have to eat their food I couldn't stand so that I never ate there and I was thin as a string no more. And how I wasn't ever going to see those kids no more and those kibbutzniks who think they're sitting up in the sky with God. (247)

When Alon, the consummate insider who shudders at the "diaspora mentality" of his fellow enlistees (54), comes to feel that he, too, falls short of the uncompromising standards of kibbutz heroism, he cannot bear to face the magnitude of that failure: his suicide casts a heavy shadow on the other men's lives in the novel's final pages. Alon's fate seems foreshadowed in the sympathetic description of one of his fellow inductees after volunteering to remain on the base over Shabbat: "He preferred to stay behind. . . . He's ashamed to go back to his kibbutz because he's a Medical Grade B recruit on Training Base Four, and where he comes from they all go to combat units and it's a big deal for them" (222). And how could it be otherwise for Alon? He has been so inculcated by duty that serving at the base for those deemed medically unfit for combat, he now feels "cut off from origins" and trapped by "his inner exile" (53). As the narrator later recalls, whenever there is a spare moment, he regales his comrades from the city about how things are in the collective:

> This is how Alon seemed to me as I saw him narrowing his eyes in concentration, his face tense, his head bursting with visions of heroism. . . . On his kibbutz, he told us, officers and fighters who came home on leave would tell the . . . younger generation about secret missions and heroic paratrooper raids, about special mysterious crack units that the public didn't know about. Alon knew the names of illustrious warriors the rest of us had never heard of, and he called them by their nicknames, as if he were one of their closest friends. (53)

Whereas others nod off during their captain's lectures on glorious military campaigns, "to Alon his words sounded like the glorious verses of an ancient epic, told by the elder of the tribe to the young warriors sitting in a circle at his feet, calling silently on the spirits of their ancestors to come and inspire their hearts and empower their arms for war" (53). No wonder, because these are the "verses" on which he was raised, and he lacks the imagination to conceive of anything beyond them. Thus, irrevocably exiled from the exalted sense of purpose and destiny to which he was born, this kibbutz youth cannot rouse himself from a sense of utter futility. His fatal self-inflicted injury seems as tragically foreordained as that of the hapless paratrooper in Amos Oz's "Way of the Wind."

4

Late Disillusionments and Village Crimes
The Kibbutz Mysteries of Batya Gur and Savyon Liebrecht

I miss savoring the experience of a day's work that I learned in Kibbutz Geva. I miss
Alumot, from whence we beheld the astonishing beauty of Emek Hayarden. I miss the
simplicity of the long walks, the wrinkled khaki clothing. I miss the flowerbeds of Kibbutz
Ashdot, the bushels of bananas on Kibbutz Degania, the plywood of Kibbutz Afikim.
I miss the dates of Kibbutz Kinneret. I miss the green fields of crops and orchards. I miss the
dairy barn, the animal pens, and the chicken coops—from which various smells emanated.
I miss the wonderful hikes just before dawn and the grazing excursions to Wadi Fijas,
where I fixed my eyes to the stars that were born with the new dawn. To this day a
vibration courses through my body whenever I hear the name "Degania." . . .
I ask myself why I miss it, just so I can figure out to whom I belong.
—*President Shimon Peres at the centennial celebration of the establishment
of Kibbutz Degania Alef, 31 March 2010*

Given that the mystery genre has often been understood as preoccupied with
the trauma of a disturbance in a world of ostensible harmony and order (hence
its classic role in exposing the secrets behind the façades of those English
country houses so frequented by Agatha Christie's Miss Marple), it seems a
wonder that no writer before or after the late literary critic and novelist Batya
Gur (1947–2005) ever took full advantage of the kibbutz's pastoral promise and
setting.[1] In each installment of Gur's exceedingly popular Israeli mystery series
featuring Inspector Michael Ohayon, the unusually sensitive and intelligent
detective struggles to glean answers from various forms of self-contained and

closed subcultures whose inner dynamics pose unique intellectual challenges to the detective.[2] Some of these dynamics may be found throughout the world—in academia, television networks, orchestras—which may account for the wide international popularity of the series. In Gur's *Linah meshutefet* (*Murder on a Kibbutz: A Communal Case*; 1991), the third in her series of kibbutz mysteries, the mounting number of murdered kibbutzniks seems to signal the demise of the idealistic values for which they toiled in life. It is not at all to her discredit as a mystery writer that what distinguishes Gur's work is her keen intellectual grasp of the peculiar sociology and the arcane rules that operate within the insular worlds that Ohayon must fathom to solve the crimes.

More often than not, Ohayon's identity as a Mizrahi Jew makes his struggle to penetrate each of these elite, Eurocentric institutions all the more difficult; indeed, long considered the ideological vanguard of Israel's Ashkenazi establishment (with a highly problematic history of failed absorption policies vis-à-vis the Mizrahi community), the kibbutz poses perhaps the greatest challenge of his career.[3] For Dvir Abramovich, there is clearly a covertly subversive quality to the Ashkenazi and Mizrahi tensions in *Murder*: "Ironically, the Mizrahi police inspector, the antithesis of the kibbutz establishment, serves as the focal point through whom questions are raised about whether the kibbutz is still vital to the sustenance of the state, or whether it has outgrown its function. Most obviously, Ohayon is the ultimate leveler" (*Back to the Future* 223). Yet his ethnic identity is not the only obstacle to overcome; he is amply warned by kibbutzniks and outsiders alike: "If you've never lived on a kibbutz . . . you'll never understand anything" (Gur, *Murder* 183). In this respect, Gur does a fine job of bringing the ideological tensions of contemporary kibbutzim) fully to life, so that even readers unfamiliar with them may easily grasp their profound consequences for the lives of its members.

Gur immediately immerses us in the idyllic surroundings of a veteran kibbutz preparing for a festive celebration of its fiftieth anniversary.[4] All the cherished stereotypes of early Zionist pioneering days seem on display. Golden bales of hay are stacked high under a dazzling blue sky, a choir of kibbutz members dressed in blue and white gathers for the event, and even the kibbutz tractors and other agricultural machines are decorated with flowers.[5] Mere moments after these alluring images are introduced, a sense of dissonance creeps into the narrative, expressed through the consciousness of Aaron Meroz, a Knesset member who no longer lives on the kibbutz. He dismisses the festive trappings as anachronisms, which veil a more complex and troubled present:

Once you took away the blue and white and the flags on the Caterpillar, the whole ceremony seemed archaic and foreign, as if it were taking place on a collective farm in Soviet Russia. . . . It was the farce of an agricultural ceremony in a place where agriculture was almost bankrupt—a kibbutz, a Zionist agricultural commune, that derived its income from an industrial plant that, of all things, manufactured cosmetics, having given its name to an international patent for a face cream that abolished wrinkles and rejuvenated skin cells and was advertised in all the newspapers with two photographs of the same woman captioned "Before" and "After." No one else seemed to be showing any recognition of the absurdity of celebrating an agricultural rite where only the manufacture and sale of face cream made it possible to go on working the land. (4)

With Aaron's rueful musings, we first glimpse the novel's fairly elaborate treatment of the disparity between the staunchly socialist, even pro-Soviet leanings of the kibbutzim's early days and their present struggle to adjust to an increasingly capitalist society for which the kibbutz is a quaint and outmoded relic of the past. As Dvir Abramovich puts it in his incisive analysis: "On the surface life ticks at a steady, stable rate, but in its subterranean layers tempestuous and turbulent forces simmer and are about to erupt" (*Back to the Future* 220). In an ironic nod to highly successful enterprises such as Ahava (a line of cosmetics based on Dead Sea minerals marketed by a conglomerate of kibbutzim), Gur illustrates the kibbutz's surrender to the decadent glorification of the self and the very bourgeois values against which it once defined itself.

Aaron especially mourns the uprooting of plum trees to make way for cactuses that produce cosmetics rather than life-giving food—and the loss of the old philosophy of individual modesty and simplicity: "How did the women of the founder's generation—with faces that had been weather-beaten and wrinkled— . . . how did they feel when they saw the women of the middle generation, looking . . . as fresh and smooth as if they'd never spent a day working in the fields?" (*Murder* 37). And yet Gur makes us aware that Aaron's nostalgic, idealized perspective ignores the new realities: the cosmetic factory's profits, he is told, subsidize the unprofitable agricultural ventures of the kibbutz, enabling members who work in the fields and orchards to feel productive—and preventing the kibbutz from sharing the fate of so many others mired in debt.[6]

Though a relatively minor character, Aaron plays a critical role as the essential insider-outsider (employed by many of Gur's antecedents) who quickly establishes the sheer alterity of kibbutz life. And thus he also serves as surrogate for the vast majority of the novel's readers who might enjoy visiting a kibbutz but who would find it hard to tolerate its paucity of distractions, its regimental routines, the monotonous demands of farm life: "The minute you walk into the door of the dining hall, your oxygen supply drops, your productivity declines; that phlegmatic calm, that slowness, they're enough to drive a person crazy" (5–6). Raised on the kibbutz, Aaron now has a more fault-finding relationship to the movement as a whole, the Knesset having recently debated its economic plight. Soon after Aaron's observations on the community's jubilee celebration, Inspector Ohayon is summoned to investigate the strange death of a young woman named Osnat, a kibbutz leader whose platform for reforming her community included a number of controversial proposals.

Violence, let alone murder, was once exceptionally rare on kibbutzim, and when Ohayon tells the members that the criminal is likely still among them, he is met at first with outright shock and denial, a kind of disassociation often linked to posttraumatic stress disorder. Gur draws comparisons between this emergency and the crisis of the early 1950s (explored in Yizhak Yeshurun's classic 1982 film *Noa at Seventeen*), when Cold War tensions wreaked havoc in the "one big family" of kibbutz society. Dvorka, a founder and ideological firebrand, recalls that destabilizing schism: "Who could have foreseen what happened in 1951, when ideology and politics split kibbutzim right down the middle? Ever since then I've thought we'd seen everything. Families destroyed. The hatred" (154). Yet, coolly managing to take the murder of her comrade in stride, Dvorka suggests that, just like the earlier crisis, which had once seemed to herald the end of the kibbutz movement, the present threat will be overcome. Only the prospect of the complete and irreversible betrayal of fundamental kibbutz ideals rattles this veteran's composure. When Ohayon asks about the possible motives of the killer, Dvorka tries to distract him with what she regards as the true calamity at hand, the cynical triumph of materialism and selfishness over socialism and altruism:

> What went wrong must be put right. . . .
> . . . There's a slow and gradual process of decay! . . . Hired labor on the kibbutz! All the kibbutzim are prostituting themselves today, they're prostituting themselves! . . .
> . . . It's a process of putting the individual above the group, putting the private person above the general good. . . .
> . . . It's all one long process—you begin by speculating on the stock exchange and profiting from bank shares, and you end up having to give our own members credit points for picking the fruit off our own trees. . . .

> For a long time now the members have regarded their private rooms as their homes instead of the kibbutz as a whole. (155)

Israeli literary critic Omri Herzog homes in on how the opposition between the personal and collective, so deeply ingrained in the surrounding culture, is in many ways the raison d'être of the kibbutz narrative: "Tension between the individual and the collective is a constituent theme in Israeli literature, its deep structure. The kibbutz is the social venue where this tension is of utmost importance, developing into secondary tensions between idealistic principles and the individual longings that the idealists portray as petty and selfish, and between an absolute sense of belonging and feelings of estrangement and alienation." As evident for some years before *Murder* appeared in 1991, the kibbutzim had already begun to place the individual before the collective, the private before the communal to a marked degree, affecting the roles not merely of individuals but of entire categories of workers such as the *metaplim* (singular, *metapelet*), who care for the younger children.[7] A character named Machluf Levy explains this shift to Ohayon: "It begins with the kibbutz nurse. . . . The kibbutz girls don't want to become nurses, it's out of fashion, so when the last one left they had to hire someone from outside, the first position they every filled with a hired person, and some of the older people there said it would be the beginning of the end of the kibbutz" (88).

When it comes to Gur's Dvorka, every incremental move toward the private realm is inherently destructive, including the new "family sleeping" arrangements, which even in 1991 were already sweeping through the entire kibbutz movement. The recent practice of taking meals in the members' private rooms provokes her because it rapidly diminishes any hope of genuinely collective life. As Dvorka (and others of her generation) see it, the ritual of togetherness once constantly reinforced their collective values at mealtimes, whereas solitary retreats contributed nothing at all to the community's sustenance. Thus, even though as an old woman she often has little strength or appetite, Dvorka imposes the discipline of attendance at all meals on herself "because," as she explains in the plainspoken sincerity characteristic of her generation, "that's when you can meet people and sit around the same table, discussing your day and keeping in touch on a daily level, which is really what it's all about. . . . We're a nonalienated society, the last bastion of a lack of alienation in today's horror-ridden world" (159–60). When Ohayon naively tries to win her over by praising the attractively designed dining room—with "all the up-to-date appliances"—she snaps back that it, too, is corrupted by "abundance. The curse of affluence" (160). At such moments, Dvorka seems to embody the guarded character of what Amos Oz once identified as the genuine "socialist psyche." As opposed to "a cozy, fireless socialism," which "gradually develops into torpid liberalism," when "genuine" socialism "seizes the reins of power it discloses a fist of iron, arrogant, authoritarian, armed with formulas, slogans and shackles, hectoring and merciless" (Oz, *Under This Blazing Light* 135). The last item in Oz's litany has particular resonance in Gur's violent story.[8]

Murder on a Kibbutz impresses not least for its willingness to examine the necessity for progress even while it movingly portrays the heroic struggle of the halutzim, whose selfless ideals will likely not survive the changing times. Throughout the novel, both adaptation to globalization and loyalty to socialist roots are explored sympathetically and intelligently in insistent counterpoint to each another. As Dvorka, the quintessential survivor of those early days of toil and ardent conviction, poignantly recalls:

> Those were different times, hard times, you can read about them . . . but you won't really understand even then. It's difficult to transmit what the first contact with the land was like. The hardship, the dryness, the water, the hunger. Especially the hunger, and the hard work. Twelve hours at a stretch sometimes, clearing and plowing and gradually building. And the heat in summer, the cold in winter, the poverty and the hunger. The men were weak with hunger and hard labor, all of us were. There were days . . . when all we had to eat were two slices of bread and half an egg a day for a pregnant woman, and a few olives. (169)

As evidenced here, Gur presents her aging characters' recollections with a degree of quiet reverence for the noble and selfless struggle between human beings and the natural world, just as she creates space for Meroz's acerbic dismissal of the social naïveté of those early days: "So much spite and envy! What a load of rubbish it is—all that talk about the ideal society! Look what it turned into! But right from the beginning, the idea of a place or a society where people would be equal, from each according to his ability and to each according to his needs—what nonsense! . . . To each according to his ability and the strength of his elbows and the loudness of his yells—that's what really happened" (184). That despairing rejoinder is notable for its scathingly ironic inversion of the founding imperative value: "From each according to his ability, to each according to his needs." With that paradigm in mind,[9] Gur proves especially adept at demonstrating that what may strike readers living in the outside world as a relatively benign process of adaptation to changing circumstances is viewed by many of those within as an insidious abandonment of the core value of self-reliance and resistance to hired labor.

To her credit, Gur manages to encompass the major tensions and contemporary crisis of the contemporary kibbutz without ever seeming either didactic or forced, reflecting discussions that were becoming common in the movement as a whole.[10] The younger generation that Gur portrays is astutely described by Alon Gan in his study of the shifting currents of the 1960s kibbutzim: "The second generation felt that their parents' world of values and slogans was losing its vitality and had gradually become irrelevant to them" (36). Examining the sentiments of some of the young people whose reflections appeared in the kibbutz journal *Shdemot* (which became an important platform for that generation's expressions of discontent), Gan invokes poet Yehiel Hazak's plaintive declaration as a representative voice both embodying the ideological erosion of that era and anticipating its outcome in the recent crisis of privatization: "The ideology no longer serves those who hold on to it. . . . From the moment that it no longer permeates our psyche, a void appears in kibbutz life, and any void carries a price. . . . I dare say that this togetherness, with its moral and cultural content, is by now devoid of the power of the ideology and this void has to be confronted on a daily basis" (qtd. in Gan 36). The essential terms of Hazak's outcry are echoed in Gur's novel by Aaron Meroz (the politician who grew up on kibbutz), here complaining bitterly about one of the kibbutz's once most highly hallowed institutions, the children's houses, which he considers the source of adult maladjustment and neurosis from the individual's early experience of emotional and material deprivation:

> You don't give them a chance to cope with the existential problems of life and the end result is a kind of stunting of the capacity for suffering, for doubt; they take everything for granted, they know nothing except the need to accumulate material possessions. That covetousness, that acquisitiveness of theirs . . . all stems from anxiety, from the fear of an independent life outside the kibbutz, and from the memory of deprivation transposed to a sphere where it didn't exist at all: The real deprivation had nothing to do with material things, it had to do with the stunting of individual growth. (*Murder* 193–94)

Gur's portrayal was particularly timely and astute, for *Murder* appeared in the triumphal wake of the rebellion against communal child rearing. Menachem Rosner, a formidable scholar of the kibbutz movement's history and sociology (and a kibbutz member), declares that this uprising, initially stirred by young mothers, caused the transformation from "an afamilistic to a highly familistic society" (qtd. in Muravschik 331).[11] Like a virus, Aaron's candor stimulates doubts and misgivings in the mind of his acquaintance Moish, who has remained on the kibbutz.[12] This loyal kibbutznik at last begins to grasp the extent of the malaise he has long denied: "The pain of loneliness and questions about the meaning of life seemed to descend on the young people all at once, as soon as they left the stifling greenhouse they were so eager to escape in order to experience new things, disorienting and alienating them from the possibility of returning to that same greenhouse and bringing up their children as they themselves had been brought up, in the sincere belief that this was the very best of all possible ways" (*Murder* 194).[13]

Many Israeli young people fresh out of the army travel abroad, but those raised on kibbutz often have an even greater sense of claustrophobia and restlessness and set off trekking around the globe, often risking their lives in dangerous environments. In Gur's novel, Dvorka sympathetically sees this phenomenon as a healthy corrective to an unavoidable lack of the genuine challenges and ordeals that gave meaning to their elders' lives: "These trips should be seen . . . as a natural and constructive reaction to a spiritual quest. We should encourage them to travel as part of the process of apprenticeship in which a person learns that the meaning of life is to be found within himself. Think about how hard it is for them. They don't have any swamps to drain. They have nothing to protect them from emptiness. It's hard to live without a challenge" (194). The child-rearing experiment that long seemed one of the kibbutzim's most thoroughly admirable innovations is later revealed to be an unintentionally callous institution where conformity and dogma overruled the heart and even common sense. Here is Moish again, in a cry of protest directed toward Dvorka and her generation of uncompromising ideologues:

> I'll tell you exactly what was wrong. There were a lot of things wrong. The first thing wrong is that we never talked about it. You didn't allow it, you didn't want to hear. . . . What do you know about us? Maybe you know when we began to walk or talk and when our first tooth arrived, but what goes on inside us you know nothing at all. We never had a chance to talk, only under cover of the jokes and skits we wrote for kibbutz celebrations. . . . I'm not saying there wasn't anything good about the way we grew up, but what about the misery, the nights when we woke up to a nonmother instead of a mother and a nonfather instead of a father. . . .

. . . Where were you before I was eighteen months old, when Miriam [a kibbutz member] told me that the memory she had of me as a baby was of a little toddler walking behind his housemother's [metapelet's] dress while the woman keeps pushing the little hand away? Where were you then? . . . That's what I want to know: Where were you? What were you thinking about then, on the nights when we were afraid? How did you come to agree to let mothers see their babies for only half an hour a day? (322–23)

As Moish's crescendo of long-suppressed resentments suggests, *Murder* adroitly encompasses the critical intergenerational tensions that cause what outsiders might assume is a staunchly settled, even static society to be one that is far from free of uneasy questioning and harsh self-criticism.[14] Moreover, it is significant, perhaps even startling that Gur's novel anticipates many of the voices heard from in Ran Tal's revelatory documentary *Yaldey hashemesh* (*Children of the Sun*; 2007). In what amounts to his *J'accuse*, Moish repudiates the selfhood-smothering form of child rearing that he and others hope to reform (a repudiation echoed in recent reassessments of kibbutz education by those raised within the system):

For the sake of the ideal of equality you organized things so we would have a group ego, but you destroyed our own, our personal egos. How healthy and secure do you think kids can be who've got only each other to turn to at night? And I'm not even talking about the beginning of adolescence and the communal showers and all your other brilliant ideas! . . . I'm fed up with being forgiving and understanding the hardships of the past. I want to understand what went on in your heads when you locked the doors of the children's house from the outside and told the night watch to check on us twice a night! Two whole times! And we would sometimes stand there the whole night banging on the door and crying and nobody came! I explode every time I think about it! (*Murder* 324)

For those of us who survived the system Moish represents or who once accepted its wonders at face value, his revisionist denunciation can be painful reading, just as the "post-Zionist" criticisms can be difficult to hear for those raised on the appealing myths of Israel's establishment. And yet both discourses are essential for coming to terms with complex realities. As his comrades waver about making the institutional changes he has called on them to make (enlarged family housing, among others), Moish shouts that he will not inflict on his children the injury inflicted on him:

> I don't give a damn about your equality . . . we're not the glory of the state of Israel or of anything else. What, I ask you, what came of it all? People accuse our kids of being materialistic and all kinds of things. What's the wonder? How else can they compensate themselves for the deprivations of their childhood?. . . .
>
> . . . Nearly all the other kibbutzim have already done it, we've got the money to do it, and we're dragging our feet . . . as if it's some trivial matter. My Asaf is going to be tucked in by me at night, you hear, Dvorka? Me and not the [metapelet], me and not the night watchman, me and not the intercom, me and nobody else. Because all you thought about was our first tooth, not our first fears, which we didn't even know how to put into words because we were so young. And I'm asking you, Dvorka, what ideal you can wave at me that's worth the fear and the loneliness of a child who doesn't know how to talk yet. . . . And that's what I've got to say to you: We're going to have family sleeping here and everything else that Osnat wanted. (325–26)

In the course of his painstaking investigation, Ohayon comes to understand the disparate social sectors of the inward-looking community, including both newcomers and hired workers. With the result that, by the novel's conclusion, we have been exposed to surprisingly divergent versions of the famous kibbutz "reality." Thus, in one version, Dave, a Canadian immigrant whose single status so disturbs the status quo that he is sent off by the elites to "all kinds of seminars and ideological weekends" (235) in search of a mate, confesses that all the reading he did about the creation of the kibbutz movement had left him ill prepared for the social conservatism, the singular devotion to the nuclear family, that he subsequently experienced. "He would never have expected them to take the institution of the family so seriously. After all, kibbutz society was supposed to be one big family . . . and the family cell was perceived as being inimical to society, and here he was, discovering every single day the conservatism of the kibbutz. In fact, he . . . said unsmilingly, it was such a bourgeois society that they hadn't succeeded in overcoming the family cell at all" (235). As an outsider, Dave inevitably has a rough encounter with the painful contradictions of kibbutz life. But he is no malcontent, and, having weathered the loss of his earliest illusions, he remains an idealist, one who has had time to carefully consider the kibbutz experiment in all its complexity. When skeptically questioned about his motives for remaining, he ardently insists: "One of the main advantages of living on a kibbutz . . . was the freedom from all kinds of things that people outside enslaved themselves to. Here too you could be a slave to material standards of living . . . but you didn't have to be. Because the minimum you were provided with here was more than enough. . . . He was not only talking about material goods but also about other worldly vanities, status and so on" (236). Through Dave's eyes, we encounter the sheer potentiality, the open-ended destiny of the kibbutz that, in spite of what other characters deem unacceptable ideological compromises, endures for him.

There is so much moral outrage and impassioned debate in the novel that it is hard to know just where Gur stood on the fragmenting world her detective penetrates. But, in at least one interview, she clearly dismisses the kibbutz's mythic stature in Israeli society:

> I never had any illusions about the nature of the Kibbutz. It drove me mad, how people really killed themselves for this ideology. They were willing to see their kids for only a half an hour a day for the ideal of communal sleeping. They tore families apart because of the issue of separation. Today, after communism simply disintegrated, I feel sorry for the people who destroyed theirs and their family's life because of this fanaticism. I ask myself—how do they justify the victims they sacrificed? What excites and attracts me is the relativity of things. How something that was once sacred, crumbles and is shown as an empty vessel. (Negev 282)

Given her subdued perspective on utopian dreaming, it is hardly surprising that on the novel's final page, Gur has her detective somberly observe, "People imprison themselves in the reality they invent" (*Murder* 350).

Perhaps because she shares Gur's familial relationship to unprecedented persecution, Savyon Liebrecht is similarly committed to exposing the violence that festers just beneath the veneer of civilized kibbutz society. Undoubtedly one of the most acerbic accounts of kibbutz life since Amos Oz's 1965 collection *Where the Jackals Howl*, Liebrecht's 2002 short story "Kibbutz" startles for its unsparing portrayal of an entire community whose callous sensibilities seem very far removed from what most readers would expect of an enlightened society. Born in Munich to Holocaust survivors in 1948, Liebrecht has received much acclaim for her novels and short fiction in both Europe and Israel and has begun to attract critical and general interest in the United States as well. "Kibbutz" and the other stories of the collection *Makom tov la-laila* (*A Good Place for the*

Night; 2002) are notable for their sobering portraits of individuals who are alienated from their ostensible homes and homelands.[15]

Liebrecht's bitter story reflects a major shift in Israeli attitudes as expressed in the kibbutz films of that time: "The changes in the cinematic articulation of the kibbutz mirror the emergence of new, alternative attitudes in Israeli society with regard to the commitment of the individual toward the collective and the commitment (or rather, indifference) of the society toward its citizens, particularly with regard to those individuals who are considered as others, the different kinds of transgressors and dissidents who do not wish, or are unable, to conform to the collectivist imperatives" (Kedem and Padva 190).

The matronly kibbutz nurse Devora is startled one day by the unexpected reappearance of Melech, whom she had known years ago as a troubled young boy, but who is now a grown man and a second lieutenant in the army ("Kibbutz" 60). Brimming with affection at the sight of him, Devora soon notices that her onetime charge is strangely distant and agitated. After informing Melech that she has proudly followed his career and posted a notice about his "outstanding officer award" on the communal bulletin board, the young man responds with hostile doubt about the goodwill of the community. Soon it emerges that Melech's visit is motivated by an urgent need to press his old caregiver for details about his parents' unhappy lives. Again and again, throughout his early childhood, Dvora had told him her own story of his origins, "in the same voice she used for fairy tales" (63). With the best intentions, Devora inculcated the boy with a harmonious myth of his origins: "She would tell him the story of his father and the story of his mother and the story of their meeting, their love, their happiness which grew greater every day until, when it was absolutely perfect, a child was born to them, the most beautiful child in the kibbutz and perhaps even in the entire area. He grew and became their pride and joy until his sixth birthday party, which was memorialized in the last picture of the three of them" (63). In the past, this was always when Devora would bring the reassuring narrative to an end. The details were so well known to both of them that "they knew the sentences by heart and would say them in unison" (63), but now Melech presses her to tell the story once again. Devora senses a hidden menace behind his request, but Melech coaxes her to tell it just as she had in years past. Soon it becomes clear that he intends to uncover the truth that Devora had long sought to shield him from. Inexorably, Melech forces Devora to reveal the true story of his parents, a far more painful one than the benign tale she had nurtured him with.

Born in a DP camp shortly after the Holocaust, Melech's father, David, was brought by his survivor parents to Israel. After his mother's death, David spent his days working with his father in a family grocery store that eventually failed, leaving David with few options in life. One day, he learned that the kibbutzim were interested in recruiting hardworking youth. Already in love with farms and the countryside, he was bursting with so much excitement that he never reached the kibbutz to which he had been assigned but got off the bus at his first glimpse of a cowshed, "stunned with joy" and in love at first sight, "the sweat-soaked bus ticket he'd clutched to tightly all the way from Tel Aviv. . . . David shouted a passionate 'Shalom' and almost fainted from the impact of the delightful smell and the velvety eyes of the cows. He had no doubt, this was where he belonged, not in the dark, stifling air of the grocery store" (71). When told by the first kibbutznik he met, who happened to be the manager of the dairy farm, that they didn't have a place for additional labor, David collapsed in tears and threw "his arms around the neck of the cow Attalia," refusing to leave. From their earliest encounter with David, the kibbutz members acidly dismissed him as an "idiot" unworthy of their respect or even goodwill. When, however, he offered to give the kibbutz the Tel Aviv apartment his late parents left him, they cynically "welcomed" him into the community.

The kibbutzniks' cynical disregard for David's willing sacrifice emerges in an even worse light when we learn that two veteran members of the kibbutz who inherited apartments held onto them as private property. Yet even David's selfless gift could not dissuade the kibbutz members from their cruel taunts and sadistic pranks:

> Not out of malice, but out of a lack of a generosity, after teasing David, the people on the kibbutz began abusing him . . . in an imperceptible, ongoing deterioration that blurred the horror of it . . . because David was amiable and seemed not to always understand the affronts, the kibbutz members could tell themselves that they teased him out of their affection. . . . At first, they merely added salt to his coffee. . . . Later they involved him in escapades that provided them with ours of laughter: how he slept on the rickety roof of the cowshed from midnight till dawn, his socks full of ice, to protect his cows from thieves; how they stood him in front of a pan of Atida's dung to look for a precious stone she'd swallowed; how they starved him for a whole day so he could do his part to help cut expenses. He was an eager participant in their schemes, keeping awake with the help of the ice he'd poured into his socks, bringing the lumps of dung close to his eyes, enduring hunger without complaint for the sake of the kibbutz budget. (76–77)

Thus Liebrecht presents us with a bitingly ironic portrait of the fate of the truly selfless individual devoted to serving the community that the kibbutz as an institution sought to foster.

Disturbed by David's increasing retreat into solitude, and even more alarmed by rumors that he had been observed passionately kissing his beloved bovine charges, Devora sat down with him for a conversation, only to discover that the one item tying David to his late parents (who died in his youth), an album of family photographs, was callously cast aside by the kibbutzniks, who sold his apartment and turned the profit over to the kibbutz—" 'They didn't take you to the apartment so you could get what you wanted?' 'No. They said it was a shame to waste a day's work' " (78). When Devora confronted one of those responsible for David's loss of the only photos of his Holocaust survivor parents, taken before the war, the guilty party tried to placate her with a secret: they had found a wife for David, in hopes of weaning him off his amorous attachment to the kibbutz cows.

From here, the story shifts back into Devora's fairy-tale version of events, which the adult Melech demands to hear again. In this tale, Rachel (Melech's mother-to-be) is discovered working in the storeroom of the Haifa-based garage where the kibbutzniks purchase parts for the kibbutz vehicles. David and Rachel fall in love and she joins him on the kibbutz, where "she was employed in the sewing shop, and on the holidays, she'd bake in the kitchen and everyone was so happy, because her cakes were the most delicious. . . . They were very, very happy together" (80). But Devora's blissful narrative is abruptly interrupted by the omniscient narrator's "truthful" one, in which David was repulsed by the photograph of Rachel: "She's black as a Negro . . . I can't marry a black woman" (81). Whether by instinct or assimilation, David shared the Eurocentric biases of his comrades and was repelled by the prospect of marriage to the Iranian-born immigrant. But when told that Rachel desired him, David immediately changed his mind.

As the story unfolds, readers discover that both Rachel and David were developmentally disabled. The two did indeed fall in love and marry, but the kibbutz members mistreated Rachel at first, just as they had her husband. Rachel proved herself a fierce "buffer between the abusive kibbutz members and her husband fighting his fights energetically and fearlessly" (85). Six months after their wedding, Rachel was pregnant with Melech. Though a specialist had already warned Devora that the couple was unlikely to have a child of "normal intelligence," she took it upon herself to encourage Rachel with illustrations from a children's book and to explain all the stages of the fetus's development. But she could not shield the isolated couple from her comrades' persistent derision. When Devora learned that the kibbutz secretary had insisted the couple adopt "a name worthy of their baby—Melech (king)—she became furious—"It's a name that invites abuse" (88)—and did her best to persuade Rachel to change her mind, but to no avail. Present at Melech's birth, Devora was relieved to see that he was a healthy, normal baby after all, but she worried about the potential for cruel jests at Melech's bris.

One day, when Melech was still a toddler, David and Rachel asked Devora to promise to care for him should anything ever happen to them. Years later, after his parents' deaths, Melech and Devora would become very close. When Melech's class was assigned a family history project, Devora accompanied him to Beersheba to visit an elderly cousin of his father's, nearly the sole survivor of Melech's entire extended family, murdered in the Holocaust. Looking at the old black-and-white photos of his murdered relatives, Melech asked the old man why nobody had rescued them and was told that "there were a lot of other bad people, not only the Nazis" (90). When Melech then asked, "And there weren't any good people?" his father's cousin told him, "There weren't enough good people" (90). (By this critical point, Liebrecht has made the connection between the immoral bystanders of the Holocaust and the thoughtlessly cruel kibbutzniks abundantly clear.)[16] Just as the two were about to depart, the old man suddenly seized Melech in a smothering embrace. Unaccustomed to experiencing such affection from anyone beside Devora, Melech gushed, "Did you see how hard he hugged me?" (91). Unlike his parents, Melech would prove to be a precocious learner and high achiever, skip two grades, win sports medals, and become immensely popular. But before all this, he was only little Melech and was aware only of the love of his parents—and Devora.

Now he tells Devora gratefully that she has been the most "stable thing in my life since I was six. Without you, I wouldn't have survived in this place" (92). At this confession, Devora becomes truly alarmed and assumes that Melech is seriously sick—but he assures her that he is healthy. From this moment, the narrative becomes a suspenseful interrogation as Melech presses her for the raw details of his parents' lives, the nature of his parents' "retardation," the gift of the apartment that apparently ensured his father's acceptance, the harsh exploitation of his father at work. Most critically, Melech is anguished by his father's status as the "kibbutz clown" and what that meant to his own identity in childhood: "Is it funny to call the sons of retards 'Melech'? Is that a kind of humor?" (94). But his deepest concern is with something far more serious.

Officially, the tractor involved in his parents' death was said to be an Oliver, but Melech has subsequently learned that the evidence submitted to the police was falsified to cover up the fact that the tractor was actually a John Deere, known to be obsolete and dangerous. When Devora, now fearing Melech's anger, insists that his parents' death was a tragic accident, Melech angrily forces her to listen to a new version of the tale she had invented for him: "Once upon a time there was a beautiful place, like in a fairytale, that was called a kibbutz. The people there were very hard-hearted and mean-spirited, and more than anything, they were very bored, and that's why they were always looking for entertainment. One day, a good, hard-working young man who was mildly retarded came to their kibbutz. He loved the cowshed and the cows, and he loved the people and their kibbutz, but that didn't make them really like him, because they had a great need for entertainment" (95). In his "revisionist" version, the kibbutzniks greeted Melech's birth with great amusement: "Their fun would be tripled because the circus had really expanded . . . but alas, the boy didn't suffer from mild retardation. . . . He was a pretty smart kid, and that's why he was also very sad, because unlike his parents, he understood very well what he saw" (96). Devora weeps to hear this version of events, which "mocked the stories she had told him with so much love" (96). But Melech relentlessly elaborates on the John Deere's fatal defect, which set the stage for "the circus people's last and best performance" (96). After all these years, a witness to the events has come forward, telling Melech that his parents were murdered, a crime that remained a secret known only to the three conspirators. One of them is dead; another, who became intensely religious and left the kibbutz, revealed these facts to Melech. The third, who "stayed on the kibbutz with his beloved wife and two lovely daughters as if nothing had happened" (97), is Devora's husband.

This final devastating revelation forces Devora to confront "with profound clarity . . . the things that had simmered at the edge of her consciousness all those years, never flowing over the edge but never subsiding either" (97). At last, the anger she has long felt toward her husband and most of all "toward the soul-crushing kibbutz" (98) rises to the surface. Melech presents her with a heartbreakingly unadorned account of the reality she had rationalized away, with what was done to this couple, "who were so . . . retarded that they thought they were members of the kibbutz, a couple like all the others, a couple with a child. They didn't know they lived here to be the kibbutz clowns. They didn't know they were taking risks that circus people take. They probably didn't even know they were actually murdered. . . . They wanted to live here in peace with the cows and the flowers and the plum cakes, and their little boy" (98–99). His concluding words chillingly reinforce the earlier bridge to the Holocaust (and its amoral bystanders) as Melech completes the story he has appropriated to give his life authentic, if tragic, meaning: "Once upon a time there were a few bad people and a few indifferent people. . . . There was also one good woman, but that wasn't enough" (99). Yet, in the end, though dramatically powerful, deeply moving, and psychologically astute, Liebrecht's "Kibbutz" presents a monochrome picture of a society whose singular cruelty bears little resemblance to the moral complexity of its real-world counterpart. In conceiving a thoroughly dystopian environment utterly unmoored from its moral antecedents, this highly gifted writer misses an opportunity to grapple with the deeper possibility of moral autonomy and selflessness alongside all the foibles and pettiness that invariably inform any human community. At the same time, her story signals the nadir of the kibbutz's sinking reputation among outsiders and anticipates the dystopian trend in the cinematic portrayals of the kibbutz examined in chapter 5.

5

From the 1980s to 2010
Nostalgia and the Revisionist Lens in Kibbutz Film

In their excellent cultural survey, Eldad Kedem and Gilad Padva trace the ironic trajectory of the kibbutz cinema from its beginnings in 1933 (with one of the first Hebrew talkies) to 2007: "In the film *Sabra* (*Tzabar*, dir. Alexander Ford), the first fiction film made in Palestine/Eretz Yisrael, Jewish settlers from Russia arrive at a desolate place in Palestine. There they establish a communal settlement that will develop into a flourishing kibbutz. Seven decades later in *The Galilee Eskimos* (*Eskimosim ba Galil*, dir. Jonathan Paz), these settlers are now elderly people, residents in a nursing home [who] discover that their families and the youths have all left and their kibbutz has been sold to a private entrepreneur" (173). Kedem and Padva note that the earliest cinematic depictions of the kibbutz (nearly all docudramas) "embrace the landscapes, the Biblical antiquities, the urban and peripheral settlements, and mainly the construction of the country: developing roads, water supply, electricity, agriculture, and industry; building houses and institutions, as well as the developing leisure culture in the bigger cities. The films are characterized by pathos-replete dialogues, glorifying voice-overs, emotional subtitles, and sentimental, stirring sound track" (174). Such films are generally devoid of indigenous Arabs, aside from the occasional shepherd or wandering camel to add local color and a sense of the immigrants' struggle to reestablish roots in the biblical landscape. They go on to explain that several films of the early 1930s captivated audiences with an ideological mapping of geographic and human landscapes that is as richly sensual as it is pragmatic in its call to action:

> Panoramic views of the kibbutzim reveal fields and settlements, reflecting both the real and symbolic aspects of the Zionist socialist ideas.

Sequences presenting agricultural work on the kibbutz (edited in a *montage* technique) create a magic and fascination, symbolizing a cosmic, actual sequence of nature's progress and the natural cyclicality of human labor: plowing, sowing, fruition, blossoming, harvest, rest, and so on. Sights of people working in the field embody a primordial memory of ownership and belonging, an ancient scene, in which possessing the land is embodied in the plow and the furrow. . . . The focus on the human body and its daily hard work in the fields, often embodied as a semi-naked male physique, emphasizes and even (homo)eroticizes the organic connection of the farmers to this particular land. (174–75)

Throughout the 1940s, as the catastrophe in Europe grew, the cinematic kibbutz was rapidly transformed from an exotic fantasia of the New Jew to a thoroughly pragmatic haven, one of quotidian experience and efficient absorption of the steady influx of immigrants from the Diaspora, "an ideal site for education and reeducation, transforming the foreigner, the other, into 'one of us'" (177). In later years, the films representing the kibbutz grew substantially more complex and interesting as the kibbutz itself deteriorated and as protagonists experienced "geographical, moral and emotional distancing" from their community, which was no longer "a familiar place" but rather "a site of memory, an estranged different space" (182).

As we have seen in previous chapters, literary fiction about the kibbutz is similarly informed by growing alienation and doubt about the meaning and limits of home in this period (1940s and 1950s), when nostalgic commemorations are strikingly rare. Moreover, quite a few of the questioning literary narratives that have emerged in recent years respond to where the problem of "at-homeness" begins for many—communal child rearing—which Edna Perlman concisely delineates: "A child's reference group was not his or her biological parents, but his peer group; the children were divided according to their peer groups and were raised and educated with their peers in children's homes; the peer group was meant to serve as an extended family" (103–4). Hence the mother and father in what is usually deemed the "nuclear family" by the rest of Western culture were required by "kibbutz society . . . to extend and share their personal parental feelings and bonding with their children with the entire community" (115). The unanticipated psychological reverberations of this system would inspire the anguished responses of the second generation of kibbutzniks in the memoirs and films of recent years. Some revisionist trends in the kibbutz cinema would portray the dispossession of Palestinian villages and farmers by the expansionist efforts of halutzim; others would grapple with the rapid degradation of the kibbutz ethos in the era of privatization. But before turning to these, we will first consider one of the most iconic renderings of the fissures in socialist ideology that began long ago.

Noa at Seventeen

In her valuable study of the critical and artistic work done by those raised in the era of ardent collectivization, Yael Darr describes how, in later weighing the experiences of their formative years, "a handful of writers and artists of this generation came together years later, forming a wave of retrospective criticism around which public discourse in Israel has revolved throughout the last two decades. In short stories, novels, exhibitions, films, plays, and television shows, ex-kibbutz members express bitter public criticism of their kibbutz childhood, bringing to the surface the heavy emotional price they have paid as a result of communal upbringing" (146). In certain respects, the earliest film in this wave is now widely regarded as a classic of the Israeli cinema, director Yitzhak Yeshurun's *Noa bat sheva-esrei* (*Noa at Seventeen*; 1982).

Set in 1951, *Noa* is most often appreciated as a gripping coming-of-age story of a rebellious young girl impatient with the banal collectivism and groupthink of her friends, one whose ardent skepticism ultimately leads to her abject banishment. Yet the film is also an incisively accurate chronicle of how Israel's ideological struggles shaped the conflict between the individual and the collective—perhaps the most critical and pervasive social dynamic of the early years of the state. Though *Noa*'s action does not directly take place on a kibbutz, the ideological force of that institution and the tense issues it gave rise to are always present. Yeshurun (who also wrote the screenplay) provides an acute and accurate portrayal both of the kibbutz's political power and mythic aura and of the crisis that overtook this vanguard of Israeli socialism in response to Soviet aggression on the eve of the Korean War, a crisis that would shatter kibbutz families and a number of kibbutzim and result in profound schisms, some of which remain unhealed more than sixty years later. Throughout the film, the values of collective life are front and center, the subject of passionate debate and rancor; the dilemmas of otherness and estrangement that it portrays mirror those faced by outsider protagonists in the classic kibbutz narratives of Israeli literature.[1] Noa (movingly portrayed by Dalia Shimko) wakes up to her own prickly individuality exactly when her friends demand unflinching loyalty to their cause. Just as she is pressured to follow them to a life of ideals and duty on the kibbutz (a path she is unsure of), the entire movement was forced to choose between Moscow and the West in the uncertain turbulence of the early days of the Cold War. The moral disenchantment with Stalin and the Soviet Union following the execution of Yiddish writers and the infamous "Jewish Doctors Trials" left the younger generation of Israelis reluctant to embrace the fervent political commitments of the past.[2]

Though it seems astonishing today, not long before *Noa at Seventeen* takes place, Stalin's Soviet Union was "at the center of Israeli identity," as Tom Segev points out in his examination of the political rivalries and controversies that raged within the left-wing party Mapam, then Israel's second-largest political faction ("'USSR Is Our Second Homeland'"). Yossi Klein Halevi aptly asserts that the "kibbutz and the Soviet Union were different aspects of the same historical march: the kibbutz an experiment in pure communism, the Soviet Union an experiment in mass communism. Both were necessary to prove the practicality of radical equality" (5–6). During the Knesset's 10 March 1949 debate on the composition of the first Israeli government, one of Mapam's leaders, Ya'akov Hazan of Kibbutz Mishmar Ha'emek, declared, "For us, the Soviet Union is the fortress of world socialism, it is our second homeland, the socialist one" (qtd. in Segev, "'USSR Is Our Second Homeland'"). Jo-Ann Mort and Gary Brenner's description of the political and social crisis that then struck directly at the heart of Zionism can help us better understand Yeshurun's approach to the positions taken by Noa, her bitterly divided family, and her ideologically passionate comrades: from the mid-1940s, a "split developed in the labor movement, which was mainly caused by different attitudes toward the Soviet Union. The majority of the Mapai Party . . . made up of both city dwellers and kibbutz members, opposed the pro-Soviet attitude of the minority. As a result, the latter created its own faction called the Ahdut Avodah Party, which was supported by a majority of kibbutz members. . . . Ideological debates raged around such esoteric concerns as which anthem to sing first, the 'Internationale' or 'Hatikvah'" (2).[3] No other Israeli film or novel has examined this period nearly as incisively. Yet, as frequently occurs in Israeli filmmaking, it was the then current moment of crisis—the 1982 Lebanon War with its resulting disenchantment and political controversies—that inspired Yeshurun to revisit the fate of the dissenter in Israel's youth and that is the emotional subtext in the film's most confrontational scenes.[4] Indeed, *Noa*'s emphasis on the limits of collective thinking and on the isolation of its nonconformist heroine by her disapproving peers reflects the angst of many unhappy artists in the years following the right-wing Likud Party's dramatic rise to power in the 1977 elections.[5]

The film's minimalist aesthetic (a melancholy musical score based on a single woman's voice alternating with a few stately notes played on a piano) and its claustrophobic interiors poetically evoke the time of austerity in which it is set; its emotional scenes, almost unbearable in their rawness, produce a sense of urgency and immediacy not often achieved in period dramas. As cultural critic Ella Shohat observes, "The simple sets and minimal camerawork . . . appropriately mirror a fictional world prizing simplicity and modesty of appearance" (*Israeli Cinema* 210). This strikingly modest and functionalist aesthetic, which prevails throughout the film, unmistakably evokes the dominant influence and ethos of the kibbutz, even without the presence of kibbutz life per se. From the perspective of an Israeli audience immersed in the all-pervasive individualism and materialism of the 1980s, *Noa*'s return to the beginning of the end of the socialist Zionist era carries surprising nostalgic force and provokes thoughts about what might have been lost in the country's shift in values. For scholar Eldad Kedem (himself a former kibbutznik), *Noa* is representative of kibbutz films in which "ideological collectivism and a totalitarian approach to equality are presented as the cause of the individual's oppression, especially of those who are different. The uncompromising idealism and group pressure are shown as the cause of destructive personal distress" (327).[6] That stress is immediately evident in the film's portrayal of Meir, Noa's father (played by Moshe Havazelet), who years earlier yielded to the demands of his wife, Bracha, and sacrificed his kibbutz dreams.

Much of *Noa* traces the direct consequences of Meir's repressed desire and the ensuing familial crisis that erupts when Meir's brother, Shraga (played by the wonderful Shmuel Shilo, who lived on Kibbutz Tze'elim from its founding until his death in 2011), a kibbutz member and Moscow loyalist, comes visiting on the inauspicious eve of a meeting with representatives from the two warring political camps. Noa's tempestuous mother, Bracha (nimbly portrayed by actress Idit Zur), is a functionary in the Labor Movement, aligned with party members eager to follow the Social Democracy Movement ascendant in European countries. Thus she and Shraga, like so many ideologues of that period, are bitter adversaries. What is most impressive about Yeshurun's examination of the warring parties in Noa's life is his refusal to sentimentalize or malign either side.[7] Though it may be tempting to dismiss the distant tumult of the early 1950s as merely a quaint relic of the past, bearing little or no relevance to contemporary Israeli society, Shohat reminds us of the profound consequences of the hardened devotion to "security" that replaced "the pioneering ideals of volunteer agricultural work and economic equality" and that lasted through successive governments into our own time: "Over the years security rather than equality or justice came to form the overriding value of Zionism" (*Israeli Cinema* 207). Thus, even as ideological struggles threaten to unravel families and friendships in the film, it is hard not to feel a deep regard for a time when ideals mattered so very much.

Noa's coming of age is dramatically staged against the collapse of sacred values and myths. As she struggles to find herself, she recoils in pain from the unyielding and wounding confrontations by the people she loves. Though long a member of a socialist Zionist youth movement, Noa grows to doubt those who care more for ideology than they do for one another and in the process discovers her inner rebel. She can no longer feel at ease, as she once did, with what she now regards as her movement's pedagogical banalities. In an early scene, we learn a great deal about both her emerging sense of individualism and her pressure-cooker environment. A steely rationalist, Noa's mother violates her privacy by reading her diary, warning her not to give in to her impulses, whereas Noa believes her instincts will lead to "justice and the truth." Moreover, she is absolutely convinced that her father's meek surrender to Bracha long ago—"My father gave up on life"—has brought him to the brink of a breakdown. At the same time, Noa is caught up in an increasingly heated conflict with her mother over her own desire to join a kibbutz with the rest of her youth group.

As part of her secret political agenda, Bracha convenes a meeting of bank officials, agricultural specialists, and political party members in order to hold a "civil conversation," even though the conflict has already entered a violent phase, that will enable the bank to fund and facilitate the "division process" in the kibbutzim that are being split apart. But at the very mention of division, passionate Shraga explodes, charging that outsiders have illegally manipulated the "Mapai majority" on his kibbutz. When the others argue that no Zionist party can afford to align itself any longer with the Soviet Union, which has just closed its "iron doors" to Jewish emigration, Shraga angrily dismisses their argument and storms out of the discussion. Noa discovers him fuming in the family kitchen and attempts to console him. For his part, Shraga questions her intention to settle on the kibbutz and gently warns her about its insular and argumentative attitudes.

The ideology-driven debates of the adults are paralleled by meetings between Noa and her friends in the youth movement. While they are planning an activity for the younger movement members at the summit of Masada (site of the Jewish rebellion against Roman occupation so central to Zionist education), Noa interrupts with a counterproposal. Rather than dwell on ancient history, the youths should instead confront the urgent ideological crisis at hand and the damage it is causing to kibbutz families and kibbutzim. One of her fellow *madrichim* (counselors), an unnamed young woman, forcefully insists that they continue with their original plan to indoctrinate the children with the question "why dying in the name of God is the right thing to do. Why is that a good thing . . . that is, unlike any other death, which is a bad thing?" Disgusted by her sanctimonious attitude, Noa demands that the youths address "real issues," to which her comrade scoffs, " 'Real issues'? Sacrificing oneself for ideals—that is a 'real issue.' One for all." Just as another youth breaks the alarming news that kibbutzniks have physically attacked their own comrades in recent days, the scene dissolves into the adults' own tempestuous meeting, where the same issue of violence is being raised.

When a furious Shraga rails against the Mapai Party for forcing the kibbutzim to absorb the new immigrants (who were largely allied against the veteran kibbutz members loyal to Moscow), the meeting collapses in a flurry of accusations and insults. After the hasty departure of the officials, a red-faced Shraga collapses onto a sofa, breathing heavily as if on the verge of a heart attack. When Meir rushes to his brother's side, Shraga sighs plaintively: "The kibbutz has failed, Meir. All those efforts . . . it was all a waste. We thought we would be the model of communism and pure equality." Shraga and Meir, both heavy men whose days of youth and vigor are long behind them, sink into weary silence. But, drawing on some deep reserve of resentment, Shraga resumes his sparring with Bracha: he blames his brother's unfortunate abandonment of the agrarian life on her; he insists that Meir's "self-destructing" silence only masks his bitter disappointment. Bracha responds by accusing Shraga of ruining his own late wife's happiness and by telling him that "if you knew how much I hated you, you would never enter this house." At this point, Meir suddenly rouses himself and startles everyone by announcing his intention to leave the family and return to farming.

In scenes that Yeshurun artfully interweaves, the world of the young people becomes as agitated as that of the adults (though further complicated by hormonal urges). When Aya, Noa's closest friend, rightly accuses her of stealing her boyfriend, Uzi, the affection-starved Noa immediately confesses: "I only wanted one kiss," but Aya leaves in disgust. Later that night, Uzi returns to find Noa distraught over her betrayal of Aya, and he tries to console her by promising that the two of them will go off on a camping trip by themselves and tour the northern kibbutzim, presumably to start a new life. Emotionally exhausted by all the turmoil in her family, Noa accepts Uzi's physical advances. The next time she sees him, however, it is in the company of another youth movement leader, and Uzi, who had once postured as a free-thinking iconoclast to gain Noa's affection, severely disappoints her by falling back into conformity and obligation, hinting that their trip is off. When the youth leader insists that Noa fulfill her obligation to lead a trip of younger children to Masada, she shrugs off his demand: "The movement is extremely narrow-minded because it assumes there is only one truth." The youth leader haughtily ripostes that the council has convened for her "to explain herself." Just before she does, however, Uzi sits down with her and quietly attempts to justify himself: "I want to belong, I do want to belong. That's why I'm willing to give up some of my self-identity." After a final tender kiss, Noa parts from her Judas and walks like a condemned prisoner to her inquisition by the young council members, all of whom are now solemnly wearing their official uniforms.

Embittered by Uzi's betrayal, Aya invokes the movement's platitudes, accusing Noa of "pure evil" for selfishly thinking only of herself and refusing to join them on the obligatory Masada trek. When she goes on to say that even Noa's skirt (which fails to conform with movement norms) is "pure evil," the council meeting rapidly descends into other petty absurdities, a grotesque mirror of the adult world's ideological excesses and ferocious enmities. These relentlessly oppressive carryings on lead Noa to a sudden epiphany about her own individuality and the impossibility of submitting to the collective will. She rails against her ex-comrades' smothering controls: "I'm all for private life. . . . You hate everything beautiful and I can't relate to that! You'd all hate flowers if you didn't have the council's approval! You'd have us share our underwear in the end! If this is socialist Zionism, I want no part of it!" The members of the youth council then rise as one and depart. In the end, after Uzi ineptly attempts to divide his loyalty between Noa and the group, Noa is left alone and cries bitterly.

When the action shifts back to the adults, Meir has returned home from the agrarian settlement, only to declare that he is departing permanently. He insists that everything will work out and that he will visit regularly. Though Bracha coldly refuses to take his reborn ambition seriously, Meir defends his dream, comparing her rigidity to that of the warring ideologies now tearing Shraga's community and other kibbutzim apart "in the name of your treasured socialism." For Meir, the socialists' precious doctrines "ruin everything. . . . Those principles drove us all insane." As in previous scenes, there seems to be no limit to the amount of emotional pain the characters can inflict on one another. Nevertheless, in the wake of the tempest, Meir quietly concludes that he will not return to farm, that "love or no love we belong together. I'm staying with you and that's the end of it." It seems a denouement worthy of Anton Chekhov.

Later, Noa tries to comfort her mother, who has broken down in tears, perhaps because she has finally understood that her husband's abandoning his dream had cost him as much as Shraga claimed it had. Though the State of Israel is just a few years old, Bracha's words all too faithfully reflect the malaise and disenchantment (and perhaps also the nostalgia) of the post-Zionist era in which Yeshurun wrote his screenplay: "We wanted to build an avant-garde society based on cooperation, sharing, and creativity. . . . You think we're all lunatics who ruin everything. But your father, Shraga, and me . . . we're not lunatics. . . . Many kibbutz members are buried here in this valley, some who made mistakes and some who didn't. Some who were disillusioned by life in a kibbutz. And your father. Your father is the best and strongest of all." When Bracha tells Noa that she wants to be alone, immobilized with emotion, Noa can only stare in wonder at the deep love and understanding her mother has just laid bare.

Noa later discovers Uzi eagerly waiting in her bedroom (he's become well acquainted with the convenience of her open window), but, unfortunately, the two cannot emulate the adults' bittersweet reconciliation. Coming to terms with her own lonely truth, Noa declares that she has "burned all my bridges behind me and you need to let go. . . . My dad gave up on his life but I don't want to give up on mine. I'm wrong for you, the group, the kibbutz." Angry at being rejected, Uzi parrots the Zionist rhetoric on which he was raised, praising those who have sacrificed their lives in the recent war and warning Noa that "everyone" they know will end up on kibbutz: "The higher up you fly with your philosophies [of life] the further you'll fall. Only a higher cause, only a supreme ideal can hold us all together. That's how it always was and that's how it will always be in this country. And those who give up on a life of fulfillment and ideals create an empty void." Repulsed by Uzi's single-minded emphasis on the abstract collective rather than the individual, Noa cries out: "'Everyone!' It's always about 'everyone'! What happens when someone's facial expression is unhappy and 'everyone' doesn't like it?!" Stung that Noa holds him in contempt, Uzi tells her that "everyone's" now aware of her lack of true patriotic feeling and dangerously "defeated attitude," that she would have dragged him down to her level had he remained with her: "Luckily though, I'm strong and I love this country."

Like self-dramatizing teenagers in very different situations, Noa cannot resist writing a final letter to Uzi. Here Yeshurun strikes just the right note in blending Noa's adolescent hubris with a hint of the sophisticated woman to come (whom we hear in a voice-over). Though still unhappy, Noa tells Uzi that she is resigned to the likely prospect "that I'll be lonely for the rest of my life." This melodramatic pronouncement expresses the essential, painful adult truth

FIGURE 9   Director Yitzhak Yeshurun with Dalia Shimko (Noa) and other cast and crew members on the set of *Noa at Seventeen*. Used by permission.

by which most genuinely self-aware individuals ultimately live. At the same time, it is a strikingly post-Zionist moment in the history of Israel's cinema, an expression of collective skepticism (fig. 9). Noa concludes, as does the film, with these self-reflective lines: "I remember when we were a forest swaying at the wind together . . . a stranger among them, I was swept away by their motion."

Palestinian Ghosts in *Rain 1949*

Ilan Yagoda's poetic 1998 documentary *Rain 1949* (fig. 10) carries us deep into the moral complexities of his family's intergenerational relationship to Kibbutz Megiddo, established in 1949 by Holocaust refugees, among them Yagoda's mother. By a rather startling coincidence, Yagoda spent four years there during

FIGURE 10   *Rain 1949* (1998), directed by Ilan Yagoda. Used by permission.

his military service (in the 1970s) without knowing about his mother's relationship to its founding days. Yagoda detaches his film from that familial story, however, by introducing a complicating factor: Megiddo was established on the site of the abandoned Arab village of Lajun.[8]

Today many kibbutzim have sold off the agricultural lands they once appropriated from abandoned Palestinian villages, a historical irony prompting political scientist Meron Benvenisti to ruefully observe, "The Zionists have always boasted that only they could feel metaphysical connection to the homeland, while the Arab peasants could only muster an emotional attachment to a well-defined place: a house, a tree, a hill. But that Zionist contention has drowned in a sea of consumerism and privatization that has turned the landscape from a national, sacred patrimony over to commercial interests, and the struggle for the Land has become a struggle for profitable zoning" (332). Since the Arab villagers who are part of the story of Yagoda's film were forced to evacuate some four months before the Holocaust survivors' arrival, the Jewish settlers had little awareness of how recently it had been inhabited by Others. For their part, the Arab villagers initially assumed that they would return after only a few days, but, of course, that was not to be.

The film's title refers to the apparently epic rains of 1949; Yagoda uses the trope of that deluge, which the Jewish settlers welcomed as an agricultural blessing and the Arab villagers took as a curse, to demonstrate the impossibility of washing away the traumas of the past—whether that of the Holocaust survivors or that of the displaced and forgotten Palestinians of Lajun. Long preoccupied by the fact that the members of Kibbutz Megiddo never told visitors the site's recent history (or even discussed it among themselves), and two decades after his service there, Yagoda felt compelled to examine the meaning of its history for Jews and Palestinians alike.[9] The Palestinians fled to the town of Umm el-Fahm, imagining that their sojourn away from their land would be temporary, not a permanent condition. An old man recalls Lajun as "my life's starting point . . . dear to my heart" but averts his eyes whenever traveling past the site. And a woman from the same generation tells Yagoda that she frequently dreams that she is carrying a water pitcher and walking "home." The dreams always leave her feeling "happy and joyful, everything is all right" and, in their wake, she allows herself to linger in the fantasy that what actually happened is merely a "nightmare."

As if in direct counterpoint to these impossible dreams of return, we hear the poetry of a Holocaust refugee, which emphasizes that life is not a circle and "you never return to your starting point. We will end up somewhere and someone else will go on. There are no circles in life." Still, even that somber wisdom does not altogether overshadow the Palestinian's plaint that Lajun is a "wound in the heart." On weekends, some of the second generation of displaced Arabs visit the ruins of their parents' homes with their own children, a poignant bridge between the exilic generations. Though they have peaceful relations with the Jews of Kibbutz Megiddo, it is clear from Yagoda's sensitively conducted yet probing interviews that many of them still feel a strong attachment to their original homes and that this attachment has made it difficult for most individuals on one side to form lasting friendships with those on the other.

There are exceptions. Ilan visits the Arabs his late father befriended, eager to learn whatever he can about their past connections, that lost world of possibilities. And, in what can genuinely be called a "pastoral scene," the elderly Jabri (showing visible signs of Parkinson's) and his Jewish friends wander companionably together through a grove of lemon trees, reminiscing about Jabri's curious sojourn at Megiddo. It seems that the kibbutz youths "adopted" him. At one point, Jabri admits that, to this day, he deeply regrets declining the amorous overtures of a kibbutz girl at a dance to which he was invited—a bittersweet moment strikingly suggestive of the plot of Atallah Mansour's novel *In a New Light*. In this and other scenes juxtaposing the traumatic and ironic convergences of Jewish and Palestinian displacements, the director achieves what Shira Stav describes as an ethics of similarity or "the adherence to traumatic personal and national history [that] demands that the Jewish collective assume responsibility for its wrongdoing to the other. . . . The question goes beyond the demand for responsibility and touches on the nature of that responsibility. The latter grows out of similarity between the Jewish and the Arab catastrophes. It is not a responsibility that grows out of the basic otherness of their experiences, narratives, and perspectives" (92).

As Yagoda himself told me, while conducting research for the film, which included frequent meetings with the Arab villagers, he was struck by the fact "that there are two groups of people similar in their struggle to overcome a major trauma from their past, their destinies are close to each other and to the same piece of land, yet they are invisible to each other." More important, he was persuaded that "participating in the film was healing for people on both sides. I hope that recognizing and respecting the pain and agony of the other side might also be the first step for a dialogue and perhaps create an opportunity for future recognition and reconciliation."[10] For the rest of us, especially those once accustomed to naively imagining the history of the kibbutz as somehow removed, or innocent, of the trauma of the Nakba, Yagoda's melancholy and intimate story of refugees begetting refugees is highly instructive.[11]

The Galilee Eskimos

In Batya Gur's novel *Murder on a Kibbutz*, as part of the kibbutz's revitalization plan, the younger generation plans to move their retired parents from their domiciles into an assisted living facility (still within the confines of the kibbutz) to make room for young families from the outside.[12] At one point, an older woman, utterly convinced that Srulke, a beloved comrade, died from a broken heart brought on by the imminent change, cries out: "You want to put us into an old-age home, that's why he died. What do you think, we did your dirty work, and now you don't need us anymore? Eskimos . . . savages . . . barbarians . . ." (38; ellipses in original).

This is precisely the unresolved question that Jonathan Paz's highly entertaining film *Eskimosim ba Galil* (*The Galilee Eskimos*; 2007; fig. 11) examines with compassion, pathos, and mischievous imagination. Due to its empathic attitude toward aging and the restoration of its elders' health, energy, and spirit, the film has sometimes been compared to Ron Howard's 1985 seriocomic science fiction fable, *Cocoon*, about the miraculous rejuvenation of a community of Florida retirees, but *The Galilee Eskimos* wisely avoids that film's sometimes condescending romanticization and its cloying elements of fantasy. Unlike Howard, who filters the experience of old age through the fetishization of youth, Paz crafts a nuanced, reverent, and often wrenching story about the dormant vigor, relevance, and humanity of a forgotten generation and its accomplishments. Paz clearly intended his film as a vehement protest: "The myth that old age represents a second-class humanity needs to be shattered!" (Hands). But perhaps the most important thing to know about *Eskimos* is that it is one of the rare instances of kibbutz storytelling that manages to be both hilarious and moving.

One morning, twelve seniors living in a sequestered home for the aging founders of a small kibbutz located on Israel's border with Lebanon wake to discover that the rest of the community has mysteriously vanished. Slowly and painfully, they rally to defend themselves against a bank that has foreclosed on

FIGURE 11   Kibbutz characters of *Eskimosim ba Galil* (*The Galilee Eskimos*; 2007), directed by Jonathan Paz. Used by permission.

the kibbutz and its lands and a bullying developer who descends in a helicopter with a plan to build a luxury casino-resort on the ashes of their socialist settlement. They go to work, restoring defunct wells, milking the cows, farming, and even preparing for armed defense. They sing and celebrate and entertain one another with scandalous tales about their younger selves as they reestablish their kibbutz and prepare for a final battle. The film's witty and empathic screenplay is written by Joshua Sobol, a former kibbutznik and one of Israel's most acclaimed dramatists. Though at times charming escapism, in its best moments, *The Galilee Eskimos* is also an unabashed and multifaceted love letter to the kibbutz dream and the resilient, prickly, and idealistically passionate personalities who lived that dream against great odds.

Yet there is also a great deal of verisimilitude here despite the film's whimsical elements of wish fulfillment. Astutely aligning the film with what he calls the kibbutz "privatization cinema," David Leach praises it for its portrayal of "the gravity of changes to kibbutz life in the real world" and for its profound illumination of "the question of what it means to be a kibbutznik" in the twenty-first century (Review). The quarrels, storytelling, and laughter of these embattled seniors bring their mythic exploits back to life even as we are made aware of how acutely irrelevant their exploits and values are to mainstream society, intensified by the kibbutz's geographical isolation from the busy coastal plain and trendy urban centers (fig. 12). Moreover, the film accurately portrays the twenty-first-century transformation of the once-pioneering heartland of the Galilee into a "post-rural" realm, an urban bourgeois invention that, largely composed of "four symbolic universes: rural style and atmosphere, agriculture and country gourmet, the experience of nature, and authenticity of place, . . . represents the voice of the urban middle class in the dynamics of place and collective identity in [twenty-first-century] Jewish Israeli society" (Z. Shavit 98). In Paz's inventive film, this transformation of the landscape's meaning is fully visible. Admiring the film's serious critique of Israeli society as a shell of what it had once been, Yael Gvirtz observes that, "contrary to what we were told as children, it has become belatedly apparent that a vacuum exists in Israeli life. Our current leadership . . . premises itself on passing the buck rather than bearing responsibility." *The Galilee Eskimos* "is illuminating in its human warmth of all that has been forgotten and left behind, and in the power of vision of those who paved the way for us vis-à-vis our weakness and our emptiness as creditors and real estate agents."

Born on Kibbutz Mizra, where he remained a member until 1971, Paz traces the inspiration for *Eskimos* to his high regard for the founders, his parents'

FIGURE 12   Cast of twelve kibbutz veterans during production of *The Galilee Eskimos* (2007). Used by permission.

generation, and what they sought to achieve. The idea emerged from a visit to his mother, who lived in the kibbutz until the end of her life: "We spoke of globalization, insensitive capitalism, and the poor state of the kibbutzim. Many of the kibbutzim had begun the process of privatization . . . no more equality and cooperation, only 'Differential Wages,' etc. . . . I asked her, 'Mother, which period of your life do you miss the most?' She answered without any hesitation, 'I would like to go back to the time when we founded the kibbutz.' I knew right then I had a story!" (Hands). Paz's recollection of his film's genesis is remarkably reminiscent of an incident in Avraham Balaban's encounter with an elderly woman in *Mourning a Father Lost*, an encounter that might serve to encapsulate all aging former kibbutzniks, the way they experience their own startling diminishment and loss of vitality, the painful intimation that their values and accomplishments will be utterly disregarded by the younger generation in the new era of globalization. Venturing into the dining hall, once the boisterous heart of collective life, Balaban is immediately struck by the life that has vanished:

> There was nothing left of the old lunchtime hubbub. Here and there sat solitary survivors of my parents' generation. Sarah, the mother of my classmate . . . smiled, then mumbled awkwardly, "What we've come to," and shuffled on. Her embarrassed words expressed sorrow: "My husband . . . died this year, and you must remember us, how we used to walk briskly to the cowshed and the orchard and the children's house. Who would have thought that one day we'd drag ourselves with difficulty from the house to the dining hall . . . who would have thought that one's body would shrivel to the size of a child's body, that we would sit by ourselves in the dining hall like scolded children, or that loneliness would hurt more, day and night, then the aching joints of the fragile, chilly body." (*Mourning* 62)[13]

The fading generation that Balaban met with during his visit was justifiably filled with anxieties about its future.[14] Joshua Muravchik describes how the severe financial challenges of the 1980s affected the veterans of the kibbutz: "The kibbutzim were facing insolvency, and although the government did arrange bailouts, the kibbutzniks knew that the nation no longer relied on them to settle the land and guard the borders. How long would it continue to underwrite them? The question haunted those at the end of their working years. Because they had never imagined reaching such a pass, no pensions had been put aside. It was assumed that the kibbutz would be there always and that it would provide" (333). In this regard, it also bears noting that since labor was the supreme value in the traditional kibbutz, older members of the community simply kept working beyond what would have been deemed retirement age elsewhere; thus they could feel as relevant to the well-being of the society as anyone else.

In their examination of the vicissitudes of aging in kibbutz life, Yasmin Asaf and Israel Doron readily affirm that, "in the past, retirement from work rarely occurred in kibbutzim, contributing to a longer and more productive old age. Since work represented the highest value in the original vision of the kibbutz, it was an ideal community in which to age. The kibbutz promised social security, a community framework, and meaningful citizenship that permitted continuing productivity and participation and in a manner that adapted itself to disability and illness" (86). The Asaf and Doron study focuses on those between fifty-five and sixty-five years of age; their respondents typically regarded work as "both a right and a duty," as defining a person's entire life experience. "When the expression 'old age' was mentioned in interviews, it bothered the interviewees, and they had difficulty locating it in their lives. Many of them were insulted by the term and asked us to use other expressions, such as 'maturing'" (91).[15] Given the prevalence of these attitudes, it is easy to see why Paz so immediately understood the creative power of his nonagenarian mother's poignant dream of recovery: "*Galilee Eskimos* [offers] these old folks the opportunity to go back . . . to their proud past, to return and build the kibbutz once again: A return to the commune, to mutual help and friendship, to the old work clothes and the communal shower, the work roster and the general meeting (democracy), to a life of culture and romances of old, even to the rearming of the kibbutz in order to guard it from external enemies" (Hands). Of the often comic adventures that ensue, one is especially worth singling out for its realism and close resemblance to the memories of Paz's mother. The kibbutz film documentarian has gathered everyone around a traditional kibbutz campfire to gaze at a slide show of milestones from their epic historical struggle sixty years earlier: the erection of the first stockade, a contentious debate over whether private tea kettles would destroy collective life, and the first kibbutz children happily at play. Set at a certain tonal remove from the surrounding high jinks, this scene carries genuine emotional force.

When asked about the far more caustic portrait of the past by fellow former kibbutznik Dror Shaul in *Adama meshuga'at* (*Sweet Mud*), also released in 2006 and discussed below, Paz calls it "a great film" but adds that his own childhood was different: "I made my film with a great deal of love, nostalgia, longing and homage to those people who founded the kibbutz. I really admire and love those people. I loved my childhood. For me and my friends, the kibbutz was a great time. We had a really happy childhood" (Hands).[16] Paz's unabated enthusiasm apparently even extends to the children's house, the same institution that has lately proved to be such a villain in the memories of other artists addressed in this study: "I fondly recall the communal sleeping arrangement as an exciting and special experience, which I look back on with great affection" (Hands). Yet even Paz couldn't resist opening his film with a flashback of a father parting from his son at night in the children's house, a father who, now elderly, gazes forlornly out of the window of the kibbutz's home for senior citizens—"The Deserter has been deserted!" as Paz himself acknowledges (Hands).[17] However, in the end, what most lingers in the minds of its viewers is the film's extraordinary statement about dignity, self-worth, and, yes, the values of socialist solidarity in an increasingly vapid Israel.

Sweet Mud

In the mid-twentieth century, portrayals of the kibbutz often focused on the willing self-sacrifices of stolid individuals sustained and supported by the community. Typical of that era is Peter Frye's film *Eshet hagibor* (*The Hero's Wife*; 1963), which examines the life of a war widow still mourning the loss of her husband, fallen in battle fifteen years before. In part due to her kibbutz's sanctimonious sentiments regarding war widows, she has been reluctant to enter into any romantic relationships until the day that a young volunteer from abroad rekindles her passion. Yet not long after the two become lovers, the youth departs and the widow pursues a relationship with a kibbutz suitor deemed more appropriate by the aggrieved community. In Yael Zerubavel's reading, although the film portrays the entire collective as "caring, nonjudgmental, and nurturing" and, in spite of the widow's temporary affections for the interloper, as capable of mustering all the resources the bereaved widow requires, "*The Hero's Wife* allows the outsider to occupy this role only within the set boundaries of a liminal phase: having released the widow from her entrapment in the role of 'the hero's wife,' the young man leaves the country soon after" ("Coping" 86). Interestingly, the portrayal of much the same scenario of a war widow's love for an unsanctioned outsider (only one less willing to conveniently exit the scene) takes a very different form in writer and director Dror Shaul's *Adamah meshuga'at* (*Sweet Mud*; 2006), as if directly challenging the banal conformity of the earlier film. More than any work we have examined, *Sweet Mud* raises the monumental question of the extent to which compassion and empathy could coexist with the rigors of socialist idealism.

Though released the same year as Paz's relatively beatific *The Galilee Eskimos*, Shaul's *Sweet Mud* is more highly representative of a tendency in the recent kibbutz cinema to relate stories of personal loss and pain rather than those of collective conflicts, as was once the norm.[18] "The internal conflicts in . . . kibbutz society," Kedem and Padva tell us, have metamorphosed into "individual traumas and devastated feelings. The sense of trauma and loss is manifested in narratives and themes of deconstruction, displacement, homelessness, wanderings, transience, and internal or external exile" (186). Even where families are portrayed, they are dysfunctional or simply "spread across the world" (186), a harshly Diasporic rebuke to the iconic image of the kibbutz as one of the sacred sites of Zionism's ingathering. In that context, Shaul's *Sweet Mud* is arguably the most searing portrayal of the isolated and traumatized individual marginalized by the indifferent collective. Its action takes place entirely on the kibbutz (thus intensifying its claustrophobic malaise) over the course of a single year (1974–75), with the four seasons representing different stages in its intensely dramatic story.

As the audibly cracked and visually fissured opening credits play, the camera slowly pans over a table with a remote loudspeaker from which we hear the wrenching sobs of an infant we do not see. As we relax into the comforting sepia-colored images, the old familiarity of that setting and furnishings lulling us into nostalgia, we are certain that someone must be on the way. But the sobs go on for what seems an unbearably long time until at last a woman moves into view and bends over a number of warming baby bottles. Grasping one, she silently exits the little room and the heaving sobs continue unabated.[19] This profoundly disturbing introduction quickly melts into a pastoral scene, the dawning of a timeless farm day. A little boy, Dvir, plays in the deep shadows of a barn as a bearded middle-aged man, Avram, enters, addressing a lowing calf affectionately. At first, this scene seems very much like the kibbutz's pleasant bucolic exteriors we have frequently encountered elsewhere. However, the viscerally shocking developments that unfold rapidly overturn that impression; they easily surpass even the most unpleasant surprises and ideological disenchantments in the literary narratives we've explored, establishing a pervasive unhappiness and even fatalism.

Casting furtive glances around him (Dvir is hidden from his view), Avram unzips his trousers and presses his penis up against the mouth of a hungry calf. In the absence of its mother's teats or a baby bottle, the creature instinctually fellates him, while the young boy looks on in horror. Thus the two alarming scenes in which the young of both human and animal are violated combine to suggest a heart of darkness within the pastoral lineaments of utopia. Ironically, in later scenes, Avram appears as the sensitive soul who soothingly serenades the kibbutz at Friday night meals with a song reminiscent of the classic Zionist songs of an earlier generation, although, of course, we cannot look at Avram with quite the same eyes as his adoring comrades.[20] These chilling scenes immediately undermine any nostalgic idealism the Israeli film audience might harbor toward socialist life, even as the filmmaker insists in other scenes on affirming a rather romanticized view of the lonely and embattled but resilient individual on the kibbutz. The young hero becomes increasingly challenged by a variety of traumatic experiences. Critic Eldad Kedem points out that numerous scenes in the film

> feature a solitary tree on a hill . . . in the background or foreground of the mise-en-scène. The tree serves Dvir as a hiding place and a refuge from personal and social chaos in some scenes and as a lookout post and a spy

224 IMAGINING THE KIBBUTZ

hole in others. Sometimes the tree is a place of forbidden pleasures, and on other occasions it is a secret meeting place for Dvir and his mother. In addition, the tree is an intersection between inside and outside, like a border marking the end of the known world, and a launching pad for sensation, experimentations, imagination, and intuition. (333)

Director Shaul replaces the heroic collective with the tormented son of an idiosyncratic woman unable to accept her community's authoritarian demand for absolute conformity.

Another early scene sets forth the pedagogy in which obligation and conformity are instilled: we encounter a class of kibbutz schoolchildren at the beginning of their "Bar Mitzvah year," their teacher ponderously instructing them to prepare for the special year ahead in which they will be given thirteen special missions that will prove their worth to the veteran members. Whatever myths the film's audience might cherish regarding "enlightened" kibbutz education are soon challenged as Maya, a strange girl who has just arrived on the kibbutz, inspires a startlingly vehement playground battle between two kibbutz boys. Dvir's mother, Miri, is an emotionally fragile woman with a checkered past. Her boys know that their father died in an "accident" of some kind and also that their mother is pining for a stranger, the "Swiss Judo champion" and restaurateur named Stephan, a man she met while institutionalized following a nervous breakdown. At the kibbutz asefa, Miri is granted her request for Stephan to visit for a month. However, Dvir, who has long fantasized about the appearance of a new heroic father (closely modeled on Zionist norms of masculinity), is deeply disappointed when a white-haired man in late middle age descends from the bus. As Miri and Stephan enter the dining hall, the kibbutz members seem to turn their heads as one; Shaul's witty choreography tells us everything he wants us to know about their insular self-regard and distrust of outsiders.

Unexpectedly, Stephan redeems himself in Dvir's eyes by working with him to build a kite that wins first place "for creativity and ingenuity" in a kibbutz competition. Yet even that uplifting moment is robbed of its full sweetness when Avram violently intrudes. Fresh from a stint in the reserves, he rages against Dvir, accusing the child of intentionally letting his pet dog impregnate Avram's. When he shoves the boy to the ground and raises his hand to strike him, Stephan rushes forward and, in the ensuing melee, breaks Avram's arm. In the next scene, the asefa sits in haughty judgment against Stephan, the outsider—"We will not tolerate such bestial behavior" (somehow overlooking that it was Avram's brutal assault on the child that precipitated Stephan's intervention). Stephan is ordered to leave, a terrible blow for Miri, whose emotional health is already precarious. Nor does the matter rest there. Avram cynically seizes an opportunity for further vengeance. On one of Dvir's habitual raids on the industrial walk-in freezer for popsicles, he is horrified to see the frozen carcass of his dog, which Avram has left to taunt and torment him. When Dvir tearfully confronts Miri with his loss in the early morning hours, she threatens Avram with a pitchfork. Other members, waking to the workday, soon arrive on the scene and quietly persuade Miri to put down the pitchfork. But their initial success in bringing the tense encounter to a safe conclusion is perversely undone when Avram unleashes a final cruel gibe: "What does she want from me? Is it my fault the Swiss guy dumped her?" At that, Miri hysterically throws herself on the bully. Later, we see her driven out of the kibbutz gates in an ambulance to be institutionalized once again.

Weeks pass, and, on Dvir's birthday, the kibbutzniks attempt to console him with the gift of a new bicycle, which he angrily rejects. He demands to see his mother but is permitted only to write her. In the autumn, Miri returns just as Eyal, Dvir's big brother, is drafted into the army. Hence one absence rapidly follows another in Dvir's increasingly unhappy childhood. In parting, Eyal sternly warns his little brother to keep their mother away from alcohol and drugs. When we next see Dvir in Miri's cottage, she is still disconsolate that Stephan has left her. When the letter Dvir has written to Stephan on her behalf ("I stayed faithful to you in the hospital") fails to lift her spirits, he desperately searches the personal ads for what he deems a suitable match. In an exceptionally tender scene, Dvir gazes lovingly at his mother as he composes his own ad to extol her charms: "Young, kind-hearted, sensitive, intelligent, a perfect dancer . . . and excellent mom." Yet this radiant happiness proves as ephemeral as before, dissolving into a grim scene in the children's house, where Dvir and the others are violently awakened by the rough overturning of their beds as gruff older youths order them out into the darkness before dawn. This is their indoctrination into the youth wing of the Labor Movement, a traditional rite of passage to which they must passively submit.

Soon it is winter, and we watch as one rainy evening Dvir (again left in charge of his own welfare during one of Miri's prolonged absences), accepts a delivery of heating kerosene from a veteran kibbutznik. As the child turns away, the man cautions him that, even though Miri will be permitted to return home, the kibbutz has collectively decided that she isn't sane and that the burden is on Dvir to keep an eye on her. The unseasonable weather (many of the remaining scenes are filmed in darkness, thunder, and heavy downpours) compounds the sense of Dvir's heavy responsibility for his still emotionally unstable mother, as does the claustrophobia of the uncaring community, and highlights the intimate bond Dvir and Miri have; they are clearly a world unto themselves amid the hostile collective. During the height of a rainstorm, Miri coaxes her son out to the empty fields to gather potatoes for roasting. This proves to be the one moment in which Dvir appears to be blissfully happy. Tossing aside his umbrella, he whirls around, shouting, "What fun!" at the top of his lungs. Later, as they eat their potatoes with the storm raging outside, Miri makes Dvir a solemn promise: "This time, I've recovered for good. Your mother is as strong as an ox," and he gazes at her in adoration. However, even more than before, what comes next effectively demolishes the precious moments of security and well-being that the child has fleetingly enjoyed—Miri suddenly announces to Dvir that she is off to visit Stephan "in an hour" (although it is clear to us that he is still in Europe). With equal resolution, Dvir quietly tells her that she isn't going anywhere. Saddled with adult responsibility and the grim knowledge that his mother may never be entirely sane again, Dvir increasingly seeks solace in the company of Maya, the young girl who has been sent to live on the kibbutz by her own dysfunctional family. At the same time, he continues to watch over Miri like a hawk. One evening, when he finds her drinking with a much older, grizzled kibbutznik, who seems eager to take advantage of his much younger mother's neediness, he hangs around until the man pretends to depart. Bidding his mother good night, Dvir notices the suitor still lurking outside in the darkness. He sighs and squats down at the cottage's entrance, an immovable object barely sheltered from the incessant rain.

Later, Dvir's invincible heart is on display once again when a woman rushes excitedly into the kibbutz laundry, bearing a letter for Miri from Stephan: "Ever since leaving Israel I haven't stopped thinking about you. You are the woman of my life, my other half . . . I believe we'll work it all out soon and be together forever. Meanwhile you must be strong and think only good thoughts." The actual composer of this (and subsequent letters) is, of course, Dvir, conspiring with Maya, who translates his words into her native French. He is convinced that his mother's life absolutely depends on these lyrical assurances of Stephan's undying love. But Dvir realizes that the letters haven't worked when he discovers his mother swinging back and forth on a children's swing one night in the rain. "I'm depressed, I'm alone," she explains to him, starkly underscoring her incongruous solitude and isolation in spite of being surrounded by a supposedly caring community. She tells Dvir that she has no more of the pills that "warm my heart," which she has taken ever since her husband's suicide. Under the weight of a responsibility no child should bear, Dvir pleads with the kibbutz nurse, only to be told that his mother has dangerously exceeded her dosage. In the very depths of despair, Dvir and Maya forge a letter from his mother to Stephan announcing her eagerness to leave the kibbutz—and Dvir's love for him, too.

One sunny spring day, on leave from the paratroopers, Dvir's older brother, Eyal, though otherwise self-absorbed with both his military exploits and his burning desire to "get laid" (one of the film's few comic interludes), suddenly notices how anguished Dvir is. He tells him not to take his mother's woes upon himself and instead to come to terms with the fact she simply will not recover from her illness. We are startled to hear Eyal casually mention that a letter from Switzerland has arrived. Dvir snatches the letter from the kit bag, where his brother stowed it, and we soon learn that Stephan has arranged for three plane tickets ("in case Eyal wants to come along") for Miri and Dvir to reunite with him in Switzerland. A further surprise arrives in the following scene when Dvir goes first to Maya, not his mother, with the letter. As they lie beside a campfire under the stars, it is poignantly clear that the two have fallen in love. Dvir secretly makes plans for all three of them to depart (substituting Maya for Eyal, who is still in the IDF) immediately after the "Fire Ceremony," a grandiose secular coming-of-age ritual that apparently serves as the Zionist equivalent of a traditional Bar Mitzvah. In the kibbutz's dimly lit communal laundry, he pleads with Miri to hold on for just two more days. When she tries to placate Dvir, her chillingly robotic repetition of his words—"We're together. We're leaving together"—has precisely the opposite effect.

The nighttime ceremony requires all the youths to dash through various hurdles, including a circle of fire, after which the parents solemnly intone a rote speech congratulating their children on their coming of age and future induction into the IDF. What *Sweet Mud* portrays is actually highly congruent with many first-person accounts by former kibbutzniks of their ordeals (even at a much younger age than the film's young characters). For instance, in Balaban's memoir, *Mourning a Father Lost*, Batsheva, a female friend from his school days, recalls her trepidation on such occasions:

> I . . . remember . . . the constant feeling that our everyday activities were only a kind of preparation, that we were little soldiers training for a terrifying future. You remember how seriously they trained us in second grade to jump from the roof onto a stretched blanket that the whole class held tight down below? Maybe the boys enjoyed it, but for me in fourth grade sliding on an omega from the water tower was sheer terror. I don't

mean just the fear of jumping. . . . I mean the sense that it was all a preparation for a future in which you'll need to use these skills or you'd be lost. (*Mourning* 97)

Batsheva compares that regimented life to "a religious order, or a military camp," which explains why so many of the kibbutz youths became the IDF's elite cadre. She describes the "code" or intense symbolism of everyday life on the kibbutz—"the hairstyle . . . length of pants . . . color and material of the clothes . . . what time you got up in the morning and went to bed. It's really weird—on the one hand, we were apparently perfectly free, almost without adult supervision, almost neglected, and at the same time we lived under a cloud of written and unwritten rules. There was a strong feeling that everything you do is recorded somewhere, that you're always picking up merits or demerits" (97). Batsheva's sense of living under the gaze of a watchful, expectant, and judgmental society certainly resonates with Dvir's precocious comprehension of his society.

As Dvir dashes to complete the Fire Ceremony course, barely containing his excitement about the prospect of their liberation, he hears Miri's voice on the loudspeaker falter: "I wanted to be a mother to you, to care for you, and to raise you. But I couldn't do it. I'm sorry. It's not my fault." Sensing her imminent breakdown, a few kibbutzniks rush forward as Miri grimaces and cries out, "I wish you a life of love. And I hope you run away from this place and never come back!" As they struggle to subdue Miri, her voice rises to a hysterical pitch: "Because this kibbutz is death! Full of evil people! You must know the truth! Your father wanted to leave, too, but they suffocated him!" Watching helplessly through the ceremony's flames in a Dantesque scene of despair, Dvir witnesses his mother's total collapse and the end of his eager hopes of normality and escape from the place that Miri has just declared destroyed his father. Alone in bed, the boy stares glumly at the now meaningless plane tickets. In the middle of the night, his heavily sedated mother rises to beg Dvir's forgiveness. But when Dvir insists that they can still leave to start a new life with Stephan, Miri tearfully asks to be left alone "to sleep." And, at last, the boy absorbs the excruciating knowledge that Miri will need to be permanently institutionalized. He goes on one last mission for her, to steal Valium from the kibbutz clinic.

Our final glimpse of Dvir is not unhopeful: on a stunningly beautiful day, he and Miri ride their bicycles together out into the kibbutz fields. If Dvir will never be able to place his complete trust and affection in the kibbutz, the abstract and unreliable collective, he nevertheless knows how to love another individual. Obligation toward systems and unfeeling authority has been replaced by loyalty to worthy individuals. For Eldad Kedem, *Sweet Mud* is representative of a decidedly oedipal trend in the cinema of the kibbutz that rebels "against the kibbutz as an ideological 'father figure' and especially against the founders of kibbutzim as a metonym for Zionism and the state. Their Oedipal focalization revolves around the question of how to reject, dishonor, and disavow the Zionist ideology as condensed in the idea of the kibbutz and how to become free of it. Aptly enough, the rebellion against the Zionist symbolic father in these 'morally critical' films is signified by images of flawed masculinity connected with madness, illness, cruelty, and deviant sexuality" (331). These elements are portrayed with honesty and verisimilitude in *Sweet Mud*, perhaps the darkest portrayal of the abasement of the kibbutz myth to date.

Dror Shaul was born and raised on a kibbutz, and his own father died before he was born. In a fascinating interview included with the film's DVD release in Israel, Shaul reflects on the fact that, though "the child in the story is not me" (and the story portrayed did not take place in a single year), most of the events in *Sweet Mud* are nevertheless based on his childhood memories. The director describes both his parents as "strong" individuals. His father was an important figure on the kibbutz, both as a musician who often performed for the members and as someone involved in security matters; his mother was a teacher and artist. After her husband's death, she lost several other close family members and sank into a severely debilitating illness that was never diagnosed, but that Shaul thinks was likely a form of manic depression. As for Shaul himself, he grew up feeling the constant absence of a father, oppressed and isolated within the small, secluded kibbutz community. Throughout this interview, Shaul continually dismisses the importance of whether his film is significantly autobiographical, at one point arguing that it is not constructive to be too concerned with "what happened and what didn't. . . . For instance, I don't think that it is important for the viewer to know whether or not my dog was killed, who beat up whom, who raped whom, and so on." Yet, when all is said and done, we might be excused from concluding that Shaul does have an exceptionally deep personal connection with this story, a conclusion that is further supported by the choice to play the same melancholy accordion music during the interview that we hear throughout *Sweet Mud* and, later, when Shaul seems quite overcome with emotion. This segment of the interview was filmed in California, where *Sweet Mud* was being screened at a number of film festivals. Standing on a hill overlooking what appears to be the beachside community of Malibu, Shaul expresses wonderment over his long journey from the events that transpired in the 1970s, to the tiny mold-infested Tel Aviv apartment where he wrote the screenplay, and to this surreal moment where both his and his mother's "once-suppressed voices" are given international expression. Growing up with his mother's sense of being treated unjustly, he now claims to feel the same sense of "victory" or vindication expressed by Dvir before his mother's final collapse. And, at this point, he loses control and the interview is brought to a close.

Children of the Sun

Immediately upon its release, director Ran Tal's film *Yaldey hashemesh* (*Children of the Sun*; 2007) received an unusual amount of attention for a historical documentary about the kibbutz movement, especially for one based entirely on archival footage derived from over eighty amateur films shot between 1930 and 1970 (with the aesthetic standards typical of home movies in those years). Eventually viewed by thirty thousand Israelis in theaters and film festivals—a startling display of public interest in a documentary film, which certainly underscores the almost mythic significance the kibbutz still holds—*Children of the Sun* received glowing endorsements from two of Israel's most prestigious writers, Yoram Kaniuk and Amos Oz.[21] *Children* is a paradigmatic example of the recent era of the Israeli cinema, in which, as Kedem and Padva explain, "the kibbutz, which previously symbolized an antimodel to the exilic Jew—through rootedness, physical work in the field, a permanent, absorbing, and supportive home—is now represented through exilic themes: a sense of displacement, wandering, transience, and homelessness" (186). Aesthetically, those interwoven motifs of unease are dis/embodied in the film by a chorus of rueful and embittered voices, veteran or former kibbutz members struggling to come to terms with childhoods that were perhaps never fully theirs, in pursuit of a noble dream of their elders. As lucidly described by Yehudah Mirsky, "This regimentation was born of a great romance, the dream of a New Man, a New Jew, the vanguard of humanity in its long but sure march to equality and justice." Although choosing not to be a part of this story (primarily because he finds the prospect of self-victimization to be distasteful on both sides of his family), Tal is demonstrably a product of the kibbutz: he left Kibbutz Beit Hashita in his twenties, and the birth of his own children stirred up disturbing memories of his kibbutz childhood. In pursuit of that emotional archaeology, Tal interviewed dozens of members of his parents' generation, pressing them for their recollections of every aspect of life pertaining to the children's houses.[22]

His film focuses exclusively on the first generation of children whose strictly regimented lives did not benefit from the subsequent modifications that would enable later generations to enjoy greater privacy and far more attention from their parents (after many kibbutzim allowed children to live at home).

Just two years before the release of Tal's documentary, and perhaps signaling that for many the time was ripe to address the unvoiced pain of the past, the controversial exhibition *Togetherness: The Group and the Kibbutz in Israeli Collective Consciousness* opened at the Tel Aviv Museum's Helena Rubinstein Pavilion. Featuring the works of twenty-four men and women raised on the kibbutz, this unprecedented artistic inquiry into the past drew unusually large crowds. Unsurprisingly, many were current and former kibbutzniks who had themselves experienced the communal sleeping arrangements, and many of these returned for repeat visits. In her account of the responses of those attendees, journalist Dana Gilerman observed the intense emotions provoked both by the artists' individual works and the overarching thesis presented by curator Tali Tamir: "That in the children's houses, the individual is swallowed up in the collective, against his will." Many attending were startled, in some instances outraged, by what they saw as a uniform response to a complex phenomenon, while others (primarily men), complained that the participating artists were merely "whiners" or "crybabies."[23]

One visitor Gilerman spoke with haughtily disavowed the cumulative impact of the exhibited work: "There were always the normal ones and the 'sensitive' ones. It appears that the artists participating in this exhibition belong to the latter breed." At least one kibbutz artist refused the curator's invitation to participate, vehemently dissenting from what the exhibition sought to convey: "I didn't intend to say how bad it was. On the contrary: I remember the children's houses as the happiest period in my life." Even one of the participating artists, Ziva Yellin, later expressed her misgivings over the homogeneous vision of the past that dominated the exhibition: "There is a huge exaggeration that creates distortion and a simplistic view. It is a cliché to say that we have all come out of the same mold, or from a machine. . . . I grew up feeling that I had the best childhood in the world" (qtd. in Gilerman). Perhaps the most interesting critique of the exhibition was offered by Galia Bar Or, art critic and director of Kibbutz Ein Harod's Museum of Art, who decried what she called a "caricature" of life on the kibbutz, lacking a nuanced understanding of the "economic, historical, social [and] ideological" factors of the past, thoughtlessly replicating a new ideological timidity that irresponsibly diminished the extraordinary value of what was attempted (qtd. in Gilerman). For Bar Or, the works of the exhibition artists simply parroted the selfish egotism of the Israeli present:

The way people relate today to the children's house system is a way of trying to deflate the society that preceded us, our parents' society, which was an agenda for them. The statement that comes out of the exhibition is that there is a terrible price for social experiments. That it is better not to experiment. This conclusion is necessary for a certain population . . . that has no social agenda or responsibility. This is Israeli society, a petit bourgeois and pseudo-liberal society that does not respect the society that preceded it, despite all the mistakes that were made. These mistakes were not made by chance, but rather because people wanted to live differently. . . . The collective sleeping arrangement was part of a whole complex comprised of pedagogical approach, of cultural creativity and with respect to these contexts, it is a fascinating phenomenon. . . .

. . . This . . . does not mean that it did not have significance, that it was a mistake. This was a move by people who were seeking an answer to a number of disturbing questions, which have not yet been solved. For example, how to make "togetherness" more tolerable. This togetherness can be very oppressive, depressing and cruel, and it can also provide solidarity, power and support. Things are complex. An art exhibition that speaks in one voice is suspect. (qtd. in Gilerman)

Though she fully acknowledged that wrongs had been done—"In every home there is a skeleton in the closet"—Bar Or clearly believed that her country's petit bourgeois and pseudo-liberal society had too hastily abandoned the creative questioning and the cooperative ideals and practices that had once characterized life on the kibbutz (qtd. in Gilerman). Her critique of the exhibition's disappointing homogeneity implicitly expresses a sense of loss, both for the artists' failure to reflect a greater historic complexity and for what Israeli society had not managed to retain from its days of greater coherence and solidarity. Yet her language of restless questioning embodies the perpetually unresolved tension between the traditional kibbutz's rigid ideology and the excesses of self-interest, the essential struggle illuminated by so many of the works we have considered.

It is also true that the exhibition's view of the past attracted equally strong and thoughtful defenders such as Dr. Ronit Plotnik, an expert on child rearing in the kibbutz movement who is concerned with the psychological and pedagogical residue of collectivism's failures. Plotnik argues that those who graduated from the collectivism of the children's houses later lacked crucial child-rearing skills: "People who grew up in them did not have the opportunity to absorb complex parental parenting. Some of them, out of a constant feeling of hunger, are with their child all the time and do not know how to set limits. However, parents who have remained on kibbutz, which is a relatively secure place, can abandon their children with the same ease. They have moved to the two extremes and do not know how to function as a loving parent who also sets limits" (qtd. in Gilerman). Clearly, the debate that raged over two decades ago still does for many, especially between those who once fiercely advocated collective sleeping and those who successfully demolished that system.

More recently, yet another exhibition of kibbutz artists provoked a similar sensitivity to the dogmatic past. The occasion was the centennial of the kibbutz movement. On display were more than fifty works by artists of the Israel Quilters Association. Though the exhibit as a whole conveys a more sanguine appreciation of the kibbutz's historical role as vanguard for Israeli society in its formative years (representing subjects such as agricultural production and pioneering), a few of the participating artists wove political and social critiques into their works.[24] In perhaps the most striking of these, Bella Kaplan's *Shared Accommodation, A Reality That Has Passed* (fig. 13), the artist sought to express

> my feelings as a young mother, who came from the bustling city to live on a kibbutz after I got married to my husband who was born and had been living on a kibbutz. The daily emotional struggle of leaving one's child, one's flesh and blood in the Children's House to sleep at night . . . that someone else would take care of him, while that person was responsible for taking care of all the other children in the children's houses. The tense nights, the heartbreaking cry of a child screaming "Mommy" in the middle of the night.[25]

Kaplan says that she was never able to adjust to that system. Whereas most of the works featured verdant fields or celebratory scenes of communal life in multicolors or earth tones, Kaplan's quilt is notable for its darkness and sense of pervasive isolation. In the desolate blackness of the kibbutz night, the wooden cribs of the era of collective child rearing appear as bleak enclosures dominating the space wherein faceless children seem passively immobilized. Above them float the stern "Thou shalt/shalt not" dictums of the pedagogues, including these unyielding imperatives: babies must be surrendered to the care of the children's house staff immediately after birth, fathers are permitted only one hour's visitation per day, crying infants should be given only sugar water at night.

FIGURE 13   *Shared Accommodation, A Reality That Has Passed*, by Bella Kaplan. Hand-dyed quilt, 2011. Used by permission.

The textual introduction to Tal's *Children of the Sun* directly invokes these new controversies, stressing that the cooperative settlements of the early twentieth century sought to abolish the bourgeois family and in its stead to raise ethical individuals "free of the ills of capitalist society" for whom the "cooperative life" would be "second nature." These utopian premises are sharply offset in many of the film's scenes and accompanying commentary. For the most part, we see vignettes of sometimes ghostly, scratched amateur films and still photographs of distant childhoods over which we hear the frequently amused, sometimes nostalgic, occasionally mortified reflections of adults, whom we glimpse only at the film's conclusion, as they look back at their earlier lives. Hearing their voices over the archival footage, we often feel as though we are sitting in the same room with them.[26] Viewing the silent footage of their younger selves in the late 1930s, they often express delight as they revisit the material artifacts of their childhood: playpens, farm implements, gymnastic equipment—the training grounds for their idealistic society's pursuit of the "New Man."[27]

The emphatic egalitarianism of those early years is underscored by the recollections of each child's sole possessions—"one pair of shoes, one shirt, one coat" and so on. "This was equality, everyone had the same," someone remarks in a tone of satisfaction. But the first hint of the dark ambivalence that will predominate in *Children* comes memorably when one unseen commentator, recognizing a certain youngster toiling to clear rocks from a field, tersely remarks, "That's Uri. He fell in the Battle of Kadesh" (in the 1948 War of Independence). This undemonstrative note of loss comes as a chilling reminder to viewers that many of the children of that day would soon sacrifice their lives for the state, in the wars of 1948 and subsequent years. Throughout, the film's silent footage bears eloquent witness to the unquestioningly dutiful nature of the youths' upbringing. We observe the rituals requiring stoicism and courage through which they were inculcated in an ethos of labor-as-religion, duty to the state, and few personal possessions. Sometimes it is hard to escape the impression that they seem to have been born for the very purpose of sacrifice.

In John Auerbach's evocative short story "A Report from Here and Now," the protagonist finds himself obsessively revisiting the kibbutz cemetery in his autumn years.[28] Located on a prominent hill, the graveyard, which he claims possesses a "magnetic field," is "one of the most beautiful and cared-for spots on the kibbutz," where "the kibbutzniks have almost identical graves: the principle of equality, so much abused elsewhere, works well in this place" ("Report" 18).[29]

On those visits, he is especially drawn to the graves of those who died as young men: "When visiting the graves of these men who died far from here at the age of 20, 24, or 27, I still remember the smell of their hair when they were little boys. It is the perfume of dry hair in summer, or fresh mown grass, with a slight addition of the heady, penetrating, sexual scent of orange groves in bloom. I feel an inexplicable longing to bury my nose in that unruly hair of these young boys, and inhale deeply, deeply. But they are all dead now, and cypress trees sway over their graves in the afternoon breeze" (18).

For better and for worse, the most powerful and resonant motif in Hebrew cultural storytelling is that of the Akedah, the binding or near sacrifice of Isaac (Genesis 22). In *Glory and Agony: Isaac's Sacrifice and National Narrative*, one of the most comprehensive studies of this fraught motif, Yael Feldman raises the uncomfortable question of just how Israeli society reached its apparently interminable quandary, quoting poet Haim Gouri, who observes, "This is how we live here, in this duality. We are overfilled with religious symbols without believing in God" (qtd. in Feldman, *Glory and Agony* 11).[30] Though sacrificial themes of one kind or another play a prominent role in shaping the values of many societies, Feldman draws attention to the special force of the Akedah in the Israeli reality, saturating its artistic, intellectual, and political life: "Obliged to recognize that what is noble for the one spells ignoble life and death for the other, Israeli intellectuals compel us to ask how far self-sacrifice is from fanaticism, and martyrdom from sanctified terror" (*Glory and Agony* 318). In her charged explication of its wounding causes and causations, she asserts that the Akedah "gained its prominence because of its double semantic potential: Janus-like, it came to represent both the slaughter of the Holocaust and the national warrior's death in the old-new homeland" (20).[31] No sector of Israeli society bore its share of that burden more than the kibbutzim. Fittingly, in Yehoshua Kenaz's novel *Hitganvut yechidim* (*Infiltration*; 1986), which follows the relationships formed between young soldiers during their basic training, the impressionable narrator is so filled with ardor for the kibbutz ethos that, before drifting off to sleep after a long day, he entertains an elaborate heroic fantasy in which every elite combat soldier bears the countenance of Alon, his kibbutz friend:

> Perhaps at that very hour a little group of paratroopers was crossing the border into Jordan or Egypt, stealing down the village paths, climbing up the mountain terraces and descending into the wadis, without dislodging a stone, without showing against the skyline. At the sound of a dog barking or a voice calling "Min hada?" in the darkness they dropped

instantly, as one man, to the ground, as if the earth had swallowed them up, making a detour around the village and coming into the fields and orchards of that ancient, mysterious land beyond the border, where another moon shone, carrying explosives on their backs to blow up a police station or an army HQ, spreading panic and dismay in the enemy ranks. Then the attackers would immediately slip away and make their way home, fleet and light of foot, brave-hearted and full of enterprise, and they all looked just like Alon, their faces sunburned and resolute as his, bearing on their shoulders the stretchers with the wounded whom they would never, never leave in enemy territory. (*Infiltration* 59)

Very possibly owing to the trauma inflicted by that unrelenting historical burden, on most occasions, the commentators of *Children of the Sun* are notably unable to express a nostalgia that is not heavily guarded or inflected by mournful irony.

In a scene reminiscent of the opening of *Sweet Mud*, the camera pans over a dozen cots of sleeping infants in a kibbutz nursery as the unseen commentator recalls that his father was eager to name him "Nahum" after his own father but was immediately challenged by "an important member," who strongly "suggested" an alternative. Incredibly enough, it seems that, as part of their mission to overcome bourgeois domesticity, what to name their children was not the parents' choice to make ("He may be your son but he belongs to the kibbutz. We are his spiritual family and the majority will decide, not you," the commentator's father was told). When the matter was put to a vote in the general assembly, "Nahum" prevailed, but only by a slight margin. This scene instructively reveals the painfully absurd and claustrophobic nature of well-intentioned idealism in those early years. In another scene, we learn of the draconian rules proscribing extensive parent-child interaction: "Parents do not put their children to bed but hand them over to the caregiver; Parents are not allowed to visit their children after bedtime"; and so forth. Yet, notwithstanding the melancholy permeating the various commentators' reminiscences, it becomes clear that their childhoods were not altogether lacking in tenderness; indeed, at one point, they spontaneously burst into singing lullabies and other children's songs. And Tal's evenhanded film also highlights radiant scenes of recreation and holidays.

Still, it seems evident that such happiness was often contingent on the children's healthy relationship with the metapelet, who was, as one of the commentators has it, "our whole world." Although a few speak of this figure in adoring tones, the voice of one commentator quavers at the memory of a metapelet he calls "the kapo"[32]—even in his old age, she looms in his mind as a brutal disciplinarian. Another still seems cowed by the metapelet who made a practice of bursting into the children's sleeping quarters to wake them up in the mornings as if waging a military campaign, jerking open the curtains and blinding them with sudden sunlight, shattering their sleep with farmworkers' jingoistic songs. Yehudah Mirsky's evocative rendering of that unsparing order provides illuminating context for what we learn here: "For the children, life on the kibbutz was a life of regimentation: only two kinds of shoes allowed; no individual toys; morning wake-ups by nannies clapping and exclaiming, 'Good morning, children, three soldiers killed along the Suez Canal last night! Time to get up!' Exactly one hour and fifty minutes a day with one's biological family." On the whole, the reminiscences of this film's aging veterans of collective child rearing tend to support the conclusions reached by Yael Darr in her study of the mission performed by children's kibbutz literature in the founding generation: "Undermining the family institution and marginalizing the role played by parents in raising and educating their children was fundamental to the system of communal upbringing that guided founding fathers and their followers" (131). Indeed, Tal's commentators agree that they spent no more than an hour and a half in their parents' modest quarters each day: "One room, a chair, and a small closet. No heating, no water, no bathroom," recalls one ruefully. One woman recalls the daily visit as "sterile"; there were no "arguments or shouting," but also "no hugging or kissing, everything was extremely orderly."

Poignantly characteristic of these commentators' spare utterances, one says simply, "There was no mother who prepares sandwiches." Indeed, there was no "mother." The children called their parents by their first names only, not "Ima" (mother) or "Abba" (father) because that would have been too "bourgeois." Another says (and these many years later the distress in his voice remains palpable): "Never once did I say the word 'Mommy.' Even today I'm actually incapable of saying it." When asked whether any of the parents ever encouraged their children to say "Ima" or "Abba," a woman emphatically declares: "No, never." Most chilling of all is the declaration of Noa, who claims that she doesn't remember her parents at all: "Those three hours of 'quality time' with the parents . . . I have no significant memory of that time. It makes no sense but I don't remember a thing. . . . When someone utters the phrase 'your childhood Noa,' I see many things . . . all connected with nighttime. I'm stuck there." Over cheerfully chaotic scenes of parents watching their children change into pajamas and brush their teeth and sometimes singing Hebrew lullabies, a man recalls that he has "pleasant memories of bedtime. There was a lot of noise . . . parents sitting next to their children." Yet even he acknowledges that "the problem was you knew it would end and you would remain alone." Later, he recalls how he "would stay up whole nights, simply afraid to fall asleep." Someone else gently qualifies his remarks by saying that his may be a very "subjective memory"—yet quietly concedes that every night there was at least one child who cried much of the night. This observation stirs a woman's painful recollection of the phenomenon of "silent crying" that overtook a few struggling not to draw attention: "I felt that there was no way I would make it through the night without my mother." Indeed, she frequently slipped into her parents' home in the middle of the night, hiding behind trees to evade the kibbutz guard on his nightly rounds: "I had my ways. All I wanted to do was sit down next to my mother. I didn't even want to get into her bed. I didn't want her to hug or kiss me. That wasn't it. . . . I simply wanted to be with her." Notwithstanding the power of this and other recollections, they cannot be said to constitute a universal agreement about the nature of the emotional bond between parents and children (it seems entirely appropriate to assume that these varied just as much as they do in the outside world). Yet, when all is said and done, we are left with an overarching sense of anguished confusion on the part of the kibbutz children over just what a parent *was*. No matter what they did, the children clearly never overcame the deep emotional strain produced by their parents' absence during their most vulnerable and lonely hours, which is what makes this film so genuine and compelling a document of the psychic costs of utopia.[33]

Here it seems worth remembering that the parents were often deeply torn about the system to which they were outwardly so loyal. For instance, Edna Perlman recounts the quiet defiance of one mother, "Anna":

> Her photo album was her means of dealing with the societal pressures and maintaining her individual outlook on parenting. She struggled to create images that would provide her the pleasure of looking, to create an album that would sustain its hold and remain impenetrable and immune to the social pressures regarding childrearing. She did so by omitting a large part of the visual signs of the collective from her private albums; the children's home, the metapelet, the room the baby slept in, the food he was served, the bath he bathed in *over there* in Anna's words. (104)

The palpable shudder in this mother's phrasing (which disturbingly calls to mind that of many Israeli Holocaust survivors referring to the Europe they fled) is striking, her poignant rebellion against an unyielding system, however modest it may seem, was clearly genuine and heartfelt.[34]

When considering the lives of kibbutz children, sentimental outsiders sometimes presume that whenever left to their own devices, those conditioned by socialist education were naturally kind to one another, that instinctively they fostered a mutually supportive environment. Yet, in the absence of the traditional family unit, as a commentator in Tal's film austerely remarks, "you had to manage in a group of children—and children are usually cruel. That's not a kibbutz invention. But the kibbutz made that group into your family." The physical separation between parent and child was reinforced by the Zionist doctrine of the New Jew, its language inspired directly by A. D. Gordon's spiritual philosophy. The rhetorical language of its pedagogues often approached neo-paganism. One of the commentators recalls being told by his father that, whereas his generation would always be "foreigners" in the land, "you are the children of the Gods. You will bring redemption to the Jewish people and to mankind." For outsiders, it is undoubtedly difficult to imagine what it must have been like to be raised with such a burdened sense of history, obligation, and destiny. As Yael Ne'eman recounts in a recent memoir, the pressure could be unbearable and the sense of unworthiness in inevitably falling short of such lofty expectations stung: "We felt that we were unworthy of the doctrine. The output had no end, for initiative could always find more and more things to do. . . . We failed to satisfy the doctrine, mute and gentle as it seemed, asking nothing for itself, seeking only considerateness, with no demands: 'to each according to his need.' But who knows what need truly is, it has no bound or limit. Our doctrine was never satisfied. We felt guilty" (qtd. in Mirsky). The vast rift between children and parents and the demands of such a stern doctrine exacted a terrible toll.

Another form of separation in the children's lives was the sheer remoteness of the world outside the kibbutz; there was no television, and one commentator recalls only rare glimpses of cars and seeing a plane only once in his first fifteen years: "We grew up ignorant of the world outside. . . . We only knew how things looked from books. You could say it was a kind of island." Indeed, the world as they experienced it, even when they were teenagers, was limited to three spheres: the kibbutz, the Youth Movement, and the Party. So what did this "island" mean in terms of the children's own sense of self and subjectivity? Tal addresses the children's lack of privacy implicitly through numerous historical images of shared bathrooms and other intimate spaces, over which two women's voices assert: "Our only identity was the group" and "Once you sleep, shower, and eat together, you become family." As Perlman's analysis of the visual culture of kibbutzim in that era ably demonstrates, even ostensibly informal photographs of children were made to serve the ends of ideology:

"Photographs of groups of children in the children's homes and during educational activities were divested of their privacy and reinstated with public emotions and interpretations. This in turn neutralized private meanings and interpretations of images for the sake of the collective ideology." Perlman sees in these static images of the past a constant war between "visions of utopia on the one hand and personal rebellious representations of motherhood and individuality on the other" (116). Of course, largely due to their isolation, the children were never aware that the rest of the world considered their lives to be exceptional, that outsiders regarded them as a startling social experiment. Among Tal's commentators, however, the female veterans are still aghast when they recall the coed showers, which continued well into puberty: "Until my dying day, I will never forget those showers," shudders one. "Until sixth grade, we had communal showers. I already had breasts, got my period, and I wore a bra. . . . I remember trying with ten fingers to try to hide and cover myself." Another recalls the humiliating exposure of public nudity and its cruel aftermath, especially if one was deemed less than a perfect physical specimen: "You were totally defenseless. If your navel was this way, or if your backside, your legs, or if your big toes were like that, you were finished. You would get a nickname relating to your defect." Although adolescence is always a time of excruciating self-consciousness, clearly, this generation faced singular challenges.

In other respects, the categorically physical nature of daily life posed further burdens to those reared in the collective system. For instance, there seems to be a consensus among the commentators that physical labor was almost a sacred imperative: the kibbutzniks were "never to be sick"; they were "to meet all demands, like soldiers in a never-ending boot camp." A few dolefully recall the social stigma of having immigrant fathers who never quite lived up to the idealized image of the Zionist farmer. Again, in words that conjure up Gordonian aspirations, a man remarks, "My father wasn't a Bedouin, or a Cossack. That's for sure. He wanted *me* to be a Bedouin and a Cossack and I remember him saying: 'There is nothing more beautiful than a half-naked child riding bareback on a colt.'" Many of the former kibbutz children naturally seem to feel they fell well short of those astral expectations. Like other ambivalent narratives of collective child rearing, however, *Children of the Sun* also presents more joyful assessments of kibbutz childhood, especially when it comes to the unparalleled degree of freedom, the hours that the children could roam the kibbutz grounds and the surrounding fields and orchards: "Everyone was friendly," recalls another man, "we could climb on any tractor, go into any home, go in any direction." On the other hand, this same man reports that those anarchic "explorations of kibbutz space came to an end" at a certain age. "We reached the frontier and the world [of the kibbutz] began to be small and pressing." What happened next?

Perhaps more than any other community of Zionist youths, the kibbutzniks were inculcated in a life of service and mission: "Life . . . had significance," says one commentator over martial-like scenes of assembling, saluting, exercising, and marching teenagers, usually wearing the uniforms of the various socialist youth movements (at times, the regimented calisthenics appear disturbingly reminiscent of the totalitarian era). A second emphasizes how "in my generation, 'values' wasn't just another word." That generation, raised to permanently replace the yeshiva world of study and crooked backs, was indoctrinated with the lofty mottos of the youth groups: "Be strong and brave. The Shomer youth tells the truth. He loves his homeland, seeks physical and spiritual perfection. Abstains from drinking, smoking, and maintains sexual purity."[35] Thus a third commentator recalls that he was effectively "brainwashed" by age eleven: "I was a loyal soldier in Poalei Zion" (Workers of Zion, which was a Marxist movement); a fourth observes that "spiritually, we felt we were the top of the world and that other people had not yet discovered justice, truth, and beauty." In contrast, reports yet another commentator, the city dweller was considered inherently "immoral . . . without values . . . not worthy of our attention."

This dedication and sense of mission was reinforced during high school graduation rituals, torch-lit ceremonies confirming the young people's understanding that they were, as one commentator puts it, the nation's "mobilized elite . . . that fulfilled the Zionist dream with its body and soul." That imperative was a great deal more than just a rhetorical plaudit insofar as the kibbutz youths served in the vanguard of the nation's most elite military units, frequently as combat officers. Over home movies of kibbutz burials and funeral processions, these unseen commentators recall the names of friends killed in battle. Yet there is a prevailing mood among them of nostalgia. Alongside their recollections of anxiety and the pervasive sense that they were indeed deprived of something in their childhood, there seems to be a strong consensus that it was intensely pleasurable to lose oneself among one's peers: "You felt as if your identity dissolved into something larger," says one without a hint of irony. "You really stopped being yourself [and] completely identified with the 'kibbutz member' inside you."[36]

When the members of this dutiful generation had their own children, they, too, surrendered them to the care of others without questioning, just as their parents had in their day. "It felt very natural," says one woman; and "I had no doubts. None," states another firmly. Nobody can recall a single instance of a mother protesting the system. It seemed entirely natural to them that they would wake in the middle of the night to dress themselves and walk over to the *bet yeladim* (kindergarten) to breastfeed their infants. But, at some indefinable point later in life, they made the melancholy "discovery" that someone else had raised their children for them. Another woman very emotionally confesses that she didn't really feel she saw her three children grow up: "That 'togetherness' robbed me of my personal, special, family life." A man recalls he was never allowed to give of himself to his children, to love or even embrace them: "It didn't feel real. Because I was messed up. You had never been loved so you didn't show love. Something inside you was dead," and he returns to that fatal flaw in the kibbutz system: "Because you were denied something." Eventually, disenchantment set in for some individuals as they came to realize "that it was a huge mistake. It was a huge mistake to raise children like that." Still another mother guiltily recalls how her child endured acute asthma attacks in her absence. When asked whether she and the other mothers feel they "missed out," they don't hesitate: "Definitely!" A few indicate that they "compensate" today with their grandchildren. If she could do it all over, a woman declares, she would raise her children by herself, and know what a "true" family is. And when asked now how they now feel about the "New Man" paradigm with which they were raised, the commentators, men and women alike in their sixties and older, simply scoff.[37] Yet when we judge what was done, perhaps, as Yehudah Mirsky contends, we should temper our judgment with compassion for the parents and the anguished conflicts they endured, "many of whom were Holocaust survivors and veterans of the brutal fighting . . . during Israel's War of Independence. As if that were not enough, they were then called upon to sacrifice parenthood's intimacies as well as the ability to provide for those of their children who chose to leave the community." Clearly, the dream of creating a thoroughly tough and resilient generation only intensified after the Holocaust.

As with Israeli society at large, these commentators recount how a palpable disenchantment took root during the dispiriting 1970s following the Yom Kippur War: one pointedly recalls that it was then that his once heady affinity for an extended family simply dissipated. Those who eventually left their kibbutzim describe those partings as sad, even heartbreaking events, for both the individuals and the kibbutzim: one recalls a man famous for his stoicism who broke down in tears on leaving and became "a wreck."[38] A few who made the dramatic transition to life in the outside world recall with wonder the gradual sense of the birth of their individualism. A woman claims that she still remembers the day she first said "I" in the aftermath of her departure and that "it sounded terrible" to her. "What do you mean 'I,'" she said to herself at the time. "There is only 'us.' It was like learning a new language. I really had to practice, like when you try a new word you don't know how to pronounce. A new concept was born—'I.'" In spite of their wondrous discovery of individuality and unfettered potential, the change was clearly wrenching for many; one man confesses that, years later, he still sheds tears of longing. A woman insists that the kibbutz endures in her imagination as her "childhood scenery," forever an intrinsic part of her. Similarly, even years of urban life in Tel Aviv doesn't diminish one man's proud sense of identification as a former kibbutznik, nor slacken the rush of welcome familiarity he feels whenever he treads the ground of any kibbutz today.

It is worth adding that, three years after the theatrical release of *Children of the Sun*, director Ran Tal spoke of his own surprising encounters during screenings, which he felt demonstrated his film's deep emotional resonance with the Israeli public: "In my travels around the country . . . I was amazed over and over again by the precision of collective memory: the children's houses and the parents' quarters; daily rituals; being put to bed at night and waking up in the morning; celebrations; the new sandals distributed during the Passover holiday; up to the day and minute when the weekly movie was screened. Viewers of my film would sit glued to the screen and with obvious delight find themselves in photos in which they did not actually appear."[39] Clearly, for such audiences, seeing *Children of the Sun* was "like jumping into the kibbutz reservoir on an especially hot summer day," as Tal said of Yael Ne'eman's *We Were the Future* (Tal, "Her Memories Are Mine").[40]

Lavi Ben Gal's *Eight Twenty Eight*

Privatization . . . entails the demise of the centralist state system, which grew
out of the historical national-collectivist foundations of Israeli nationalism.
The house built by "Zionist socialism," its institutions and beliefs,
was thrown in the 1990s into the dustbin of history.
—*Uri Ram*

One of the most personal entries among the new wave of kibbutz documentaries explores a much later generation than the children's house veterans we encounter in *Children of the Sun*. Lavi Ben Gal's *Shmona esrim v'shmona* (*Eight Twenty Eight*; 2007), which premiered the same year as Tal's film, concerns twenty-eight-year-old Gal's receipt of a letter from his kibbutz informing him that he has reached the age when he must either commit to return or formally relinquish his rights there. The film consists largely of a series of interviews with aging kibbutz members accompanied by idiosyncratic vignettes of places that formed the landscape of Gal's childhood. Many of these sites, like the aging members themselves, are in serious decline. In the first of his conversations, a woman who hasn't seen him for years remarks archly of his belated appearance: "You come home and there's nothing left." In a tone blending both pathos and irony, Gal points out iconic images of his childhood home as someone passing on a motorbike shouts to the camera, "What are you filming . . . the abandonment?" And we are shown the remnants of several children's houses of his memory, now mostly abandoned or converted to storerooms.

As Eldad Kedem observes, *Eight Twenty Eight* is composed entirely around "an absent home and fantasies of a lost paradise . . . of blocked and oppressed desire." Gal quietly introduces us to the nine kibbutz paths that made up his entire childhood world and then applies cinematic strategies "of improvisation, creativity, and experimentation. . . . Each path gives out a sensation of texture, materiality, noise, rhythm, direction, composition and atmosphere" (Kedem 335). Along these paths, we encounter kibbutzniks who pause to converse (though some refuse), such as the metapelet who essentially raised Gal as a toddler. It is Friday afternoon and, almost in spite of himself, Gal feels compelled to visit the synagogue, only to discover that there aren't enough old men to form a minyan (the quorum required for a Jewish prayer service). It's a painful realization, and Gal is demonstrably uncomfortable at being coerced to join them: "What do I have to do with this prayer? I don't belong here. But you can't just leave in the middle," he tells us. Of course, the crucible of "leaving" and not genuinely belonging is the sad subtext of this autobiographical film. In the end, even though enough Mexicans arrive and he is "liberated," he can't bring himself to move, frozen by the gaze of an old man who cannot quite place who Gal is, yet recalls every word of the ancient prayer.

Throughout, Gal juxtaposes troubling signs of the new kibbutz economy (private cars, members struggling to generate income through what resemble American garage sales) along with the reliable and familiar sights of friends from the older generation gathering on one another's lawns every day to reminisce about the old days, the children taken on daily walks to watch the milking in the cowshed (now run by Thai workers). Visiting the kibbutz kitchen and dining room proves a strangely dissonant experience when Gal discovers that, instead of the old system of mandatory shifts, a catering company employing Russian workers now runs everything. The hired workers tell one another in Russian that Gal is "kookoo" for taking interest in their activity, and the restless camera moves on.[41] In this eccentric and often perversely melancholic film, a recurring visual trope is the sight of a kibbutznik's back as Gal lags behind, always out of step and unseen. In one such instance, his father pauses, patiently waiting for him to join him on the path, but Gal remains where he is, a stubborn but invisible presence, hidden just beyond the camera lens. One cannot but wonder precisely what he means to Gal to declare, as he does repeatedly throughout: "This is my kibbutz." Our last view of the community is of a perfunctory performance by a few of the hired Thai workers, singing on stage during the kibbutz anniversary.[42]

Degania: The First Kibbutz Fights Its Last Battle (2008)

One of the most pernicious myths hastening the end of socialist collectivism in Israel is that the traditional kibbutz inhibited economic progress. As J. J. Goldberg (former secretary-general of Kibbutz Gezer) explains:

> Over the past two decades, supposedly, those kibbutzim smart enough to recognize this truth have gone private. They've created incentives for productivity, rewarding the best and brightest with higher salaries. The non-privatized kibbutzim, presumably, have remained mired in socialist stagnation. But the truth is just the opposite. The kibbutzim that maintained classic kibbutz socialism are the ones that thrived economically over the past generation. Their members have kept innovating regardless of kibbutz structure, developing and marketing high-tech irrigation systems, operating state-of-the-art printing, plastics manufacturing and even financial services. It turns out that when money comes in, nobody minds sharing. It's when the kibbutz treasury runs dry and living standards are slashed that bickering erupts.

For this and related reasons, of all the recent documentaries about wrenching changes in the kibbutzim, none is quite as painful as Yitzhak Rubin's film *Hakrav ha-aharon al Degania* (*Degania: The First Kibbutz Fights its Last Battle*; 2008), a painful glimpse of the flagship of the entire kibbutz movement and the model adopted by more than four hundred kibbutzim. Filmed during the days of its unraveling as the community lurched toward privatization, *Degania* is a major exemplar of the late kibbutz film documentaries, whose sympathies are almost invariably divided between individual members and the collective as a whole. If only for its symbolic significance, Rubin's account of what many would call the self-destruction of the very first kibbutz must surely be considered the nadir of the kibbutz decline.[43] As *Degania* begins, subtitles situate what follows in relation to two pivotal events: the fall of the Berlin Wall in 1989, celebrated as the West's triumph over world communism, and the financial collapse of Wall Street in 2009, which gave rise to "deep questions and unease . . . over unfettered capitalism." Kvutzat Degania ("wheat of God"), as the kibbutz was first called, was founded in 1910. Ironically, that was precisely one hundred years before the making of the film, an occasion that might have been celebrated as the centennial of collective life but instead marked the triumph of privatization and, from the perspective of many of us, the tragic demise of the most successful socialist experiment in world history.

Far from evoking the immediacy of that crisis, the first scene is reminiscent of the pastoral scenes celebrating the kibbutz in so many of the narratives we have examined. It is dawn on Degania, and a grizzled worker, perhaps in his late fifties, tells us what the life of a farmer means to him: "You get up in the morning with a song in your heart." For years, Degania has been the proudest of those veteran Galilee kibbutzim where five generations of one family still live together; with that in mind, Rubin lets us hear from the aging children of the first halutzim as well as from their descendants. Surveying the "Founders' Cemetery," a member recalls with a palpable sense of wonder the life of his grandfather, who, as a nineteen-year-old from a Hassidic family in Eastern Europe, came to the Jordan Valley in 1908 to make sacrifices and undergo profound personal changes. Many of the headstones in the cemetery are engraved with the same stubborn epitaph: "Devoted to work and to the group." Other members, their voices suffused with nostalgia, recount the early efforts of the pioneers and the halcyon years that followed. A visit to the kibbutz archives reveals that the Degania experiment attracted the admiration and intense interest of a range of luminaries, including Albert Einstein, Franz Kafka, and Tomáš Garrigue Masaryk, president of the Czechoslovak Republic, who was among its early visitors.

Almost pitilessly, the film abruptly shifts from scenes in the cowshed and other farm settings, sites of the earliest memories of the founders' labor, to the fluorescent-lit office of Shai Shoshani, kibbutz secretary, resolute leader of the Privatization Movement. Shoshani says that he is kept awake contemplating the measures that must be taken to preserve what he repeatedly calls "the myths" or "taboos" of kibbutz ideology. In later scenes, we track the efforts of the "Privatization Supporters Coalition" to engage other members in talks about their vision of the future. Much of this interaction takes place in the dining hall, the traditional site of the kibbutz asefa, where the "Degania Model" is presented at a tense gathering. Yet, though the privatization process is often viewed as an intergenerational struggle in which the younger generation advocates capitalism, it is clear that many younger members dismiss the "Degania Model" as a cynical and selfish grab for a bigger piece of the pie, an abnegation of the core principle of mutual responsibility. After the initial meeting, a member declares to the camera: "If a society wants to commit suicide, there's no power on earth to stop it." Another simply charges that "it's a crazy rush for money." Rubin takes care to visit the social institutions that once mattered more than wealth to Degania's members, notably the home for its aging residents. Rather than being shunted aside or sent to outside institutions, the parents were always treated with reverence and housed within the community's own nursing home despite the enormous expense.

As the privatization steering committee proceeds with its plans, preparations are made for a suburban neighborhood adjacent to Degania where disaffected youths from the kibbutz may live even if they choose to opt out of membership. Unabashedly, the committee members argue that the entire kibbutz should be reenvisioned as a suburban community. As many reel in outraged disbelief at the news, meals in the once sociable kibbutz dining hall rapidly become acrimonious affairs; embittered members shout at one another: "Go live in a suburb yourself!" and "It's all about money and greed!" Many siblings as well as parents and children end up on different sides of the ever more heated dispute. We see the clashes between privatization supporters and foes grow increasingly bitter; the supporters complain that the current system only encourages parasitism, and the foes assert that the traditional system of love and mutual support is worth preserving, even if they must work harder to support those who work less or are unemployed. One member captures the deteriorating situation in language with which both camps in the wounded community would likely agree: "The social relations here are so bad that saying 'dog eat dog' is putting it mildly." He is thankful that his parents are not alive to see these days.

At one point, a young foe of privatization observes to the camera that those among his comrades obsessing over money forget that having "nothing" also means that one is debt free. Invoking the biblical language "He comes into the world naked and leaves nothing behind," he declares: "I find it fabulous. I look at myself, born to kibbutz parents, and I think it's awesome that they get to live in dignity and to know they are doing okay for the rest of their lives, they're financially sound and not leaving me any debts." One of the more acerbic and far-reaching moments in this achingly intimate and observant documentary comes when another foe remarks with quiet but stinging irony that the kibbutzniks in the privatization camp are like traditional Jews "in the Diaspora . . .

they are no longer farmers but businessmen." At the meeting in which the kib-butz's economic and ideological fate will be determined, an older foe of priva-tization invokes the chilling biblical passage: "Your destroyers will come from within you" (Isaiah 49:17). The next day, a member of the antiprivatization camp holds up an article titled "Kibbutzim That Didn't Go Through the Privatization Process Are Healthier." But the news has clearly come too late for the members of Israel's founding kibbutz.[44]

The Kibbutz Video Art of Oded Hirsch

The extraordinarily inventive Oded Hirsch (b. 1976) has enjoyed critical acclaim in the New York art world for four videos (all made in the Jordan Valley) that combine performance art with unusual cinematography to creatively comment on both personal and collective aspects of his kibbutz years and his rather bleak assessment of the kibbutz's future. Each installment in this cerebral, compassionate, and at times almost hallucinatory series depicts a strange, seem-ingly senseless labor undertaken by silent individuals and groups often leading to dubious or anticlimactic outcomes. Esteemed art critic Roberta Smith cap-tures the essence of their dreamlike quality, highlighting their cumulative rendering of "oddly pointless physical feats in spectacularly isolated land-scapes."[45] In a profile of Hirsch, journalist and filmmaker Dalia Karpel suc-cinctly describes the cumulative trajectory of his four art videos: "He likes to pry into the collective memory of the kibbutz movement and explore where the community ends and the individual begins." Like these critics, I am struck by how, throughout his oddly meditative and uncanny portraits of arguably mindless labor, Hirsch achieves a tense balance between alienated portraits of labor and the community.[46] Though raised on Kibbutz Afikim, Hirsch had a particularly traumatic childhood: his father suffered a horrific spinal injury in a truck accident that left him permanently paralyzed. His artist son's acute awareness of how lonely kibbutz existence can become for those who fall out-side the healthy and vigorous norm seems to have begun in those painful days.

Because Oded was only five at the time, perhaps it was inevitable that his father's injury would transform him into an unwelcome outsider, the trauma that shaped *50 Blue* (2009; fig. 14), the first video in the series, which opens with the father being painstakingly hoisted aloft in a wheelchair to the top of a lonely tower situated on the edge of Lake Kinneret (Sea of Galilee). As Hirsch explains,

FIGURE 14   *50 Blue* (2009), directed by Oded Hirsch. Used by permission.

the bigger I got, the more I looked down at him, because he was in the wheelchair and I was getting taller. I had this recurring dream in which I lifted him up and placed him on a big boulder, or on a tower, and looked up at him from below. *50 Blue* grew out of a desire to deal with the baggage of the past and with the pain of the child who was ashamed of his father. It's not easy to live in a closed and claustrophobic kibbutz society. As a child I felt different. Everyone else's fathers were like big heroes who could walk while my father, whom I saw as a hero, wasn't perceived that way by the collective. The film reaches a peak when he is hoisted up in his wheelchair to the top of the tower. (Karpel)

In his recasting, or rather subverting, of the painful betrayal of this relationship, Hirsch is keenly attuned to the heavy burden of the Akedah in Israeli culture and narrative.[47] His vision of redeeming humanity's enduring drama of human sacrifice and fanatical devotion inspires this opening scene, which grew into a parody of the most sacred tropes of the Zionist enterprise itself:

> It's the sacrifice of Isaac in reverse. I'm interested in the tension between the individual and the group, so in the film . . . a group of people hoist him up to the tower. Essentially he's dependent upon them, and they are not human but mechanized characters. I try to take the heroic ethos of the pioneer and to make it ridiculous to the point of being absurd. If the symbolic going up to [Kibbutz] Hanita in 1938 was a heroic act of settlement, and they were photographed carrying poles and ascending the mountain to establish a "tower and stockade" settlement, then I'm taking the tower and sticking it in an absurd location and, instead of legendary pioneers carrying poles, my brother is rolling our father in the wheelchair along the muddy paths. Much ado about nothing. (Karpel)

Another of Hirsch's potent gestures to his father's generation is evident in the next video of the series, *Ha-baita* (*Home*; 2010), wherein twenty-one women and men in their sixties gaze fixedly toward an unseen horizon (fig. 15). The camera pulls back to reveal that they are standing passively in an anchored boat surrounded by the Kinneret's waters against a hazy, almost indeterminate landscape (fig. 16).

These dignified and vaguely mysterious figures are as motionless as the boat they are in, their mouths tightly pursed, their expressions hauntingly oblique. The soundtrack features only the incessant splashing of wavelets against the shore. *Ha-baita* (*Home*) quietly destabilizes the signifiers of immigration, homeland, and rootedness. Regarding his use of these steadfast elder sentinels, Hirsch remarks: "If a person is a product of his childhood landscape, in the film I wanted to create an opposite situation—the person as detached from his childhood landscape . . . people that are stuck. Above them is the blue sky, and all around them are the waters . . . but they aren't moving anywhere. There is hardly any movement at all in the frame apart from a light ripple on the water." (Karpel)

In striking contrast, *Tochka* (2010; fig. 17), the third and also the longest video of Hirsch's experimental series, offers notably greater movement and a deeper sense of environment.[48] The video opens on a dozen muddy laborers,

FIGURE 15   *Ha-baita* (*Home*; 2010), directed by Oded Hirsch. Used by permission.

dressed in blue kibbutz work clothes, whose absurdly outsized *kova tembels* (soft cloth hats of the pioneering workers that became one of Israel's most iconic symbols) fully shield their eyes from view. Throughout *Tochka*, discordant and hollow metallic noises and other labor-related sounds can be heard, but (as in the rest of the series) nobody speaks—and that pervasive absence of human speech is just one of the features of Hirsch's aesthetic that pointedly reduce any notion of individuality or personality. Bearing unwieldy yellow buckets and hauling an absurd collection of rusty farm tools, the men struggle stoically in a foggy landscape. When they occasionally pause, the effect is that of an incongruously suspended tableau; indeed, as Karen Rosenberg observes, *Tochka* has the appearance of "a Millet or van Gogh."

Arduous labors whose significance is utterly unfathomable unfold before us, their meticulous exactitude only bewildering us further: the passing of buckets of water, the haphazard digging, the painstaking brewing and heating of a mysterious concoction under the men's devoted care. For no apparent reason, two men valiantly strain to push a huge iron wheel up a steep incline. Eventually, a strange behemoth-like construction arises over the landscape, perhaps a parody of the stockade and watchtower practice of settlement that marked the establishment of the first kibbutzim, as recounted by the pre-state kibbutz writers with whom we began (notably, Arthur Koestler in his 1946 novel *Thieves*

FIGURE 16   *Ha-baita* (*Home*; 2010). Used by permission.

of the Night). In the end, the structure is revealed to be a rickety bridge clumsily laid across a slight ravine in the landscape, a structure that manages to appear both massive and precarious. Kaelen Wilson-Goldie memorably describes the film's cumulative impact as "crafty, nostalgic, highly inefficient yet still somehow emancipatory and sublime." As the camera pans over the surroundings, the surreal absurdity of the entire enterprise becomes manifestly apparent: the ravine could have easily been avoided, and the bridge, as Hirsch himself admits, clearly "leads nowhere" (Karpel).[49]

Nothing New (2012; fig. 18), the final installment in the series, is inspired by the director's early encounter with Amos Oz's canonical short story "Derech haruach" ("The Way of the Wind"; 1962), from the collection *Artzot hatan* (*Where the Jackals Howl*, discussed in chapter 2), and is perhaps the most ambitious, featuring a cast of roughly 200 members of Jordan Valley kibbutzim. For Hirsch, the process of bringing together so many kibbutzniks from around his former community for three days in order to create the video had its own special meaning in light of recent events that had badly frayed the social ties of Kibbutz Afikim, especially the closure of the factory that had once played a

FIGURE 17   *Tochka* (2010), directed by Oded Hirsch. Used by permission.

prominent role in its social coherence. Hirsch found something resonant and almost intimately familiar in the story of Gideon, Oz's hapless protagonist, who dives out of a plane with his fellow paratroopers as part of the Independence Day festivities and gets badly tangled in power lines. Hirsch is haunted especially by the role of Gideon's father in the story, who "has a classic Zionist activist look" and tells his son, "'Jump! Jump!' But the terrified paratrooper is unable to meet . . . his father's expectations to be brave and bold. Humiliated, he puts a hand out to touch the wires . . . and dies." Hirsch explains that his cinematic retelling "relates to something that I felt as a teenager. The burden of expectations that I grew up with resonated with Oz's story. The son who doesn't fulfill the father's expectations. In my films, the solution that society proposes is always an absurd solution" (Karpel). Perhaps for that reason, *Nothing New* begins with the brutal denouement of "The Way of the Wind": a lifeless body is hanging as if crucified from the power lines poised over a verdant Jordan Valley landscape.

FIGURE 18   *Nothing New* (2012), directed by Oded Hirsch. Used by permission.

Whereas a living person is winched aloft in *50 Blue*, here the collective low-ers a sacrificial corpse back to earth. In Hirsch's version of Oz's story, nobody is there to witness the sacrifice until a young girl accidentally stumbles onto the scene. The corpse, wearing goggles from another era, seems to gaze steadily down on her, but we cannot see its eyes. Later, a crowd of kibbutzniks marches toward the site, some shouldering crude farm implements, as if to a place of pilgrimage. Companionably, they sit silently around a campfire, directly beneath the martyred figure. In another scene, workers of every age bear wheelbarrows and buckets of earth, pausing at one point to lift their faces reverently upwards toward the tattered parachute with its tangled body. One worker climbs the pylon while others below tether him, and, in a communal effort, they lower the young man's body, laying it out on an earthen mound. Given that the title of

Oz's story is "The Way of the Wind," perhaps it is apt that, throughout, only the mournful voice of the wind can be heard.[50]

Hirsch recently returned to Israel (where he is yet not well known), having earned rave reviews in U.S. venues such as *Artforum* and the *Village Voice*. Jerry Saltz, a formidable Manhattan-based art critic for *New York Magazine*, was struck by the "richly textured" qualities of these videos: "Hirsch evokes our eternal need to build towers of Babel to touch the gods." Roberta Smith praised Hirsch's haunting imagery, wherein a "medieval yet timeless mood prevails; the fragile predicament of Israel is enacted in terms that Bosch or Brueghel would recognize." Perhaps the kibbutz does embody Israel's "fragile predicament" in a national sense, yet it is always clear that Hirsch has foremost in mind the impossible realization of the kibbutz experiment (its unsettlingly audacious utopian dreaming) always foremost in conceiving this related video series: "There's something awkward about the kibbutz idea. . . . Admirable totality. . . . They took the utopian idea of equality to crazy and wonderful extremes" (Karpel). In envisioning the totality of his art video project, Hirsch likens it to "a person out walking in nature who is supposed to get from Point A to Point B. He comes across a small crevice and instead of just skipping over it, he builds a large construction—a bridge that leads to nowhere. This construction symbolizes pipe dreams" (Karpel). Presumably, that grandiose image best captures the essence of the kibbutz—the impossible abundance and ultimate indeterminacy of what was attempted.[51]

As previous chapters have sought to demonstrate, the growing surge of entries in the kibbutz cinema only underscores the fact that writers and other artists have provocatively illuminated the myriad ways that the kibbutz, from its very inception, has confronted wrenching changes that have shaken the equilibrium of what appear from the outside to be the bland and static environs of utopia. That turmoil has proved a bittersweet blessing, for, as kibbutz writer Aliza Amir-Zohar explains, "if a person has no sense of distress, or dissatisfaction, or imperfection, then he simply exists like an inanimate object" (Rosenfeld 178). Yet, lately, the acceleration of change driven by the new managers of the kibbutzim, accompanied by a lack of deep reflection about long-term social consequences, has come at a significant cost both to individuals and to the social integrity of communities. In their study of cooperative behavior in kibbutzim in the age of privatization, Richard Sosis and Bradley Ruffle demonstrated that "members of collectivized kibbutzim exhibited higher levels of in-group cooperation than members of privatized kibbutzim, suggesting the importance of ideological commitment in promoting cooperation" (109). But perhaps the deterioration of the kibbutz was inevitable.[52] For her part, however, Shula Keshet, a member of Kibbutz Givat Brenner and senior lecturer in the Graduate Faculty of the Kibbutzim College of Education, Technology, and the Arts, has argued that the most indispensable changes, namely, those required to bring about "the restoration of equilibrium between the individual and society, were suppressed for many years, until they reached crisis point" ("Kibbutz Fiction" 162). Though that is surely the case, it is also true that this struggle has been a remarkably potent catalyst, inspiring some of Israel's most soul-searching and imaginative engagements with both the allure of ideals and the high price exacted in their pursuit. No writer has better summed up the entwined grandeur and frailty at the heart of the kibbutz enterprise than Assaf Inbari: "I view the kibbutz story as tragic, not as pitiful. Tragic is heroic. I find it a story of people who possessed a tragic greatness. A greatness that was required in order to even try to realize such a far-reaching dream, which amounted to a conscious challenge to human nature. A common misapprehension is that they didn't understand human nature. They did understand it and they set out to defy it. To defy it in terms of family, possessions, privacy, ego" (Avrahami).

Afterword
Between Hope and Despair
The Legacy of the Kibbutz Dream in the
Twenty-First Century

We have made the acquaintance of the fundamental tenets of kibbutz ideology and
have not refrained from hinting at a few deviations from them; we are writing about
human beings, after all. . . . As the kibbutz truck driver puts it, people
are flesh and blood, not myrrh and frankincense.
—*Amos Oz*

Slowly they were realizing their untenable situation: they were socialists bound to a
capitalist system. Some suspected they were caretakers of a beautiful idea that had almost
worked, and that their task was to provide a dignified burial for the utopian dream.
—*Yossi Klein Halevi*

Here it is important to pause from our contemplation of both the sweet and
the bitter revelations in literature and film to take stock of what has happened
to the kibbutz's mission and to address contemporary realities. Let us begin
with Joshua Muravchik's magisterial assessment of the diverse and often tragic
paths that world socialism took in the last century, as made by this wizened
political veteran of the world stage on his belated pilgrimage following the
global collapse of communism:

> From New Harmony to Moscow, from Dar es Salaam to London, the
> story of socialism was the story of a dream unrealized, a word that would
> not be made flesh. The little utopias erected by the likes of Owen disin-
> tegrated soon after they began. . . . But the societies the Communists

created were a miserable caricature of the socialist vision. . . . And Third World socialism made a sorry tale. There was, however, one exception to this unbroken record of disappointment. In the biblical promised land, the promise of socialism was at last fulfilled. It took the form of communities called kibbutzim . . . where, on average, four to five hundred people lived a life of sharing, cooperation and mutual support. Small as those settlements were, socialists of many stripes took heart from them. When Gorbachev visited Israel some six months after the dissolution of the Soviet Union, he toured Kibbutz Ein Gedi and exclaimed: "This is what we meant by socialism." (321)

Even taking into account the recent erosion of the kibbutz values that once inspired Muravchik's global socialists, the sheer scope of their endurance is still fairly astonishing. Uri Zilbersheid places that endurance in a more historical perspective: "The kibbutz movement grew steadily within successive state frameworks: the Ottoman Empire until its fall in 1918, the English rule from 1918 to 1948 (most of the time as the English Mandate of Palestine), and the State of Israel since 1948." For many of those years, the idealized reputation of the kibbutz excited the passionate interest of both researchers and volunteers from all over the world.[1] In its heyday, the kibbutz was touted by Jewish intellectuals from philosopher Martin Buber to literary critic (and unrepentant socialist) Irving Howe and, of course, by many non-Jewish luminaries who were equally stirred by its promise of a truly renewed society. And, with just cause, the kibbutz was long one of Israel's most cherished icons for Jewish Israelis themselves.

In what might be considered the movement's Golden Age, the kibbutz enjoyed the kind of reverence given to mythical founding icons anywhere— roughly like that given to America's pilgrims. And that reverence largely endured for as long as the surrounding society itself embraced socialism. Indeed, Israel's quintessential national style has its genesis in the kibbutz's pervasive influence. As Amos Oz remarks, "there are many kibbutz genes in Israeli society. There is a certain directness, a certain lack of hierarchies, a latent anarchism in Israeli society which I regard as the heritage of the kibbutz and I think it's a good heritage" (Estrin). And Shula Keshet, a kibbutznik and member of the Graduate Faculty of the Kibbutzim College of Education, Technology and the Arts, observes that "ever since the early kibbutz settlement of the Jordan and Jezreel Valleys, the kibbutz concept has been perceived by many as the principal innovation of the Jewish people in Eretz Yisrael. The utopianist lifestyle, which was not put in abeyance until the End of Days but realized in everyday life, was set in the collective consciousness as a symbolic site that represented pioneering Israeliness at its best. The human experiment touched not only the people who lived it but also many others who found the dream captivating, even if they were unable to fulfill it themselves" ("Freedom of Expression" 195). For a very long time, there were good reasons for such adulation. Though their members never accounted for more than 7 percent of the country's population and frequently much less, the kibbutzim were long admired for their highly practical role in meeting crucial national challenges in settlement, agricultural development, and especially security.[2]

By the late 1930s, Eliezer Ben-Rafael declares, the kibbutz had become paramount to the nationalist ethos:

> Youngsters enrolled themselves en masse . . . in kibbutz-oriented youth movements, which confirmed the kibbutzniks' sense of being an elite. They had taken this role ever since the onset of the kibbutz venture when they formed a militant cohort that upheld social and national ideals, and, above all, implemented the model of the revolutionary utopia as the universal social regime of the future. Moreover, this prestige stimulated an equally basic political drive. Kibbutz members were recruited from the political mainstream, and not from its margins; they come from youth movements that identified with the political parties and the establishment of the society-in-the-making, which existed in Palestine before Israel was founded. (130)

Such a lofty position naturally prompts us to consider what led to the kibbutz's sharp decline in our own time. Ironically, it appears that the very success of the kibbutz led to its loss of social prestige. For, if the pioneering ethos required continued sacrifice, which the surrounding society revered, then the kibbutzim's later affluence presented outsiders with an image of prosperity, a contradiction that seemingly justified their later resentment of an institution that received a large share of the nation's resources in the form of subsidies and other support.

The same processes that created a path for Israel to enter the elite membership of the world's wealthiest countries presented acute challenges for the kibbutz, which had once proved its adaptive spirit by reallocating a great deal of its human resources from traditional agricultural endeavors to industrial ones (the most successful kibbutz enterprises were often factories). Beginning in the 1990s, Uri Ram became alert to "the dichotomous nature of the changes that swamped Israel: postmodernity in Tel Aviv versus neofundamentalism in

Jerusalem; high-tech industrial parks in the center versus sacred sites of veneration in the peripheries; an exclamation of constitutional revolution versus an adherence to ethnonationalistic principles" (viii). In his *Globalization of Israel* (2008), Ram identifies "a dialectical dynamic" at the heart of contemporary Israel, "metaphorically between Tel Aviv as a site of McWorld and Jerusalem as a site of Jihad" (5). Much of what he asserts focuses on the complexities of Israel's position in a hostile neighborhood and its dependence as a client state of the United States: "Israel is straddled geopolitically between McWorld and Jihad, between being a protégé of the United States and being situated in the Middle East, the heart of world Islamic resistance to the United States. . . . Israel also undergoes inside it the same bifurcation and tension between the capitalist and tribal dimensions of McWorld and Jihad that take place in the world at large. [Indeed, a] dialectical struggle between a global, capitalist, civic trend and a local nationalist-religious trend takes place within Israel" (6).[3]

The decline of the kibbutz is a long and rather complex story of neglect and shifting priorities, exacerbated by other factors such as immigration, that lies beyond the scope of this study and has been ably addressed by others.[4] However, it seems appropriate to offer at least a brief sketch for readers unfamiliar with what transpired. In the late twentieth century, members of the Likud (politically and economically akin to Ronald Reagan and Margaret Thatcher) wasted no time after their party's dramatic rise to power in 1977, immediately settling scores festering since the 1930s; after gaining control of the Finance Ministry, they abruptly halted loan guarantees that the kibbutzim had received under successive Labor governments. In 1984, the Israeli economy nearly collapsed under the staggering rate of inflation; to stabilize the economy, debts were restructured and renegotiated for manufacturers, retailers, and unions, but, due to the cynically divisive national politics of the day, not for the kibbutzim.

That exclusion, whose disastrous consequences still reverberate, occurred precisely when the kibbutzim found themselves caught up in the most trying circumstances of their history. As J. J. Goldberg, former founding member and secretary-general of Kibbutz Gezer, points out: "Kibbutzim didn't receive even partial debt restructuring until 1989. By that time, the combined kibbutz movement debt was near $6 billion, or about $50,000 per kibbutznik. Draconian debt repayments were emptying kibbutz treasuries and driving down living standards, except on the wealthiest kibbutzim." What seems especially ironic is that in precisely this period, the kibbutzim were not only economically viable but terrifically productive: "In 1990, kibbutzim accounted for about 2% of Israel's population, but were responsible for 7% of its gross domestic product and fully 15% of its exports. . . . The problem was that the banks were getting the money instead of the kibbutzniks." As of this writing, most of Israel's kib-butzim have undergone hafrata, or privatization; fewer than one-third of them have retained the old egalitarian model. In Goldberg's terse lament, "the institu-tion of the kibbutz has survived its first century, but the hope of pioneering a new and better model of human society has not. Over the past quarter-century, most of Israel's 270 kibbutzim have abandoned the founders' socialist credo, 'from each according to his ability, to each according to his need,' and replaced it with the new 'privatized' kibbutz. Today's kibbutz boasts differential salaries, shuttered dining halls, individual home ownership, private bank accounts and investment portfolios and, of course, richer and poorer kibbutzniks." Given the magnitude of the changes Goldberg enumerates, we should take note of the new formal classifications of kibbutzim that emerged in their wake. The "collec-tive kibbutz" (*kibbutz shitufi*) embraces the values and economic model of the socialist past, whereas the "renewing kibbutz" (*kibbutz mitkhadesh*) adopts one or more of the following: privatization and ownership of homes; differential salaries; distribution of cooperative shares of kibbutz enterprises to kibbutz members (Ben-Rafael and Topel 251).

Though this reorganization clearly has profound implications for the ethics and values of individual communities, it is worth noting that the most collec-tivist (*kibbutzim shitufim*) tend also to be the richer kibbutzim, "which means that members of this type of kibbutz may be willing to remain loyal to the original value orientations [since] their kibbutz can 'afford' it" (Ben-Rafael and Topel 251). But it is also clear that, for those kibbutzim which have forsaken the earlier cooperative model, much has been lost. Thus, in my former kibbutz, Yahel, the now middle-aged members who once toiled side by side picking tomatoes and other field crops in their youth for equal benefits often live very unequally today. One single mother I've known for years barely gets by (on a minimal allocation that financial bureaucrats have called a "safety net," in place of the old egalitarian model of shared income), whereas some of her neighbors own cars and private apartments or even houses in the city and can afford lavish vacations that she cannot.[5]

Given the unanticipated insecurity and inequality that my friend and many others struggle with, it seems worth considering what else has been lost in the wake of the abandonment of the founders' ideology. In an ambitious interdis-ciplinary study led by anthropologist Richard Sosis and economist Bradley Ruffle, the research team determined not only that "members of collectivized kibbutzim are more cooperative than city residents" (as one might expect) but that their anticollectivist peers, or "members of kibbutzim that have abandoned socialist ideology (privatized kibbutzim), are no more cooperative than city residents" (89).[6] Ironically, the very cohesion of the meticulously restructured "privatized" kibbutzim is now likely in peril. What remains to distinguish their members from the surrounding population, to shape their lives in meaningful ways, and to prevent the disintegration of these kibbutzim as unified communities?

As Sosis and Ruffle point out, "unlike most of the traditional populations studied by behavioral ecologists, kibbutz members are a self-selected population; they have chosen to live their lives in a communal environment and have ample opportunity to leave their kibbutz and join the surrounding population with whom they share a common religion, language, ethnicity, and national identity. Therefore, maintaining cooperation on the kibbutz is dependent on the kibbutz's ability to foster ideological commitment among its members" (91).[7] In contrast, other researchers seeking to defend the privatized model argue that members of collectivized kibbutzim had severely overspent in relation to their income for many years, reflecting a growing middle-class drive that grew out of the evolving familial proclivities of kibbutz society. This is often described as an utterly inevitable, "natural" process. As the influence of individualism and the private nuclear family (both once anathema to kibbutz life) grew, so did rampant consumerism.[8] Yet still others have a very different story to relate, one more complicated than the usual argument that the late twentieth-century kibbutz "naturally" failed under the onslaught of the market.

After interviewing past kibbutz federation secretary-generals and half a dozen kibbutz treasurers, Goldberg arrived at an account of what occurred that differs considerably from the one circulated most frequently:

> We've all heard the explanations. The socialist dream succumbed to the realities of the market and of human nature. Communal enterprise couldn't compete in the free-wheeling economy of the late-20th century. Collective life stifles ambition and rewards laziness. Kibbutzim got by on idealism for several generations, but by the mid-1980s the stagnation of the commune couldn't compete with the glitter of capitalism. Now kibbutzim are wising up and trading their impractical ideals for hard-headed market realism. It's a dramatic story. . . . But if you listen to the leaders and financial managers who were running the kibbutz movement during the crisis that undermined the kibbutzim during the 1980s, you get a very different story. The way they tell it, the old kibbutz dream didn't die out. It was more like murder. A combination of malice and neglect by government officials and incompetence by planners in the central kibbutz federation in the

1980s short-circuited a social and economic system that had been working fine for decades.

As a former kibbutznik of the preprivatization era, I write in unabashed support of Goldberg's vigorous critique and also in rebuttal to a few recent studies. In particular, one of the most important of these, Jo-Ann Mort and Gary Brenner's *Our Hearts Invented a Place* (2003), leaves me distinctly uneasy. Notwithstanding the romantic sentiment of their study's title, the authors resoundingly affirm the success of hafrata (privatization) but essentially ignore the very values that long stood at the core of the kibbutz movement. They examine the prickly financial issues of privatization that so preoccupy many kibbutzim, such as inheritance laws, property allocations and divisions, and differential salary structures, with relative grace, but they overlook the furthest-reaching *consequences* of the privatization process itself.[9] Uncritically and without a hint of ambivalence, they lend support to the transformation that overtook Israel as socialism was sacrificed on the altar of privatization and globalization.[10] Although their ostensible mission was to document the variety of responses to the economic challenges confronted by three representative kibbutzim, it is manifestly apparent in chapters with titles like "End of Kibbutz or a New Beginning" that their agenda is to advocate for the kinds of accelerated shifts toward capitalist structures and practices that have demoralized and damaged the well-being of so many kibbutzniks. And whereas, for the sake of appearing open-minded, Mort and Brenner assiduously quote from many who dissent from the new platform of dramatic changes, they rarely pause to consider the deep logic of pleas for cleaving to traditional kibbutz values.[11] Instead, they pointedly applaud those favoring sweeping changes, glossing over the raw urgency of one of their respondents, a veteran kibbutz member who warns: "There are . . . conditions that determine whether the kibbutz is a kibbutz. If one of them falls, then there is no more kibbutz. If we cross the redline, we are in postkibbutz" (141).[12]

Even when taking note of the controversial selling off of agricultural lands (including those once farmed by Palestinians before the Nakba) for commercial development, their enthusiasm proves relentless, again effectively disregarding the far-reaching consequences of such actions, consequences decried by artists and intellectuals such as Jonathan Paz, kibbutz-born director of the film *Eskimosim ba Galil* (*The Galilee Eskimos*; 2007), in his wonderful homage to aging, memory, and the kibbutz dream. Like a number of other recent artists and filmmakers addressed in this study, Paz perceives privatization as unambiguously ruinous: "Privatization killed the kibbutz. . . . The kibbutz as defined in the old days is gone. The very few kibbutzim that still exist are not like the old collective kibbutz. That's one of the tragedies of my parents' generation" (Hand). Of course, as the kibbutz writers we have encountered readily acknowledge, from the very beginning, life on the kibbutz was stressed by day-to-day incremental compromises between what Muravchik calls "the stringent communist ideals of the founders and the germ of egoism" (332). Here Muravchik recounts the very earliest challenges to pure egalitarianism and common property:

> The early kibbutzniks had decided to foreswear possessing even their own clothing. Garments were handed in to the central laundry each week, and clean ones of the appropriate size . . . were received in exchange. After a couple of years the women could stand this no longer, and the kibbutz made its first bow to private property. Typically, the second bow . . . occurred when the men who had volunteered for the British army in World War II returned with electric teakettles or some other small furnishing. The kibbutz could not force members to relinquish such prizes, but they introduced an intolerable element of inequality. The solution? Buy a kettle for each household. However, with a teakettle in each dwelling the first step had been taken in undermining communal dining. In subsequent similar cycles, each member was furnished with a refrigerator and then a television. (332)

Yet, having granted the legitimacy of this view of the kibbutz revolution as *always* adjusting and compromising, a reasoned consideration ultimately demands that we ask (as does the veteran member cited in Mort and Brenner's study): just how far can the painfully strained term "kibbutz" be extended before it loses its meaning altogether? At what point is a kibbutz, no matter what its self-identification, effectively no longer a kibbutz?[13] Members of the early kibbutzim felt themselves endowed with a profound social, even spiritual mission: to enlarge the possibilities for authentic human community. But, even after our long journey through the myriad stories that have been told about the classic kibbutz, it is still uncertain whether its imperfections outweigh its considerable achievements.

And, in the present moment, we have Israeli courts contending with evidence of deep malaise and mistrust between individual members and their privatized kibbutzim. In May 2013, Avi Ben-Aharon, dismissed from his management position in the kibbutz fishery by Kibbutz Tel Yosef in the Jezreel Valley, sued for compensation in the Nazareth Labor Court. The judge determined that Tel

Yosef's legal status as a privatized kibbutz represented "a far-reaching change in comparison to the traditional kibbutz in which members worked according to their ability and according to what the kibbutz decided, and received equal pay without reference to their work." The judge determined that there "was no longer a place to test the relations between the member and the kibbutz against the backdrop of the cooperative society where there was complete equality" (qtd. in Ashkenazi). In other words, the Labor Court ruled that the kibbutz's special communal character *no longer existed*, and hence its conduct of employer-employee relations should be considered the same as in the normative society. That the incidence of such once unprecedented litigation is increasing suggests a growing anxiety on the part of many members of privatized kibbutzim over the abandonment of the old values of mutual responsibility and mutual aid and over the new so-called social safety net, which leaves them feeling helpless and unprotected.

If the kibbutz of today is to thrive and avoid that breakdown of basic trust, it will have to find a mission, a larger meaning to inspire future generations, whether its own children or outsiders disenchanted by the economic injustices now proliferating in Israel and other Western societies. Many criticize the movement for its failure to assume a crucial role in national life (such as absorbing new immigrants, as it once did so well).[14] Without an urgent mission, the kibbutz's reputation will surely continue to decline. As Yakov Oved, kibbutznik and historian, rightly points out: "There is a fundamental contradiction between the kibbutz and its environment. We build our status on this difference; it is on behalf of this difference that we want to influence the society at large. The Israeli commune, like many other communes in the world, is [one] which must influence society in order to justify its existence. Such a commune is doomed to a permanent experience of the dialectics of difference—interfering with the society, being influenced by it."[15] Though rapid immigrant absorption was once one of the national burdens the kibbutzim shouldered in the past, that role has clearly waned.[16] There are other salient instances in which the *national* impact of the kibbutz's internal crisis is acutely felt, however. Consider the fate of just one important institution—the Israel Defense Forces (IDF). As is well known, from the earliest years of Israeli statehood, kibbutzniks played a predominant role in elite volunteer combat units, from the paratroopers to the Naval Commando (S-13) unit as well as the Air Force. As Zeev Drory notes, they were "above and beyond their numbers in the broader population. Kibbutz youths were omnipresent in combat and volunteer units, and many of them reached command roles in the companies and battalions of the IDF's infantry and armored corps brigades, both in the conscripted army and even more so in the reserve units" (176).[17] Yet, by the late 1990s, a military commission noted a severe drop in the "motivation" of kibbutz youths—who, until then, had consistently served the military as its main source of volunteers for its officer corps and most elite combat units.[18]

With the gradual eclipse of the kibbutz as preeminent source of the military's elite cadre of officers and combat soldiers, Jewish fundamentalists (indoctrinated in right-wing academies) have ambitiously positioned themselves within the military hierarchy. Drory suggests that the privatization processes have had a directly deleterious impact on IDF enlistment among kibbutz youths: "As the privatization process in the kibbutzim gained speed, suspicion and alienation increased in the kibbutz community towards the state, accompanied by reservations about the army and military service. . . . The crisis of values . . . adversely impacted the fundamental values of collectivism and contribution to the community and the state" (178, 186). Here I would argue that this startling transformation has striking implications for the oppressive circumstances endured on a daily basis by Palestinians in the occupied territories. For, in place of kibbutz youths at the head of combat units in the IDF, we now find the graduates of fundamentalist yeshivas: those raised in the tradition of secular humanism have been replaced by those inculcated in the values of national-religious extremism. As widely reported in the media both within Israel and abroad, this has led to egregious human rights abuses on a previously unprecedented scale and to growing violence and bloodshed between Israelis and Palestinians, such as the 2008–2009 Gaza conflagration, with its bleak record of indifference to civilian casualties on both sides (Bronner).[19] In contrast to these developments, however, we should note that members of the kibbutz movement have long had a disproportionate presence in the peace camp.

Although news about the present state of the kibbutz is clearly disconcerting, from the very beginning, the self-critical narrators of the kibbutz experience have never shied from portraying the daunting challenges that their enterprise faced. And when it comes down to it, the kibbutz *has* proved to be a remarkably enduring institution. Thus, for many people, Amos Oz's 1968 declaration that the kibbutz "is the least bad place I have ever seen. And the most daring effort" (*Under This Blazing Light* 124) might yet hold true.[20] But, for one accustomed to the old values of egalitarianism and communal identity, the kibbutz's dramatic metamorphosis calls for an honest and sober assessment.

Though it might seem a highly unlikely model for understanding the current crisis of the kibbutz, Smadar Lavie's *The Poetics of Military Occupation: Mzeina*

Allegories of Bedouin Identity Under Israeli and Egyptian Rule is surprisingly instructive for what it suggests about the rationales constructed by all homogeneous communities in turmoil. Lavie considers the severe challenge to traditional Bedouin culture posed by its painful abandonment of nomadism. What new self-understandings and rationales emerge?[21] After sojourning among the Mzeina tribe of the southern Sinai Peninsula and studying their self-narration in the form of oral allegories, Lavie concludes that the prominent currents of their storytelling "sustain the Mzeina belief in the immortality of their collective tribal past, yet all the while, they repeatedly make the Mzeinis confront and mourn the extent to which they are entrapped within the global fluctuations of the present. They attempt to represent the image of the tribe as being a noble whole . . . but this is impossible, in fact, because in recent history the Mzeina as a tribe has never had a political and economic existence independent of the colonial powers or an occupying nation-state" (318). Perhaps the contemporary kibbutz movement is also something of an idealized form of tribe, and its pivotal discursive tropes—"progress," "adaptation," and so on—are iterations that mask an underlying understanding of how much has been lost, of the necessity and impossibility of bridging what cannot be bridged.[22]

In that regard, it may be useful to examine the kinds of sweeping changes that have overtaken other modern sites of turmoil, changes that were neither coordinated nor planned. Kibbutz sociologists Eliezer Ben-Rafael and Menachem Topel (each a former or current kibbutznik) consider decolonization during the 1960s, international student revolts in the same period, the breakup of Communist regimes in Eastern Europe in the last two decades of the twentieth century, and the various manifestations of the Arab Spring in our own time. They argue that such upheavals have relevance to the kibbutzim because, just as others faced specific problems in the general circumstances of their respective crises that affected them as a whole, "in each case, [kibbutz] members faced specific problems in general circumstances of crisis that hit the kibbutz sector as a whole. In many kibbutzim, this crisis caused a genuine breakdown of legitimacy of the social order that brought about claims for radical change and the invention of new patterns" (257). Yet it also caused a great number of contemporary communities to embrace systems that would have disqualified them from being identified as kibbutzim in days past, giving rise to a marked degree of anxiety and internal dissent.

In a 1992 study conducted with thirty-six leaders within the United Kibbutz Movement, the respondents "unanimously" expressed dismay that their comrades no longer viewed the kibbutz's former mission to positively influence Israeli society as relevant, "that the general mission of the kibbutz is the concern only of a small cohort within the kibbutzim" (Ben-Rafael 142). In his collab-orative research with Menachem Topel, an expert on the sociology of kibbutz transformation, Eliezer Ben-Rafael sought to examine the self-understandings of kibbutzniks amid the monumental changes (a project not unlike Lavie's inquiry into the transformed lives and identities of the Sinai Bedouin). Their respondents included more than three hundred members of twenty-five "diverse" kibbutzim. The overwhelming consensus that emerged was their belief that "the kibbutz has rejected its original values and aspirations—especially the value of equality and involvement in Israeli society. . . . They believe that the kibbutz now stresses individualistic values such as the search for quality of life and economic security" (255). It seems especially notable that, even though all respondents felt that the kibbutz was a "distinct and unique social setting," the more a kibbutz had abandoned the traditional model, the less its members cherished the values of the past: "The survey revealed that there are significant differences between kibbutzniks who belong to the two extremes on the kib-butz continuum, running from firmly *shitufi* [the original cooperative model] to determinedly *mitkhadesh* [the privatized or "renewing" model]" (255).[23] Not surprisingly, the researchers concluded that "members of the first type show significantly stronger loyalty to "classic" kibbutz values than do members of the second." Furthermore, "the more shitufi their kibbutz, the more respon-dents stress their kibbutz identity; the more mitkhadesh the kibbutz, the less importance respondents give to their kibbutz identity" (256).

By now it should be clear that the ramifications of this diminished sense of purpose and identity are highly consequential for Israeli society itself: there is growing evidence that the older model encouraged greater empathy for Israel's marginalized and underprivileged populations in development towns and for blue-collar workers in the cities (even for those who saw themselves as closer to the urban middle class in terms of their own economic situation): "As opposed to the more mitkhadesh kibbutz, members of the more shitufi kibbutz type express a stronger allegiance . . . to non-kibbutz members who eke out a living from blue-collar work. Moreover, the kibbutzniks of more shitufi kibbutzim are . . . more convinced that the kibbutz has contributed positively to society as a whole" (Ben-Rafael and Topel 255, 256).[24] Though their study obviously reveals a greater kibbutz identity felt by the members of the more classic kib-butz, Ben-Rafael and Topel's conclusions have profound implications not only for the communal enterprise itself but also for the fate of solidarity and com-passion, for a sense of a common humanity in and beyond Israeli society. As our encounters with kibbutz narratives often highlighted in previous chapters, that struggle to find a balance between the "I" and the "We," in all its myriad variations, is the central drama that has inspired the socially engaged artistry and self-questioning of generations of the kibbutz's insiders and outsiders. That long-sought balance might yet be achieved, and if so, it may prove to have surprising resonance in the surrounding society increasingly oppressed by the unanticipated economic, social, and ideological losses incurred by privatization.[25]

In 1987, poet and fiction writer Elisha Porat (1938–2013) spoke incisively of the time-honored equipoise between the antagonistic currents in kibbutz life:

> The burning issues of the kibbutz today are the same as they were in the past . . . the struggle between forces that tend to undermine and dismantle and divide the kibbutz into tiny, egotistical units, and forces that want to see in it a single collective unit, to solve current problems in kibbutz-like ways. You might say that there are two schools. According to one school, the kibbutz exists for the sake of the member. This school sees the kibbutz as a means for achieving the comfort and pleasure of the member. . . . It would be bad for this outlook to gain ascendancy in the kibbutz, because these people want to divide the cake into little crumbs and give them to the members.
>
> On the other hand, there are those who hold down the fort, who stubbornly guard every principle and cause a lot of tension because of their inflexible attitudes. The end product is a sort of balance, and this balance is important to everyone, but we must be aware that the balance is very delicate. It is possible only because there are people struggling for each of the two camps. If one of the camps should weaken and the balance be disturbed, I can't predict what sort of kibbutz there would be, but it's clear that it wouldn't be the kibbutz as we know it. I am always glad when I see that in dealing with some kibbutz problem . . . both camps argue their separate viewpoints, because I know that as a result of this fight, this tension between them, the kibbutz will preserve its balance. (Rosenfeld 175)

When Porat wrote these words, he clearly considered this estimable equanimity so finely tuned that it would reign for years to come—yet the stresses have already proved too great for the center to hold. And one side has clearly prevailed if today over two-thirds of the kibbutzim are no longer collective and their members receive differential salaries based on their work (Pavin). As

Ben-Rafael argues, "Kibbutzniks are faced, like anyone else, with the exigencies of individualism, achievement, and social egoism. They differ from non-kibbutzniks only by confronting these exigencies much more acutely and directly in their daily endeavor, as contradictions with their opposite; that is, sharing egalitarianism, partnership, and societal ambitions. These codes, which are no less an essential part of the society's culture, do not just constitute for kibbutzniks a general frame of moral reference, but force them to ponder their significance, in the ongoing organization and re-organization of the community life, the economic enterprise and the relation to the environment" (228).

In his homage to that constant and imperfect struggle, Assaf Inbari, raised in Kibbutz Afikim and author of the best-selling novel *Ha-baita* (*Home*; 2009) about kibbutz life from its earliest years to its decline, speaks of the movement's fading days with elegiac tenderness: "I view the kibbutz story as tragic, not as pitiful. Tragic is heroic. I find it a story of people who possessed a tragic greatness. A greatness that was required in order to even try to realize such a far-reaching dream, which amounted to a conscious challenge to human nature. A common misapprehension is that they didn't understand human nature. They did understand it and they set out to defy it. To defy it in terms of family, possessions, privacy, ego" (Avrahami). Yet there are vibrant examples of new permutations suggesting that Inbari's tragic vision is not a foregone conclusion. Not so long as kibbutzniks rally and strive to counter the challenges that will otherwise undermine the utopian dream.

According to a report in the *Guardian* that appeared in July 2012, Inbari's own kibbutz may be thriving after all the turmoil: "In the last two years, Afikim's membership has increased from 500 to 600, and there is now a waiting list of people wanting to join"; the contemporary kibbutz is run with a "progressive taxation system: the more you earn, the more you pay into the collective fund. There is a 'safety net' minimum income for all, and the kibbutz subsidizes healthcare, education, social needs and care for the elderly" (Sherwood 20).[26] Though the prospect of home ownership is undoubtedly a factor these days, young individuals and married couples continue to cite the attraction of a close, supportive community and the overall quality of life on the kibbutz, including education and the environment, as the reason they decided to become members. Moreover, in May 2008, in his talk "The Kibbutz: Reports of Its Death Are Greatly Exaggerated," Gavri Bargil, secretary general of the United Kibbutz Movement, triumphantly proclaimed that not only are today's kibbutzim experiencing a net gain in members (including a returning young generation), but that only 30 of 272 kibbutz communities remain in economic difficulty. Bargil proudly cited statistics demonstrating that the meager 1.6 percent of Israel's population lately residing in kibbutzim (roughly 120,000 people) still manages to produce nearly 7 percent of the country's GDP ("Changes on Kibbutz").[27]

Even now, a surprising number of kibbutzim remain devoted to ensuring their enduring relevance through creative dedication to urgent humanistic pursuits that include protecting the environment, overcoming the global crisis of desertification, engaging in social action and peace studies, and promoting the original, lofty ideals of egalitarianism and antimaterialism to which the earliest kibbutz generations selflessly sacrificed themselves.[28] Indeed, the most recent kibbutz established, Eshbal (2007), is the home of a highly praised Jewish-Arab school that encourages social activism among and coexistence between Jews and Arabs; the kibbutz has also undertaken a number of important multicultural and bilingual leadership initiatives in the Galilee and throughout the country.[29] In fact, there are myriad ways in which the kibbutz movement might regain at least some of its lost stature—and ensure its relevance not only for the generation of children being raised on kibbutzim at the time of this writing and future generations, but also for Israeli society—and indeed even the world far beyond.[30]

For too many, it has become too easy to uncritically reject the kibbutz ideal as utterly outmoded, old history.[31] Yet Goldberg passionately reminds us that the pernicious lies and distortions that brought down the most sustained, successful realization of the socialist dream still dog Israeli society: "The same cynical arguments brought against the kibbutz at a time of crisis—it never worked anyway, idealism is naïve, greed rules, dog must eat dog—are being hurled these days against every effort at a kinder society, from health care reform to minimum wages to pensions to consumer credit protection. It was bunk back then, and it's bunk today." Given that often unspoken truth, it is heartening that some see real hope in the phenomenon of communal groups that have emerged throughout Israel over the last three decades, particularly their progressive and socially transformative work in development towns and other peripheral urban areas. Many of the members of such groups (dubbed by some "irbutzim" or urban kibbutzim) share certain characteristics, identified by Yuval Dror:

> Many of them grew up in a kibbutz or spent at least a few years there. Many of them considered the youth movement as their natural home; the experience was meaningful to them and made an impact on their life. The factor most significant to them was their year of social service prior to their military service. This pre-military year enabled them to

experience intimate life in a close-knit group, usually accompanied by study of various Jewish-Zionist and social texts. The military units in which most of them served together . . . enabled them to . . . foster their sense of group cohesion and the collectivist ethos during their military service as well. (320)

Dror's research into these predominantly left-wing communities demonstrates that they transformed their critique of Israeli society into educational activism within their surrounding communities. Interestingly, the evidence he uncovers suggests that these groups are staunchly opposed to the privatization of the kibbutzim from which they themselves sprang (321).[32]

Such findings vigorously underscore the fact that, no matter how intensely individualism, hedonism, and materialism have transformed mainstream Israeli culture, a yearning for a meaningful life under a more collectivist ethos inherited from the past stubbornly endures in the youngest generation of Israelis (all the more so among those whose formative years were shaped by the communal experience). Moreover (perhaps owing to their more intimate connections with one another), the members of these communities may not succumb to the alienating pressures and stifling conformity that led many young people to abandon the traditional kibbutz in the 1970s. Dror argues that the urban collectivities represent "a completely different mode of kibbutz life" (323), one that successfully synthesizes the most enduring ideals of the past with the norms of postmodern culture. In some respects, especially with regard to education, they aspire to be more inclusive than the traditional kibbutz, striving to overcome the elitism that once separated the kibbutzim from the lesser affluent communities surrounding them:

> They are intimate manifestations . . . comprising a few dozen partners, not a large community of hundreds of people; they are communal (in a "modern" way that permits the use of external resources), but not privatized in a way that flaunts the original principles that hearken to the kibbutz ethos; they are based on personal autonomy and choice with respect to ways of self-actualization and advancement less on collective needs and systemic and individual constraints; they are committed to community values as a whole, with communality and commitment complementing each other; they actually live in urban development areas, and do not turn into patronizing external sponsors for [limited] periods . . . and they are a society eager to learn together on a weekly basis, not only a community that enables individuals to study. (324)

It is, of course, much too soon to tell how long these communities will endure, whether their vision will succeed in attracting new members, and, if so, whether they will have as profound and lasting impact on Israeli society, as the traditional kibbutzim once had.[33] Yet it is certainly inspiring to note that this revitalizing experiment owes its existence to what Amos Oz calls the "kibbutz genes" of Israeli society. At the very least, it is tempting to share Dror's tantalizing hope that "this kibbutz-born revolution will have an impact on 'the old kibbutz' from which it grew" (324).

And now it seems we have come full circle: the members of one such kibbutz have adopted one of the earliest kibbutz novels discussed in this study, David Maletz's *Ma'agalot* (*Young Hearts*; 1945), as a "textbook for the group in their attempts to construct a more effective communal group" (Keshet, "Kibbutz Fiction" 164). There seems something manifestly promising in that conscientious return to sources and origins, for though he never underestimated the daunting struggle to create a radically new society, Maletz also affirmed the spiritual and social resilience of collective life.[34] Thus even the literature of the distant kibbutz past proves its lasting relevance to the communal imagination of the present. And therein lies not merely a nostalgic consolation in what was once achieved, but also a genuine pragmatism and a wellspring of inspiration and hope for the future. May the dream that inspired me and my fellow former kibbutzniks stir many others toward a greater vision and awareness of what human community might be.

ACKNOWLEDGMENTS

Above all, this book is dedicated to Michal Kofman, who introduced me to the vibrant complexities and nuances of Cuban society while pursuing her own research, and for whose unqualified love and support I am and will always be profoundly grateful. My work would not have been possible without the close cooperation of scholars as well as dozens of kibbutz members, current and former, who were generous with their time and candor. I would like to single out Nancy Reich of Kibbutz Yahel, Hanan Ginat and Gigi Strom of Kibbutz Samar, Mark Naveh, Liset Sela, and Alex Cicelsky of Kibbutz Lotan for their candid reflections on the challenges faced by young desert kibbutzim. And both kibbutz life and my military service were enriched beyond words by lifelong friendships formed in "Regev," my Nahal cadre. Today those cherished connections and warm memories flourish through frequent reunions with Rafi Ber, Avi Camhi, Shmulik Friedman, Yonaton Gold, Robert Hoffman, Shlomo Mordechai, Chip Nobil, Tsvika Rubin, "Gingi" Motti Shlomo, and Mark Weiser (enabling me to travel back to a time of youthful idealism, adventure, and memorable misbehavior so blissfully remote from the stuffy spaces of academia).

My deepest appreciation goes to filmmakers Oded Hirsch, Jonathan Paz, Ran Tal, Ilan Yagoda, and Yitzhak Yeshurun for the evocative images of their extraordinary cinematic statements about Israel's collective past. My thanks as well to Amotz Peleg, archivist of Kibbutz Hulda, for his generous assistance in locating and making available rare photos from Hulda's resplendent history. The Frankel Institute for Advanced Judaic Studies at the University of Michigan afforded me a wonderful opportunity to work on this project and to receive invaluable critical feedback from an exceptional range of gifted colleagues there. My heartfelt appreciation goes to faculty members Maya Barzilai, Lois Dubin, Jennifer Glaser, Harvey Goldberg, Tatjana Lichtenstein, Deborah Dash Moore, Andrea Siegel, Orian Zakai, and especially Carol Bardenstein and Shahar Pinsker, among others, for their friendship and interdisciplinary acumen, as well as to Jonathan Freedman, who conducted our lively weekly workshops with skill and genuine warmth, and to Avery Robinson, a resourceful young scholar, who served as my research assistant in Ann Arbor during the fall of 2012. A generous University of Miami Provost Research Award enabled me to complete the final phase of writing. Jeffrey Lockridge is the most diligent copyeditor I have ever worked with; many thanks to him as well as Samantha Baskind, general editor of the Dimyonot series, and Patrick Alexander, director of the Pennsylvania State University Press.

I owe an incredible debt to Adam Rovner, literary critic and translator extraordinaire, and, above all, genuine mensch, for his incisive review of the entire manuscript, a review that inspired me to make important improvements. I would also like to express my strong appreciation to Michal Palgi of the University of Haifa and to Shulamit Reinharz of Brandeis University for helping me grapple with the ramifications of this project at an early stage and to Allan Arkush for his thoughtful reflections on my approach to Amos Oz's *Between Friends*. I was profoundly inspired by the superb work of film documentarian Toby Perl Freilich. My stimulating conversation with Toby one beautiful summer morning in a café in Jerusalem's German Colony both confirmed a great deal and raised important new questions that inspired my approach. For anyone who has not yet viewed her splendid, deeply engrossing documentary film *Inventing Our Life: The Kibbutz Experiment*, I cannot begin to praise it enough for its critical yet empathetic presentation of the travails of the utopian dream as it encountered the sharp realities of social change and human limits. David Leach's generous encouragement and insights were also invaluable, and I encourage anyone interested in the kibbutz to seek out his well-informed and utterly captivating blog "Look Back to Galilee: A Hundred Years of Communal Life" <http://lookbacktogalilee.blogspot.com/>. And I owe an affectionate debt to Ellis Shuman and Jodie Kaufman Shuman for their wonderful kibbutz memories and especially for their deeply sustaining friendship over many years. Finally, my transformative sojourn at Kibbutz Yahel, which began in Yahel's early days and was an astonishing adventure lasting over a dozen unforgettable and life-changing years, as well as shorter periods of service and visits with kibbutz members living in Beit Zera, Ketura, Kfar Blum, Kfar Hamaccabi, Ketura, Lotan, Samar, and Yotvata—all these have helped form my understanding of this subject over the past several decades. I am profoundly grateful to all who shared their time with me during those visits. Their lives of dedication continue to inspire me and shape my thinking and values in indelible ways. Most of all, they left me firmly persuaded that the kibbutz is far from an anachronism and that, though its future is yet unknown, its time has not yet passed.

NOTES

INTRODUCTION

The epigraphs to this introduction are drawn from Shaham, *Other Side* 222, and Manguel.

1. I remember the tractor accidents and other agricultural mishaps that likely occurred because of how worn out we were. And there was a very dedicated young woman of my acquaintance from a neighboring kibbutz who was roused by the night guard to milk the dairy herd at 3:30 A.M. and startled her coworker when she showed up bleary-eyed wearing only her milking apron and boots.

2. For example, while I was writing this study, one of many examples of the kibbutz's far-flung popularity came to me from my colleague Tatjana Lichtenstein, who spoke about the remarkable impact of the kibbutz ideal on her native Denmark, which endured even amid rising sympathy for the Palestinians in the occupied territories: "Denmark, as you know, is a country with a strong social democratic (and further left) tradition. I do think that the left-leaning Jewish state and especially the kibbutz movement was something that kept alive a positive, romantic, adventurous image of Israel in Denmark. This was probably especially true in the 1960s . . . [, when] people were engaging in all kinds of social experimentation. . . . Obviously some left-leaning groups cared very strongly about the Palestinian struggle, but that did not really make it into public consciousness until the First Intifada. At that time, Danish Friends of the Kibbutz (Danske Kibbutz Venner DAKIV) still had a very strong infrastructure in place for young Danes who would spend their gap year on a kibbutz (when I say 'gap year,' I also mean people without university ambitions). Between the 1960s and the early 2000s, about 40,000 Danes volunteered on a kibbutz (a Danish website talking about the organization's demise. It closed down in 2001). . . . The kibbutz was central to the left's positive attitude towards Israel beyond 1967. Prominent lefties here talk about balancing their excitement for the social experiment in the kibbutz with an emerging awareness of the plight of the Palestinians in the 1970s" (pers. comm., 6 November 2012).

3. As a fifteen-year-old, Judt "adored" his experience of "Muscular Judaism" on a kibbutz in the mid-1960s. What he came "quickly to understand if not openly acknowledge," however, "was just how limited the kibbutz and its members really were": "The mere fact of collective self-government, or egalitarian distribution of consumer durables, does not make you either more sophisticated or more tolerant of others. Indeed, to the extent that it contributes to an extraordinary smugness of self-regard, it actually reinforces the worst kind of ethnic solipsism."

4. I like Alberto Manguel's wry framing of the Jews' utopian imagination: "The first Jewish utopia was a garden where, according to the Book of Genesis, God himself liked to stroll in the cool of the evening. It didn't end well. Almost 6,000 years later, in 1909, a group of young Jews decided to recreate that original garden in Ottoman Palestine and on the southern tip of the [Sea] of Galilee set up a kibbutz (or 'gathering') which they hopefully named Kvutzat Degania ('Wheat of God')."

5. Emily Eakin recounts the idiosyncratic nature of the famously ephemeral American utopias: "The historical record is not auspicious in this regard. Fruitlands, founded in 1843, near Harvard, Massachusetts, by the progressive educator Bronson Alcott, lasted just six months, its goal of self-sufficiency doomed by its members' extremism: they were vegans who refused to wear cotton, wool, or leather because these were products of either animals or slaves, and they tried to till the soil by hand, in order to avoid exploiting oxen and horses. They began each day with a cold shower and believed that sex should be passionless or avoided altogether" (73).

6. Like so many of the scholars consulted for this study, Daniel Gavron is a former kibbutznik. He has lived in Israel since 1961.

7. Halevi's *Like Dreamers* documents Israel's political shifts through the later lives of the young men from the legendary 55th Paratrooper Reserve Brigade, many of whom hailed from the kibbutzim.

8. The works discussed in these pages occasionally allude to the names of specific kibbutz movements. Created in 1927, Hakibbutz Hameuchad (United Kibbutz Movement) sought to instill a common approach to the building of a labor society in Palestine and drew from many separate youth Zionist movements. Hakibbutz Haarzi Hashomer Hatzair (National Kibbutz Movement of the Young Guard) was also established in 1927; its ideological tenets stressed the Zionist agrarian ideal as well as the class struggle, and it sought to pioneer a socialist society. Precisely because its members came from a variety of movements, Hakibbutz Hameuchad eventually was filled with internal political and social controversies, largely as a result of the growing intensity of the struggle between the political factions of the left-leaning Mapai and the more centrist Mapam and the subsequent decision of Mapai to establish its own cultural and educational institutions. (This schism is particularly relevant to my discussion of the film *Noa at Seventeen* and other works portraying the heated politics of the 1950s in chapter 5, and readers unfamiliar with the Stalinist affinities of some kibbutzim may find that a fascinating story.) At a meeting of the movement's council, those kibbutzim with a Mapai majority seceded and formed Ihud Hakibbutzim, which joined with Hever Hakevuzot to form Ihud Hakibbutzim ve-Hakevuzot (Union of Collective Settlements). For some time, the Ihud was the most liberal of the kibbutz movements, imposing less ideological or political discipline on its member kibbutzim; it was within this movement that children first began to sleep in parental homes in some settlements in the early 1970s. Over time, especially amid the economic stresses of later decades, the sharp ideological differences between kibbutz factions softened considerably. In 1979, the two kibbutz organizations, Hakibbutz Hameuchad and Ihud Hakevutzot ve-Hakibbutzim, reunited after twenty-eight years of separation to form the Hatenuah Hakibbuzit Hameuhedet (Takam, or the United Kibbutz Movement). A small number of kibbutzim were formed under the auspices of Hakibbutz Hadati (the Religious Kibbutz), a movement established in 1935 by religious pioneer groups from Poland and Germany and dedicated to creating a spiritual synthesis of religious practice with labor.

9. As political scientist Shlomo Avineri notes of the classic days when socialism reigned in Israel (1940s–1960s), the kibbutzniks had always regarded themselves as a "serving elite"; historian Tom Segev identifies them as the "nobility and priesthood of the national ideology" (qtd. in Muravchik 327–28).

10. Preeminent Israeli military historian Zeev Drory observes that kibbutz soldiers accounted for 18.5 percent of all Israeli soldiers killed in the "Second Lebanon War," or seven times more than "the proportion of the kibbutz population within the general population" (185).

11. Gan also quotes the words of Benko Adar, a young man who had recently fought in the 1967 War and whose reflections suggest he was an especially eloquent and self-knowing spokesperson of this new sensibility: "Until now the kibbutz was perceived mainly as a tool, and so was the individual—as a soldier on the line, called upon to sacrifice, serve certain aims, give up for the sake of. . . . That is the way of all great revolutions at their inception. . . . Gradually a new percep-

tion takes hold, emphasizing the kibbutz as an aim in itself, as a framework—not as a fighting unit committed to the execution of missions of national importance. This leads to a change in the attitude to the individual. The person becomes an aim, an end in itself. The individual, his happiness, joy. . . . Today our task—that of the younger generation—is to build on the foundations laid down by the generation of the first settlers, a society enabling each person to assert himself, realize himself, to fulfill the potential of his personality. A society of happy people, not people sacrificing themselves 'on the altar.' Not 'kibbutz' as a group of people living for the sake of the kibbutz itself, but kibbutz as the people living in it, its aim being the people themselves" (qtd. in Gan 40–41). Yet another young person who embodies the urgent need to wander and to fulfill oneself can be found in Amos Oz's novel *Menuhah nehonah* (*A Perfect Peace*; 1982) in the figure of Yonatan. Years after his army service, Yonatan wistfully calls for opportunities that he and his generation missed: "I think there must be some kind of procedure enabling people—in particular young people—to wander and develop their personality to the full" (*Perfect Peace* 41).

12. Today it seems to me that, growing up as we did amid the Civil Rights Movement and the utopian political dreams of the 1960s, my generation was the last to be quite so thoroughly captivated by the promise of the kibbutz.

13. "Nahal" is the Hebrew acronym for Noar Halutzi Lohem (Fighting Pioneer Youth), an organization unique to Israel that combines military service with civilian support to newly established or struggling kibbutzim and other communities.

14. For example, kibbutz memoirist Alfy Nathan traces the decline of authentic communal life to the disappearance of communal showers: "Communal showers meant that you got the opportunity to joke around with one another; laughing and singing could be heard a good distance away. The men's and women's showers were separated by a corrugated wall. You could hear the ladies going through the same routine as us and friendly banter would go back and forth" (though the same writer does not evince nostalgia for the older days of bathing via "old cucumber cans"). After showers were installed in the homes, he and others felt that "it came with a price . . . a steep one; a decline in the communal life of the kibbutz. It may seem like a small thing but I think it was significant" (Nathan with Sklare 141).

15. Hence my exasperated wife's insistence on printing me a T-shirt that reads in Hebrew, "BECAUSE ONCE I WAS A KIBBUTZNIK."

16. At the same time, *Imagining the Kibbutz* demonstrates that, in each literary generation, though genuinely fraught with responses to the challenges and contingencies of life on the kibbutz and with the kinds of existential issues taken up by other modern literary works, kibbutz narratives also exhibit a rich capacity for addressing gritty practical matters entailed by the shift from an intense communal framework to a privatized one, such as the decline of the children's dormitories and eating in family homes rather than the collective dining rooms.

17. When *Ma'agalot* appeared in translation as *Young Hearts*, its publisher touted it as "the first genuine modern Israeli novel to be printed in English."

18. Not long after Oz arrived at Hulda as a fourteen-year-old, he befriended Balaban, who had been born there and was then eight, and gave him books of modern poetry to encourage his own precocious efforts.

19. By way of conclusion to their study of cooperative behavior in twenty-eight kibbutzim, comparing individuals on traditional "cooperative" kibbutzim with those in privatized communities, Sosis and Ruffle offer the intriguing speculation that "because secular ideologies are exposed to greater vicissitudes of examination, they are less durable than religious ideologies and less successful at promoting long-term commitment and cooperation among adherents" (112). Notwithstanding the merits of this argument, among all the historical examples of secular communal living, the traditional kibbutz has proved to have unprecedented endurance.

20. For readers unfamiliar with the later evolution and recent history of the kibbutz, it will be helpful to keep in mind that, as of 2014, the kibbutz population exceeded 106,000, with more

than 20,000 children; the 273 kibbutzim included 16 members of the Hakibbutz Hadati Movement that regard themselves as Orthodox Zionist. Of the total number of kibbutzim, 190 (70 percent) had undergone privatization by 2010, a model also referred to as the "Renewed Kibbutz" (also known as the "security net" framework), whereas 65 kibbutzim (24 percent) still adhere to the traditional ideals of the "Communal Kibbutz." Yet a third model, known as the "Integrated Kibbutz," was adopted by 9 kibbutzim (3 percent). In the traditional communal kibbutz, income is entirely equal, with no linkage between income and vocation. Following privatization, the "Renewed Kibbutz" adopted a differential income structure based on salary index and earning ability. In this system, the greater the individual salary, the greater the individual share of the community's income. A percentage of gross salary is deducted and applied toward both community expenses and "security net" income to support those whose salaries fail to reach the minimum income established by each kibbutz. In the Integrated Kibbutz, three factors contribute to the individual member's income: an equal portion shared by all, a percentage based on the member's seniority (years of membership), and finally, the member's salary or deemed contribution. The implications of these income systems are addressed at greater length in the afterword.

CHAPTER I

The epigraphs to this chapter are drawn from Shaham, *Other Side* 151, and Shavit 4.

1. As Zeev Drory recounts, "Nahal was one of the most important tools in the IDF's involvement in Israeli society. Its main activity was consolidating settlement core-groups, supplementing members in outlying kibbutzim, and setting up new settlement outposts along the borders and in peripheral regions. On 12 September 1948, the General Staff published an Order that included a special section on the foundation of the Nahal. The order stipulated the framework, goals, and the special modus operandi of the Nahal. . . . [The] first commander was Elik Shomroni, who was close to Ben-Gurion and a member of Kibbutz Afikim. Shomroni was among the architects of the idea of the Nahal and a central figure in its formation . . . who imprinted his ideas on [its] first regulations and first patterns: the contract with the kibbutzim, the core-group procedures, arrangements for Shalat (Hebrew acronym for Voluntary National Service), the year's division into army exercises and agricultural; work, recruitment arrangements, the Nahal's symbol, the agricultural college, the Nahal entertainment troupe, the *Bemahaneh Nahal* weekly magazine, and all the other elements that together created the special mosaic of this force" (172, 173).

2. These founding writers include Aliza Amir-Zohar (b. 1932), Yossl Birstein (1920–2003), Zvi Luz (b. 1930), David Maletz (1900–1981), Amos Oz (b. 1939), Nathan Shaham (b. 1925), Moshe Shamir (1921–2004), Amnon Shamosh (b. 1929), and Dan Shavit (b. 1944). Novels of the pioneering effort (dubbed in Hebrew as the genre of the "settlement novel" by Gershon Shaked) were also written by those with no kibbutz affiliation, including Yosef Aricha (*Bread and Vision*), Alexander Carmon (*Man and Soil*), and Israel Zarchi (*An Unsown Land*), among others. See Keshet, "Kibbutz Fiction." For the sake of my intended audience, most of my focus here will address works that are also available in English translation, with judicious comparison to other salient Hebrew works that, as yet, are not.

3. There may even be a precursor to the kibbutz literary tradition. Iris Milner considers a 1909 short story by Y. H. Brenner titled "Agav urcha" ("By the Way") as a sort of ur-text, both written and set during the Turkish and British struggles over Palestine: "Before the first kibbutz actually came into being, it describes the rise and fall of an experiment in communal life involving six fervent Zionist pioneers, on their way to Eretz Yisrael" (159). Brenner himself immigrated to Palestine in 1909 and became the most illustrious literary figure in Hebrew letters of his day, credited with shifting the center of Hebrew culture from Europe to Palestine. Arab rioters killed him in 1921. In contrast, Brenner's settler characters voyage en route from Trieste to Alexandria; poi-

gnantly, they never arrive in Palestine (a fate characteristic of Brenner's pessimistic vision of life as unending toil leading to disaster). "By the Way" would thus seem to anticipate many of the narratives of doubt, incompleteness, and unease that my study undertakes to address. But then, Jewish culture is always one of deferral.

4. As both scholar and literary author, Inbari is in a strong position to appreciate the unique situation of the kibbutz writer (for whom what we usually assume about the conventional demarcation of the public and private realms simply does not hold). In "Kibbutz Novel," he reflects that "the very literary separation between the private . . . and the social-national-historical one . . . does not at all reflect the experience of most of the kibbutz founders and their children, since their strongest and most significant personal experiences have been those of being kibbutz members, settlers, pioneers, founders, farmers, and fighters. Their self-consciousness was a devotional, Zionist-socialist one, and, therefore, the personal story of each one of them was that of his or her participation in the national and communal story" (143).

5. The full sentence from Buber and the one immediately following it read, "And, psychologically speaking, it is based on one of the eternal needs, even though this need has often been forcibly suppressed or rendered insensible: the need of man to feel his own house as a room in some greater, all-embracing structure in which he is at home, to feel that the other inhabitants of it with whom he lives and works are all acknowledging and confirming his individual existence. An association based on community of views and aspirations alone cannot satisfy this need; the only thing that can do that is an association which makes for communal living." See Buber 140.

6. An anecdote from kibbutz poet Mira Meir's 1940s childhood lends remarkable credibility to Shaham's portrayal of poetry's lowly status among many of the Zionist pioneers: "I remember myself at a Hashomer Hatzair Movement camp. At the time, the anthology *The Songs of the Siren* [*Sherei hasirena*], edited by [Avraham] Shlonsky, had just been published. I brought the book with me to camp and read it. All but my best friends jeered at me and said, 'Why on earth are you reading poetry?' But I continued reading, and they made my life a misery to such an extent that I decided to transfer to another work camp . . . where the members were more capable of tolerating someone as unusual as myself. This was in 1947, in the 'forest group,' which was then considered an intellectual group *par excellence*. And even they couldn't digest anyone who read poetry" (Ring 161–62).

7. A. D. Gordon (1856–1922) was an early paragon of the Labor Movement, aligning that effort with the spiritual revitalization of the Jews of the Yishuv (pre-state Palestine). As Arthur Hertzberg recounts, "If Herzl was Zionism's president-in-exile . . . Gordon was the movement's secular mystic and saint" (369), insisting on forging "the metaphysical bond between the Jew and the land of Israel. . . . The Jew would become whole again by living the life of nature" (371). Hertzberg ruefully concludes that, though Zionism's "greatest teacher" and "heterodox Hasidic master of the Labor-Zionist movement," Gordon, like most utopian thinkers, has been "more admired than followed" (371). However, it is worth emphasizing here that Zionist youth movements were profoundly influenced by his teachings (the members of one such movement, Gordonia, even embraced his name as the prophetic call for their work). Gordon was buried in Degania, the first kibbutz, where he lived out his final years.

8. Exceptions to that reticence include historical novels that focused on the development of individual settlements, such as Ever Hadani's *Tzrif ha-etz* (*Wooden Hut*; 1930), Shlomo Reichenstein's *Raishit* (*Beginnings*; 1943), and *Adama lelo tzel* (*A Land Without a Shadow*; 1951) by Alexander and Yonat Sened (Milner 160).

9. The rough equivalent, "pioneers," doesn't begin to capture the rich significance of the halutzim in the Israeli imagination, their glorified position in Israeli national history, culture, and education. Israeli iconography from propaganda posters to state-issued banknotes celebrated the rugged and tanned images of labor-loving Hebrew settlers who arrived in organized waves of settlement from groups such as Bilu and Hovevei Zion. Like other secular Zionist terms, the

reverent expression was appropriated from biblical language denoting the military conquest of Canaan by the Israelites, and applied to the Jewish migrants transformed into agricultural laborers who settled the frontiers of the expanding New Yishuv, as memorialized in the language of Israel's Declaration of Independence. As Israel's Declaration of Independence narrates, they "made deserts bloom . . . built villages and towns, and created a thriving community controlling its own economy and culture . . . bringing the blessings of progress to all the country's inhabitants, and aspiring towards independent nationhood" (Israel Ministry of Foreign Affairs, 14 May 1948). Some Israelis would argue that the term "halutzim," connoting being at the vanguard or forefront, is far from an anachronism and that the spirit of *halutziut* (pioneerism) still drives Israel's entrepreneurial spirit, producing innovations in drip irrigation, solar water heating, the flash drive, and a variety of other groundbreaking agricultural and technological developments.

10. For years, antipathy toward writers prevailed on the kibbutz. Amos Oz has often recounted the unfavorable conditions under which he wrote his second, more psychologically accomplished novel, *Mikha'el sheli* (*My Michael*; 1968; a huge success, eventually translated into nearly thirty languages). "The kibbutz granted him only one day a week . . . for literary writing," Omri Herzog reports. "So, in addition, each night, after he returned from working in the fields and spent a little time with his family, he would shut himself into the tiny bathroom, in order not to disturb his wife and children's sleep. He sat on the closed lid of the toilet, a heavy art book that the couple had received as a wedding present on his knees, and wrote longhand with a lit cigarette between his fingers. By the middle of the night his eyes would begin to close with fatigue, mingled with sorrow for the character whose story he was writing, and he would leave the bathroom and go to sleep in his bed."

11. In August 2012, Deputy Education Minister Menachem Eliezer Moses, of the United Torah Judaism Party, gleefully reported that, for the first time in Israeli history, religious Jewish children made up more than 50 percent of Israeli preschoolers (Bar'el).

12. See also Hanna Naveh's related account of the early literary entanglements with socialist ideology during the 1920s.

13. As I demonstrate in chapter 5, recent movies, documentary films, and other visual art productions have largely appropriated the skeptical role once performed by kibbutz fiction.

14. Moderator Israel Ring launched this 1986 literary symposium with an expression of unease about the "silence" of most kibbutz writers on certain topics in kibbutz life, notably, "childhood and youthful experience in collective education and in relations between parents and children . . . it is hard to find anyone wrestling directly, penetratingly with these themes. I find it difficult to recall works expressing a happy or unhappy childhood, enthusiasm, curiosity—the depth of childhood and youthful experiences." Speculating aloud about the relative absence of "full daring . . . of full expression of all the pain" experienced in the framework of collective education (while highlighting exceptions inherent in the work of a very few authors) and citing "evidence of the gap existing between that which is locked up in kibbutz children and that which they are prepared to reveal in their [published] works," he called on the assembled writers to grapple with the reasons for that fraught silence (151, 153). As my study suggests, though the reasons remain unclear, it would be nearly two decades before writers and other artists ventured into that void.

15. Literary writers were often trapped between a rock and a hard place, discouraged by their movement ideologues, on the one hand, and by the high priests of art, on the other. Even as they struggled to capture the social reality of the new revolutionary settlements in Palestine, novelists were derided by critics. Thus Baruch Kurtzweil, perhaps the most esteemed literary critic of the 1940s and 1950s, asked, "Has our life in the village, kibbutz, and farming community of Eretz Yisrael consolidated to the point of actually being able to serve as the raw material of epic work?" And to make perfectly clear that the answer to his rhetorical question was a foregone conclusion, Kurtzweil imperatively asserted that "a young world, lacking coherent lines, groping in semi-

darkness for its place, is not the appropriate spiritual soil for the novel and story" (qtd. in Inbari, "Kibbutz Novel" 131).

16. Assaf Inbari draws attention to the daunting challenge faced especially by kibbutz writers to address a tumultuous history "still in the making." Writers had to contend with the "storm of multicultural immigration waves, of shifting from Turkish rule to English rule to self-rule under American patronage, of the shock of the Holocaust. . . . The writers of Eretz Yisrael in the pre-state era, as well as the Israeli writers after the establishment of the state, did not live in a cohesive social world, such as that in which the writers of Victorian England, Tsarist Russia, or the East European shtetl worked. Consequently, Israeli writers and critics have repeatedly claimed that, in such a dynamic historical reality, the writing of a realist social novel is a nearly impossible task. The challenge faced by kibbutz writers was even greater, not just because of the even greater dynamism of the kibbutz as an arena of social experimentation, but also due to the incongruity between a positive, common experience—such as that of realizing national and social ideals—and the personal, gloomy themes expected from 'good literature'" ("Kibbutz Novel" 129).

17. The two other Hebrew novels of the 1940s are David Maletz's *Ma'agalot* (*Young Hearts*; 1945), addressed later in this discussion, and Emma Levin-Talmi's *Zman ha-olahim* (*Time of Tents*; 1949).

18. Shamir's 1959 drama, extolling the mythos of tragic heroism so critical to the 1948 generation, is notable for being the first play to be performed after the founding of the Jewish state and is widely considered the most popular work of its day. Soon after the 1967 War, it was adapted as a film starring Assi Dayan (handsome son of Defense Minister Moshe Dayan). According to Mikhal Dekel's critically astute discussion, the original staged version "was seen by no less than a third of Israel's Jewish population at the time . . . an instant success. It was performed around the country, often before soldiers, and became known as the Israel Defense Forces' 'secret weapon' and a morale booster among combatants. The play touches on many themes: the hardship and drama of kibbutz life, relations between Sabras and immigrants, gender arrangements in the new state, and the Yishuv's take on the Holocaust" (198). Above all, *He Walked Through the Fields* (in all its variations) addresses the self-sacrifice of the citizen soldier. Although the protagonist's identity as the kibbutz's firstborn is crucial to Shamir's narrative (he himself was a member of Kibbutz Mishmar Haemek), because Shamir does not treat kibbutz life in depth, I address the work only briefly here. Suffice it to say that other works of the period address its themes in congruent ways.

19. In the 1987 dialogue of kibbutz writers published in *Shdemot* (literary digest of the kibbutz movement), the issue of the artist's freedom versus fealty to the collective appears to have been largely settled. Nevertheless, it seems remarkable that it even arose at that time. A few representative reflections on the writer's "obligation" prove revealing. Zvi Luz: "As a writer, I feel a deep obligation toward human society as a whole, and my human society is the kibbutz. I have a duty to the kibbutz, not as an institution, but as a place in which people live. . . . I am not, of course, obliged to preach any 'truths' or support any cause in my writing, but rather to give shape, with artistic tools, to what seem to me real situations and real problems." Elisha Porat (with perhaps just an ironic hint of the ambivalence recorded in Franz Kafka's famous 8 January 1914 diary entry: "What have I in common with Jews? I have hardly anything in common with myself"): "I make an absolute distinction between a social, personal obligation, and literary obligation. I have no literary obligation to anyone including the kibbutz—hardly even to myself!" A pressure of a more pragmatic nature seems evident in writer Amnon Shamosh's response. Claiming that he felt responsibility to ensure that his "product" be considered as lucrative as any other kibbutz branch of work, Shamosh cited the "obligation to see that my work brings in maximum income, as I would do if I had to support a family outside the kibbutz, or as I did when I managed an agricultural branch in the kibbutz" (Rosenfeld 164–65).

20. It bears noting that the lofty theme of self-sacrifice was already an important presence on the 1930s Hebrew stage. The era of defense, wartime heroism, and pioneering shaped the emerging

Hebrew dramaturgy in ways that left little room for nuance, skepticism, or the presence of more than one narrative of "justice." An important exemplar of this largely self-righteous tradition (and the first play staged in the newborn state), *Be'arvaot Hanegev* (*On the Plains of the Negev*; 1949) by Yigal Mossensohn (1917–1994), was performed immediately after the War of Independence and enjoyed an impressive run of thirteen years, viewed by nearly a quarter of a million audience members. As Dan Urian describes it, Mossensohn's drama portrayed "the story of the founding of a kibbutz in the face of Arab attacks during the War of Independence, and the death of a kibbutz son while carrying out his mission to evacuate the wounded. The dramatis personae include figures from the second generation, native-born, and fighters. In *On the Plains of the Negev*, the love for the motherland encounters two generations: the father, Abraham, objects to evacuating the besieged kibbutz, declaring: 'I want to look into the eyes of my Danny as a fighting man and not as a miserable refugee who fled from his land. . . . This is the only land that does not turn us into refugees and beggars.' The kibbutz is saved, but Danny, the *sabra* son, is killed in battle. The audience that watched the play at Habima Theatre in Tel Aviv shared with the actors the same spirit of sacrifice and patriotism" (283).

21. Representative of those exulting in Yizhar's literary legacy is Gabriel Piterberg: "Yizhar . . . remains the greatest Hebrew author among those born in Palestine/Israel whose first language was Hebrew, as distinct from those who had emigrated from Europe like Bialik, Brenner and Agnon. Yizhar's aloofness and lack of marketing acumen or motivation have resulted in his relative anonymity in the past few decades, nationally and internationally. This anonymity, however, must not be allowed to hide the vast superiority of his literary gift. . . . Yizhar's expansive landscape descriptions as well as stream of consciousness have impelled modern Hebrew prose to unsurpassed peaks" (205–6).

22. After praising Yizhar's "Ephraim" as "psychologically complex" and "beautifully written," with clear mastery of "interior monologue and stream of consciousness" techniques, David Aberbach criticizes the work for its "overly romantic" tendencies and for its "immature . . . portrayal of relations between men and women." Aberbach notes the unlikely mismatch between that romanticism and the demands of the kibbutz's agrarian socialism and its putative promise of gender egalitarianism, citing Ephraim's (and apparently also young Yizhar's) "idealized, semi-mystical view of goddess-like women [as] incongruous in the rough and tumble—not to mention the socialist ethos—of kibbutz life." As my discussion of other narratives of the period suggests, the latter tendency is often evident in the Yishuv writer's bucolic renderings of both landscape and gender relations.

23. Though less poignantly biographical than Avishai Margalit's exegesis, Aberbach's speculation over what lies behind this seemingly trifling debate in "Ephraim" seems equally well founded: "There may be symbolism here: alfalfa is used for animals while oranges feed humans, and Ephraim's public grievance is that he is merely a beast of burden, an instrument of the collective will."

24. Many years later, in his belated return to writing kibbutz fiction, Amos Oz has a character named "Nina" suggest much the same in "Deir Agloun" in the collection *Be'in haverim* (*Between Friends*; 2013).

25. I am profoundly grateful to David Leach for sharing many of his critical insights regarding Koestler's early Palestine years. Michael Scammell's gripping biography, *Koestler: The Literary and Political Odyssey of a Twentieth-Century Skeptic*, also served as an invaluable introduction to the writer's conflicted and vacillating responses to Zionism. Many twentieth-century intellectual giants underwent tremendous paradigm shifts in their lifetime, but few embodied the monumental pendulum swings of the restless Koestler (from ardent Zionist to anti-Zionist, Communist to anti-Communist, existentialist to antiexistentialist, fierce advocate of empirical science to enthusiastic advocate of parapsychology—to mention a few), and Scammell does full justice to that complexity.

26. Later, to research *Thieves*, Koestler spent time at Kibbutz Ein Hashofet, where, according to biographer Scammell, "the high point of his stay was an expedition to the summit of an arid

hill some miles away to plant a new settlement" (254), and this clandestine mission inspired the novel's title.

27. LEHI is the Hebrew acronym for Lohamei Herut Israel (Fighters for the Freedom of Israel), otherwise known as the "Stern Gang" (named after its founder, Avraham Stern). LEHI, labeled a terrorist organization by the British, was responsible for the assassination of Lord Moyne as well as attacks on the British authorities and Palestinian Arabs. The Irgun (National Military Organization in the Land of Israel) was a militant offshoot of the Jewish Zionist paramilitary organization Haganah. The Irgun's attacks on native Arabs and the British resulted in formal condemnation by the World Zionist Congress in 1946. Ideologue and founder of Revisionist Zionism, Ze'ev Jabotinsky (1880–1940; born in Odessa) called for military struggle until Hebrew independence over the entire land of Israel was achieved. He was "Supreme Commander" of the Irgun until his death in 1940. In later years, Koestler turned decidedly against the Irgun and reviled "any form of terrorism" (Scammel 333).

28. In a Shabbat sermon dated 31 January 1947, Harold Saperstein, a rabbi of the Reform Movement, insisting that "I don't believe in terrorism," acknowledged his mixed emotions as a reader of *Thieves* when confronted with Koestler's portrayal of the intransigent British and the Jews languishing in DP camps: "How would you feel if you were a Jew in Palestine, who had left all his family behind, hoping some day to bring them to join you. . . . Then the war comes, and a black curtain cuts you off from all contact. When it is lifted, you learn that almost all of them . . . 'went up in smoke,' met their death in the gas chambers . . . only one survived . . . who at least was still alive and looking forward to being reunited with you. You can't wait. But . . . the months go by and stretch into years . . . and your brother or sister is still in a DP camp. Let us understand that this kind of experience is what makes the psychology of the terrorist. My friends, let the British quit their moral posturing and their political hypocrisy and their condemnations of terrorism" (*Thieves* 139–40).

29. Leon Uris's 1958 novel *Exodus* repeated the same plot device of the young Jewish woman victimized first by Nazis and later murdered by Arab fedayeen.

30. Not until the 1970s did serious fissures begin to appear in the self-righteous portrayals of kibbutz settlement. Most notable was Joshua Sobol's famous drama *Leil ha'esrim* (*The Night of the Twentieth*; 1977), which so forcefully responded to the post–Yom Kippur War zeitgeist. First performed at the Haifa Municipal Theater, the play presented the settlement of a prototypical kibbutz in the Galilee during the 1920s. Its feverishly idealistic members engage in fierce debates over the displacement of native Arabs and the values the Jewish settlers carry with them. Some leave, others commit suicide, and the drama raises sharp, previously muted questions about the myths surrounding the achievements of the kibbutz pioneers that had nurtured previous generations. In retrospect, Sobol traces the origin and inspiration for his play to the pervasive unease and disillusionment of the post-1973 era: "After the war, I investigated the roots upon which Israel is founded, as well as the cultural and spiritual world of the Yishuv [pre-state Jewish community in Palestine], in order to understand how we'd reached the point we were at. The search for these roots led me to the nightly discussions at Bitaniya. That led me to write *The Night of the Twentieth*. The question raised there was how to deal with the Arab population and what sort of relations to establish with them. I demonstrate how that question, posed at the outset of the [modern settlement] enterprise, was later cast aside and repressed" (Rotem).

31. From Wisse's perspective, the "most serious internal flaw" of *Thieves* "is that its advancement of Zionism comes at the expense of the Jews it was intended to help," and thus she concludes that Koestler, like his protagonist, Joseph, seems to lack "any corresponding affection for his fellow Jews" (255).

32. Scammell emphasizes that Koestler was "a lightning rod for controversy," especially for his unapologetic pro-Irgun views, throughout his time as a foreign correspondent in Palestine. He became infamous for boisterous arguments with other journalists in which he defended every

Jewish act of terror short of the massacre at Deir Yassin and the hanging of two British sergeants: "In an extension of the message of *Thieves in the Night*, Koestler argued that 'ruthlessness was essential for human progress' and that the end could justify the means at decisive moments in history. He compared the Irgun to the IRA during the Easter Rising and saw it as a catalyst for human progress" (Scammell 328).

33. A number of intellectuals, many of them supporters of Koestler's earlier work (including George Orwell himself), were alarmed by the ease with which the "logic of the Ice Age" might be used to justify any totalitarian movement. When the British sculptor Daphne Hardy (a close confidante) accused him of betraying his principles, Koestler was unapologetic: "On the whole I think that acts of sabotage with due preliminary warning, passive and active resistance against the prevention of immigration, and even retaliation for floggings may be historically justified," though he also felt that "indiscriminate assassinations cannot be justified either on ethical or utilitarian grounds" (qtd. in Scammell 283).

34. Maletz's biographer, Moti Zeira, asserts that *Ma'agalot*, which received an unprecedented number of reviews, was circulated from individual to individual in Israel, eventually reaching soldiers serving in the Jewish Brigade in Europe. A kibbutz member of Ein Harod stationed abroad wrote Maletz of the tremendous demand for his book among his "few dozen comrades," who "formed a queue . . . immediately, and in fact it is being read by three people at once, for we each have time to read at different times of the day" (qtd. in Keshet, "Kibbutz Fiction" 148).

35. Similarly, scholar and kibbutz novelist Assaf Inbari asserts that "the pattern of the realist novel was realized by most kibbutz writers as an erotic intrigue set on the kibbutz." In spite of that titillation, Inbari regards Maletz himself as a serious student of Tolstoy and Dostoyevsky, "a perceptive writer, educator and essayist, who . . . wrote his novels in order to express his spiritual, moral, and ideological misgivings, not to entertain his readers" ("Kibbutz Novel" 137).

36. "Se'arat vikuhim ba-kibbutzim beshel sifro shel Maletz," *Ha-Boker* 11 February 1945. In her study, Keshet considers a striking range of documentary materials (kibbutz movement journals and newsletters, daily newspapers, public records of assemblies held at workers' councils in rural and urban communities, and dozens of readers' letters) bearing witness to the stormy public debate that raged in the kibbutzim and the surrounding Yishuv society. What this raging controversy revealed, Keshet concludes, is the pioneers' deep unease at being challenged in the most cherished tenets of their orthodox ideology: "The kibbutz members who stubbornly adhered to the dream, and whose Spartan new life demanded so much sacrifice and hard work, could not accept with equilibrium a book that questioned the worthiness of their endeavor. Criticism threatened to open cracks and bring down the entire structure. Maletz's book was the first that dared to pose questions" ("Kibbutz Fiction" 153). Drawing on reception theory, Keshet cogently argues that Maletz's fellow kibbutz readers were the "product of sociocultural norms" and thus largely "controlled by a dominant normative system" they had internalized: "An independent stance will be very rare in a society with a total ideology like kibbutz society during the period in question, which demanded absolute loyalty to the group's norms in every sphere of life" (153). Yet Maletz himself clearly dared to question those norms.

37. The intensity of attacks on *Ma'agalot* (*Young Hearts*) seemed to vary depending on the nature of the venue. According to Keshet, "the most vehement attacks on the book appeared in the daily press and the kibbutz movement journals, i.e., in public platforms. The more public the platform, the more heated the attack, and vice versa—when the response was expressed in a more closed circle, in kibbutz bulletins and personal correspondence, the criticism was more moderate and the level of identification . . . rose accordingly. The most virulent attacks appeared in the daily press that also served as a platform for party-political attacks; in the kibbutz movement journals there was almost a balance between those who supported and opposed the criticism; while in the kibbutz newsletters, which were the intimate mode of expression of a single kibbutz, not intended for dissemination beyond internal discussion, there was greater willingness to acknowledge the

value of the social criticism expressed in the novel. The highest level of identification with the author and the human distress he dared to express in his book can be found in personal correspondence. In these letters some of the writers share with Maletz their own experiences in coping with life in the 'kibbutz machine,' and even tell him of similar events in their own life. It seems that the more intimate the platform, the more the oppositionist, subterranean voice is heard, seeking to free itself from the shackles of the demand for conformity" ("Kibbutz Fiction" 157–58). The reception history that Keshet illuminates offers early portents of the bolder literary dissent—and some readers' empathic receptivity and even demand for such questioning—that has come to distinguish the kibbutz narrative and the Israeli literary canon itself.

38. Maletz's novel *Ma'agalot*, published in Tel Aviv in 1944, was awarded the Brenner Prize by the Palestinian Authors' Association. Maletz had immigrated to Palestine from Poland in 1920 and joined the settlement of Ein Harod two years later. He was also the author of critically acclaimed short stories.

39. At a writer's conference held in 1987, John Auerbach (1922–2002), a short-story writer from Kibbutz Sdot Yam (who has drawn praise for his portraits of the pain of lonely individuals), declared simply that "when I deal with kibbutz life I usually write about the 'outsider' or 'nonconformist.'" At the same event, Elisha Porat delved even deeper into the literary allure of outsider sensibilities, or what he called "types from the fringes, characters pursued by an unhappy fate; each of them will have an unfortunate story. In effect, they will be tragedies, and not simply tragedies, but life stories in which are concentrated many elements which are actually found in every life, but don't reach such tragic proportions. Most of their lives will end in an unnatural manner . . . whether by suicide, in disasters, or in terrorist attacks, they will come to unnatural, violent, ends. They lead their lives at the periphery of the kibbutz; they are pushed to the fringes either because that is how they want it, or because the kibbutz doesn't really understand what it is that they want. They see nothing bad about the fringes. They are happy to be there—in fact if not at the periphery they couldn't exist in the kibbutz at all. And their existence and movement at the periphery is a most illuminating reflection of the center of the kibbutz as a whole" (Rosenfeld 171, 172).

40. In the author's note to his novel *Menuhah nehonah* (*A Perfect Peace*; 1982), perhaps in acknowledgment of Maletz's death the previous year, Oz described his indebtedness to the earlier writer: "In 1959 a novel, *The Locked Gate*, was published by David Maletz against the backdrop of kibbutz life; several threads connect my own book with Maletz's; such things have been known to happen" (*Menuhah nehonah* 382; translation mine). In his account of this acknowledgment, Assaf Inbari argues that "Oz lets us know that he is not a mere epigone of Maletz . . . but, rather a writer who consciously, out of thoughtful, artistic choice, continues to follow the proven formula of the kibbutz novel" ("Kibbutz Novel" 139).

41. Compare this passage with another on the marginalization of the aging in Oz's 1963 short story "Artzot hatan" ("Where the Jackals Howl"): "The old people of the kibbutz are still at rest in their deck chairs. They are like lifeless objects, allowing the darkness to cover them and offering no resistance" (*Jackals* 5). Oz's empathy for the poignant condition, sad inconsequentiality, and incomprehension of this "Desert Generation" is even further apparent in his first novel, *Makom aher* (*Elsewhere, Perhaps*;1966): "Many years ago, in [the Ukrainian town of] Kovel, when the future founders of our kibbutz were carried away by their enthusiasm for the Zionist youth movement, their parents tried to stop them, some with anger. . . . But in time the tables were turned, and they were forced to seek refuge here with their obstinate progeny. In consequence, they behave toward their sons and daughters, and even toward their grandchildren, with extreme politeness and even respect. They do not proffer advice, as old people elsewhere do. They submit uncomplainingly to all the regulations of the kibbutz. A silenced terror seems to govern all their dealings with the kibbutz institutions. . . . In the presence of the kibbutz secretary or treasurer or sanitary officer they behave as if he represented a tyrannical Gentile authority. Every evening they shuffle weakly to their children's rooms to have coffee with the family and to look—but only look—at

their grandchildren. They would never dare play with the little children or tell them stories for fear of breaking the unfathomable educational rules. . . . Their old age is apparently protected against every want and humiliation. But they are isolated in their own quarters. They try to avoid being in the way. An air of sadness envelops them" (*Elsewhere, Perhaps* 184).

42. A generation later, some of the kibbutz writers participating in a 1986 literary symposium (nearly all in their fifties) indirectly echoed Maletz's concerns over the "emotional shallowness" and "narrowness of spiritual and cultural horizons" that they felt was pervasive in their communities. Moderator Israel Ring provocatively questioned whether the cause was due to "a constant togetherness in a standardized society"; moments later, the writer Eli Alon (Kibbutz Ein Shemer) speculated uneasily: "Have we not built here, with the purest of intentions, and quite unwittingly, an almost non-human 'togetherness machine'? Almost a Kafka-like punishment machine?" (Ring 152, 154). Undoubtedly, Alon had in mind Franz Kafka's nightmarish indictment of authoritarian culture in his short story "In the Penal Colony" (1914). Invoking yet another famous Jewish writer of the Diaspora, kibbutz-born poet Elisha Porat (Kibbutz Ein Hahoresh) criticized the daunting factors inhibiting the expression of creativity among the younger generation: "If a parent . . . came to the kibbutz to live a collective and egalitarian life . . . he sends out a simple *petit bourgeois* message to his beloved offspring. . . . 'Cut out all this artistic trash. First and foremost, learn some useful trade, and then you can run wild!' To rebel one needs to be really very strong. . . . We are, in fact, returning to Shalom Aleichem's dilemma: Why be an artist? Why be a madman? Why live like a disturbed character, unproductive and unprofitable? You'll be left behind your friends from the start" (Ring 155–56). In this discussion, Porat later provided an exemplar of the stultifying conformity weighing on the kibbutz writer recalling the words of the late Mira Mintzer, a kibbutz writer of his acquaintance: "She said, 'When I finally get a day for writing, when I go down to my shelter to do some writing, I see 300 pairs of eyes piercing the concrete however thick it may be'" (Ring 156). Similarly, the renowned musician Meir Ariel, who once served as secretary of Kibbutz Mishmarot, left it for Tel Aviv during the 1980s, in part because of his sense of its spiritual vacancy. As Yossi Klein Halevi recounts it, "Meir's disappointment with kibbutz life was also spiritual. The kibbutz had been an experiment in human transcendence, yet it remained, in its way, material, concerned primarily with organizing the physical needs of its members. The kibbutz, Meir believed, had failed to recognize its own spiritual essence" (Halevi 432–33).

43. Milner addresses the salient example of Maletz's staid conformist vision: "The couple Menachem and Hannah . . . despite the continuous humiliation they suffer and the various pressures inflicted upon them, and [despite] their acknowledgement of the malfunctioning of the commune in terms of . . . support of the individual, and its rigid adherence to irrational rules . . . develop a strong sense of belonging to the kibbutz and experience it as their extended family" (167). Derek Penslar finds that, though *Young Hearts* reveres the kibbutz's "creation of a flourishing physical space, economy, and community," Maletz's novel "also [raises] concern over its concentration on productive labor at the expense of individual creativity and spirituality, and its capacity to be more stifling than empowering" (6).

44. Similarly, Keshet sees Maletz struggling against the suppression of spirituality, noting that, in 1929, Maletz had warned that the "material" would come to dominate life in Israel "like the golem lurking for its creator" (qtd. in "Freedom" 203).

45. The term "kvutzah" used throughout *Young Hearts* is Hebrew for "group" and was the original name for any of the new forms of communal life in the Yishuv; it was later replaced by "kibbutz" (derived from the Hebrew word for "to gather"), as membership of the intimate family-like groups rapidly grew. Maletz consistently uses the earlier expression in this novel.

46. A little later, Menahem wistfully echoes Klein's concern (though without voicing "it aloud" which is typical of his passivity throughout): "The trouble was that the collective didn't permit people a quiet development. True life required time and quietude, but here everyone was in a hurry and there was no room for contemplation" (*Young Hearts* 161).

47. That struggle is fully evident in Maletz's description of Klein's appeal to his skeptical or otherwise indifferent comrades—one of them seems to speak for all in his supercilious dismissal: "You . . . are a philosopher. You have deep thoughts. But . . . we cannot live by philosophy. Let me tell you something—what we need is compote. Yes, compote and not philosophy" (*Young Hearts* 147). And another character rejects the exemplar of the pious Arab in Orientalist terms, the casual racism that Maletz must have heard expressed in his own community: "You envy the Arab whom you saw praying to Allah, though you know as well as anyone that his life is a mass of superstition, fanaticism and savage instincts. Yet you hold up his life as meaningful" (152).

48. Keshet points to important instances where Maletz's editor, Berl Katznelson, insisted on softening or omitting much of *Ma'agalot's* erotically explicit language (quite tame by today's standards), some of which appears to have been restored in the English translation. See Keshet, "Kibbutz Fiction" 158–61.

49. Grumberg argues that essentially little has changed for women in Israeli society: "This feature of early twentieth-century Zionism has weathered the historical storms of war, independence and statehood, and it continues to inform Israeli discourse and praxis to this day. . . . Motherhood is one of the most powerful forces in Israeli women's lives, in no small part because it is a legacy of Zionist conceptions of women's roles. In light of the link between mothering and nationalism, which relegates women to the most private recesses of the public sphere, the fact that men dominate a public culture as militarized as Israel's is no surprise" ("Female Grotesque" 146).

50. *Young Hearts* is ridden with skepticism over the successful metamorphosis of the enervated shtetl Jew of either gender. In a later moment in the novel, Hannah expresses disgust over the recidivist bourgeois tendencies of her female comrades: "Our women . . . would drive anyone wild. I would never have believed that it could be like this among us. They'll make the biggest fuss over some paltry rag. They're the same 'Yentes' as their grandmothers. Everlasting jealousy and envy and argument and gossip" (*Young Hearts* 195).

51. Hever's deconstructive elaboration on the internal contradictions of the kvutzah Jew's identity is instructive: "The 'New Jew' is an invention whose essence is the denial of exile (*shlilat-ha-gola*) and the return to origins: skipping over the time, space, nature, and conditions of exile creates an illusion of eternity that begins at the 'real' place of origin, at the early 'beginning' in Eretz Yisrael. Eternality continues while skipping over an interruption, a disruption in the resolute grip of the origin as a constant presence in space; this disruption is the 'sojourn' in exile, there and not here; and then, after this leap, eternality recurs and continues to reinvent the origin. But the very fact of its reconstitution is decisive proof of this origin's fragility, its temporariness, the possibility of its disappearance. Therefore, in fact, the proof disproves the origin's eternal existence at the very moment when it tries to ratify it" (8).

52. Such disparagement of youths wearing glasses was startlingly pervasive in Israel for decades after independence. In a recent conversation with me, novelist Meir Shalev (b. 1948 in Nahalal, the first moshav) recalled that, when a teacher told his parents he needed glasses, they both visibly recoiled, seeing it as a terrible shame or stigma—as if Zionism had utterly failed. Shalev's mother simply turned the teacher away and said he was wrong about Shalev's eyesight (pers. comm., 10 April 2013).

53. See Joshua 9:27: "And Joshua made [the Gibeonites] that day hewers of wood and drawers of water for the congregation, and for the altar of the Lord" (KJV). In invoking the alien tribe of the conquered Gibeonites, who were made to work as menial drudges, Srulik underscores Menahem's outsider status.

54. Four decades later, at the literary symposium moderated by Ring in 1986, writer Miriam Dror complained that the kibbutz was a wasteland when it came to the spontaneous experience and expression so essential for cultivating individuality: "Go and see what happens in educational groups and also in adult kibbutz society and you'll find almost a total lack of spontaneity. Everyone knows his exact place in the system and will usually not dare to deviate from it. . . . And

without spontaneity—without taking an individual stance, with everyone leaning on the togetherness and relying on its support—there is no creative personality" (Ring 159).

55. That Menahem has successfully metamorphosed into a virile pioneer deserving of the settlement's most sought-after woman is underscored by an unintentionally comic section of overheated prose depicting a chaste episode in which the pitchforks of clover wielded by Hannah and Menahem tangle together: "'Oh, excuse me,' he said and a hot current ran through his limbs. He felt as if he were coming in contact with Hannah's flushed, beloved body" (*Young Hearts* 57–58). Soon after that quaintly purple passage, we are told that Hannah is pregnant.

56. In his public remarks on the tenth anniversary of the Labor Zionist ideologue's death, Maletz exulted that "Gordon was one of the great individuals and intellectuals in the generations that were privileged to come face to face with their god" (Weitz).

57. Many later writers were inspired by Maletz's descriptive attention to the contours of utopia. Thus, in the beckoning opening to his novel *Makom aher* (*Elsewhere, Perhaps*; 1966), Amos Oz describes the (imaginary) Kibbutz Metsudat Ram as follows: "Its buildings are laid out in strict symmetry at one end of the green valley. The tangled foliage of the trees does not break up the settlement's severe lines, but merely softens them, and adds a dimension to weightiness. The buildings are whitewashed, and most of them are topped with bright red roofs" (*Elsewhere, Perhaps* 3). Just beyond this civilized space, however, the kibbutz members are constantly aware of "the border between our land and that of her enemies" (3).

58. As Maletz portrays the growing tensions between Jews and Arabs over the Jews' acquisition of more land for settlement (which he both witnessed and participated in), it is impossible to avoid how ironically his description of that uneasy beginning anticipates the way, seven decades later, the fortress state of Israel seems to require an external Other to ensure any semblance of internal solidarity. "Even as the kvutzah wrestled with its crisis, troubling rumors began to come in from different parts of the country. In outlying districts Jews were being attacked on the roads. At first only individuals were molested. Then little towns were attacked. In Hebron and Safed pogroms broke out. The rioting spread all over the country. The unrest penetrated even to their own valley where the Jewish population was large. At night the hills of Gilboa lay black and threatening. Strange lights would appear upon the hills, would move about and vanish. Stray shots were heard. The villages tensely awaited attack. All dissension was put aside. They gathered their forces to meet the shock. . . . Menahem's village . . . saw its way through its crisis. All of a sudden everyone knew what had to be done. An emergency council was set up. Under peril the entire community braced itself for defense. The settlement experienced a tremendous surge of unity. The different departments functioned like magic. Gloom disappeared. Instead there was the warmest sort of cooperation" (*Young Hearts* 188). This quietly observed episode is a "distant mirror" (to borrow historian Barbara Tuchman's memorable phrase), reflecting with prescient force the situation in Israel today.

59. The decisive turning point for Menahem seems to follow his encounter with an older man, an immigrant from Germany, who says of the young pioneers, "You are children still . . . that is why you completely overlook the blessings of this way of life . . . you have built a paradise without knowing it. Back in Germany I was in the lumber business for many years. . . . You might say I was my own master and did as I pleased. But I tell you that I was a slave. We were all slaves there—slaves to money, and money is the cruelest of tyrants. Where it rules, man is capable of killing his brother for a penny. Money is a madness that enslaves man. If you have a hundred marks you want to have two hundred. You chase after money as if the devil were at your heels, and you chase after others on account of money. There is never a minute's rest. But you here have done away with money; you've driven the evil from your midst and have recaptured peace of heart. I rather think that a man has to experience all the evil in life before he can truly appreciate . . . the good that is in collective living" (*Young Hearts* 221–22). Whatever doubts have been uttered along the way, for Maletz's readers, as for Menahem, the anticapitalist ideologue has the final, definitive say about the inestimable worth of their achievement in a mammon-obsessed world.

60. Even during the early days of their first child, Menahem found the children's house "forbidding and depressing. . . . The atmosphere of such a place, Menahem felt, ought to be warm and friendly; he could not help finding it otherwise" (*Young Hearts* 65). Later, as his own sons are raised in the children's house, he has deep misgivings about the dysfunctional ways they seem to mirror the failure of adults to achieve egalitarianism in the kibbutz, wherein "the dominant personalities accomplished little beside humiliating their less aggressive comrades" (158). He finds the children's house to be "a microcosm of the larger world of the kvutzah" (158), noticing "a cruel streak of destructiveness running through the presumably innocent lives. . . . Among the children, too, there was no equality. Some were aggressive and others found themselves pushed aside" (159). Menahem is deeply dismayed to discover that his own son Yaakov is one of the "chief aggressors" in a large crowd who victimize the quiet and sensitive types who "were like frail little plants," who remain on alert to "the possibility of outside attack" (159). Here we find an early explicit instance of cruelty in a narrative about the kibbutz, anticipating the harrowing portraits of sadism that would appear in more recent narratives such as Dror Shaul's film *Adama meshuga'at* (*Sweet Mud*; 2006) and Savyon Liebrecht's bleak tale "Kibbutz" (2005), in which ideology fails to redeem human nature.

61. At one point, Maletz felt compelled to defend his protagonist against his detractors, who found Menahem an "illegitimate" representation of the heroic pioneering enterprise. In a letter to the labor newspaper *Davar*, Maletz wrote that Menahem "possesses some very worthy psychological traits. From his childhood he brought a longing for equilibrium, for putting down roots. He knows how to listen to the flow of water, the growth of plants. These are things that we also prayed for when we went to Eretz Yisrael, to the village, to create a Hebrew field. And we aspired to something else too—less urgency, less haste. More roots, growth, and these are to be found in [Menahem]. He possesses spiritual wealth—perhaps as compensation for his incompetence in organization and society. He also knows how to love, a great, loyal love. And that too is a God-given gift" (qtd. in Keshet, "Kibbutz Fiction" 157).

CHAPTER 2

The epigraph to this chapter is drawn from Balaban, *Mourning* 36; the Shaham and Balaban epigraphs to its sections are drawn from Rosenfeld 167 and Lori.

1. Many years later, when asked about the contrast between Kibbutz Hulda and Arad, Oz implied that he had merely exchanged one intimate community for another: "I like small places. [Arad's] a quiet place but it's also very cosmopolitan. There are Jews from 36 different countries of origin and many Arabs as well. I enjoy sitting down in a street café. Strangers recognize me because I'm on television sometimes and they immediately gather around my table and start a political argument with me. I enjoy that tremendously. They try to save my soul for me and I try to save their souls for them. And when I want to be on my own I have the privacy of my study" (Round). In 2013, having reached his seventy-fourth year, Oz moved to a quiet neighborhood in north Tel Aviv.

2. It is worth noting that, some years later, Hulda granted Oz the opportunity to divide his time between writing and teaching in a kibbutz high school; over the years, he has alluded to other stints on the kibbutz, serving as night guard and even as waiter in the dining hall.

3. I am grateful to Nitzan Meltzer for reminding me of this revealing and evocative passage in Oz's memoir.

4. On the other hand, according to the kibbutz-born writer Miriam Dror (who seems to speak for many), such an outsider status was actually enviable. Collectively addressing the "joiners" (writers such as Oz), she vigorously asserts that "we don't stand on the same ground! What we term the initial crystallization of the personality and place in the world, so vital to the creative

personality however you may have passed through it—in poverty, distress, hunger, in a forest, on all sorts of paths—you passed through as *individuals*. We passed through it as a *group*" (Ring 160; emphases in original).

5. In the same interview with *New York Times* reporter Herbert Mitgang, Oz described how it was the American writer Sherwood Anderson who had first alerted him to the value of looking very closely at what, and who, was very near: "I had a Hungarian teacher at Kibbutz Hulda who never set foot in America but who told me to read [Anderson's] *Winesburg, Ohio* after it was translated into Hebrew. She knew I was a secret poet and wanted me to write prose. I had thought the real world was outside—in Jerusalem or New York or Paris. *Winesburg* showed me that the real world is everywhere, even in a small kibbutz. I discovered that all the secrets are the same—love, hatred, fear, loneliness—all the great and simple things of life and literature."

6. The Seneds were recipients of important national literary awards, including the Prime Minister's Prize, the Brenner Prize, and the Agnon Prize. During Israel's War of Independence, the couple arrived in Israel as illegal immigrants to join Kibbutz Revivim in the Negev. Alexander Sened eventually served as chief editor of Hakibbutz Hameuchad Publishing House.

7. As Adam Kirsch remarks in his thoughtful assessment of what motivated the young Oz to write his earliest stories, "It is surely impossible to take upon yourself the burden of the name 'strength,' as Oz did, without paying some kind of psychic price. What does it mean to be born into a country, and into an ideological movement, where strength is the ultimate virtue? How do the children of Zionism live up to its necessary demands and its nearly superhuman legacy?"

8. Also in "Thoughts on the Kibbutz," Oz affectionately invokes Martin Buber's famous phrase "exemplary non-failure" to note the ironic, even farcical outcome that "revealed . . . the unreformable deformities of the human condition. . . . Only when the hills of 'social ill' had been scaled" did "the towering peaks of cosmic, metaphysical ill" emerge from their dormancy. Yet, in the end, Oz affirms that the kibbutz endures as "the least bad place I have ever seen. And the most daring effort" (*Under This Blazing Light* 124).

9. In his richly comparative analysis of Oz's "Nomad and Viper," Yair Mazor finds an additional source of biblical intertextuality: the kibbutznik and Bedouin communities embody the hostile rivalry between Cain and Abel. As farmers, the kibbutzniks are associated with Cain ("the archetypal tiller of the soil"), whereas the wandering Bedouin are linked to Abel ("the shepherd"). This association produces fascinating ironies and moral reversals: "The formal system of norms embedded in the story emphasizes the moral and social superiority of kibbutz society over nomadic society, the supremacy of agriculturalists, permanent settlers over shepherds who drive their flocks through the fields and orchards of the kibbutz, destroying crops and property. . . . The formal system of norms is based on a clear-cut distinction between 'good guys' and 'bad guys.' The tillers of the soil are the 'good guys,' whereas the nomadic shepherds are the 'bad guys.'" Mazor points out the biblical reversal: "Cain the farmer, the permanent settler, becomes a nomad, like the shepherd, while Abel, the nomadic shepherd, becomes a 'permanent resident' of the same soil whence his blood cried unto the Lord." So just how does Oz complicate the bible's ironic reversals even further? Mazor notes that the victims in "Nomad and Viper" are, initially, the settled kibbutzniks whose property is repeatedly violated by the marauding nomads. But, ultimately, "when the tillers of the soil in the story carry out their vengeful raid, they lose their moral superiority over the nomads and, in fact, adopt the behavioral model that until now had made them victims . . . they cease to be the victims, or at least they suspend their victim status by assuming the reprehensible aggression of Cain" (10–11). In Mazor's illuminating and utterly cogent reading, there is plenty of room to accommodate both Genesis texts as legitimate wellsprings of Oz's intertextual play with irreconcilable difference, belonging, and justice.

10. In this regard, Oz slyly engages, and ultimately overturns, the authoritative narrative voice that had traditionally dominated previous kibbutz narratives for decades. As ably described by Milner, that voice guides us through the sacred sites of kibbutz life and "is typically auctorial (an

all-knowing narrating voice, not identified with any of the literary characters) and seldom conceals its freedom to witness private affairs and to enter the inner lives of all participants alike: it follows the different figures along the narrow footpaths between the various public sites and their family or bachelor tents or rooms, peeps through windows, walks into the nursery and the communal showers, stops by the tables at the collective dining room and listens to conversations, goes out to the working places and catches details of tensions and disputes, and follows the kibbutz members' inner thoughts and reveals their most hidden secrets." Milner sees in both the blurring of private and public realms and the role of the auctorial voice "a panoptic strategy of regulation and control, where every place and every move is constantly under surveillance, with no available hiding place from the watchful collective eye" (163–64, 166–67).

11. From his earliest memories, Oz seems to have been torn between the austere pioneering ethos of his father's Zionism, which was secular, rational, and optimistic to the core, and the Diasporic influence of his mother's dark tales of European forests, demons, and Jewish mysticism and her own mysterious inwardness. Although, in novels such as *My Michael* and *A Perfect Peace*, Oz had long aspired to reconcile these oppositions, in the memoir *A Tale of Love and Darkness*, he is painfully honest in exposing the insurmountable abyss that ultimately divided his parents. Although it is clear that Oz has very deep reservoirs of sympathy for both parents, it is also clear that his father's insufferably cheery but ultimately impatient pragmatism left little room for his mother's deeper emotional depths. The wrenching breakdown in relations between his parents and eventually the tragedy of his mother's suicide when Oz was only twelve eventually led to his departure for Kibbutz Hulda, where he would remain for four decades.

12. Despite Oz's brief allusion to the resemblance of "The Way of the Wind" to the unfolding of Greek tragedy, Kirsch recognizes the story's rich biblical intertextuality in Oz's ironic retelling of "the biblical tale of Jephthah, from the Book of Judges. Jephthah is the warrior-judge who goes off to battle promising God that, in exchange for victory, he will offer as a sacrifice the first thing he sees on his return home. This turns out to be not an animal as he expected, but his own daughter, whom he duly kills."

13. The most compelling issue that drives Yael Feldman's inquiry is just how an ancient parable against human sacrifice came to mean something quite different: "How has Isaac, the *passive* survivor of a *near*-sacrifice, come to stand for the necessity for active military self-sacrifice, for a warrior's *glorious death* in battle?" and "how could Israelis have turned around a biblical scene traditionally read as a trope of obedience . . . into a trope of violence, synonymous with the oedipal conflict?" (*Glory and Agony* xiii, 7; emphases in original). Elsewhere, considering "the psychological inferiority complex" of the sons of the founding fathers, Feldman draws a comparison with that experienced by Holocaust survivors in the same generation. She quotes Eli Alon, a young poet and native of Kibbutz Ein Shemer, whose anxious reflections in a 1969 collection of kibbutz conversations (*Communal Talks in the Kibbutz Movement*) include the following observation: "The thesis of the founding fathers was so powerful, that I doubt if we, the shadowed plants of their spirit, will ever be able to state our truth with the same force of conviction. . . . One of the noticeable characteristics of the kibbutz second generation is their very late spiritual maturation" (qtd. in *Glory and Agony* 220). Feldman's important book also addresses the salient role of the kibbutz journal *Shdemot* (in its successive incarnations *Kibbutz Currents* and *Kibbutz Trends*), founded by Avraham Shapira (Kibbutz Yizrael), which began publication in 1960 and thrived for three decades as an arena for the second generation to set forth their spiritual, emotional, and social concerns. Feldman calls this venue an "open mike" of sorts, asserting that it sought "to foster, amid the left-wing socialist climate of the kibbutzim, a counter pro–'Jewish culture' movement" and that its early period was distinguished by contributions "articulating various modes of painful and bewildered wrestling with personal trauma, mourning, and melancholia" (223, 225).

14. As Yossi Klein Halevi observes, for the kibbutz founders, May Day was "sacred" and effectively "transformed them from a footnote to a harbinger: they weren't merely a private experiment

in altruism in a tiny country in the Middle East fighting for survival but a model that would no doubt be adopted one day, in one form or another, throughout the world" (16).

15. Many years later, in the experimental free-rhyme narrative *Oto hayam* (*The Same Sea*; 1999), perhaps the most personal of all his fictional works, Oz would ruefully, yet perhaps also with a degree of affection, recall "the bad old days of his youth when he used to run away at night to be all alone in the reading-room of the kibbutz where he would cover page after page with jackals' howls" (*Same Sea* 41).

16. In a wry nod to the New Hebrew, however, the illegitimate offspring of the scandal that has so preoccupied kibbutz members in *Elsewhere, Perhaps* is an altogether indeterminate being, underweight, her facial features as yet indistinct, her eye color as yet unsettled.

17. Though alluding to the typical male protagonist of the Israeli novel of the 1960s, Nurith Gertz's formulation still serves as a revealing portrayal of the antihero's existential situation in Oz's 1982 novel *A Perfect Peace*: "alien, disconnected from himself and from the world around him, living in misery and desolation. Therefore, he cannot understand what he misses, or what is missing from the reality around him. This is an unconscious hero, who feels uncomfortable in his cultural environment and is drawn, through incomprehensible and unexplained actions, to nature, to its destructive representatives, to contact with unclear, mystical forces, to contact with a woman. . . . Nor does he find refuge in society or family. The society is fake and degenerate, and its pioneering Zionist values have turned into hollow clichés. The protagonist yearns to break out of his desolate and alienated condition" (Gertz 77–78; translation mine).

18. For a more elaborate treatment of *A Perfect Peace*, see my " 'Disgrace to the Map.' "

19. Oz clearly has Yonatan outwardly mirror the popular notion of the brash and ever-youthful Sabra, the "authentic" representative of the native-born Israeli often portrayed in the nation's literature and civil rhetoric as "wild and untamed, yet innocent and sincere" (Weiss 25–26). And, as Yael Zerubavel observes, this figure was but one part of a deterministically scripted binary opposition: "The Jew of exile was portrayed as uprooted, cowardly and manipulative, old and sickly, helpless and defenseless in face of persecution, interested in materialistic gains or conversely, excessively immersed in religion. . . . In contrast, the New Hebrew . . . was characterized as young and robust, daring and resourceful, direct and down-to-earth, honest and loyal, ideologically committed and ready to defend his people to the bitter end" (" 'Mythological Sabra' " 115). Paradoxically, though perceived as ruggedly "individualistic," the Sabra figure actually embodies Zionist collectivism, raised under cultural imperatives that link self-fulfillment to the successful pursuit of national goals often requiring violent sacrifice. Little wonder that the unsettled desert eventually tempts Oz's protagonist as a refuge from the stifling demands of socialist conformity.

20. Yair Mazor traces the bitter reference to Ben-Gurion in Yolek's nightmare to 1 Samuel 14, where Jonathan fails to hear his father Saul's order to his troops not to consume any food until victory. On hearing that his son has tasted some honey in the field, the king orders his execution, but Jonathan is saved by the active will of the people (43). Nehama Aschkenasy concurs, seeing Oz's development of Yolek as a "modern-day version of the tragic King Saul, who fell out of favor with God and failed to establish a dynasty," and of Yonatan, "lacking his father's political aspirations . . . yet still performing courageously on the battlefield" as "the modern counterpart of King Saul's heroic son Jonathan" (130).

21. In the final pages of *A Perfect Peace*, Srulik, the conscientious kibbutz member who replaces Yolek as secretary by the novel's end, wonders to himself "with what weapon can we repel this interior wilderness?" (363). This figure, a member of Yolek's founding generation, is made even more sympathetic when he writes in his journal of his own alienation from the dictums of socialism: "I have lived my life here to the music of a marching band, as if death had already been abolished . . . and the whole universe nothing but a giant arena for political and ideological quarrels" (226).

22. Before the Anglo-Jewish writer and activist Israel Zangwill wrote that "Palestine is a country without a people; the Jews are a people without a country" in 1901 (in the *New Liberal Review*), Christian proto-Zionists had already been articulating variants of the phrase for decades, most famously Anthony Ashley-Cooper, Earl of Shaftesbury, in a letter to Prime Minister Aberdeen (George Hamilton Gordon) in 1853. For further details regarding the historiography of this controversial slogan, see Garfinkle.

23. This seems to be a lightly mocking self-portrait, for, in his youth at Kibbutz Hulda, Oz was a voracious reader of Spinoza. Balaban concludes that, in those early years, "Spinoza's pantheism appealed to Oz because it emphasizes the sanctity that permeates the world, and the harsh determinism that it implies. . . . But Oz did not find Spinoza's religious concepts wholly satisfactory. The harmonious totality that characterizes God in Spinoza . . . lacked the drama and the strife that were part and parcel of Oz's life experiences" ("Secularity and Religiosity" 69–70).

24. Balaban draws our attention to a strong biographic resonance: "Oz reached Kibbutz Hulda at the age of fourteen. Decades later, upon reading *A Perfect Peace*, his classmates on the kibbutz would remember his tireless efforts to impress them and make himself well-liked. The novel tells the story of Azariah . . . coming to the kibbutz, a strange outsider who wants to win the love of the kibbutz members immediately" (*Between God and Beast* 24). Balaban cannot help further noticing that "the layout of Kibbutz Hulda (the dining room, the swimming pool, the cultural center, the youth group buildings, the barns, and the rest), the fields around it . . . provided the model for descriptions of the kibbutz" throughout Oz's kibbutz fiction (24).

25. Balaban aptly observes how Yonatan and Azariah "move in opposite directions: one moves outward from inside the circle, the other moves from the darkness beyond the circle inward toward the center. . . . In contrast to Yonatan, born on the kibbutz, trying to uproot himself from the soil of his homeland, Azariah, the persecuted refugee, wants to take root in that soil" (*Between God and Beast* 216–17).

26. Dismissing the sexual scandal Yonatan's mysterious absence has provoked, Azariah offers this hyperrational explanation of his fortuitous appearance to Srulik, the new kibbutz secretary, who has lately replaced Yolek: "I want you to know, Comrade Srulik, that it was Yonatan who invited me into his home. It's as simple as that. You can even announce it at the next general meeting. He wanted someone to be there. He even showed me where he kept all his tools so I could replace him. Just as you've replaced Yolek" (*Perfect Peace* 249).

27. For a comprehensive discussion of these issues, see Lavi.

28. Compare Yonatan's haunting memories of Palestinian ghosts with my discussion in chapter 3 of those haunting Atallah Mansour's Arab protagonist, Yusuf.

29. As befits Oz's interest in the romantic imagination of children, in Yonatan's childhood recollection, we can hear faint yet distinct echoes of William Wordsworth's disturbing lyric "Nutting," with its intimation of the latent darkness and violence within, which the Romantic poet composed following an encounter with Nature in his early adolescence.

30. Yonatan's anguished reflections on the ruined village and the legitimacy of Zionist dispossession of Arabs and appropriation of their lands strikingly resemble those of Udi Aviv, a kibbutznik from Gan Shmuel and a paratrooper in the 1967 liberation of Jerusalem. After he returned to his kibbutz from the Six-Day War, the nearby ruins of Cherkas, an Arab village destroyed by the IDF in 1948, thoroughly unsettled him: "As a child Udi and his friends had gone there to pick mulberries; Udi had feared being stranded among the abandoned stone houses without roofs, as though its ghosts would possess him. . . . The army offered the fields bordering the road to Gan Shmuel; the kibbutzniks voted to accept the offer. They had just emerged from a war of survival . . . they weren't about to argue. . . . No one in Gan Shmuel talked about Cherkas. But now Udi found that silence unbearable. How had their parents simply watched Cherkas vanish without protest?" (Halevi 131).

31. Ironically, "hirba," the modern Hebrew word for "ruin," is an Arabic borrowing.

32. Elsewhere, Azariah, whose outsider status is accentuated when we learn he is a Holocaust survivor, denounces the young men of the kibbutz, "who do nothing all day but talk about killing the Arabs. This is a snake pit, not a country. A jungle, not a commune. Death, not Zionism" (*Perfect Peace* 289).

33. In his enthusiasm for what he considers the typical structure of Oz's narratives, Mazor sees the repetition of "subtle, hesitant steps toward moderation and accommodation . . . for the warring sides to inch their way to the middle ground, to steer away from the path of perpetual strife. Reconciliation, however fragile and tenuous, is given a chance. . . . The power struggle between the two rivals is far from terminated, and probably will never cease, but a soft, placating, almost caressing breeze is suddenly felt on the frantic, sweaty neck" (2). In particular, he embraces "the conciliatory note" that distinguishes the conclusion to *A Perfect Peace*: "One realizes that there is room for compromise, that there is no need to take sides, to triumph absolutely. Gradually, perhaps with time and maturity, one accepts the middle road, the golden mean, the existence of a reality that can accommodate opposing extremes." Thus, Mazor concludes, "if not perfect peace, this is at least a truce" (43).

34. Even the novel's title presumes this teleology: "a perfect peace" is a phrase from the Jewish service for the dead, strongly suggesting that Oz views his hero's quest for an alternative identity as a fata morgana from the outset.

35. In this interview by Niva Lenir, Oz credits the kibbutz for teaching him "much of what I know about human nature" and that if he had spent those decades elsewhere "I would not have had the slightest chance of becoming so intimately acquainted with 300 souls."

36. Compare Dagan's remarks to those of Alon, the haughty kibbutz soldier in Yehoshua Kenaz's novel *Hitganvut yechidim* (*Infiltration*; 1986), who observes disparagingly of the Mizrahi immigrants that "the army . . . is our only hope. Only the army can educate them, turn them into Israelis, until they're like us. They don't know the country outside their *ma'abarot*, they don't know its history, its beauty, its culture. When they bring them to their new settlements, they don't want to get off the trucks. They're not used to hard work and living in the country and farming. So how can we expect them to like our songs? The army has to educate them—at least the young ones because the old ones may as well be written off. The generation of the wilderness" (*Infiltration* 92).

37. Oz's "Little Boy" should hold special interest for those familiar with Ran Tal's spellbinding documentary *Yaldey hashemesh* (*Children of the Sun*; 2007; discussed in chapter 5), which features the gripping, often rueful reminiscences of veteran or former kibbutz members struggling to come to terms with childhoods that were perhaps never fully theirs, in service to their parents' noble dream.

38. Oz is hardly alone in making such slyly meaningful comparisons. Consider the comments of Assaf Inbari, author of *Ha-baita* (*Home*; 2009), a novelistic chronicle of Kibbutz Afikim, where he lived the first two decades of his life: "Ask yourself, in the 20th century, what Jewish community fulfilled the values of Judaism in a more vital way. Within a culture that sanctifies the land of Israel, the Hebrew language, the tradition of the holidays, they were the most intensive Jews in terms of how detailed a lifestyle they put forward. Take their list of regulations. Every Orthodox Jew will place the halakha [Jewish religious law] above himself. On the kibbutz, the most unique thing about it was that it was a 'halakhic' community. A community that debated and argued over the pettiest of issues. This is the Jewish approach, which has no equal in other cultures. The kibbutz was the expression of Judaism in the 20th century" (Avrahami).

39. In accepting the Heine Prize in 2008, Oz remarked that "Israel—even today—carries European chromosomes" and that "the cross-roads is the only place where I am at home, where I really belong."

40. I am grateful to my colleague Allan Arkush for this intriguing observation.

41. Chekhov was a discernible influence even in Oz's early career. Thus, in *Elsewhere, Perhaps*, an embattled young woman discusses leaving behind the disgrace of bearing a child out of wedlock

and moving abroad: "Living along one long groove. Dead straight. Calmly. Clenched teeth. Living drily" (248). But, in his autumn years, the novelist seems to find even greater significance, both politically and psychologically, in that Chekhovian ethos of disillusioned and stoic endurance.

42. Compare this declaration with the messianism embodied in the collective narrator's voice in Amos Oz's first kibbutz novel, *Makom aher* (*Elsewhere, Perhaps*; 1966): "Those who believe in an ultimate justice hold that even suffering is a sign of divine Providence, since without suffering there is no happiness and without hardships there is no redemption or joy. We, on the other hand, who yearn for a reformed world, do not believe in this kind of justice. Our aim is to eradicate suffering from the world and to fill it instead with love and brotherhood" (*Elsewhere, Perhaps* 15).

43. A few years after the publication of Shaham's "The Salt of the Earth," Prime Minister Menachem Begin made controversial remarks designed to exploit the class resentment felt by many of the Mizrahi constituents who had swept him into power. According to Anita Shapira, "several months after the 1981 elections, Israeli television broadcast a program including a segment in which a member of Kibbutz Manara on the Lebanon border was seen swimming to his heart's content in the kibbutz pool. Menachem Begin, in an interview on Israel Radio on the eve of Rosh Hashanah, referred to this by then notorious kibbutznik and the pool as an arrogant expression of a culture of excess: 'That man on a kibbutz, lounging in the pool as if [you were watching] . . . some American millionaire and talking with a good deal of condescension? Did I sit at that swimming pool? I have no such luxury.' Begin's crude and demagogic use of the 'ethnic card' reflected his awareness that the kibbutz, for all its faults and weaknesses, still posed an alternative to his new regime. Moreover, it still symbolized an idealistic society, the best of the Israeli nation. If Begin wished to rewrite the history of Israel and give voice to groups like his own Irgun, which had been excluded from the Zionist narrative, he had to undermine the symbolic keystone of the Labor movement—the kibbutz—by depicting its members as people living off the fat of the land while they exploited hired workers and denied these workers' children admission into kibbutz schools" ("Kibbutz and the State" 9).

44. As Joshua Muravchik puts it, Begin's "characterization might easily have been laughed off, but it came as a shock to people who saw themselves as a selfless vanguard" (328). The economic truth behind the financial crisis that the kibbutzim found themselves in is somewhat more complex. Although it is true that the kibbutzim had failed to invest and had used their earnings to increase their standard of living, Muravchik argues that the "impulse to do this did not grow out of hedonism, but in the hopes of stemming the loss of members" (328) and, by extension, their children, or the third generation and beyond.

45. For resonant examples of such characters, consider S. Yizhar's passive witnesses to wartime misdeeds in *Khirbet Khizeh*, A. B. Yehoshua's firewatcher in "Facing the Forests," or any number of Amos Oz's troubled male protagonists, such as Yonatan, the kibbutznik who cuts short his escape to the desert in *A Perfect Peace*, or Fima, the title character of *Matsav hashelish* (*Fima*; 1991), a man with many dreams who seems incapable of acting on any of them.

46. Alas, we should note that even the object of the young woman's fantasy life seems to be the antithesis of the "New Jew." In sharp contrast to "Big Yitzhak" ("good-looking, tall, solid . . . his arms are strong and muscular"), her secret love Theo's "narrow shoulders, caved-in chest, and thin arms hardly indicate masculine vigor" (136). And yet, for all that, Theo's compassion for a stray dog from a nearby Arab village and his apparent spiritual nature arouse her interest (and may win her greater sympathy from Shaham's readers).

47. Numerous scholars of the kibbutz movement have described its failure to live up to its lofty claims of gender equality. Edna Perlman, for one, argues: "Kibbutz society aspired to be an egalitarian society; but in point of act, it was an androcentric society, which took a male view of the world, and in which power and control were in the hands of men. Although kibbutz society had pretensions of being an egalitarian society and upheld principles of gender equality, it operated by means of male-centered concepts and worldviews. Women were designated for female

roles in the kibbutz; education, laundry and health. Today women testify about the frustration they experienced within the social system that spoke in two voices; which in actuality contradicted the ideological principles that it claimed to espouse: by discriminating against women in terms of the occupational roles they were permitted to fulfill within the kibbutz, and in terms of the status they were permitted to achieve" (104). This is a useful context for considering the plight of Shaham's aptly unnamed character.

48. Even today, as a recent study concludes, "gossip and social ostracism continue to be the primary social control mechanisms used to discipline those who free ride, over-consume, or express beliefs deviating from the community's ideals" (Sosis and Ruffle 92).

49. Ultimately, although the psychological verisimilitude of Shaham's "The Other Side of the Wall" cannot be denied, its protagonist faithfully adheres to the plot of reconciliation that, Iris Milner argues, distinguishes the classic kibbutz narrative: "Only an absolute eradication of individual interests and needs, with no exception, may enable the accomplishment of the hopes of resettlement in the extremely harsh and demanding Jewish homeland" (168).

50. In addition to his book of criticism on Oz, *Between God and Beast*, a work widely perceived as canonical (and widely quoted in my study), Balaban is the author of four books of poetry, seven scholarly works on writers such as Amalia Kahana-Carmon, Nathan Alterman, and A. B. Yehoshua, and two novels.

51. Readers interested in the contemporary kibbutz memoir (and literate in Modern Hebrew) should also seek out Asaf Inbari's esteemed work *Ha-baita* (*Home*; 2009), which the historian Anita Shapira has called "a requiem" for his birthplace, Kibbutz Afikim. Through letters, notes, diaries, and minutes of meetings, Inbari artfully reconstructs the story of his birthplace, from its genesis in the Soviet Union during the 1920s, through its flowering in the Jordan Valley, to its recent decline under the onslaught of privatization and hyperindividualism.

52. Dror concluded her remarks to the kibbutz literary symposium by declaring that the kibbutz as she experienced it "has created a society which is basically non-creative. It can certainly be that this was unintentional, but this is the situation . . . there are very few significant creators among those born in the kibbutz . . . very few know where to go on from here, and those who do, or think they do . . . pay a heavy price which erodes their ability" (Ring 160).

53. In the same interview by Aviva Lori, Balaban remarks, "I was lonely my whole time in the kibbutz children's society. Totally solitary. I was very agile in work, an outstanding athlete and very active in society, but solitary, because I didn't really fit in. I wasn't able to cultivate the thick skin that life in the children's house demanded." Balaban recalls an "avid longing for parental security" that generally went unfulfilled, with one poignant exception: "there was sometimes this moment—special and unique—in which my mother made black coffee and the whole family sat around the table, like in a bubble, and for an instant we were not kibbutz members. We were a regular family. Because most of the time when we visited our parents we saw only their backs—they stood there and prepared a parcel for us, or something to eat. I'm sure they were not ill-intentioned, but they made a great many mistakes along the way."

54. In her groundbreaking essay, Yael Darr discusses the role of children's literature in the kibbutz movement during what she calls the "ardent" decades of the 1940s and 1950s, when "the principle of communal sleeping was still widely applied in all kibbutz movements" (129). Of the kibbutz publishing houses, which included Hakibbutz Hameuchad, Sifriyat Poalim, and Am Oved, established in the late 1930s and early 1940s, the first two "explicitly aimed their publications at kibbutz children, their parents, and their educators" (131). Yet their impact greatly exceeded their primary audience, for during the ardent decades, they published "the overwhelming majority of Israeli classics for children. . . . In most of them, the rural settlement and the young collective peer group take center stage, serving as the direct, explicit message" (139–40), which confirms the tremendously disproportionate influence that kibbutz life had on the nation's collective imagination.

55. In her examination of young people who left their kibbutzim to live as expatriates in Los Angeles, Naama Sabar cites a study conducted during the 1970s in which "half" the participants (all raised on kibbutzim) spoke of "their relationship with their parents as complex, filled with tension and frustration. . . . Most . . . spoke about the weakness of the parent-child relationship on the kibbutz, a relationship they would not want to return to under any circumstances. The main point of criticism was the parents' limited involvement in the children's lives . . . beginning with the toddlers' group through the children's house and the elementary or high school" (117).

56. This friend almost echoes Balaban's own sense of abandonment: "How they chucked us, aged two or three, into a children's house that was the furthest building in the kibbutz, right by the fence. You remember that poem—'Wizened and quiet, my mother laid me down by the fence'—it was read out on some occasion in school, and for a moment I thought it was a poem about me" (*Mourning* 97).

57. See, in this regard, Yossi Klein Halevi's poignant portrait of a kibbutz childhood in his epic historical study of post-1967 Israel: "Uri and Tova Adiv were worried about their son, Udi. But they didn't know how to show their concern. As a boy Udi hadn't been hugged or kissed by Tova, who considered such gestures a form of spoiling. Udi's father, Uri, a big silent man, found speech almost painful; whatever he had to say he conveyed in practical ways. He had served as kibbutz secretary general and was sometimes dispatched by the movement to help organize a struggling kibbutz. He had little left for his children. Young Udi would fall asleep at night on the windowsill in the children's house, hoping to catch a glimpse of his father returning from the fields" (137).

58. Compare Balaban's nostalgic account with Zerubavel Gilead's reminiscences of his kibbutz's elaborate commemoration of Passover in earlier days, a meticulously choreographed spectacle lasting many hours, envisioned as celebrating both the traditional exodus from enslavement in Pharaoh's Egypt and a spring agricultural festival: "The kibbutz members, with their families and guests—often more than four hundred—assemble in front of the dining hall and walk in procession to the field, music from loudspeakers accompanying us all the way. Sitting on bundles of straw . . . we watch the ceremony against a backdrop of the glinting waters of the kibbutz fishponds and the towering Gilboa. The ceremony begins by reading passages from the Bible that exalt and bless the harvesting for the first crops, imitating what our biblical forefathers did at this season. The words are then matched by the deed, depicted in a scene that might be titled 'The Reapers.' A group of kibbutz men carrying scythes appear and proceed in rhythmic order to cut down a long patch of the first ripened wheat while singing lines from a poem by Bialik inspired by Genesis 3:17–19 and Psalms 127:2: 'Not dry bread / Not quail, not heavenly corn / But the bread of sorrow you will eat / The fruit of the labor of your hands.' The reapers include a small number of veterans who actually scythed the crops in their youth and a much larger contingent of young men who have learned the art of scything for this ceremony. Meanwhile, the kibbutz combine harvester stands nearby, as if watching with interest the performance of a primitive ancestor. As the reapers withdraw to loud applause, they are replaced by young mothers and their children who gather the swathes into heaps to the accompaniment of fresh music and song. Then follow 'The Dancers,' young girls . . . dressed in long, flowing robes of biblical-oriental style in vivid colors . . . gracefully miming the traditional prayers of thanksgiving for the first crops. A visitor once remarked that they looked like biblical figures out of a Poussin painting" (Gilead and Krook 283–84).

59. Kibbutz Kfar Blum's archivist Shimon Schwartz describes the three phases of the dining room's culture: "First there was the 'instead' period. In the early days the food was served on trolleys and everybody got the same thing. If you didn't like it you could ask for something else instead, and then you got something else, which was usually of lesser quality, and if you didn't like that either, it was your problem. There were no other options. The second period was the 'variety' period, which more or less started in the 1970s. That's when the dining hall switched to self-service, which was the only way more variety could be introduced. And the third period, which started in

the 1990s and is still going on today, is the 'privatization' period. The moment you started paying for the food, it got better and more varied, and the quantity wasn't limited anymore either. Before you couldn't have more than one piece of chicken or two sausages at lunch, now you can have as much as you want, since you're paying for it. But privatization also meant that communal dining rooms started closing down, either entirely or partially. Even before the privatization process, most kibbutzim stopped serving dinner. Then they stopped serving breakfast. Now most privatized kibbutzim serve only lunch, if they're open at all" (qtd. in Kessler).

60. The announcement writer's fatalism seems fully justified today: only one-quarter of Israel's 274 kibbutzim now operate any form of a cooperative dining system, and many are managed by external catering companies.

61. Rachel Elboim-Dror, who grew up in moshavim and is a scholar of Zionist education practices, argues in her review of *Mourning* that Balaban "cannot bring himself to forgive the paucity of his father's love, who was devoted to his work and concerned with his status, which depended on his dedication to the collective—at the price of neglecting his parental duties. Balaban's antagonism toward his father is so deep that even seeing the old broken man in a sorry state during the last stage of his life, he feels no compassion" (Review 156–57). Elboim-Dror poignantly confesses that "it felt as if I were reading a biography of my own childhood: the yearnings for an ever-absent father, who was devoted to collective goals; my fears of the howling of jackals, while being left alone throughout the night; and life among rigid and closed-minded revolutionary pioneers" (158). She draws on this background in her novel *Clean Death in Tel Aviv* (2003), and she concludes her largely favorable review of Balaban's *Mourning* by calling for a "dialectical synthesis" between "the sweet, but false nostalgia for a reality that never was, and the empty rhetorical slogans [and] the equally false bitter anger and alienation towards the pioneering heroics of that early period" (Review 159).

62. Today, Balaban seems more reconciled to the past, if also a little harder on himself, matter-of-factly telling an interviewer that, in portraying his father, "I didn't let him off lightly. I described him very harshly and unsympathetically. He wasn't a bad man . . . mainly a devoted pioneer and a wounded person. And those two elements prevented him from being a good father. I am sorry that in his last years I never mustered the strength to embrace him powerfully, as one embraces a hurt child, like a parent who tries to imbue in his crying child something of his strength. That was a test I failed" (Lori).

63. Another memoirist of the generation that grew up in the 1970s, Avner Avrahami, speaks of his collective upbringing with similar ambivalence: "In certain ways, I had a wonderful childhood. In other ways, I had a wounded childhood. And I think this is the honest and mature answer for anyone. In principle, I do not respect or accept the victim stance which I feel is a childish position to take."

CHAPTER 3

1. Mansour was born in the village of Al-Jish in the Upper Galilee and attended school in Lebanon from 1946 to 1950. He returned to Israel illegally in 1950 and managed to obtain Israeli citizenship a decade later. Over the years, he has published fiction and journalistic articles in Arabic, Hebrew, and English. As for his brief kibbutz sojourn, Mansour told me how he and seventeen other young Arabs were selected by Mapam as part of the party's pilot program to introduce its ideals to the Arab sector and how they were made to follow a rigorous schedule of working forty-five hours and studying for nine hours each week. In his memoir *Still Waiting for the Dawn*, in a tone of almost wistful regret, Mansour recalls that he and his Arab comrades were not afforded the opportunity to "become genuine kibbutzniks," although they "felt grateful to Mapam and the kibbutzim. They told us most of the Jews in Israel would not have trusted Arabs enough to live so closely with them. But [the kibbutz members] were bold enough to take the risk" (54).

2. Mansour told me in Nazareth that he envisioned *In a New Light* as an examination of how the purported collective ideals of the kibbutz stood up against the desire of a single individual on the periphery of Zionist society to belong (pers. comm., 15 June 2012).

3. Compare Mansour's description of utopian simplicity with the narrator's impression of kibbutz space in Amos Oz's first novel: "It radiates a delicate, unpretentious elegance" (*Elsewhere, Perhaps* 6). In her article discussing "the planning of the total kibbutz space," Esther Zandberg identifies the kibbutz as one of three preeminent historical examples of spatial engineering toward furthering egalitarian goals: "Along with the kibbutz, other notable examples of improving the world through spatial planning are the Ebenezer Howard's English social garden city and Soviet urbanism. The three are rooted in the principle of collective ownership of the land, creating a community of a size that can be managed 'efficiently, fairly, democratically and inclusively,' and in the connection of the communities to an ideological network. The experiments were distorted. Howard's garden city turned into a bourgeois garden city venture after being embraced in a bear hug by the capitalist establishment and became responsible for many of the ills of modern urban planning. The revolutionary Soviet experiment was shattered by the cruelty of the Communist regime." As Zandberg points out, the kibbutz outlasted the other two models, though, after a century of adaptive change, privatization proved "one change too many" and "in effect ended the experiment."

4. Here is one of the early hints of the conflicted insider-outsider nature of Mansour's narrator, which only becomes fully understandable much later, with the revelation that he is in fact an Arab.

5. Here, too, Mansour's memoir sheds light on the attitudes of the time. He describes a brief flirtation with a Jewish girl and its abrupt conclusion: "I remember one day, while acting as *sadran avoda* (work organizer), I met one of the kibbutz girls. I befriended her to some extent in the course of our subsequent 'official' meetings. Then, after a few weeks, she suddenly refused to talk to me. She left me confused for some time. When we met again, by accident, on one of Haifa's streets, she came up to me to apologize for her behavior. Her group leader had advised her 'not to encourage an Arab'—especially since we were living temporarily in the kibbutz" (*Still Waiting* 55). Mansour's *In a New Light* seems to build on the tantalizing utopian "what if" that must have long lingered in his imagination after that episode—an alternative history of what might have been (both in terms of the prospect of the kibbutz as a permanent dwelling and a union with a Jewish girl) had xenophobia and deep distrust of the Arabs not prevailed among the same kibbutzniks who sought Arab support for their political party.

6. The naive enthusiasm of Mansour's protagonist for the rapid transformation of the native landscape can be profitably read alongside another interpretation, which serves as ironic counterpoint. In the same period in which *In a New Light* takes place, Jacqueline Kahanoff observed the Zionists' "'European' obsession" that Israel, with its lively landscape, so harmoniously unique unto itself, should become a little Switzerland. Bulldozers erase delicate contours to give rise to buildings which can be seen anywhere in the world and have no particular relevance as an expression of this land and people except that they are 'modern.' The charming old parts of Jaffa rot away because we cannot accept their 'alien' beauty" (208).

7. Compare Yehudah's comments with Avram's in David Grossman's masterpiece novel *Isha borachat mi-besora* (*Until the End of the Land*; 2008), where, traumatized by his torture at the hands of his Egyptian captors during the 1973 War, Avram is horrified by the very prospect that he may be a father.

8. For a worthy account of Arab Israeli critics' reception of Mansour and his novel, see Kayyal.

9. These events are clearly modeled on Mansour's recollections of the attempts of the "Arab Department" of Mapam (United Workers Party), then the second-largest party in Israel, to reach out to young Arab-Israeli villagers in the early 1950s (*Still Waiting* 52–61).

10. It should be noted that, for readers in twenty-first-century Israel, the taboo against miscegenation between Arabs and Jews probably remains as potent as it was when *In a New*

Light was first published nearly fifty years ago; indeed, romantic relations between them are as controversial as ever among ultra-Orthodox rabbis and others who rail against this relatively rare phenomenon.

11. The Ninth of Av, or Tisha B'Av, is an important fast day in the Hebrew or Jewish calendar, commemorating the destruction of both the First Temple and Second Temple in Jerusalem; in some traditions, it includes other notable Jewish tragedies that fell on this day, including the expulsion of the Jews from Spain in 1492. It falls in July or August of the Western calendar.

12. Rivkah's utopian declaration stands in intriguing counterpoint to an episode in Mansour's life, shortly following his kibbutz sojourn, when he began to explore the possibilities of working as a journalist. After writing Prime Minister David Ben-Gurion to complain that Israeli Arab youths were experiencing widespread discrimination, the young Mansour was startled to receive "a long personal letter in which he assured me that he did not discriminate between one man and another and that if there was any discrimination, it had to be eradicated. He added, 'You are cordially invited to visit me any time you find it convenient'" (*Still Waiting* 58). In those days, the Arabs of the Galilee still lived under military rule and, in spite of Ben-Gurion's invitation, Mansour encountered bureaucratic obstacles in getting a travel permit. When at last he was admitted to the prime minister's home in Kibbutz Sde Boker, Mansour found the leader in the company of a right-wing Knesset member. The subsequent conversation that Mansour reports in his memoir is memorable for many reasons, not least for an abrupt interrogation by Ben-Gurion's wife, Paula, before the two men spoke to each other: "Do you plan to marry a Jewish girl?" Taken aback, Mansour responded, "I certainly plan to marry a girl that I shall love!," which he thought would satisfy her. Instead she huffed, "You look [like] a pleasant young man, but you are in fact another diplomat, like most of Ben-Gurion's friends" (60). Nevertheless, Mansour describes the ensuing exchange with great enthusiasm since the prime minister emphasized the need to "treat all citizens equally" (61). According to Mansour, he was the first Palestinian Arab to have met Ben-Gurion in two decades.

13. Rachel Brenner cogently argues that the cumulative impact of the writings of Arabs and Jews in Israel, despite their disparate sociopolitical perspectives, effectively "restores the visibility of the Arabs in the 'empty' land and calls into question the unequivocal Zionist claim to the land."Indeed, "the story of the suffering that the triumphant Jews inflicted on the defenseless, defeated Arab population invokes the history of Jewish persecution and victimization in the Diaspora. Against the doctrine of exclusion, the literary representations reassert in the Israeli consciousness the denied histories of the Palestinian Arab and the Diaspora Jew" (*Inextricably Bonded* 9). As I suggested in the main text of chapter 3, Brenner's *Inextricably Bonded* strongly warrants our appreciation and attention as one of the most innovative studies of modern Hebrew literary criticism, especially for its forceful demonstration that the identity politics of both Israeli Arab and Israeli Jewish writers has produced a dynamically "bi-ethnic" rather than a narrowly "national" body of literature.

14. As a sadly ironic coda to this discussion of Mansour's portrayal of minority citizenship, the pretenses of kibbutz idealism, and the poignant struggle to belong, it is worth noting that, in 2004, as his wife was dying from cancer, Mansour's Israeli-born daughter, Samar, was unable to live in Israel and help care for her mother because she was married to a Jordanian citizen with whom she was raising a daughter. According to a report in *Haaretz*, "the Shin Bet [Israel Security Agency] received an order from the prime minister [then Ariel Sharon] to stop all the examination procedures, due to his policy to block the immigration of Palestinians and citizens of Arab states to Israel" (Benziman).

15. Lital Levy distinguishes Eli Amir as a writer who, in pursuing an integrationist path, "by and large adopted the Zionist narrative, eliciting tempered criticism of Israel's immigration and absorption policies but not of the ideological premises of Zionism . . . this might be termed *bikoret be-havanah*, a 'forgiving' or 'sympathetic' criticism" ("Reorienting" 155). Nevertheless, even Levy

concedes that Amir remained demonstrably "preoccupied with the cultural environment of his formative years" (129).

16. In her study of Iraqi Jewish immigration, historian Esther Meir-Glitzenstein observes that "the kibbutz was the most absolute, the most demanding of all absorption models in the country, and at times it did not leave the individual any breathing space" (83).

17. Between 1949 and 1951, more than six hundred and fifty thousand immigrants arrived in Israel from North Africa, Yemen, Iraq, Iran, and Turkey.

18. Even much younger Mizrahi children than those described in *Scapegoat* were exposed to these pressures. In her marvelous study *The Rise of the Individual in 1950s Israel: A Challenge to Collectivism*, Orit Rozin describes the activities of a program called "Korat Gag" ("A Roof over Their Heads"), which placed children from six to twelve years old in boarding schools and kibbutzim, largely as a humane gesture to protect them from exposure to the winter elements in the tent camps. Others, even younger, were placed in day-care facilities, a program that "had negative consequences, with some Mizrahi children developing feelings of inferiority. They sought to emulate their Ashkenazi hosts and escape their ethnic identities. Given the negative attitude that many old-timers had toward the education provided by Mizrahi families, it is hardly surprising that some sought to persuade the children they hosted to abandon their parents and enter kibbutz. . . . These pressures were exerted on the children without their parents' knowledge" (171). Whereas Mizrahi mothers "were compelled" to cooperate with this arrangement, "immigrant mothers from Europe were never forced to do so" (167).

19. The kibbutz's exclusion of immigrants is inevitably reflected in and memorialized by the institution of the kibbutz cemetery. In her marvelously incisive study *Place and Ideology in Contemporary Hebrew Literature*, Karen Grumberg observes that "the myth of kibbutz egalitarianism has been widely contested by women, Mizrahim, and Israeli Arabs, and the inequality that they argue existed in kibbutzim is reflected in the kibbutz graveyard as well. . . . Its fence makes the final determination of belonging, eternally banishing those outside the collective and embracing those within it" (104, 106–7).

20. Established between 1952 and 1954, the ma'abarot, or immigrant transit camps, housed more than one hundred and eighty thousand immigrants in tents and tin shacks at more than one hundred sites.

21. This episode alludes to a historical promise made by Ben-Gurion in the early years of the state to award a "reproduction prize of one hundred Israeli lirot [pounds]" to every mother who gave birth to ten children.

22. Also frequently overlooked were the educational backgrounds and potential the immigrant youths brought with them. Esther Meir-Glitzenstein notes that these youths were the "sons and daughters of petty merchants, craftsmen, and office workers . . . urbanites from Baghdad, Basra and other cities, and most of them had secondary education" (84).

23. The gatekeeper's casual slur, a distant but unmistakable echo of Herzl's prophetic pronouncement (23), reflects the Eurocentrism and Ashkenazi hegemony so pervasive in Israel at the time and even to this day. Herzl's original German text first appeared in 1896.

24. At such moments, Amir's narrative anticipates the more multicultural space that has lately opened in Hebrew fiction for Mizrahi writers, whose works urgently address a tradition of shared cultures in the Middle East, a tradition that Zionists and Arab regimes after 1948 sought to ignore, yet one that, at the time portrayed in *Scapegoat* (mid-1950s), was still a vital connection to the Arabic language and culture as well as to Islam itself.

25. Amir's portrayal of these no-nonsense figures of authority is also supported by Meir-Glitzenstein's study of young Iraqi immigrants: "The kibbutz appointed *madrichim* (counselors) for them who helped with the ideological and social unification of the [training groups]." Each of the agricultural and socialist training units "maintained a separate group framework and managed its own independent social life" (83).

26. Many who choose to immigrate to Israel also choose to Hebraize or otherwise change their original names, but, in the case of these youths and others sent off to kibbutzim, that decision has been made for them.

27. Eventually, many of the Youth Aliya girls in *Scapegoat* adopt the strategy of "Nilly-knickers," the dominant member of their group, who, on the kibbutz, dresses promiscuously—"she flaunted her body and wagged her backside shamelessly"—but, at home on leave, wears long skirts and modest sleeves (138). Amir evocatively portrays the confusion inherent in her painful struggle to transcend her distant origins and appear as brazen and liberated as any of the native girls: "Something was seething inside Nilly-knickers, burning her up and not giving her or us a moment's peace. She came from a remote village in the north of Iraq, and the Arabic dialect she spoke was greeted with gales of laughter and mockery. . . . [She] looked for excuses to go up to the regional school. She had discovered a new world there and she prowled its fringes wide-eyed, hesitating on the threshold, daring and not daring to enter" (138–39).

28. On another occasion, the Mizrahi youths attend a musical quiz at the regional school and are again cowed by the proud natives: "Quiet as mice we crossed the threshold, almost on tiptoe, so as not to disturb the singing. We huddled together. . . . Hardly any of them deigned to honor us with a glance. In a full-throated, resonant choir they went on singing their songs, as broad as the valley over which they had galloped on horseback since the dawn of their childhood" (*Scapegoat* 122–23).

29. In another idyllic moment, Nuri proudly participates in the kibbutz commemoration of the agricultural festival of Shavuot (here called "Festival of the First Fruits"), a scene of teeming prolificacy reminiscent of other fictional portrayals of the kibbutz's secularization of religious observance: "I stood in my best Sabbath clothes in a . . . sunlit field of stubble. All the branches of the farm had put their first fruits on exhibition: chickens and chicks, sheaves of wheat and barley, baskets full of fruit and vegetables, spotted calves and, of course, the big bull who contemplated the festivities from his cage like a bored king. Scores of children roamed about with baskets on their shoulders and garlands of flowers crowning their heads, like little princes, and the whole kibbutz was one big, happy, celebrating family. The loudspeakers blared forth with accordions and drums and a thunderous singing, which rolled in wave after conquering wave over the entire Jezreel Valley" (*Scapegoat* 194). That sense of ebullient fecundity is intensified by Nuri's struggle with his own lustful urges, culminating in the first erotic encounter of his young life.

30. Cf. a similar scene in *Hitganvut yechidim* (*Infiltration*; 1986), Yehoshua Kenaz's epic novel about young soldiers of different cultural backgrounds, where the narrator observes as an immigrant from the Arab world named "Rahamim Ben-Hamo" briefly rebels against the strict conformity and arduous training of basic training as well as the bias of those from Ashkenazi backgrounds by performing an ethnic dance, in spite of some who react to his performance with "contempt . . . violent revulsion and disgust": "The expression of concentration on his face grew more acute, and the chains were us, his spectators, our faces observing him, our eyes barring his way. His body writhed and twisted, refusing to surrender to the hostile forces trying to paralyze him, straining to snap the chains and escape far away from here. The Arabic song, so ugly to me in its tearful tone, its wet, guttural consonants, its dissonant trills, its repulsive moans, took possession of the room and everyone in it. No longer a beggarly outcast, its foreignness and ugliness were transformed into a source of strength. The laughter and catcalls died down. We stood in a circle around the dancer . . . watching silently. . . . The ugliness of the animal-like writhing and the moans that accompanied it, of the savage beating on the drum, was so powerful, dark, and fascinating that it hardly seemed ugly at all. Rahamim must have sensed our feelings from the way we stood there. . . . A happy smile spread gradually over his face, a smile of gratification and relief. He went on shouting, rhythmic shouts, and the sounds emerging from his throat now sounded like cries of victory" (*Infiltration* 95). Here the contrast seems clear: the Mizrahi inductee's performance, at least momentarily, transforms his environment and the sensibilities of his fellow soldiers, who are utterly transfixed by the performance.

31. Today's Israeli readers cannot fail to take note of how many decades would have to pass before Arabic music would find mainstream acceptance, or would even be broadcast on Israeli airwaves.

32. Though it appears utterly impossible to find common ground between the Ashkenazi and Mizrahi perspectives during this wounding period, it seems worth listening to at least one kibbutz "insider" whose memoir addresses the disunity from the other side. Zerubavel Gilead arrived on Kibbutz Ein Harod in 1924 at age eleven with his mother, who later became an emissary for the Working Youth Movement among the impoverished neighborhoods of Tel Aviv. Gilead insists that "the kibbutzim would have been ready to take in the new 'Oriental' immigrants as members, but the vast majority of them had no desire whatever to join. . . . They knew nothing about socialism, they didn't understand the cooperative-egalitarian principles of the kibbutz, and what they came to understand they didn't like." He acknowledges the immigrants' "desperate" need for employment but condescendingly dismisses them as "unskilled, often illiterate." Without seriously addressing the kibbutzim's reluctance to absorb the Mizrahim as full members, he describes the ideological quandary that ensued: "Ben-Gurion appealed to the kibbutzim to take in the new immigrants as hired laborers, even though to do so would oblige them to set aside their cherished egalitarian principle, which tolerated no employer-employee relationship. . . . Ben-Gurion's appeal created a severe dilemma for the kibbutzim. Most of them resisted; some capitulated, willing to try it out on an experimental basis, and the hired-labor question became a hotly disputed ideological issue throughout the 1950s." Writing as a seasoned veteran kibbutznik in the 1980s, Gilead seems to regard this as almost inevitable, given the socioeconomic circumstances, yet also a sad moment of opportunism and a critical juncture of ideological decline from which there was no turning back: "There was a strong temptation to hire unskilled workers from the neighboring development towns, whose people were constantly seeking employment. Many kibbutzim did, and some became rich as a consequence; but they lost a good part of their kibbutz character in the process, and members of these affluent kibbutzim often felt considerable moral discomfort at the knowledge that they owed their ever rising standard of life, partly at least, to the labor of hired hands" (Gilead and Krook 273).

33. As for the many immigrant members who left the kibbutz, Meir-Glitzenstein says that their exodus led to the concentrations of oriental populations that prevail in present-day Tel Aviv (especially Shekunat Hatikvah, a working-class neighborhood in southwest Tel Aviv) and other Israeli cities: "Here they went back to working in fields of commerce and craftsmanship as they had in [Iraq], they kept in touch with their extended families, they observed their religious tradition at one level or another of strictness, they prepared their traditional foods, they spoke in Arabic among themselves, and they listened to the Arab music they liked. All of this diminished the scope and depth of the personal-social revolution demanded of them by socialist-Zionism" (98).

34. There were, of course, notable exceptions to the generalization that most, if not all, immigrant members left the kibbutz. Donna Rosenthal reports that, as of 2003, half of the members of Kibbutz Ein Harod were immigrants from Iran, Iraq, Morocco, and Algeria (107).

35. The Likud was opposed to the European-styled socialism of the Histadrut (Federation of Labor, a national trade union) and related institutions, to which the kibbutz was loyal for good cause, receiving support from Mapai members and serving Mapai's interests. For its part, in the 1960s and 1970s, the Likud drew significant support from the new Jewish immigrants from the Arab world, who had no prior familiarity with socialism or leftist sentiments and who had good reason to resent the country's Ashkenazi leadership; indeed, their votes brought down the Labor government in 1977. In a process that combined shifting ideologies and demographics with Israel's emerging "bourgeoisie," the political ascendancy of the Likud was caused in part by its "nationalistic position, which defies the supposed divisiveness of the nation by class interests, and in part . . . by its petite bourgeoisie constituency, which comprised urban merchants, contractors, and entrepreneurs that abhorred the ostensible socialism of the ruling party" (Ram 49). For the kibbutz, this

meant a serious reversal, from which it has never recovered; with the fall from power of the socialist parties, the kibbutz movement lost the economic subsidies and resources that had always ensured its material well-being. In other words, as the political crisis coincided with economic woes and ethnic rage, the entire kibbutz system was engulfed in a "perfect storm" of sorts.

36. The left-of-center Labor Party was established in 1968 with the joining of three socialist parties: Mapai, Ahdut Avodah, and Labor Rafi.

37. The Likud's victory led to the undoing of the Histadrut, which had long protected the rights of workers, Jews and Arabs alike. Founded in 1920 and far more than a national trade union, the Histadrut played a vital role in building the State of Israel; indeed, it was widely understood as a "state within a state" and had essentially functioned as a government entity. The owner of numerous businesses and factories, the union was also the largest employer in Israel for many years; as late as 1983, more than one-third of all Israelis were still members. It oversaw a variety of health, welfare, and educational enterprises. Of these, the most popular was its national health insurance network of services (Kupat Holim), the program most responsible for its workers' unwavering loyalty. From its earliest days, the Histadrut served as an important source of loans that enabled the economic development of the kibbutzim; it developed a marketing co-op to sell their agricultural goods in the cities. The union also sponsored new kibbutzim and moshavim and created the Kibbutz Industries Association, which financed and structured as many as three hundred industrial enterprises in the kibbutzim.

38. All of Kenaz's ten novels and short story collections have been best sellers in Israel, and several of his works have been made into movies. Kenaz received notable literary awards, including the Alterman Prize (1991), the Agnon Prize (1993), and the Bialik Prize (1997). In 2007, *Infiltration* was voted one of the ten most important books since the creation of the State of Israel. A film adaptation was released to critical acclaim at the Jerusalem Film Festival 2010.

CHAPTER 4

The epigraph to this chapter is drawn from Ashkenazi, "100 Years On."

1. As Carole Kismaric and Marvin Heiferman note, "The golden age of detective fiction began with high-class amateur detectives sniffing out murderers lurking in rose gardens, down country lanes, and in picturesque villages" (56). In this regard, such "golden age" detective novels have long struck me as reenactments of the primal murder scene of Genesis, wherein the agrarian landscape is irreparably violated by fratricide until the divine utterance renders up the guilty Cain. Other ancient works that have been considered as possible antecedents include the story of Susanna and the Elders (Apocrypha: Susanna) and Sophocles's *Oedipus Rex*, wherein Oedipus struggles to discover the fate of his murdered father.

2. In this respect, Ohayon bears a family resemblance to P. D. James's poet-detective Adam Dalgliesh, who probes into hermetic English institutions such as publishing houses and monasteries.

3. In each of his cases, and in spite of promotions, Ohayon fears being "'out of his element,' . . . the alienation that caused the tension he felt every morning upon awakening, an acute, undefinable, unfocused anxiety, which also produced the insomnia characteristic of the periods when he was working on a particularly difficult case" (*Murder* 139–40). Confronted by the necessity of upsetting the cream of the Ashkenazi Zionist establishment, Ohayon's angst is often evident during the current case.

4. The introduction to many a kibbutz narrative functions like a camera lens, sharply capturing the orderly, harmonious elements that Karen Grumberg delineates: "They are usually verdant sites, with sprawling lawns, numerous trees, and modest white homes arranged in relation to a range of collective buildings like the dining hall and the clubhouse. Neat paths wind among the various structures. Farmland and agricultural spaces, such as chicken coops and stables, are arranged around or at the edge of the kibbutz" (*Place and Ideology* 33).

5. Such scenes from Gur's novel have a distinct verisimilitude and call to mind similar moments in Balaban's *Mourning a Father Lost*, which describes "harvest and vintage, bushel and scythe, furrow, first fruits and husbandry. The voices lifted in song at Passover, Pentecost, and Tu Bishvat reveled in the festive words, and the speakers set them like jewels in their speech. . . . Girls come up on the stage, which is edged with rolls of hay, to do the dance of the priestesses. Their white dresses glow against their wheat-colored suntan, their eyes are wide open, as though they're listening to a melody the rest of us can't hear. Blushing a little, aware of their beauty, they turn slowly, like sorceresses, their arms holding up invisible sheaves—they seem to be offering their youth to the four winds. The audience is sitting . . . on bundles of straw, amid festive decorations and slogans. The biblical verses ringing in the afternoon breeze turn the prickly straw into bricks of gold. If we're patient, we shall see Boaz and Ruth coming in from the field" (*Mourning* 38, 39). This evocative passage aptly sums up the bridge of decorous continuity forged by the kibbutz movement between biblical antiquity and the modern reclamation of the land by Jewish settlers.

6. My reading of such passages largely agrees with Dvir Abramovich's: "Gur delights in opening a window to the earthshaking changes that transformed kibbutz life, showing, for instance, how farming is now no more than a leisure pursuit in the kibbutzim. The kibbutz, we learn, relies on cosmetics manufactured in an industrial plant . . . rather than on the traditional working of the land. It is not without irony that the cacti used to mass-produce the cream that abolishes wrinkles [are] grown on land from which plum trees were uprooted, a symbolic marker of the decline of the Zionist agricultural ethos" (*Back to the Future* 224).

7. The caregivers of the younger children of the kibbutz are usually described as *metaplim* (singular, *metapelet*), Hebrew terms so familiar to the global communal movement that even some communes outside of Israel have adopted them.

8. To prevent the abuses of a bullying personality like Dvorka, Oz's prescription seems apt: "Any socialist system needs to aim at the flexibility, complexity, plurality, paradox and humor which are characteristic of human life, even at the expense of consistency" (*Under this Blazing Light* 137).

9. It is increasingly observed throughout the kibbutz movement that this imperative has been effectively revised to "From each according to his preferences, to each according to his needs."

10. Consider the plaint of poet and veteran member of Kibbutz Ein Harod Zerubavel Gilead (1912–1988) about the losses caused by affluence in the post-1950s kibbutzim: "The 'materialization' or 'bourgeoisization' of the kibbutzim has been another consequence of industrialization. The steep rise in the income of the kibbutzim with the most successful industries has led to a parallel rise in their standard of living. They can afford to give their members bigger houses, bitter furniture, air conditioners, TV sets, increased personal allowances, and private telephones (considered a great amenity), as well as higher education for those who want it, leave of absence for travel abroad, and other 'treats' that were inconceivable in the 1950s. This has resulted in a greater preoccupation with the material things of life, at the expense . . . of the spiritual, cultural, and ideological" (Gilead and Krook 276). Gilead penned the Palmach's anthem as well as numerous books of Hebrew poetry, short stories, and nonfiction studies.

11. Shlomo Avineri (whom Muravchik calls "Israel's foremost socialist thinker") similarly stresses that this transformation wreaked havoc with collective life, leading to the "privatizing of many things . . . an across-the-board reorganization of public and private space" (qtd. in Muravchik 331).

12. Once again, Gur's *Murder on a Kibbutz* successfully delineates a source of pervasive unease in actual kibbutzim. In her numerous conversations with former kibbutzniks, Naama Sabar often heard "complaints that . . . ideology was imparted, not in open discussion or through open persuasion but by preaching. . . . While their parents had chosen kibbutz life for ideological reasons, the next generation never had experienced the challenge of having to choose a life, but were born into the kibbutz reality." Sabar reports that "many spoke of the intense frustration they experienced at

having been deprived of the ability and the right to make their own decisions, either big or small. As they put it, they tried to make up for this deprivation by later establishing a family whose lifestyle was decided exclusively by the two spouses" (123, 128).

13. Interestingly, the suggestion that the kibbutzniks' first tentative step toward their often-permanent separation from the kibbutz and its way of thinking usually follows their first expansive encounter with the outside world is also supported by critical studies. See especially Sabar's *Kibbutzniks in the Diaspora*.

14. Of course, the emotional pain caused by the enforced communal child-rearing system was borne by parents as well. Kibbutz researcher Edna Perlman describes the plight of the typical kibbutz mother who was "unable to outwardly defy the norms of communal child rearing. . . . Her option was to leave kibbutz or accept them. She acknowledged the fact that staying on kibbutz meant compromising her maternal desires." In the terse words of one subject Perlman spoke to, "*Those who couldn't abide by the rules are not here today*" (102–3; emphasis in original).

15. Each story in *A Good Place for the Night* is set in a specific locale (Hiroshima, Munich, a postapocalyptic landscape), in which characters endure extreme forms of dislocation and loss. Throughout this thematically integrated collection, "there is a physical or emotional distance from home," where "'home' is merely a longing for our place of birth and the people we love." Institute for the Translation of Hebrew Literature. <http://www.ithl.org.il/page_14278>.

16. Liebrecht's entire oeuvre, especially as expressed in the thematically unified stories of *Tapuchim min hamidbar* (*Apples from the Desert*; 1986), represents an intense investigation into the ethics that genuine Holocaust consciousness demands, and which she finds deficient in Israeli society. For Dvir Abramovich, that is often expressed through intergenerational tension: "Liebrecht's stories tap the abrasive and anguished vein of relationships between Holocaust parents and their conflicted children and grandchildren. . . . Liebrecht limns the aftershocks that reverberate through the lives of the survivors' offspring as the memories of the Holocaust come to the fore. The basic method of Liebrecht's writing is to present the reader with two antithetical world views, two opposed aspects of the same inseparable reality. She peoples her diegesis with characters who are emotionally crippled from direct or indirect effects of the Holocaust and who are trying to repress or preserve memory. Typically, the horrific past that engages the characters is fully realized and dramatized in scenes where it is either revealed piecemeal, or less commonly, flares up in an uncontrolled outburst" ("Post-Holocaust Identity" 12).

CHAPTER 5

The epigraph to the section "Lavi Ben Gal's *Eight Twenty Eight*" is drawn from Ram 62.

1. In this regard, it is worth looking at the cautionary approaches taken to individualism and alienation in early kibbutz narratives, which suggest that, like other enclosed societies, the kibbutz afforded many opportunities for exclusion. As described by Iris Milner, "immediate triggers" typically included "the harsh struggle for survival in face of an extremely demanding reality, or more personal issues such as loneliness, envy, homesickness (for the home abandoned back in Europe), a frustrated desire for individual expression, love intrigues . . . or bitter disputes between a single member . . . and the entire commune. The personas involved many be central figures or marginal ones, veterans, or newcomers. In all cases alike, however, the options of joining in or staying on the outside, holding on or abandoning, being accepted or being rejected expose a constant collision between centrifugal and centripetal forces, drawing the protagonists into and out of the communal entity and what it stands for" (165–66).

2. Such reluctance was exemplified by Avital Geva of Kibbutz Ein Shemer, one of the memorable paratroopers of the 1967 War portrayed in Yossi Klein Halevi's *Like Dreamers*. Somehow Geva's kibbutz (and a number of others) had weathered the ideological storms of the previous

decade, but the Soviet Union's support for the Arab armies proved a step too far. Yet, even for Geva, who had lost cherished friends in the battle to liberate Jerusalem's Old City, the emotional momentum, lacking critical analysis, behind the new rift with the Soviet Union raised unsettling questions about the excesses of any communal conformity: "The ideological shift had happened too abruptly, without introspection. Avital was struggling to understand how a community of decent, even noble human beings had been so blind to evil and threat. They had behaved no differently from the religious fanatics they loved to despise. *Worse, comrades: we turned a mass murderer and anti-Semite into a saint!* They had walled themselves off from the rest of the nation, reading only the movement's newspaper and dismissing all criticism of their ideology as lies. Unless they tried to understand how they had gotten to that point, they could make a similar mistake again" (*Like Dreamers* 136–37; emphasis in original).

3. Joshua Muravchik describes the devastating impact of this period on the life of one kibbutz. Though the schism was "not about any practical matter, but over socialist theory and how to assess the Soviet Union," it "tore Ein Gev down the middle, and the impassioned disagreement proved intolerable within the intimate community of the kibbutz. Some 140 of the more pro-Soviet members of Ein Gev left and joined Ginosaur" (326), a more radical kibbutz. Kibbutz Givat Haim split in two, resulting in Givat Haim Meuchad and Givat Haim Ihud. Aside from continuing to share the lucrative Prigat factory (producer of fruit juice and canned goods), there was no other form of cooperation until the summer of 2012, when the kibbutzim decided to select a single community director. That is perhaps a hopeful sign, but many members still seem emotionally scarred from those years. Tamar Lang-Raz, a member of Givat Haim Ihud, admitted to a *Haaretz* reporter that "there are people here who say they can't stand the smell of anyone from the Meuchad kibbutz. Some are still carrying around the trauma. There was a huge fight here; families split apart and that left a deep mark" (qtd. in Ashkenazi, "Two Warring"). Another prominent example of the traumatic schism is that of Kibbutz Ein Harod, founded in 1921, which split into Ein Harod Ihud and Ein Harod Meuchad (site of the original) in the early 1950s. Their rivalry became so intense that they each built separate elaborate performance halls separated by only a few dozen yards "to demonstrate ideological superiority by means of architecture" (Dvir). Due to its prominent status and early history, Kibbutz Ein Harod has been the subject of numerous books and essays by kibbutz members and researchers.

4. Many have noted the anguished questioning of the period following the invasion and occupation of Lebanon in 1982. Sidra Dekoven Ezrahi tells how the "cracks in the armor" revealed in the Yom Kippur War of 1973 culminated in "the breakdown of the internal consensus over the role of the Israel Defense Forces and the justness of Israel's military posture in the world" (294). And Glenda Abramson argues that, "of all Israel's wars, the 1982 Lebanon War . . . aroused the bitterest reaction in Israel. It instigated an unprecedented political crisis in Israel that also severely damaged Israel-Diaspora relations," provoking demonstrations on the Left and counterdemonstrations on the Right. These developments were further intensified by Israeli writers' growing attention to the injustices that stoked the first Palestinian Intifada, ultimately inspiring a creative storm of vehement protest narratives by David Grossman, Yitzhak Laor, Nathan Zach, and many others (Abramson 221).

5. For the first time in history, the right-wing coalition led by the Likud won a majority in the Knesset, bringing a startling end to nearly thirty years of rule by centrist and left-leaning Labor governments. It is particularly jarring to recall that, as late as Yitzhak Rabin's first government (1974–1977), six of his ministers (a full quarter of his cabinet) were kibbutz or moshav members. It also bears recalling that five Labor Party Israeli prime ministers (David Ben-Gurion, Levi Eshkol, Golda Meir, Ehud Barak, and Shimon Peres) lived for significant periods on kibbutzim or were themselves members.

6. Similarly, Miri Talmon highlights *Noa*'s engagement with "the decline of collectivism and socialism as ideological and social norms. . . . Kibbutz society . . . began to be exposed as crum-

bling frameworks holding onto ideals that have lost their strength in Israeli society" (qtd. in Kedem 337).

7. As Ella Shohat observes: "The force of [*Noa at Seventeen*] lies in its capacity to present both individualist and collectivist polarities without caricature" (*Israeli Cinema* 210).

8. Yagoda later told me that, during his years there, he felt haunted by Lajun's ruins: "At nights I dreamed of the Arab residents coming back to their houses, to their fields, to their grave-yard" (pers. comm., 23 August 2013).

9. Yagoda said that the narrative of the kibbutzniks encompassed biblical history as well as the eschatological story of Armageddon but not the more recent past. Yet he insisted that he never blamed them for that omission: "I didn't judge or blame the Kibbutz members for that because I was familiar with this mechanism of suppression and erasure of the past from home. They, like my parents, were Holocaust survivors . . . and this was their pattern of not dealing with their past in order to be able to go on with their lives" (ibid.).

10. Ibid.

11. Lawrence Joffe notes the painful ironies embedded in the kibbutzim's relation to the displacement of the Palestinians. Although long assailed from the right, increasingly, "the leftist flagships have recently faced criticism from others on the left too. Anti-Zionists accuse them of playing a crucial role in the incremental pre-1948 dispossession of Palestinian peasantry, and of avarice and aggression in war." And: "Mapai kibbutzim accused Hashomer kibbutzim of acquiring Arab property and harvesting vacant Arab fields; a Mapai circular named Kibbutz Mishmar Haemek as the first to demand destruction of neighbouring Arab villages. [Benny] Morris quotes a despairing Hashomer director, Aharon Cohen, reflecting on Arab flight from Haifa in early May 1948: 'As a socialist I am ashamed and afraid; to win the war and lose the peace, the state, when it arises, will live on the sword.' But Yitzhak Ben-Aharon of Ahdut kibbutzim countered: increasing the number of Arab refugees 'also increases our security.' While Mapam political secretary Leib Levite said, 'War has a logic which must be carried through' and he 'justified and endorsed every conquest and every eviction of every Arab settlement necessitated by the war.'" Yet, in the end, Joffe eagerly stresses that "at least Mapam and the kibbutzniks debated the issue in mid-war; no other party did that."

12. Dvir Abramovich describes Osnat's ambition to propel the kibbutz into an era of "egalitar-ian elitism," which would place "a renewed emphasis on the individual [to] ensure the continued existence of the Kibbutz into the new millennium" (*Back to the Future* 219).

13. It is instructive to compare Sarah's comments about the kibbutz dining room with those of former kibbutz members interviewed by Dafna Arad. A female member explains to Arad with some ambivalence that "the dining room is a very fraught place. . . . It arouses many emotions, both positive and negative, and it isn't easy to enter it. There are others who are sad to see it closed, who miss it a lot, and for others it is quite a traumatic place. I was one of those . . . flooded with many memories of the holidays and the togetherness." Another offers her the more pointed obser-vation that "the kibbutzim in the worst shape are the ones where the dining hall isn't active. They are finished as a kibbutz. The people no longer get together, and everything that united them—the heart of the kibbutz—has stopped beating. Everyone shuts himself in to his own corner, and that's very sad. There is tremendous longing for the food, as a symbol for a community that used to exist and doesn't anymore. . . . At many kibbutzim, they insist on keeping the dining hall because they understand that, without it, it wouldn't be a kibbutz." Arad also cites the collective paean of Kibbutz Lohamei Hageta'ot, "Requiem for the Dining Hall," to commemorate the 1970 closure of the original structure after a new one was built: "Farewell to thee, dining hall! Farewell to thee, kitchen! Farewell to the bleach, the pots, the frying pans, the kerosene stoves, the dripping faucets, the fly tracks on the walls, the limping bread slicer, the big rats that will be miserable (until they find their way to the new dining hall). What, what, didn't we do here? Here we spoke in Yiddish at general meetings. Here we sang, until daybreak, songs of the Jewish Agency, songs of the illegal

immigration, songs of the Palmach and songs of 'comrades going' in pure Russian, not to mention the (few) Polish songs. Here we gathered when the bell rang."

14. There is a wryly humorous moment in Aliza Amir-Zohar's "Finally" where the aging protagonist distracts herself during a kibbutz meeting by gazing around the room at the decrepit countenances of her peers. Her gently deprecatory musings expose the pitiful impossibility of mortal humanity ever fully realizing the egalitarian dream: "So long as people are flesh and soul and blood and not flat cardboard characters with rigid joints, they cannot be equal. They may consume the same quantity of bread and clothes and shoes; one may allot them the same number of square meters for housing and the same number of vacation days, but they do not all gain an equal share of love, of happiness, of imagination, of pain. So how can they be equal? Of what use are socks and an armchair as opposed to Olga whose raven hair is now streaked with white, whose eyes are dimming, and who is shrinking before our eyes, a graying old spinster? So what! Can one take a bit from Cooper and give it to Olga? Or maybe from Serina, who has everything and nevertheless has very little, and whose face is tense and mouth bitter? No, from Serina one can take nothing to give to Olga" (135).

15. Thus an older woman named "Shoshana" declared to Asaf and Doron, "I'm not one of those people who dreams of a retirement in a café. . . . At heart, I am a working person" (86).

16. Paz claims that he only left the kibbutz because of his desire to attend film school (Hands).

17. Evoking yet another form of abandonment, a different character in *The Galilee Eskimos* remarks, "We left our parents and our children left us." Though in most Western societies, that is generally the norm, the case is quite different in Israel, where parents and children frequently live in close proximity and intergenerational Shabbat family gatherings are common. Hence Paz says that he sought "to emphasize . . . that Israeli tradition is different: children don't leave their parents for long. That's why the founder of the kibbutz [portrayed in *The Galilee Eskimos*] is in shock" (Hands).

18. Perhaps this trend is owed in part to the late-life reminiscences of the fading generation of those still capable of recalling the kibbutz's halcyon days. More than sixty years ago, Ruth Gefen-Dotan, a member of Kibbutz Ayelet Hashahar, wrote a biweekly journal for *Bamaaleh*, newspaper of the Histadrut's youth group, reflecting its burning idealism ("A kind of purity of that generation"). Today she is proud of the kibbutz legacy even as it falls apart: "We remain a few people with good hearts, and there is help and care." As is the case with most kibbutz veterans, nostalgia rarely colors her clear-eyed view of the past: "It was not paradise. My dreams were that there be ice cream and a toilet in the house. There was indescribable poverty. I do miss the people who died, and the language, the culture, the behavior. I don't miss that you couldn't tell the children fairy tales—Sleeping Beauty, for example—because it wasn't the socialist reality. I don't miss that you couldn't hug your children" (qtd. in Ashkenazi, "Kibbutznik 1948 Diary").

19. Shaul's judgment on the coldly utilitarian approach to the babies' nighttime needs is reinforced in a later troubling scene in which two children are put in charge of this task.

20. In this regard, it is worth mentioning the important dramatic role of music throughout *Sweet Mud*. Nostalgic accordion music frequently plays in the background, in ironic counterpoint to the diminished social reality, especially the commune's inhumane treatment of its most vulnerable members; a mournful Hebraic chorale is sung over the closing credits.

21. *Children of the Sun*'s publicity materials quote Kaniuk's and Oz's enthusiastic reviews: "Not only is *Children of the Sun* a brilliant and beautiful film, but a film that depicts the history of the beauty of shattered dreams" (Kaniuk); the film "depicts the early years of the Kibbutz movement with neither nostalgia nor slaughtering sacred cows, but with a keen eye, enthralling insight and unforgettable editing" (Oz). *Children of the Sun* ran for forty-five weeks in Tel Aviv, far longer than most commercial films.

22. Tal's birthplace, Kibbutz Beit Hashita, was founded in the eastern Jezreel Valley in 1928 by a cadre of pioneering youths that included his grandparents on both sides.

23. In his rather caustic assessment of the *Togetherness* exhibition, renowned Israeli historian Tom Segev criticized its pervasive tone of self-pity as well as its failure to engage with Israel's "true story": the exhibition artists' "story contains no Mizrahim—Jews of Middle Eastern descent—and no Arabs who tried to be accepted, but were rejected; the trauma of the Holocaust survivors in the kibbutzim is also nonexistent. . . . The elitist insularity, the hypocrisy, the exploitation and the waste—it's as though they never happened" ("Kibbutz Coup de Grace").

24. Twenty-one of the original fifty-six quilts exhibited in Israel were featured in the *A Century of the Kibbutz Art* exhibition by the Israel Quilters Association, which traveled to venues in Europe in 2011 and North America in 2013 (Ghert-Zand).

25. Pers. comm., 10 August 2013. Kaplan's quilt was awarded second place in this juried exhibition.

26. Critics seemed to unanimously agree that Tal's voice-over strategy was successful, the amateur archival films telling their own singular story without the need for interference.

27. Tal's reminiscing commentators are the miraculous New Hebrews arrogantly introduced to us by the impersonal collective narrator of Amos Oz's first kibbutz novel, *Elsewhere, Perhaps*: "Look at them. Aren't they a credit to us? Look how tall they are, the girls as well as the boys. They are all good-looking. Any exceptions there may simply prove the rule. . . . Their walk is agile, their movements are graceful and lithe. They have been brought up from early childhood to physical labor, saturated with sunshine and fresh air, toughened by long, arduous expeditions, exercised with sport and games. All of them are sun-tanned, most of them are fair-haired. Their hands are strong and well formed. The hubbub of voices radiates cheerfulness. Though some of them may suffer from an excess of poetic aspirations, they know how to keep them well under control" (35). Of course, the unforeseen cost of that repression, just hinted at in that last sentence, still haunts the old children who collectively narrate Ran Tal's film.

28. John Auerbach was born in Warsaw in 1922 and served as a soldier in the Polish army in the early days of the World War II. During the German occupation, he escaped from the Warsaw Ghetto but was later sent to the Stutthof concentration camp. After the war, he smuggled refugees to Israel until captured by the British, who detained him in a Cyprus camp for two years. Following his release he joined Kibbutz Sdot Yam. Auerbach's son was killed in the 1973 War. He wrote and published twelve books of short stories and novellas, including the short story "The Owl," which was awarded First Prize in the PEN/UNESCO Awards of 1993. He died in 2002.

29. Though the treatment of grave sites could sometimes vary by community, the normative kibbutz cemetery, as explained by Yoram Bar-Gal, was the product of "never-ending debate and discussion over decades, the kibbutz world drew up rules, regulations and technical prescriptions. . . . With reference to burial . . . kibbutzim preserve egalitarianism meticulously: tombstones are uniform and inscriptions completely regular" (77). Yet even here, as Bar-Gal speculates, the far-reaching effects of privatization may even transform this hallowed site of egalitarianism: "What will happen in the cemeteries and at personal commemoration sites in the kibbutz when they, too, carry a price tag as in capitalist societies? There will be a bill for a burial plot, a charge for a headstone, a fee for a page in the memorial book . . . a price to maintain a file in the kibbutz archive, an outlay for a funeral, and more. Is it to be expected that the future landscape of the kibbutz cemetery will appear more capitalist, less representative of the founding fathers and the collective myth and of the original vision in all its purity?" (83).

30. See note 13 to chapter 2. Indeed, it seems a tragic sign of the urgent timeliness of the Israeli-born Feldman's reflections on the powerful work that metaphors do in the Jewish state's militarized society, that, as I reread Auerbach's haunting "Report," a controversy raged in Israel over a female combat soldier's supposed "cowardice" in seeking shelter rather than charging a terrorist unit on the Egyptian border. Complicating that debate, the older sister of a male combat soldier wrote an open letter to the woman commending her behavior, in terms directly evoking the Akedah: "My little brother is also a combat soldier. . . . To him I say: If you ever find yourself

in a situation in which terrorists are shooting at you and there is no backup—there is only one thing your family wants you to do, and you know what that is. To us, you will be a hero. Israelis tend to sanctify death more than they do life, but the fact of the matter is that cowards stay alive. So, I say to my brother, remain a coward forever. . . . Those accolades on the altar of death are not for you. Leave them for others. Let them be remembered as heroes while you start a family. So you won't be called a hero . . . but you will be alive! . . . I am not asking that other people fight your battles for you. I simply ask that the . . . words 'at any cost' not prevent you from protecting yourself and that the title 'hero' won't blur your senses" (qtd. in Katzir).

31. That duality, Feldman reiterates throughout *Glory and Agony*, undoubtedly is owed in part to the fact that ancient Hebrew makes no distinction between "sacrifice" and "victim."

32. An allusion to the Jewish trustees of the Nazi concentration camp, notorious for their harsh treatment of their fellow inmates.

33. While gathering archival materials for his memoir, Balaban came across a kibbutz newsletter from 1941 setting forth the basic rules for the children's houses, the first rule setting the tone for those to follow: "Parents do not enter the children's houses, even if they hear their child crying and screaming" (*Mourning* 144).

34. Perlman reports that Anna "objected to raising children in the children's home . . . and had a difficult time reconciling herself to the demands of kibbutz life. She said that it was especially difficult for her to take leave of the children at night and turn them over at bedtime to the metapelet at the children's home. She also said that it was even more disturbing to her that while she was working as a metapelet, putting to bed other children, a different . . . metapelet was putting her own children to bed. She admits that she feels guilty for having left the children in the children's home at nights. In Anna's words: 'I remember that we had to take our children back to the children's home at a quarter to eight every night even if your child slept the whole afternoon and you had no time to spend with him. . . . If we wouldn't cooperate, then the kibbutz movement might collapse. They had to maintain very strict rules. There were very few who didn't abide by the rules and brought their children over at eight. And they were reprimanded'" (110). Anna's kibbutz was one of the last kibbutzim to abandon their commitment to communal child rearing.

35. This last point might come as a surprise for those who assumed that close proximity between the genders meant casual sex. Another commentator in *Children of the Sun* explains that, though "we had all the opportunities to realize all our fantasies, we were too closed emotionally, we weren't open at all." Moreover, sexual relations within such a tight-knit group would in essence have been akin to "incest," still another concludes.

36. This point about togetherness and the dissolution of the self in *Children of the Sun* was driven home for me in Balaban's memoir, precisely because it is such a ruthlessly unsentimental narrative: "You remember the singing and dancing in the dining hall at festivals and weddings?" he asks his sister. "Since leaving, I've danced at a number of parties, and I always felt it was a feeble imitation of the real thing. . . . There was a valuable quality about it, a feeling that we were special and wonderful, maybe not each one individually, but all of us together . . . when we were singing and dancing we were first of all Israelis, first of all kibbutz children, and this togetherness was wonderful. . . . I'd give anything to experience that unity one more time. . . . I often weep in . . . dreams, from sheer longing" (*Mourning* 42).

37. *Children of the Sun* ultimately documents the shift that took place incrementally in the kibbutzim as, one by one, the children's houses were closed and the children brought back to stay in their family homes. The practical difficulty and expense of expanding the family homes seems to have been the only practical obstacle that prevented a more rapid transformation.

38. There is nothing sadder than a kibbutz that has lost its people, as Balaban's memoir makes abundantly clear: in contrast to years past when the kibbutz was "busy as a beehive," filled with young people and activities such as a choir, educational courses, and sports, he finds "a desert. It's years since a baby was born here" (*Mourning* 79).

39. In Edna Perlman's illuminating theoretical discussion of the memorialization work of kibbutz photo albums (which she treats as a narrative genre), she describes how, in the albums, "the same signs are read differently by the same kibbutz members over different periods of time, in which kibbutz society went through structural transformations in its lifestyle and ideology. Contemporary kibbutz society has found itself in a state of change; the ideological and institutional order has lost its grip, creating a platform for kibbutz members to release hidden meanings that previously did not correlate with kibbutz ideology and social trends" (101). Thus, as the coherence of old value systems atrophies, there is more room for individual dissonance and the past itself gains greater complexity. The question Perlman investigated in relation to a family that lived on a kibbutz in the Negev was the extent to which their private photo album "reflected a personal representation of their individual and emotional reality . . . and to what extent . . . the album [was] marked by the public collective, socialist visual" norms (100). Her study also drew on interviews with families who had raised children on kibbutzim belonging to the Hashomer Hatzair Movement (the most intensely ideological of all the kibbutz movements) between 1948 and 1967, a period that was relatively stable in terms of the kibbutz value system.

40. As a social phenomenon, Tal's *Children of the Sun* subsequently provoked the musings of a surprising number of writers and artists, many of whom rhapsodized over the quality of their own childhoods while empathizing with others'. Looking back on his early kibbutz years, novelist and film producer Yossi Uzrad remarked, "As far as I was concerned, that was the way of the world. Not for a moment did I have doubts about whether it was good or not. For me it was excellent. I know now that for others who were with me in the same room, it was an awful nightmare. I had a marvelous childhood experience. I don't feel a drop of bitterness about the kibbutz. Only compassion for those people and a great deal of appreciation, because there really was a genuine desire to change the world, to do something good, a hard-core ideology—which no longer exists." Yet immediately after expressing a sense of nostalgic regard, Uzrad hastened to add that as a seventeen-year-old looking critically at his own society, he could already perceive that the same sunny world of routine and obligation that worked well for many could prove stifling for more creative or intellectually restless individuals: "There is no doubt that a kibbutz member who got up in the morning and went to work, then ate a breakfast of salad and dark and light bread, and afterward went back to work and didn't have many doubts, had a really lovely life, but—and I say this with discomfort—those people did not stand out for their wisdom and intelligence. They saw the world as it was and accepted it, and so did not get bogged down in fundamental questions. Life as such was pleasant and good. . . . It was precisely people who were not brilliant who fit well into the kibbutz movement" (Shani). Yet, as is so often the case in the epic story of the kibbutz, we can always count on hearing a vociferous and equally persuasive "second opinion." Here is one from Alfy Nathan, a founder of Kibbutz Kfar Hanassi in his 2010 memoir, *Alfy: An Incredible Life Journey*: "Despite the fact that much of the work we were doing was physical, many of our members were cultured, well-read, and intellectually curious. You could find them reading and engaging in spirited discussions about a whole range of topics. We had an active choir and our most literate members published an interesting newsletter. Had they not decided to go to Israel and join the kibbutz, many of our members would have become scientists, engineers, artists, and teachers. They chose kibbutz because they wanted to build up the country. They were willing to sacrifice. It shows you the tremendous allure of idealism" (146).

41. Dafna Arad relates the rise and fall of this essential collective space in moving detail: "The dining hall nourished the collective with socialist ideology and chicken soup. It was planned as a building that would express the spirit of the kibbutz and was situated at the center of public life. In addition to being a place for eating and food preparation, it also served a variety of other functions: the place for celebrating holidays and greeting the Sabbath; the place where people quarreled and reconciled, caught up on the news and whispered gossip. Today, the abandoned

dining halls, the cash registers and caterers, the cooking and eating in private kitchens and dining nooks, are clear markers of the change that has taken place." And Jonathan Cummings notes, "The first permanent building in a new settlement, the dining room often dwarfed the modest members' housing and the wide lawns that encircled them. . . . The architecture of the dining room was a statement, a monument to the communal, modern and secular values of the kibbutz movement. It played multiple roles in the life of the community. Without any means of cooking at home, there was no alternative to eating together. It was also the arena in which communal dramas were played out. In the great Mapai-Mapam schism of the early 1950s over the extent of Israel's pro-Soviet orientation, which eventually resulted in several [kibbutzim] physically splitting into two, rival groups ate in roped-off areas for fear of ideological contamination. . . . Sadly, now, as the kibbutz morphs in a new Israel, the huge buildings stand largely silent."

42. This last image of Gal's *Eight Twenty Eight* is quietly damning and one of the most revealing in the recent Israeli cinema. As most readers will recognize, even though Israel, like much of the world, now relies on the labor of foreign migrants for agriculture, construction, and even home care for aging parents, the Zionist founders were so hostile to Jewish dependence on anybody but themselves that they called such dependence *avoda zara*, a phrase borrowed from the Hebrew Bible, where it refers to idolatry among the Israelites. Thus, in judging the earlier generation of First Aliya immigrants, David Ben-Gurion decried their employment of Arabs as a modern heresy, which carried "the idol of exile to the temple of national rebirth" (qtd. in Yadid). "A supreme—almost divine—importance was placed on socio-economic self-sufficiency as the key to achieving independence," Judd Yadid tells us in his etymology of the phrase, "with Ben-Gurion saying that 'if we do not do all kinds of work, easy and hard, skilled and unskilled, if we become merely landlords, then this will not be our homeland.' . . . Labor was billed as transformative, and the New Yishuv's leaders were adamant that Jews again do the hard work, the dirty work, and the dangerous work. Not only would they be doctors and lawyers and usurers, but builders and farmers and guardsman—laying roads, draining swamps, and building towers and stockades." Because *avoda zara* was directly antithetical to the Zionist project of reclamation, one cannot imagine a more discordant, though honest, conclusion to Gal's film. In place of *avoda zara*, an antithetical new paradigm was advanced—*avoda ivrit* ("Hebrew labor"). Whereas *avoda zara* was cast as polluting, *avoda ivrit* was lionized as liberating.

43. Lawrence Joffe lists the most prominent of Degania Alef's illustrious progeny: "Five years after its foundation, in May 1915, the community celebrated the birth of the world's first native-born kibbutznik, one Moshe Dayan. Thousands of other sons and daughters of the movement followed, including Ehud Barak, Amos Oz, Shimon Peres (who later founded Kibbutz Alumot), Arthur Koestler, the painter Avigdor Arikha, and the outstanding Hebrew poet Rachel, who lived and is buried at Degania."

44. Studies have shown the falling rate of productivity of the kibbutzim in spite of the new ideological model of "efficiency" demanded by the managerial elite above all else. "The introduction of the differential wage system has been accompanied by the rise of the ideology of efficiency," Uri Zilbersheid explains. "Productive activity has ceased to be perceived and shaped, at least partially, as a kind of self-fulfillment bearing a creative character. Efficiency is now demanded from every single member. . . . Branches of the economy that were maintained because of the satisfaction they offered to the members working in them have been scrapped in all the differential kibbutzim, unless they could prove plausible profitability. The partial abolition of the division of labor has been scrapped as contradicting the principle of efficiency. Members are not supposed to change branches in order to increase their satisfaction from work and their feeling of self-fulfillment. Efficiency, and its concomitant concept of profitability, is the sole criterion dominating production in the differential kibbutzim. Amazingly, and undoubtedly [instructively],

the rate of labor productivity of kibbutz industry as a whole has been deteriorating since the early 1990s and has permanently been below that of Israeli industry. Instrumental productive activity and its criterion, efficiency, are not a guarantee of higher productivity. Suppression of creativity may negatively affect productivity."

45. Art scholar Karen Rosenberg was struck by how the laborers in Hirsch's art videos "communicate urgency and dedication, but the larger purpose of their actions is . . . unclear."

46. In yet another critical take on the cumulative impact of Hirsch's artistry, Kris Scheilfele finds that Hirsch "makes everyone pull together both literally (on ropes) and metaphorically (as a support system), but the actions are so stiffly stylized and methodically choreographed that aspersions are cast on the ties that connect but also bind."

47. A few critics have singled out *50 Blue* as the most emotionally resonant of Hirsch's poetically sorrowful series. Indeed, the video's image of figures in yellow sou'westers arduously lifting a handicapped man to the serenity of an extraordinary natural vista of sea and sky has a mysterious, even breathtaking power. *50 Blue* was acquired by the Israel Museum for its permanent collection in 2013 and was on display at the time of this writing.

48. "Tochka," originally a Russian term for a geological or military point on a map, was adopted as the name of a Soviet Hashomer Hatzair Youth Movement kibbutz founded in 1925. In 1939, the kibbutz was renamed "Afikim" (Hebrew for "riverbeds") by the founders. During the 1948 War, Kibbutz Afikim was subject to heavy shelling by the Syrian and Iraqi armies.

49. Of course, Hirsch was not the first visual kibbutz artist to critique the foundering values of the kibbutz. In the 1970s, former paratrooper and disaffected kibbutz artist Avital Geva mounted a conceptual exhibit featuring a shelf of moldy and worm-infested books encased in cement in the plaza of the Tel Aviv Museum of Art. As Yossi Klein Halevi recounts it, by the time Gush Emunim's early settlement victories in the occupied territories first began to overtake kibbutz socialism, Geva had grown "obsessed with decay. In one exhibit he displayed bones and false teeth; in another, a plastic pond filled with fedoras and dead fish preserved in salt. How else to describe what was happening in the country? Leading members of the Labor Party were being accused of bribery and embezzlement. The kibbutz movement, once Israel's moral conscience, was paralyzed by inertia. The Zionist revolution was founded on Jewish labor; but now Arabs were working the fields and building the houses" (308).

50. The filmmaker's father, Yoel, recounts how Hirsch relied on a collective and cooperative ethos for the successful fruition of his artistic vision: "He asked us to gather 200 people to take part in the film. He came from New York, gave talks at kibbutzim and handed out flyers, but only a few responded. . . . My wife managed to convince 200 older folks to be in it, including some in their seventies and eighties, and one fellow who was 90. It was hot and somebody had to organize a rest tent with refreshments, so I was also the cook. Everything is based on communal connection and goodwill" (qtd. in Karpel).

51. As Hirsch himself says, in summing up his kibbutz tetralogy, "My process is not limited solely to the finished work. I am fascinated first and foremost by the social and communal endeavor itself" (pers. comm., 30 July 2012).

52. What has happened to the kibbutzim corresponds to sweeping global transformations. Indeed, Zilbersheid tells us, "the dystopian transformation" of the kibbutzim "occurr[ed] in a period characterized, in both Israel and the world, by the rise of economic and political neoliberalism and the concomitant destruction of the welfare state. In Israel itself, the economic crisis caused by neoliberalism and 'cured' by the government along a neoliberal line, which directly affected the kibbutzim, exacerbated the economic situation with which the kibbutzim had to cope in the mid-1980s and have had to deal with since. Those groups in the kibbutzim, mainly at managerial level, and the 'masses' misled by them who have supported the radical changes, have transformed two-thirds of the kibbutzim into a bad society."

AFTERWORD

The epigraphs to this afterword are drawn from Oz, *Elsewhere, Perhaps* 80, and Halevi 431.

1. As Amos Oz reports, back during his years at Kibbutz Hulda, "every several months, a group of volunteers . . . arrives at my kibbutz. Among them are Jews and non-Jews, almost all of them very young, from the campuses, with revolutionary ideas, all of them seeking absolute universal justice, without compromises, immediately" (*Until Daybreak* 7).

2. Here are demographic statistics taken from the national census in the early decades of the state: in 1948, there were 46,940 people residing in 177 kibbutzim, or 6.5 percent of Israel's Jewish population; in 1960, 67,500 residents in 214 kibbutzim, or 5.6 percent of the Israel's Jewish population. This proportion declined to 4.5 percent during the 1960s and 1970s and to a mere 1.8 percent by 2010.

3. What Ram says about the tensions between messianic fundamentalism and liberal cosmopolitanism within present-day Israel can, of course, be usefully applied to understanding the anxieties and uncertainties reverberating with greater violence in the surrounding region in the troubling aftermath of the Arab Spring. From my own perspective, however, Ram overlooks an additional tension that represents no less a monumental contrast, namely, that between American-styled individualist capitalism and the socialist ethos that once was responsible for the state's development as well as for the coherence of society. In most other respects, especially the vantage point afforded by socioeconomics, his argument about this process is invaluable. Ram considers the most recent phase of Israeli national development, "postindustrialization," as "a transition from labor-intensive material industries to knowledge-intensive informational industries and the expansion of services" (30). Like everything else in Israel, economic transformation has been remarkable for its sheer intensity and pace, exceeding other societies in its compression of technological process. Ram observes that "in fewer than five decades, Israel had experienced in condensation the full path of modern industrialization of the past two centuries, from the mechanical and textile revolution in the first third of the nineteenth century, mostly in England, through the chemical and electrical centered in Germany and the United States in the late nineteenth century, to the electronic and then digital revolution that developed initially in the United States and spread to western Europe, Japan, and Southeast Asia in the second half of the twentieth century and at an intensified pace since the 1990s" (32–33). This final dramatic transformation was accompanied by a political earthquake, a sort of "bourgeois" revolution that Ram says was "all the more palpable on the background of the quasi-socialist and collectivist history of this society, in which Labour had been the 'natural' party of governance ever since the times of agricultural communes in the 1920s and up to the times of the military-industrial state conglomerate of the 1970s" (44).

4. Though the kibbutzim once played a critical role in the absorption of immigrants, this role rapidly declined, so that by the 1950s, they were absorbing only 3.6 percent of Israel's new immigrants each year (Ben-Rafael 134). Their role in sheltering and settling thousands of immigrants cannot be exaggerated, however. One popular estimate of those channeled through Kibbutz Kfar Giladi alone suggests that, between 1922 and 1948, as many as 10,000 immigrants were sheltered, including many children who were put up in chicken coops and cowsheds. Between 1945 and 1948, this kibbutz brought 1,300 children out of Syria in an operation known as "Mivtzah Ha'elef" ("Operation Thousand").

Among the best works on the decline of the kibbutz are Eliezer Ben-Rafael, *Crisis and Transformation: The Kibbutz at Century's End* (1997); Michal Palgi and Shulamit Reinharz, eds., *One Hundred Years of Kibbutz Life: A Century of Crises and Reinvention* (2011); and Raymond Russell, Robert Hanneman, and Shlomo Getz, *The Renewal of the Kibbutz: From Reform to Transformation* (2013).

5. Uri Zilbersheid explains the tremendous impact of the differential wage system that has played such an important role in the privatization process: "The new course began in the mid-1990s

and has since then been introduced in many kibbutzim, mostly in the 21st century. The introduction of the new system is defined as the establishment of a direct connection between labor, or economic contribution, and remuneration. Typically enough, the place of the kibbutz member in the economic hierarchy, that is, the office held by him, has become the main, and practically the sole, factor determining the salary level." Thus, Zilbersheid concludes, the differential salary (which has benefited mostly the top-salaried members) must be considered "as a dystopian moment in the New Kibbutz—the deliberate building, by a leading group, of a bad society by a sophisticated distortion of the essence of common ownership."

6. Sosis and Ruffle also compared the secular and religious varieties of traditional collective kibbutzim and determined that the individual "members of religious kibbutzim are more cooperative than their secular counterparts" (89).

7. In pursuing their study of the fate of ideology in the contemporary kibbutz, Sosis and Ruffle were stirred to respond to what they perceived as an obvious gap in anthropological and economic scholarship (their respective fields): "Throughout human history ideological commitment has served as a powerful catalyst for human behavior. Indeed, modern human history devoid of nationalism, communism, Nazism, feminism, Islam and Christianity, among many others, would be almost unrecognizable. Large-scale cooperation among unrelated individuals, which many consider a hallmark of humanity, generally follows from ideological motivations. Nevertheless, modern evolutionary scholars have largely ignored the relationship between ideological commitment and building cooperation" (113).

8. As sociologist Eliezer Ben-Rafael asserts of this later phase: "The kibbutz . . . sees itself as a privileged part of society, and does not easily accept an underprivileged condition, even when it is dictated by the exigencies of the enterprise"; he blames the unresolved "competition between the private and the collective" for the tremendous debts it accumulated (124, 128).

9. Jo-Ann Mort and Gary Brenner also ignore the profound impact that kibbutz values had on the structures of the surrounding society—the essentially symbiotic relation that endured for decades. Zilbersheid points out that "the kibbutzim, playing a leading role in the Israeli labor movement, which was the major political force in Israel until the late 1970s, were also very active in establishing and furthering the system of the welfare state in Israel, thus creating a supportive socioeconomic environment that helped them exist and flourish. The welfare state did not function in this regard as an interim stage in which new humans would develop, as Marx and Herzl envisaged, but rather as a system that substantially reduced the pressure of capitalism, thus helping the people in the kibbutzim, a small minority in Israeli society, to live as new human beings. The partially planned economy, which included subsidies for agriculture, enabled the kibbutzim to be viable and—mostly–successful economic units, thus making the choice to live in a kibbutz, i.e. in an existing utopia, an easier matter. The partial destruction of the Israeli welfare state that has taken place since the 1980s has created a much less favorable environment for the kibbutzim."

10. The term "privatization" entered wide usage in Israel during the 1980s. Not merely understood as an economic policy, privatization was a societal paradigm shift that sought to undo the welfare and other socialist policies of the state as well as class-oriented social and political movements and institutions (Ram 46).

11. Notwithstanding Mort and Brenner's affecting title, their study lacks heart. Though it ably presents data and statistics, it generally evades questions about enduring values or the ultimate relevance of the kibbutz to the increasingly troubled state of Israel. And in that regard, it's not clear why the authors undertook their study to begin with. Neither of them was raised on a kibbutz and only one of them has even lived on a kibbutz for a significant period. The practice of outsiders attempting to write book-length studies about the intricacies of kibbutz life dates back at least as far as Bruno Bettelheim's *Children of the Dream*, notorious for its author's drawing its data and sociological insights exclusively from a three-week visit to Ramat Yochanon. In that respect, I should emphasize that, aside from participating for thirteen years in the growth of a very

young kibbutz, Yahel, I lived for various periods at several of Israel's most veteran settlements, including Bet Zera, Kfar Blum, Kfar Hamaccabi, and Yotvata and still have close ties with active members of these kibbutzim, a number of whom agreed to be interviewed for this study.

12. The speaker here is Rafi Ashkenazi, a member of Kibbutz Gan Shmuel and one of its leaders, alluding to the economic and ideological crisis his community struggled with in 2000.

13. Ronen Manor is representative of many kibbutz critics of hafrata who have lately argued that the privatized kibbutz no longer deserves to be called a kibbutz "because there is no equality among members—not in their revenues, not in their consumption, nor in their production. Kibbutzim pay differential wages, and in their search for cheap labor they prefer to employ outsiders and not kibbutz members, meaning that even the value of self-employment is disregarded. Furthermore, due to the drastic cutbacks in community services, not much remains of the mutual guarantee principle, and members increasingly need to rely on themselves (49).

14. Whether it should be interpreted as a further diminishment of the kibbutz, the deterioration of Israel's political climate, or both, it bears noting that 2013 saw the first Israeli Knesset in history with only a single representative of the kibbutz movement, Zvulun Kalfa, from the far-Right Habayit Hayehudi (for decades, most Knesset members from the kibbutzim were identified with the Left). As a grim Yossi Sarid tersely observed, "The kibbutzim are out and the settlements are in." That development stands in stark contrast to the years when the Zionist enterprise was inconceivable without the leadership and values of the kibbutzim. Twenty-six kibbutz members served in the first Knesset, far surpassing their percentage of the population, and, over the years, many kibbutz members sat on cabinets that were formed by successive governments (Sarid). On the eve of those elections, Gideon Gazit of Kibbutz Tel-Katzir, once politically active as an organizer in the Labor Party, spoke disconsolately: "We won't have any Knesset members and aren't represented in the government. We've done our part, we settled along the borders and defended them, and now we're no longer needed" (qtd. in Ashkenazi, "Kibbutzim No Longer Bitten").

15. In a similar vein, another kibbutz sociologist, Ephraim Yuchtman-Yaar, insists that the participation of a kibbutz in national life is intrinsic to its existence: "Political involvement in the society is an organic aspect of kibbutz identity, just like equality or sharing. The question is not: 'For what purpose are we involved?' but 'How should we be involved?' This is the concept of shlichut, that is, mission" (qtd. in Ben-Rafael 138–39).

16. Consider the indifference of the recent wave of Russian immigrants, whose antipathy to all vestiges of socialism is substantial. Aside from being "the least Jewishly aware immigrants in Israel's history," Donna Rosenthal points out that, "unlike earlier Russians who came to 'build and to be rebuilt' in a parched land, who greeted each other as comrade or . . . sang the 'Internationale' and put on May Day workers' celebrations, most Russian-speaking newcomers are keen capitalists who detest socialism. When offered housing on kibbutzim, few accept. A kibbutz reminds them of a kolkhoz, the failed Soviet experiment in collective farming. These consumers crave condos in Haifa or Tel Aviv. Flights back to Kiev and Moscow are filled with briefcase-wielding Israeli Russians on the hunt for lucrative business deals" (134).

17. Drory invokes the 1956 Sinai Campaign, in which half of all the air force's fighter pilots came from the kibbutzim, as a representative example. He further cites an important study conducted by the psychologist Yehuda Amir ("Kibbutz Youth and the IDF") in 1966: "The research engaged with the questions: what were the basic data that kibbutz youth brought to the IDF on conscription, and were kibbutz youth indeed better soldiers than others. The research population encompassed all the young men who enlisted between 1961 and 1964. The results showed clearly that kibbutz youth in the IDF outstripped other segments of the population at that period—in intelligence levels, education, knowledge of Hebrew, and adaptive ability. Kibbutz youth tended to serve in the combat-volunteer units more than their counterparts did" (Drory 175, 176).

18. Ram cites statistics indicating that, whereas, in previous decades, kibbutz conscripts composed roughly 50 percent of pilot trainees, by 1997, they numbered only two individuals (88).

19. A soldier quoted in Bronner's report, which ran on the front page of the *New York Times*, remarked that, during the campaign, "the rabbinate brought in a lot of booklets and articles and their message was very clear: We are the Jewish people, we came to this land by a miracle, God brought us back to this land and now we need to fight to expel the non-Jews who are interfering with our conquest of this holy land. This was the main message, and the whole sense many soldiers had in this operation was of a religious war." Throughout the first forty years of the young Jewish state's existence, the army was dominated by kibbutz members who were well educated, secular, and liberal. In the past ten or fifteen years religious nationalists, many drawn from the settler movement, have rapidly ascended the top ranks of military authority. Though no army as active as Israel's could ever claim an entirely unblemished record, there is strong evidence that the replacement of the secular humanist youths of the kibbutzim by the graduates of religious seminaries subjected to right-wing ideology has led to greater dehumanization of (and violence toward) Palestinians in recent years as well as to what many have described as an increasing coarsening of Israeli society as a whole.

20. Elsewhere in *Under This Blazing Light*, Oz, writing then as a member of Kibbutz Hulda, reports that "I look around and I see a social system that, for all its disadvantages, is the least bad, the least unkind, that I have seen anywhere" (128), noting his Jerusalem urbanite upbringing and extensive travel. But Oz's work, based on adherence to the very principles that have fallen by the wayside, now makes for painfully ironic reading. "The kibbutz is the only attempt in modern times to separate labour from material reward" (128) is now a woefully anachronistic statement wherever privatization has supplanted the traditional collective model.

21. My interest in exploring this unlikely affinity was further sustained one day by a stimulating conversation with filmmaker Toby Freilich (*Inventing Our Life: The Kibbutz Experiment*) over lunch in a sun-drenched café in the German Colony of Jerusalem in June 2011. Her striking comparison of the challenges faced by contemporary kibbutzim and the Bedouin of Israel's Negev immediately confirmed my sense that, when one compares the radical upheavals faced by each, it is easy enough to grasp their common ground. Both, after all, are "traditional" communities, minorities engulfed by an impatient and largely indifferent society, facing unprecedented pressures under capitalism and privatization (pers. comm., 16 July 2010).

22. Most poignantly, Lavie observes that, "for the Mzeina, their identity as Bedouin is what is at stake, and it may indeed never have existed as they yearn for it to be. . . . [They] draw their idealized identity from the image of the nomad, all the while being forced to subsist on wage-labor" (319, 320). And this related issue of an irrecoverable idealization may be equally applicable to the communal enterprise, in spite of the pervasive nostalgia in certain circles for what has ostensibly been lost. Whenever I visit kibbutzim, I am interested in gauging the way that the "native informants" who host me and share their candid understanding of their lives and society invariably present self-narratives that rationalize and gloss over the outcomes of difficult choices. In some ways, what I encounter sometimes seems to entail a certain form of forgetting.

23. It is also important to keep in mind, as Ben-Rafael and Topel remind us, how far this continuum of kibbutz norms and values has really shifted. What would have been perceived as less virtuous in the 1950s and 1960s, or "very liberal," is today regarded as "classical," whereas the mitkhadesh model "would not have qualified as 'kibbutz' at all" (257).

24. In this respect, the members of shitufi kibbutzim seem roughly analogous to the overwhelming majority of Jewish Americans, who, as many scholars have noted, share a tendency to vote against their economic self-interest in supporting the Democrats, whereas others with similar class backgrounds and economic situations repeatedly vote for the Republicans.

25. A report issued on 14 May 2013 by the Organization for Economic Cooperation and Development indicated that Israel is the most impoverished of the thirty-four economically developed countries, with a poverty rate of 20.9 percent. As of this writing, Israel remains one of the countries

with the largest income inequalities, ranking fifth. <http://www.oecd.org/els/soc/OECD2013 -Inequality-and-Poverty-8p.pdf>.

26. Kibbutz Afikim seems to reflect a growing trend that marks the reversal of decades of declining communities in the wake of bankruptcies and privatization, and the total population of all kibbutzim has reached one hundred forty-three thousand. That is in fact the highest in the movement's 102-year history, according to figures kept by the United Kibbutz Movement. These statistics are published by the Central Bureau of Statistics (C.B.S.) of the State of Israel.

27. It is important to stress that the kibbutz continues to be a site of exciting innovation and productivity on a number of fronts. Ori Zisling, a kibbutz dairy farmer at Ein Harod, reported to Donna Rosenthal that "our dairy cows are world champions in milk production." Rosenthal goes on to note that "five of his sons have worked in the dairy; one, an engineer, is developing milking robots. . . . Israeli chickens produce more eggs than anywhere in the world. . . . Israeli cotton farmers hold the world record for most cotton produced per acre. The kibbutz's electronically controlled fish ponds produce enormous amounts of carp, bass, and St. Peter's fish. . . . Kibbutzniks use computerized drip irrigation/fertilization systems that make optimal use of scarce water. Innovative Israeli agricultural techniques are used all over the world. Experts in plant genetics are breeding new fruits and vegetables that thrive on brackish water. Kibbutzim [still] produce half of Israel's agriculture, although most of their income no longer comes from toiling the land" (105).

28. Kibbutz Ketura, Kibbutz Lotan—"Tend organic vegetables and fertilize your mind," says Lonely Planet (73) of Lotan's innovative ecovillage—Kibbutz Neot Smadar, and Kibbutz Samar, all located in the Arava Desert, as is Kibbutz Yahel, where I lived between 1978 and 1988, have each embraced organic and other ecological-minded practices. In 2012, Yahel became the first solar-powered kibbutz, and no doubt other Arava kibbutzim will soon follow. In addition, Russell, Hanneman, and Getz identify Kibbutz Nir Oz, Kibbutz Sasa, and Kibbutz Sde Eliyahu as having "taken up the cause of environmental protection" (115–16).

29. The Galil School, located at Kibbutz Eshbal, strives to maintain equal numbers of Arab and Jewish students; each class has two teachers, one Arab and one Jewish, and the school is directed by two co-principals, Arab and Jewish.

30. When Anne Heyman (1962–2014), a pioneering Jewish philanthropist born in South Africa, established a youth village for victims of the Rwanda genocide, the preeminent social model that guided her efforts were the kibbutzim. In founding the Agahozo-Shalom Youth Village for the Rwanda war orphans, she was inspired by the kibbutzim's critical role in absorbing Holocaust orphans in their own time. Over the years, still others have sought to demonstrate the ways in which aspects of the kibbutz model and structural design might be applied to the challenges faced by urban communities. One of the more exemplary of these is David Leach, who in "Kibbutzing Your 'Hood'" (even as he acknowledges that though the kibbutz once sought to transform the world, the world irrevocably transformed the kibbutz), argues passionately that the inherent activism and free-flowing human-oriented spaces of the kibbutz engender the kind of interactive and socially cooperative communities with their own collective memories, shared stories, and identity that progressive urban designers seek to foster. Invoking what he calls the kibbutz's "architecture of hope," Leach finds inspiration for conscientious twenty-first-century development "one less fence and one more story at a time." Equally tantalizing is a recent development concerning the return of several former refugees to Juba, the capital of South Sudan, after they no longer needed to take shelter in Israel. One of them worked in agriculture at Kibbutz Yotvata for seven years, where he learned about how its residents had transformed the desert decades earlier. Today the friends plan to create their own kibbutz on the banks of the Nile. After establishing a basic infrastructure and planting crops, they plan to bring over Israeli kibbutzniks to help them in the advanced stages of planning (S. Oz).

31. Consider popular Israeli novelist Assaf Gavron's novel *Hagiva* (*The Hilltop*; 2013), wherein Hilik Yisraeli, a settler from a small zealous settlement in the occupied West Bank, is a doctoral student writing his dissertation largely as a postmortem of the pioneering movement, whose national and ideological significance he and his community regard themselves as triumphantly usurping: "The working title . . . was 'Pioneering, Land Redemption, Ideology: The Pre-State Kibbutz Movement as a Failure-in-Waiting.' In his paper, Hilik sought to point out a wide range of warning signs, arguing that the manner in which the kibbutzim were established and evolved, beginning with the appropriation of land . . . the receipt of state credit and benefits . . . the reliance on slogans and ideology, and . . . also the condescension and arrogance of a closed society, alienated and on a pedestal, functioning according to its own set of rules—signaled the failure of the Kibbutz Movement some fifty years before the onset of its actual demise. Or something to that effect" (*Hilltop* 117). As I attempt to demonstrate in this afterword, many might yet find cause to regard this fictional Ph.D candidate's acerbic dismissal as premature.

32. Yuval Dror is himself a kibbutznik and kibbutz educator, living at the time of this writing in a self-identified "community neighborhood" within Kibbutz Kfar Ruppin.

33. Uri Zilbersheid's perspective on the potential impact of what he dubs the "Egalitarian Stream" of the kibbutzim (what most other researchers label the "collective" model) is perhaps too sanguine, but it is certainly an alluring vision: "The Egalitarian Stream in the kibbutz movement is a proof, I would say a sociopolitical proof, that even under opposing 'bad' circumstances humans can build a good society—even so good as to be defined as utopian. The kibbutzim that belong to the Egalitarian Stream do not confine themselves to the building of their own good society. As a matter of fact, they are closely involved in the attempts made in Israel to restrict neoliberalism and rehabilitate the welfare state. The latter is understood by them as both the building of a moderately good society for the large public and the creation of a socioeconomically supportive framework for themselves. A new Israeli welfare state would help them secure their prosperity and enlargement. Their efforts in this direction could, if supported by other political groups, become the starting-point of the resurrection of Israeli society itself."

34. See Shula Keshet's discussion of this development in "Kibbutz Fiction" 162.

BIBLIOGRAPHY

Aberbach, David. "S. Yizhar (1916–2006)." *Jewish Quarterly: A Magazine of Contemporary Writing, Politics, and Culture* 203 (Autumn 2006). <http://www.jewishquarterly.org/issuearchive/article6e27.html?articleid=226>.

Abramovich, Dvir. *Back to the Future: Israeli Literature of the 1980s and 1990s*. Newcastle upon Tyne: Cambridge Scholars, 2010.

———. "Post-Holocaust Identity and Unresolved Tension in Modern-Day Israel: Savyon Liebrecht's *Apples from the Desert*." *Women in Judaism* 3.1 (2002): 1–13.

Abramson, Glenda. "Oh, My Land, My Birthplace: Lebanon War and Intifada in Israeli Fiction and Poetry." *Narratives of Dissent: War in Contemporary Israeli Arts and Culture*. Ed. Rachel S. Harris and Ranen Omer-Sherman. Detroit: Wayne State UP. 221–40.

Almog, Oz. *Hasabbar—Dyoqan* [*The Sabra: The Creation of the New Jew*]. Tel Aviv: Am Oved, 1983.

———. *The Sabra: The Creation of the New Jew*. Trans. Haim Watzman. Berkeley: U of California P, 2000. Trans. of *Hasabbar—Dyoqan*.

Alter, Robert. *Modern Hebrew Literature*. New York: Behrman House, 1975.

Amar, Amram, dir. *Hafuga* [*Ceasefire*]. Israel. Atzmaout Films, 1950.

Amir, Eli. *Scapegoat*. Trans. Dalia Bilu. Tel Aviv: Am Oved, 1987. Trans. of *Tarnegol kaparot*.

———. *Tarnegol kaparot* [*Scapegoat*]. Tel Aviv: Am Oved, 1983.

Amir-Zohar, Aliza. "Finally." *Shdemot: Cultural Forum of the Kibbutz Movement* 28 (1987): 132–49.

Antin, Mary. *The Promised Land*. Boston: Houghton Mifflin, 1912.

Arad, Dafna. "Cookbook for One and All: Recipes from the Kibbutz Dining Hall." *Haaretz* 28 September 2012. <http://www.haaretz.com/weekend/week-s-end/cookbook-for-one-and-all-recipes-from-the-kibbutz-dining-hall.premium-1.467281>.

Asaf, Yasmin, and Israel Doron. "The Meaning of Aging Among Mature Kibbutz Members." *One Hundred Years of Kibbutz Life: A Century of Crises and Reinvention*. Ed. Michal Palgi and Shulamit Reinharz. New Brunswick: Transaction, 2011. 83–100.

Aschkenasy, Nehama. "Deconstructing the Metanarrative: Amos Oz's Evolving Discourse with the Bible." *Symposium* 55.3 (2001): 123–34.

Ashkenazi, Eli. "Israeli Court Orders Privatized Kibbutz to Compensate Fired Member." *Haaretz* 2 May 2013. <http://www.haaretz.com/news/national/israeli-court-orders-privatized-kibbutz-to-compensate-fired-member.premium-1.518717>.

———. "Kibbutzim No Longer Bitten by Israel's Political Bug." *Haaretz* 22 January 2013. <http://www.haaretz.com/news/national/kibbutzim-no-longer-bitten-by-israel-s-political-bug.premium-1.495695>.

———. "Kibbutznik 1948 Diary Longs for 'Purity of That Generation.'" *Haaretz* 4 May 2008. <http://www.haaretz.com/print-edition/news/kibbutznik-1948-diary-longs-for-purity-of-that-generation-1.245174>.

———. "100 Years On, the Kibbutz Movement Is Alive and Kicking." *Haaretz* 1 April 2010. <http://www.haaretz.com/hasen/spages/1160341.html>.

———. "Two Warring Sister Kibbutzim Mend Fences." *Haaretz* 13 August 2012. <http://www .haaretz.com/news/national/two-warring-sister-kibbutzim-mend-fences.pre-mium-1.457746>.

Auerbach, John. "The Owl." *The Owl and Other Stories*. New Milford, CT: Toby Press, 2003. 3–10.

———."A Report from Here and Now." *Shdemot: Cultural Forum of the Kibbutz Movement* 28 (1987): 6–19.

Avrahami, Avner. "Native Son." *Haaretz* 2 April 2009. <http://www.haaretz.com/native-son-1.273407>.

Balaban, Avraham. *Between God and Beast: An Examination of Amos Oz's Prose*. University Park: Pennsylvania State UP, 1993.

———. *Mourning a Father Lost: A Kibbutz Childhood Remembered*. Trans. Yael Lotan. New York: Rowman & Littlefield, 2004. Trans. of *Shiv'ah*.

———. "Secularity and Religiosity in Contemporary Hebrew Literature." *Middle Eastern Literatures* 15.1 (2002): 63–79.

———. *Shiv'ah* [*Mourning a Father Lost*]. Tel Aviv: Hakibbutz Hameuchad, 2000.

Bar'el, Zvi. "A State of All Its Religious Citizens." *Haaretz* 29 August 2012. <http://www.haaretz .com/opinion/a-state-of-all-its-religious-citizens.premiu m-1.461297>.

Bar-Gal, Yoram. "Landscapes of Death—the Kibbutz and the Cemetery." *Jewish Journal of Sociology* 54.1–2 (2012): 67–86.

Ben-Aharon, Yariv, and Avishai Grossman, eds. *Bein tze'irim* [*Among the Youth*]: *Communal Talks in the Kibbutz Movement*. Tel Aviv: Am Oved, 1969.

Benbassa, Esther, and Jean-Christophe Attias. *The Jew and the Other*. Trans. G. M. Goshgarian. Ithaca: Cornell UP, 2004.

Ben-Rafael, Eliezer. *Crisis and Transformation: The Kibbutz at Century's End*. Albany: State U of New York P, 1997.

Ben-Rafael, Eliezer, and Menachem Topel. "Redefining the Kibbutz." *One Hundred Years of Kibbutz Life: A Century of Crises and Reinvention*. Ed. Michal Palgi and Shulamit Reinharz. New Brunswick: Transaction, 2011. 249–58.

Benvenisti, Meron. *Sacred Landscape: The Buried History of the Holy Land Since 1948*. Berkeley: U of California P, 2000.

Benziman, Uzi. "The Case of Atallah Mansour." *Haaretz* 16 May 2004. <http://www.haaretz.com/ print-edition/opinion/the-case-of-atallah-mansour-1.122580>.

Bergstein, Fanya. *Bo elay parpar nehmad* [*Come to Me, Sweet Butterfly*]. Tel Aviv: Hakibbutz Hameuchad, 1945.

Bettelheim, Bruno. *The Children of the Dream*. New York: Macmillan, 1969.

Bloome, H. J., dir. *Halome ami* [*Dream of My People*]. Israel. Palestine American Film Company, 1934.

Brenner, Rachel Feldhay. "'Hidden Transcripts' Made Public: Israeli Arab Fiction and Its Reception." *Critical Inquiry* 26 (Autumn 1999): 85–108.

———. *Inextricably Bonded: Israeli Arab and Jewish Writers Re-Visioning Culture*. Madison: U of Wisconsin P, 2003.

Bronner, Ethan. "A Religious War in Israel's Army." *New York Times* 22 March 2009: 1, 6.

Buber, Martin. *Paths in Utopia*. Trans. R. F. C. Hull. London: Routledge and Kegan Paul, 1949.

Buechner, Frederick. *Wishful Thinking: A Seeker's ABC*. New York: Harper & Row, 1986.

"Changes on Kibbutz." *Partners for Progressive Israel* (blog) 4 June 2008. <http://blog.partners 4israel.org/2008/06/changes-on-kibbutz.html>.

Cummings, Jonathan. "Digging Deep into the Collective Kitchens of Israel." *Jewish Daily Forward* 19 April 2013. <http://forward.com/articles/174716/digging-deep-into-the-collective-kitchens-of-israe/?p=all>.

Darr, Yael. "Discontent from Within: Hidden Dissent Against Communal Upbringing in Kibbutz Children's Literature of the 1940s and 1950s." *Israel Studies* 16.2 (2011): 127–50.

Dekel, Mikhal. "Citizenship and Sacrifice: The Tragic Scheme of Moshe Shamir's *He Walked Through the Fields*." *Jewish Social Studies* 18.3 (2012): 197–211.

Dror, Yuval. "The New Communal Groups in Israel: Urban Kibbutzim and Groups of Youth Movement Graduates." *One Hundred Years of Kibbutz Life: A Century of Crises and Reinvention*. Ed. Michal Palgi and Shulamit Reinharz. New Brunswick: Transaction, 2011. 315–24.

Drory, Zeev. "Societal Values: Impact on Israel Security—The Kibbutz Movement as a Mobilized Elite." *Israel Studies* 19.1 (2014): 166–88.

Dvir, Noam. "A Kibbutz Architectural Icon Frozen in Time." *Haaretz* 16 August 2012. <http://www.haaretz.com/news/features/a-kibbutz-architectural-icon-frozen-in-time.premium-1.458576>.

Eakin, Emily. "The Civilization Kit: A Utopian Self-Sufficiency Plan." *New Yorker* 23 December 2013: 70–79.

Elboim-Dror, Rachel. *Clean Death in Tel Aviv*. New York: iUniverse, 2003.

———. *Mavet naqi* [*Clean Death in Tel Aviv*]. Trans. Rachel Elboim-Dror. Tel Aviv: Sifriat Poalim, 1999. Trans. of *Clean Death in Tel Aviv*.

———. Review of *Mourning a Father Lost: A Kibbutz Childhood Remembered*. *Utopian Studies* 16.1 (2005): 155–59.

Eliot, George [Mary Ann Evans]. *Daniel Deronda*. Edinburgh: William Blackwood and Sons, 1876.

Estrin, Daniel. "Amos Oz, 74 Years Old and a National Treasure, Still Dreams of Life on the Kibbutz." *Tablet* 23 September 2013. <http://www.tabletmag.com/podcasts/145655/amos-oz-interview>.

Ezrahi, Sidra Dekoven. "From Auschwitz to the Temple Mount: Binding and Unbinding the Israeli Narrative." *After Testimony: The Ethics and Aesthetics of Holocaust Narrative for the Future*. Ed. Jakob Lothe, Susan Suleiman, and James Phelan. Columbus: Ohio State UP, 2012. 291–313.

Feldman, Yael S. *Glory and Agony: Isaac's Sacrifice and National Narrative*. Stanford: Stanford UP, 2010.

———. *No Room of Their Own: Gender and Nation in Israeli Women's Fiction*. New York: Columbia UP, 1999.

Flantz, Richard, ed. *Until Daybreak: Stories from the Kibbutz*. Selected and with an introduction by Amos Oz. Tel Aviv: Hakibbutz Hameuchad, 1984.

Freilich, Toby Perl, dir. *Inventing Our Life: The Kibbutz Experiment*. Israel/USA. First Run Features (USA), 2010.

Frye, Peter, dir. *Eshet hagibor* [*The Hero's Wife*]. Israel. Lancet Fry Films/Hatzvi Films, 1963.

Gal, Lavi Ben, dir. *Shmona esrim v'shmona* [*Eight Twenty Eight*]. Israel. Claudius Films, 2007.

Gan, Alon. "From 'We' to 'Me': The Ideological Roots of the Privatization of the Kibbutz." *One Hundred Years of Kibbutz Life: A Century of Crises and Reinvention*. Ed. Michal Palgi and Shulamit Reinharz. New Brunswick: Transaction, 2011. 33–46.

Garfinkle, Adam M. "On the Origin, Meaning, Use, and Abuse of a Phrase." *Middle Eastern Studies* 27 (October 1991): 539–50.

Gavron, Assaf. *Hagiva* [*The Hilltop*]. Tel Aviv: Yediot Aharonot, 2013.

———. *The Hilltop*. Trans. Steven Cohen. New York: Scribner, 2014. Trans. of *Hagiva*.

Gavron, Daniel. *The Kibbutz: Awakening from Utopia*. New York: Rowman & Littlefield, 2000.

Gertz, Nurith. *Hirbat Hiz'ah veha-boker she-lemaharat [Generation Shift in Literary History: Hebrew Narrative Fiction in the Sixties]*. Tel Aviv: Hakibbutz Hameuchad, 1985.

Ghert-Zand, Renee. "100 Years of Kibbutz Quilting." *Jewish Daily Forward* 10 June 2013. <http://blogs.forward.com/the-arty-semite/178916/-years-of-kibbutz-quilting/>.

Gilead, Zerubavel, and Dorothea Krook. *Gideon's Spring: A Man and His Kibbutz*. New York: Ticknor & Fields, 1985.

Gilerman, Dana. "Too Much Togetherness?" *Haaretz* 5 August 2005. <http://www.haaretz .com/misc/article-print-page/too-much-togetherness-1.166003?trailingPath=2.169%2C2 .216%2C>.

Golan, Menahem, dir. *Shmonah be'l'kvot ehad [Eight Against One]*. Israel. Noah Films, 1964.

Goldberg, J. J. "What Actually Undermined the Kibbutz." *Jewish Daily Forward* 16 April 2010. <http://forward.com/articles/127122/what-actually-undermined-the-kibbutz/>.

Green, David B. "Yossi Klein Halevi: I Am Looking for the Vanished Israel." *Haaretz* 20 October 2013. <http://www.haaretz.com/culture/.premium-1.553443>.

Grossman, David. *Dvash araiot [Lion's Honey]* Tel Aviv: Yedioth Ahronoth, 2005.

———. *Isha borachat mi-besora [Until the End of the Land]*. Tel Aviv: Hakibbutz Hameuchad; Siman Kriah Books, 2008.

———. *Lion's Honey: The Myth of Samson*. Trans. Stuart Schoffman. New York: Canongate, 2006. Trans. of *Dvash araiot*.

———. *Until the End of the Land*. Trans. Jessica Cohen. New York: Knopf, 2008. Trans. of *Isha borachat mi-besora*.

Grumberg, Karen. "Female Grotesque: Orly Castel-Bloom and the Israeli Woman's Body." *Nashim: A Journal of Jewish Women's Studies and Gender Issues* 23 (2012): 145–67.

———. *Place and Ideology in Contemporary Hebrew Literature*. Syracuse: Syracuse UP, 2011.

Gur, Batya. *Linah meshutefet [Murder on a Kibbutz]*. Jerusalem: Keter, 1991.

———. *Murder on a Kibbutz: A Communal Case*. Trans. Dalya Bilu. New York: HarperCollins, 1994. Trans. of *Linah meshutefet*.

Gvirtz, Yael. Review of *The Galilee Eskimos*. *Ynetnews* 12 January 2007. <http://www.ynetnews .com/articles/0,7340,L-3351224,00.html>.

Habiby, Emile [Imil Habibi]. *The Secret Life of Saeed the Pessoptimist*. Trans. (from Arabic) Salma Khadra and Trevor LeGassick. London: Zed, 1985.

Hadani, Ever. *Tzrif ha-etz [Wooden Hut]*. Tel Aviv: Mizpah, 1930.

Halevi, Yossi Klein. *Like Dreamers: The Story of the Israeli Paratroopers Who Reunited Jerusalem and Divided a Nation*. New York: HarperCollins, 2013.

Hands, Stuart. "Interview with Jonathan Paz." *Beyond the Toronto Jewish Film Festival* (blog) 13 January 2009. <http://tjff09.blogspot.com/2009/01/interview-with-galilee-eskimos -director.html>.

Havatzelet, Ze'ev, dir. *Havurah she'kazot [What a Gang]*. Israel. Geva Films, 1962.

Hawthorne, Nathaniel. *The Blithedale Romance*. Oxford: Oxford UP, 2009.

Heiferman, Marvin, and Carole Kismaric. *The Mysterious Case of Nancy Drew and the Hardy Boys*. New York: Simon & Schuster, 1998.

Hertzberg, Arthur. *The Zionist Idea: A Historical Analysis and Reader*. Philadelphia: Jewish Publication Society, 1997.

Herzl, Theodor. *The Jewish State: An Attempt at a Modern Solution of the Jewish Question*. Houston: Halcyon Press, 2010.

Herzog, Omri. "Amoz Oz's Sober Look at What It Means to Be a Stranger Among Friends." *Haaretz* 28 May 2012. <http://www.haaretz.com/culture/books/amoz-oz-s-sober-look-at -what-it-means-to-be-a-stranger-among-friends.premium-1.432933>.

Hever, Hannan. *Nativism, Zionism, and Beyond*. Syracuse: Syracuse UP, 2014.

Hirsch, Oded, dir. *50 Blue*. USA. Thierry Goldberg Gallery, 2009. Video.

———. *Ha-baita [Home]*. USA. Thierry Goldberg Gallery, 2010. Video.

———. *Nothing New*. USA. Thierry Goldberg Gallery, 2012. Video.

———. *Tochka*. USA. Thierry Goldberg Gallery, 2010. Video.

Hochberg, Gil. "A Poetics of Haunting: From Yizhar's Hirbeh to Yehoshua's Ruins to Koren's Crypts." *Jewish Social Studies* 18.3 (2012): 55–69.

Horn, Bernard. "Sephardic Identity and Its Discontents: The Novels of A. B. Yehoshua." *Sephardism: Spanish Jewish History and the Modern Literary Imagination*. Ed. Yael Halevi-Wise. Stanford: Stanford UP, 2012. 189–210.

Horowitz, Amy. *Mediterranean Israeli Music and the Politics of the Aesthetic*. Detroit: Wayne State UP, 2010.

Inbari, Assaf. *Ha-baita [Home]*. Tel Aviv: Yedioth Ahronoth / Hemed Books, 2009.

———. "The Kibbutz Novel as Erotic Melodrama." *Journal of Israeli History: Politics, Society, Culture* 31.1 (2012): 129–46.

Joffe, Lawrence. "100 Years of Kibbutzim." *Jewish Quarterly: Contemporary Writing, Politics, and Culture* July 2010. <http://jewishquarterly.org/100-years-of-kibbutzim/>.

Judt, Tony. "Kibbutz." *New York Review of Books* 18 January 2010. <http://www.nybooks.com/blogs/nyrblog/2010/jan/18/kibbutz/>.

Kafka, Franz. "Before the Law." Trans. Willa Muir and Edwin Muir. *The Complete Stories*. Ed. Nahum N. Glatzer. New York: Schocken Books, 1971. 3–4.

———. *The Diaries of Franz Kafka, 1914–1923*. Ed. Max Brod. Trans. Martin Greenberg with Hannah Arendt. New York: Schocken Books, 1965.

———. "In the Penal Colony." Trans. Willa Muir and Edwin Muir. *The Complete Stories*. Ed. Nahum N. Glatzer. New York: Schocken Books, 1971. 165–92.

Kahanoff, Jacqueline. "Ambivalent Levantine." *Mongrels or Marvels: The Levantine Writings of Jacqueline Shohet Kahanoff*. Ed. Deborah A. Starr and Sasson Somekh. Stanford: Stanford UP, 2011. 193–212.

Karpel, Dalia. "Reinventing the Wheel: Kibbutznik-Turned-Filmmaker Conquers NY Art Scene." *Haaretz* 26 July 2012. <http://www.haaretz.com/weekend/magazine/reinventing-the-wheel-kibbutznik-turned-filmmaker-conquers-ny-art-scene.premium-1.453861>.

Kashua, Sayed. *Aravim rokdim [Dancing Arabs]*. Moshav Ben-Shemen: Modan, 2002.

———. *Dancing Arabs*. Trans. Miriam Schlesinger. New York: Grove Press, 2004. Trans. of *Aravim rokdim*.

Katzir, Roni. "Cowards Stay Alive." *Ynetnews* 29 September 2012. <http://www.ynetnews.com/articles/0,7340,L-4286805,00.html>.

Kayyal, Mahmoud. "'Arabs Dancing in a New Light of Arabesques': Minor Hebrew Works of Palestinian Authors in the Eyes of Critics." *Middle Eastern Literatures* 11.1 (2008): 31–51.

Kedem, Eldad. "Kibbutz Films in Transition: From Morality to Ethics." *Israeli Cinema: Identities in Crisis*. Ed. Miri Talmon and Yaron Peleg. Austin: U of Texas P, 2011. 326–39.

Kedem, Eldad, with Gilad Padva. "From *Sabra* to *Children of the Sun*: Kibbutz Films from the 1930s to the 2000s." *One Hundred Years of Kibbutz Life: A Century of Crises and Reinvention*. Ed. Michal Palgi and Shulamit Reinharz. New Brunswick: Transaction, 2011. 173–93.

Kenan, Amos. "Interview with Dan Omer" (Hebrew). *Prozah* August–September 1977: 4–13.

Kenaz, Yehoshua. *Hitganvut yechidim [Infiltration]*. Tel Aviv: Am Oved, 1986.

———. *Infiltration*. Trans. Dalya Bilu. South Royalton, VT: Zoland Books/Steerforth Press, 2003. Trans. of *Hitganvut yechidim*.

Keshet, Shula. "Freedom of Expression in an Ideological Society: The Case of Kibbutz Literature." *One Hundred Years of Kibbutz Life: A Century of Crises and Reinvention*. Ed. Michal Palgi and Shulamit Reinharz. New Brunswick: Transaction, 2011. 195–213.

———. *Hamahteret hanafshit: Al reshit haroman hakibbutzi* [*Underground Soul: Ideological Literature: the Case of the Early Kibbutz Novel*]. Tel Aviv: Hakibbutz Hameuchad, 1995.

———. "Kibbutz Fiction and Yishuv Society on the Eve of Statehood: The *Ma'agalot* (*Circles*) Affair of 1945." *Journal of Israeli History: Politics, Society, Culture* 31.1 (2012): 147–65.

Kessler, Dana. "Kibbutz Cuisine Gets Its Due." *Tablet* 16 January 2013. <http://www.tabletmag .com/jewish-life-and-religion/121640/kibbutz-cuisine-gets-its-due>.

Ketzner, Tzvika, and Akiva Tevet, dirs. *Atalia*. Israel. Jerusalem Capital Studios, 1984.

Kirsch, Adam. "The Burden of Israeli Strength." *Tablet* 16 August 2012. <http://www.tabletmag .com/jewish-arts-and-culture/books/109356/the-burden-of-israeli-strength>.

Kismaric, Carole, and Marvin Heiferman. *The Mysterious Case of Nancy Drew and the Hardy Boys*. New York: Simon & Schuster, 1998.

Koestler, Arthur. *Thieves in the Night: Chronicle of an Experiment*. New York: Macmillan, 1946.

Kritz, Reuven, and Ori Kritz. *Sipurei ha-kibbutz* [*The Kibbutz Tales*]. Vol. 1. Tel Aviv: Pura, 1997.

Lanir, Niva. "Amos Oz Makes Room for His Loneliness." *Haaretz* 15 March 2012. <http://www .haaretz.com/weekend/magazine/amos-oz-makes-room-for-his-loneliness-1.418823>.

Laqueur, Walter. *A History of Terrorism*. New Brunswick: Transaction, 2001.

Lavi, Zvi, ed. *Kibbutz Members Study Kibbutz Children*. New York: Greenwood Press, 1990.

Lavie, Smadar. *The Poetics of Military Occupation: Mzeina Allegories of Bedouin Identity Under Israeli and Egyptian Rule*. Berkeley: U of California P, 1990.

Leach, David. "Kibbutzing Your 'Hood.'" *TEDxVictoria*. 10 January 2012. <http://www.youtube .com/watch?v=OFRMyKVF7j0&feature=youtu.be>.

———. Review of *The Galilee Eskimos. Look Back to Galilee* (blog) 26 May 2010. <http://look backtogalilee.blogspot.com/2010/05/review-galilee-eskimos.html>.

Lehmann-Haupt, Christopher. "Books of the Times." *New York Times* 14 November 1973. <http://www.nytimes.com/books/97/10/26/home/oz-elsewhere.html>.

Lerski, Helmar, dir. *Avodah*. Israel. Palestine Pictures, 1935.

Levin, Meyer. *Compulsion*. New York: Simon & Schuster, 1956.

———. *The Old Bunch*. New York: Simon & Schuster, 1937.

———. *Yehuda*. New York: Jonathan Cape & Harrison Smith, 1931.

Levin-Talmi, Emma. *Zman ha-olahim* [*Time of Tents*]. Tel Aviv: Sifriat Poalim, 1949.

Levy, Lital. "Nation, Village, Cave: A Spatial Reading of 1948 in Three Novels of Anton Shammas, Emile Habiby, and Elias Khoury." *Jewish Social Studies: History, Culture, Society* 18.3 (2012): 10–26.

———. "Reorienting Hebrew Literary History: The View from the East." *Prooftexts* 29.2 (2009): 127–72.

Liebrecht, Savyon. *Apples from the Desert: Selected Stories*. Trans. Marganit Weinberger-Rotman et al. New York: Feminist Press, 1998. Trans. of *Tapuchim min hamidbar*.

———. "Kibbutz." *A Good Place for the Night*. Trans. Sondra Silverston. New York: Persea Books, 2005. 59–100. Trans. of *Makom tov la-laila*.

———. *Makom tov la-laila* [*A Good Place for the Night*]. Tel Aviv: Keter, 2002.

———. *Tapuchim min hamidbar* [*Apples from the Desert*]. Tel Aviv: Sifriat Poalim, 1986.

Lind, Jakov. *Counting My Steps*. New York: Macmillan, 1969.

Lonely Planet. *Israel and the Palestinian Territories*. 5th ed. Footscray, Australia: Lonely Planet, 2007.

Lori, Aviva. "All You Need Is Love: What Happened to the Ideal Mother of Israel's Early Days?" *Haaretz* 15 July 2010. <http://www.haaretz.com/weekend/magazine/all-you-need -is-love-1.302132>.

Loshitzky, Yosefa. *Identity Politics on the Israeli Screen*. Austin: U of Texas P, 2001.

Maletz, David. *Ma'agalot* [lit. "Circles"; *Young Hearts*]. Tel Aviv: Am Oved, 1945.

———. *Young Hearts: A Novel of Modern Israel.* Trans. Solomon N. Richards. New York: Schocken Books, 1950. Trans. of *Ma'agalot.*

Manguel, Alberto. Review of *Between Friends* by Amos Oz. *Guardian* 8 May 2013. <http://www .guardian.co.uk/books/2013/may/08/between-friends-amos-oz-review>.

Manor, Ronen. "The 'Renewed' Kibbutz." *Journal of Rural Cooperation* 32.1 (2004): 37–50.

Mansour, Atallah. *B'or hadash* [*In a New Light*]. Tel Aviv: Kami, 1966.

———. *In a New Light.* Trans. Abraham Birman. London: Vallentine, Mitchell, 1969. Trans. of *B'or hadash.*

———. *Still Waiting for the Dawn: A Long Life for a Palestinian with His Stepfather, Israel.* Seattle: CreateSpace Independent, 2013.

Margalit, Avishai. "Israel: The Writers' Writer." *New York Review of Books* 24 September 2009. <http://www.nybooks.com/articles/archives/2009/sep/24/israel-the-writers-writer/>.

Mazor, Yair. *Somber Lust: The Art of Amos Oz.* Trans. Marganit Weinberger-Rotman. Albany: State U of New York P, 2002.

Meir-Glitzenstein, Esther. "Ethnic and Gender Identity of Iraqi Women Immigrants in the Kibbutz in the 1940s." *Jewish Women in Pre-State Israel: Life History, Politics, and Culture.* Ed. Ruth Kark, Margaret Shilo, and Galit Hasan-Rokem. Waltham: Brandeis UP, 2008. 83–99.

Mendelson-Maoz, Adia, and Liat Steir-Livny. "The Jewish Works of Sayed Kashua: Subversive or Subordinate?" *Israel Studies Review* 26.1 (2011): 107–29.

Meyer, Lisa. "Employing Language in the Service of Peace: Amos Oz Knows Words Can Heal as Well as Wound." *Los Angeles Times* 28 January 1998. <http://articles.latimes.com/ print/1998/jan/28/news/ls-12760>.

Milner, Iris. "Agitated Orders: Early Kibbutz Literature as a Site of Turmoil." *One Hundred Years of Kibbutz Life: A Century of Crises and Reinvention.* Ed. Michal Palgi and Shulamit Reinharz. New Brunswick: Transaction, 2011. 159–72.

Mintz, Alan. "Tellers of the Soil." *New Republic* September 1991: 39–41.

Mirsky, Yehudah. "We Were the Future." *Jewish Ideas Daily* 2 June 2011. <http://www.jewish ideasdaily.com/895/features/we-were-the-future/>.

Mitgang, Herbert. "Amos Oz, a Kibbutznik in the Colorado Rockies." *New York Times* 6 July 1985: 9.

Mole, Gary D. *Lévinas, Blanchot, Jabès: Figures of Estrangement.* Gainesville: UP of Florida, 1997.

Mort, Jo-Ann, and Gary Brenner. *Our Hearts Invented a Place: Can Kibbutzim Survive in Today's Israel?* Ithaca: Cornell UP, 2003.

Mossensohn, Yigal. *Be'arvot Hanegev* [*On the Plains of the Negev*]. Tel Aviv: Habimah, 1949.

Muravchik, Joshua. *Heaven on Earth: The Rise and Fall of Socialism.* San Francisco: Encounter Books, 2002.

Nathan, Alfy, with Joshua M. Sklare. *Alfy: An Incredible Life Journey.* Fort Lauderdale: Monte-fiore Press, 2010.

Naveh, Hanna. "Dyokan hakvutza agav urcha—Haya o lo haya? Od Meshel Y. H. Brenner" ["A Portrait of the Group 'By the Way': Had It Ever Existed? More of Y. H. Brenner"]. *Safrut ve-chevra ba-tarbut ha-ivrit hahadasha* [*Literature and Society in the New Hebrew Culture*]. Ed. Yehudit Bar-El, Yigal Schwartz, and Tamar Hess. Tel Aviv: Hakibbutz Hameuchad and Keter, 2000. 82–100.

Near, Henry. *The Kibbutz Movement: A History.* 2 vols. Oxford: Oxford UP, 1992.

Negev, Ayelet. *Sichot intimiyot* [*Intimate Conversations*]. Tel Aviv: Yediot Ahronot, 1995.

Omer-Sherman, Ranen. "'A Disgrace to the Map of Israel': The Wilderness Journey of the Citizen-Soldier in Amos Oz's *A Perfect Peace.*" *Journal of Modern Literature* 27.3 (2004): 97–114.

———. *Israel in Exile: Jewish Writing and the Desert*. Urbana: U of Illinois P, 2006.

———. "The Kibbutz and the Disenchanted: Representations in Contemporary Israeli Narratives." *One Hundred Years of Kibbutz Life: A Century of Crises and Reinvention*. Ed. Michal Palgi and Shulamit Reinharz. New Brunswick: Transaction, 2011. 139–57.

Oz, Amos. *Artzot hatan* [*Where the Jackals Howl*]. Tel Aviv: Massada Press, 1965.

———. *Be'in haverim* [*Between Friends*]. Jerusalem: Keter, 2012.

———. *Beor hathelet ha'aza* [*Under This Blazing Light*]. Jerusalem: Keter, 1979.

———. *Between Friends*. Trans. Sondra Silverston. London: Chatto & Windus, 2013. Trans. of *Be'in haverim*.

———. *Elsewhere, Perhaps*. Trans. Nicholas de Lange. New York: Harcourt Brace Jovanovich, 1973. Trans. of *Makom aher*.

———. *Fima*. Trans. Nicholas de Lange. New York: Harcourt Brace, 1993. Trans. of *Matsav hashelish*.

———. *Makom aher* [*Elsewhere, Perhaps*]. Tel Aviv: Sifriat Poalim, 1966.

———. *Matsav hashelish* [lit. "The Third Condition"; *Fima*]. Tel Aviv: Keter, 1991.

———. *Menuhah nehonah* [*A Perfect Peace*]. Tel Aviv: Am Oved, 1982.

———. *Mikha'el sheli* [*My Michael*]. Tel Aviv: Am Oved, 1968.

———. *My Michael*. Trans. Nicholas de Lange. London: Chatto & Windus, 1972. Trans. of *Mikha'el sheli*.

———. "Nomad and Viper." *Sleepwalkers and Other Stories: The Arab in Hebrew Fiction*. Ed. Ehud Ben-Ezer. Boulder: Lynne Rienner, 1999. 119–34.

———. *Oto hayam* [*The Same Sea*]. Jerusalem: Keter, 1999.

———. *A Perfect Peace*. Trans. Hillel Halkin. New York: Harcourt Brace Jovanovich, 1982. Trans. of *Menuhah nehonah*.

———. *The Same Sea*. Trans. Nicholas de Lange. London: Vintage, 2002. Trans. of *Oto hayam*.

———. *Sipur al ahava ve-hosheh* [*A Tale of Love and Darkness*]. Jerusalem: Keter, 2002.

———. *A Tale of Love and Darkness*. Trans. Nicholas de Lange. Boston: Houghton Mifflin Harcourt, 2005. Trans. of *Sipur al ahava ve-hosheh*.

———. *Under This Blazing Light*: Essays. Trans. Nicholas de Lange. Cambridge: Cambridge UP, 1979. Trans. of *Beor hatkhelet ha'aza*.

———. *Where the Jackals Howl and Other Stories*. Trans. Nicholas de Lange and Philip Simpson. New York: Random House, 2005. Trans. of *Artzot hatan*.

———, comp. *Until Daybreak: Stories from the Kibbutz*. Intro. by Amos Oz. Tel Aviv: Hakibbutz Hameuchad and the Institute for the Translation of Hebrew Literature, 1984.

Oz, Amos, and Fania Oz-Salzberger. *Jews and Words*. New Haven: Yale UP, 2012.

Oz, Sheri. "Former Refugees Have a Dream: A Kibbutz in South Sudan." *Haaretz* 29 August 2013. <http://www.haaretz.com/news/features/.premium-1.544095>.

Palgi, Michal, and Shulamit Reinharz, eds. *One Hundred Years of Kibbutz Life: A Century of Crises and Reinvention*. New Brunswick: Transaction, 2011.

Pavin, Avraham. *The Kibbutz Movement: Information and Numbers*. (Hebrew). Tel Aviv: Yad Tabenkin, 2005.

Paz, Jonathan, dir. *Eskimosim ba Galil* [*The Galilee Eskimos*]. Prod. Jonathan Paz. Israel. Israeli Films, 2007.

Peleg, Yaron. "Writing the Land: Language and Territory in Modern Hebrew Literature." *Journal of Modern Jewish Studies* 12.2 (2013): 297–312.

Penslar, Derek J. "Special Issue: The Kibbutz in Israeli Society: New Perspectives Introduction." *Journal of Israeli History: Politics, Society, Culture* 31.1 (2012): 5–7.

Perlman, Edna Barromi. "'In My Eyes, Each Photograph Was a Masterpiece': Construction of Children's Photos in a Family Album on Kibbutz in Israel." *Social Semiotics* 23.1 (2013): 100–118.

Piterberg, Gabriel. *The Returns of Zionism: Myths, Politics, and Scholarship in Israel*. New York: Verso, 2008.

Plato. *The Republic of Plato*. Trans. and ed. Francis Macdonald Cornford. New York: Oxford UP, 1945.

Ram, Uri. *The Globalization of Israel: McWorld in Tel Aviv, Jihad in Jerusalem*. New York: Routledge, 2008.

Reichenstein, Shlomo. *Raishit [Beginnings]*. Tel Aviv: Am Oved, 1943.

Ring, Israel, moderator. "Kibbutz-Born Creators, a Symposium: Kibbutz Artzi Conference of Writers." Trans. Yehudith Agassi. 16 July 1986. *Shdemot: Cultural Forum of the Kibbutz Movement* 28 (1987): 150–63.

Rosenberg, Karen. "Oded Hirsch: 'Nothing New.'" *New York Times* 22 March 2012. <http:// www.nytimes.com/2012/03/23/arts/design/oded-hirsch-nothing-new.html>.

Rosenfeld, Susan, ed. and trans. "*Shdemot* Queries—Authors Respond." *Shdemot: Cultural Forum of the Kibbutz Movement* 28 (1987): 164–80.

Rosenthal, Donna. *The Israelis: Ordinary People in an Extraordinary Land*. New York: Free Press, 2003.

Rotem, Tamar. "The Israeli Playwright Who Foresaw the Illusion—and Arrogance—of Israel's Might." *Haaretz* 25 September 2013. <http://www.haaretz.com/jewish-world/high-holy -days-2014/yom-kippur-war-40-years-later/.premium-1.549007>.

Roth, Philip. *The Counterlife*. New York: Farrar, Straus & Giroux: 1986.

———. "Goodbye, Columbus." *Goodbye, Columbus and Five Short Stories*. Boston: Houghton Mifflin, 1959.

———. *Operation Shylock: A Confession*. New York: Simon & Schuster, 1993.

Round, Simon. "In Praise of Compromise: Simon Round Interviews Amos Oz." *Fathom* 31 January 2013. <http://www.fathomjournal.org/conversation/in-praise-of-compromise/>.

Rozin, Orit. *The Rise of the Individual in 1950s Israel: A Challenge to Collectivism*. Waltham: Brandeis UP, 2011.

Rubin, Yitzhak, dir. *Hakrav ha-aharon al Degania [Degania: The First Kibbutz Fights Its Last Battle]*. Israel. Teknews Films, 2008.

Russell, Raymond, Robert Hanneman, and Shlomo Getz. *The Renewal of the Kibbutz: From Reform to Transformation*. New Brunswick: Rutgers UP, 2013.

Sabar, Naama. *Kibbutzniks in the Diaspora*. Trans. Chaya Naor. Albany: State U of New York P, 2000.

Sagi, Avi. "The Wondrous Trembling of the Soul." *Shalom Hartman Institute Spotlight* (blog) 30 June 2010. <http://hartman.org.il/Research_And_Comment_View.asp?Article _Id=518&Cat_Id=323&Cat_Type=research_and_comment>.

Saltz, Jerry. Review of Oded Hirsch's *Nothing New*. *New York Magazine* 20 March 2012. <http://www.odedhirsch.com/press/new-york-magazine-review-by-jerry-saltz>.

Saperstein, Harold. *Witness from the Pulpit: Topical Sermons, 1933–1980*. New York: Lexington Books, 2000.

Sarid, Yossi. "Israel's First Kibbutz-Free Knesset." *Haaretz* 24 December 2012. <http://www .haaretz.com/news/israeli-elections-2013/israeli-elections-opinion-analysis/israel-s-first -kibbutz-free-knesset.premium-1.489741>.

Scammell, Michael. *Koestler: The Literary and Political Odyssey of a Twentieth-Century Skeptic*. New York: Random House, 2009.

Scheilfele, Kris. "Fitzcarraldo Joins a Kibbutz: Oded Hirsch at Thierry Goldberg." *Artcritical: The Online Magazine of Art and Ideas* 10 March 2012. <http://www.artcritical .com/2012/03/10/oded-hirsch/>.

Scliar, Moacyr. *The Centaur in the Garden*. Trans. Margaret A. Neves. Madison: U of Wisconsin P, 2003. Trans. of *O centauro no jardim*.

———. *O centauro no jardim* [*The Centaur in the Garden*]. Rio de Janeiro: Editora Nova Fronteira, 1980.

Segev, Tom. "Kibbutz Coup de Grace." *Haaretz* 8 July 2005. <http://www.haaretz.com/kibbutz -coup-de-grace-1.163284>.

———. "'The USSR Is Our Second Homeland,' Said One Kibbutznik when Stalin Died." *Haaretz* 9 March 2013. <http://www.haaretz.com/weekend/the-makings-of-history/the -ussr-is-our-second-homeland-said-one-kibbutznik-when-stalin-died.premium-1.508137>.

Sened, Alexander, and Yonat Sened. *Adama lelo tzel* [*A Land Without a Shadow*]. Tel Aviv: Hakibbutz Hameuchad, 1951.

Shaham, Nathan. *Kirot etz dakim* [*The Other Side of the Wall*]. Tel Aviv: Am Oved, 1977.

———. *The Other Side of the Wall: Three Novellas.* Trans. Leonard Gold. Philadelphia: Jewish Publication Society of America, 1983. Trans. of *Kirot etz dakim.*

Shaked, Gershon. "Livnot u'lehibanot ba: Al roman hahityashvut" ["To Build and to Be Rebuilt in It: On the Settlement Novel"]. *Proceeedings of the Sixth World Congress for Jewish Studies* (1973): 517–27.

Shalev, Meir. *The Blue Mountain.* Trans. Hillel Halkin. New York: Aaron Asher Books, 1991. Trans. of *Roman russi.*

———. *Roman russi* [*The Blue Mountain*]. Tel Aviv: Am Oved, 1988.

Shamir, Moshe. *He Walked Through the Fields: Four Israeli Plays in English Translation.* Trans. Aubrey Hobes. Jerusalem: World Zionist Organization Department for Education and Culture, 1959. Trans. of *Hu halach ba-sadot* (play).

———. *Hu halach ba-sadot* [*He Walked Through Fields*] (novel). Tel Aviv: Sifriat Poalim, 1947.

Shammas, Anton. *Arabeskot* [*Arabesques*]. Tel Aviv: Am Omed, 1986.

———. *Arabesques.* Trans. Vivian Eden. New York: Harper & Row, 1988. Trans. of *Arabeskot.*

Shani, Ayelett. "Television and Film Producer Yossi Uzrad on the Demise of the Medium." *Haaretz* 22 June 2013. <http://www.haaretz.com/weekend/magazine/television-and-film -producer-yossi-uzrad-on-the-demise-of-the-medium.premium-1.531029>.

Shapira, Anita. *Israel: A History.* Trans. Anthony Berris. Waltham: Brandeis UP, 2012.

———. "The Kibbutz and the State." Trans. Evelyn Abel. *Jewish Review of Books* 2 (Summer 2010). <http://jewishreviewofbooks.com/articles/246/the-kibbutz-and-the-state/>.

Shaul, Dror, dir. *Adama meshuga'at* [*Sweet Mud*]. Perf. Tomer Steinhof and Ronit Yudkevitz. Israel: GlobusUnited, 2006.

Shavit, Dan. "Introduction." *Shdemot: Cultural Forum of the Kibbutz Movement* 28 (1987): 4–5.

Shavit, Ze'ev. "The Bourgeois Construction of the Rural: An Israeli Case." *Israel Studies Review* 28.1 (2013): 98–119.

Sherwood, Harriet. "Israel's Kibbutz Movement Makes a Comeback." *Guardian* 23 July 2012: 20.

Shiffman, Smadar. "Forging the Image of Pioneer Women." *Jewish Women in Pre-State Israel: Life History, Politics, and Cuture.* Ed. Ruth Kark, Margalit Shilo, and Galit Iasan-Roken. Waltham: Brandeis UP, 2009. 131–40.

Shohat, Ella. *Israeli Cinema: East/West and the Politics of Representation.* Austin: U of Texas P, 1989.

———. "Remembering a Baghdad Elsewhere: An Emotional Cartography." *Jadaliyya* 1 April 2013. <http://www.jadaliyya.com/pages/index/10908/remembering-baghdad-elsewhere _an-emotional-cartogr>.

Shuman, Ellis. *The Virtual Kibbutz: Stories From a Changing Society.* New York: iUniverse, 2003.

Smith, Roberta. "Sharing a National Identity, Emerging Artists Engaging in a Visual Language." *New York Times* 11 August 2010: C5.

Sobol, Joshua. *Leil ha'erim* [*The Night of Twentieth*]. Tel Aviv: Proza, 1977.

Sosis, Richard, and Bradley J. Ruffle. "Ideology, Religion, and the Evolution of Cooperation: Field Experiments on Israeli Kibbutzim." *Research in Economic Anthropology* 23 (2004): 89–117.

Stav, Shira. "Nakba and Holocaust: Mechanisms of Comparison and Denial in the Israeli Liter-ary Imagination." *Jewish Social Studies* 18.3 (2012): 85–98.

Tal, Ran. "Her Memories Are Mine." *Haaretz* 3 March 2011. <http://www.haaretz.com/life/books/hebrew-fiction-her-memories-are-mine-1.346912>.

Tal, Ran, dir. *Yaldey hashemesh [Children of the Sun]*. Israel. Lama Films, 2007.

Urian, Dan. "Representations of War in Israeli Drama and Theatre." *Narratives of Dissent: War in Contemporary Israeli Arts and Culture*. Ed. Rachel S. Harris and Ranen Omer-Sherman. Detroit: Wayne State UP, 2012. 281–99.

Uris, Leon. *Exodus*. New York: Doubleday, 1958.

Weiss, Meira. *The Chosen Body: The Politics of the Body in Israeli Society*. Stanford: Stanford UP, 2002.

Weitz, Yechiam. "David Meletz, a Rare Kibbutznik." *Haaretz* 30 November 2011. <http://www.haaretz.com/misc/article-print-page/david-meletz-a-rare-kibbutznik-1.398746?trailing Path=2.169%2C2.203%2C2.205%2C>.

Wilson-Goldie, Kaelen. "The Workers." *Artforum* April 2012. <http://artforum.com/index.php?pn=picks&id=29259&view=print>.

Wisse, Ruth. *The Modern Jewish Canon: A Journey Through Language and Culture*. New York: Free Press, 2000.

Wordsworth, William. "Nutting." *The Collected Poems of William Wordsworth*. Intro. by Antonia Till. Ware, UK: Wordsworth Editions, 1998. 215–16.

Yadid, Judd. "Avoda Zara." *Haaretz* 26 June 2013. <http://www.haaretz.com/news/features/word-of-the-day/.premium-1.531512>.

Yagoda, Ilan, dir. *Rain 1949*. (Hebrew) Israel. Israel Film Service, 1998.

Yehoshua, A. B. [Abraham B.]. *Hameahev [The Lover]*. Jerusalem: Schocken, 1977.

———. *The Lover*. Trans. Philip Simpson. New York: Dutton, 1977. Trans. of *Hameahev*.

———. *Mul haye'arot [Facing the Forests]*. Tel Aviv: Hakibbutz Hameuchad, 1968.

Yeshurun, Yitzhak [Isaac Zepel], dir. *Noa bat sheva-esrei [Noa at Seventeen]*. Israel. United King Films, 1982.

Yizhar, S. [Yizhar Smilansky]. *Ephraim chozer la-aspeset [Ephraim Goes Back to Alfalfa]*. 1938. Reprint, Tel Aviv: Hakibbutz Hameuchad, 1978.

———. "Ephraim Goes Back to Alfalfa." Trans. Misha Louvish. *Midnight Convoy and Other Stories*. London: Toby Press, 2007. 1–61. Trans. of *Ephraim chozer la-aspeset*.

———. *Hirbet Hiz'ah [Khirbet Khizeh]*. Tel Aviv: Sifriat Poalim, 1949.

———. *Khirbet Khizeh*. Trans. Nicholas de Lange and Yaacob Dweck. Jerusalem: Ibis Editions, 2008. Trans. of *Hirbet Hiz'ah*.

———. *Yemei Tziklag [Days of Ziklag]*. Tel Aviv: Zmora-Bitan, 1958.

Zandberg, Esther. "From Utopia to Suburbia." *Haaretz* 6 October 2011. <http://www.haaretz.com/print-edition/business/environment-from-utopia-to-suburbia-1.388477>.

Zangwill, Israel. *The Melting-Pot: Drama in Four Acts*. New York: Macmillan, 1909.

Zeira, Moti. *Sipur hayav veyetzirotav shel David Maletz [He Flew on Broken Wings: The Life and Work of David Maletz]*. Tel Aviv: Hakibbutz Hameuchad, 2011.

Zerubavel, Yael. "Coping with the Legacy of Death: The War Widow in Israeli Films." *Israeli Cinema: Identities in Motion*. Ed. Miri Talmon and Yaron Peleg. Austin: U of Texas P, 2011. 84–95.

———. "The 'Mythological Sabra' and Jewish Past: Trauma, Memory, and Contested Identi-ties." *Israel Studies* 7.2 (2002): 115–44.

Zilbersheid, Uri. "The Israeli Kibbutz: From Utopia to Dystopia." *Critique: Journal of Socialist Theory* 35.3 (2007). <http://libcom.org/library/israeli-kibbutz-utopia-dystopia-uri-zilbersheid>.

INDEX

Negev, 39, 69–70, 71, 151, 171, 183, 185, 320n21; desert space, 97–98

New Hebrew (New Jew), 30, 42, 44, 52, 56, 58, 133, 144, 148, 167, 289n51, 297n46; in Amos Oz, 87, 94, 108, 294n16, 294n19; film portrayals, 205, 230, 240, 312n27. *See also* Sabras

New Jew. *See* New Hebrew

1948 Generation (War of Independence), 10–11, 26, 91, 118, 147, 164, 173, 235, 243, 284n20, 295n30

1956 Sinai Campaign, 319n17

1967 War (Six-Day War), 91, 140, 278–79n11, 295n30, 308n2

1982 (First) Lebanon War, 207

Noa at Seventeen (Noa bat sheva-esrei), film, 19, 20, 190, 206–13, 278n8

"Nomad and Viper" (Oz), 70–73, 75, 91, 105, 292n9

North Africa, 19, 105, 160, 183–84

Nothing New (film), 253–56

Old Bunch, The (Levin) 35

Orientalism, 36, 71, 101, 143, 161, 168, 289n47

"Other Side of the Wall, The" (Shaham), 122–29

Ottoman Empire, 259

Ottoman Palestine, 277n4

Oved, Yakov, 266

Oz, Amos, 2, 15, 17–18, 67–113, 114, 129–30, 151, 230, 258, 311n21, 315n43; Abraham Balaban, friendship with, 279n18; Baruch Spinoza, affinity for, 295n23; Arad years, 103, 291n1; "Artzot hatan" ("Where the Jackals Howl"), 73–75, 287n41; "At Night," 109; Be'in haverim (*Between Friends*), 55, 84, 97, 103–13, 284n24; Beor hathelet ha'aza (*Under This Blazing Light*), 71; children's houses portrayed, 107, 291n60; David Maletz' influence on, 52, 287n40; "Derech haruach" ("The Way of the Wind"), 76–84, 92, 186, 253–56, 293n12; "Esperanto," 110–13; "Hakibbutz ha-yom" ("The Kibbutz At the Present Time"), 71; gender in kibbutz, 105; Hulda years, 67, 68, 76, 84, 85, 103–5, 111, 282n10, 291n1, 291n2, 293n11, 295n24, 317n1, 320n20; on human nature, 71, 103–4; jackals as trope, 109; *Jews and Words*, 107; on "kibbutz genes" of Israeli society, 259, 274; "Little Boy," 107; "Machshavot al hakibbutz" ("Thoughts On the Kibbutz"), 71, 292n8; Makom aher (*Elsewhere Perhaps*), 2–4, 84–90, 290n57, 296n41, 297n42,

312n27; Menuhah nehonah (*A Perfect Peace*), 18, 34, 52, 79, 82–83, 90–103, 105, 279n11, 287n40, 294n21; Mikha'el sheli (*My Michael*), 282n10; "Minzar hashatkanim" ("The Trappist Monastery"), 73; Negev and, 69–72; "Nomad and Viper," 70–73, 75, 91, 105, 292n9; Oto hayam (*The Same Sea*), 294n15; Palestinians and, 98–100, 113, 205; Peace Now and, 76; precision in language ethos, 111; savage and civilized dichotomy in, 74–75, 84–85, 151; Sabra myth and, 83, 86, 96, 98, 294n17, 294n19, 312n29; Sipur al ahava ve-hosheh (*A Tale of Love and Darkness*), 18, 67, 68, 76, 80, 107, 111; Sherwood Anderson, influence of, 292n5; socialism and, 192, 307n8; suicide of mother, 293n11; *Under This Blazing Light*, 192; *Where the Jackals Howl*, 18, 70; Yizhar's influence, 110; as Zionist writer, 103

Oz-Salzberger, Fania, 107

Padva, Gilad, 162, 204–5, 222

Palestine, 40–41, 42, 47, 55, 61; in Amos Oz' fiction, 98–100, 113, 124. *See also* Yishuv

Palestinians, 26, 39, 56, 91 97–100, 205, 214–16, 309n4, 310n11; West Bank, 140; Attalah Mansour's protagonist, 142–60. *See also* Arabs

Palgi, Michal, 317n4

Palmach, 18, 307n10, 311n14

Passing (identity), 140, 143–58

Passover, 99–100, 131, 138, 299n58, 307n5

Paz, Jonathan, 20, 311n16; communal childrearing, reflections on, 221; *The Galilee Eskimos* (Eskimosim ba Galil), 20, 204, 216–21, 222, 311n17

Peace Now, 76

Peleg, Yaron, 75–76

Penslar, Derek, 24, 52

Peres, Shimon (Israeli president), 161, 187, 309n5, 315n43

Perfect Peace, A (Oz), 18, 34, 52, 79, 82–83, 90–103, 105

Perlman, Edna, 56, 205, 239, 240–41, 297n47, 308n14, 313n34; on memorialization work of kibbutz family photo albums, 314n39; "mythologies of collectivity," 35

pioneers, 57, 85, 281n9, 286n36. *See also* halutzim

Piterberg, Gabriel, 284n21

Plato, 28

Plotnik, Ronit, 232–33